THOMAS BABINGTON MACAULAY

SELECTED WRITINGS

Classics of British Historical Literature

JOHN CLIVE, EDITOR

Thomas Babington Macaulay

———

Selected

Writings

EDITED AND WITH AN INTRODUCTION BY

JOHN CLIVE &
THOMAS PINNEY

The University of Chicago Press
CHICAGO AND LONDON

ISBN: 0–226–49996–0 (clothbound); 0–226–49997–9 (paperbound)
Library of Congress Catalog Card Number: 78–171350
The University of Chicago Press, Chicago 60637
The University of Chicago Press, Ltd., London

Contents

CONTENTS

Series Editor's Preface

This series of reprints has one major purpose: to put into the hands of students and other interested readers outstanding—and sometimes neglected—works dealing with British history which have either gone out of print or are obtainable only at a forbiddingly high price.

The phrase Classics of British Historical Literature requires some explanation, in view of the fact that the two companion series published by the University of Chicago Press are entitled Classic European Historians and Classic American Historians. Why, then, introduce the word *literature* into the title of this series?

One reason is obvious. History, if it is to live beyond its own generation, must be memorably written. The greatest British historians—Clarendon, Gibbon, Hume, Carlyle, Macaulay—survive today, not merely because they contributed to the cumulative historical knowledge about their subjects, but because they were masters of style and literary artists as well. And even historians of the second rank, if they deserve to survive, are able to do so only because they can still be read with pleasure. To emphasize this truth at the present time, when much eminently solid and worthy academic history suffers from being almost totally unreadable, seems worth doing.

The other reason for including the word *literature* in the title of the series has to do with its scope. To read history is to learn about the past. But if, in trying to learn about the British past, one were to restrict oneself to the reading of formal works of history, one would miss a great deal. Often a historical novel, a sociological inquiry, or an account of events and institutions couched in semifictional form teaches us just as much about the past as does the "history" that calls itself by that name. And, not infrequently, these "informal" historical works turn out to be less well known than their merit deserves. By calling this series Classics of British Historical Literature it will be possible to include such books without doing violence to the usual nomenclature.

JOHN CLIVE

Editors' Introduction

In his own day, Macaulay was the most honored of all English authors. He did not have the universal popularity of Dickens— what other writer ever did?—but all educated opinion, in England, on the Continent, and in America, agreed that he was the most distinguished man of letters that England had to show, and the list of his honors is eloquent testimony to this conviction. In 1853 he was able to write to a friend that he could sign himself "T. B. Macaulay, F.R.S., M.R.I.A., M.P., late fellow of Trinity College, Cambridge, late Lord Rector of the University of Glasgow, Knight of the Order of Merit of Prussia, Member of the Royal Academies of Munich and Turin, Member of the Historical Society of Utrecht, and . . . Member of the French Institute in the Department of Moral Science! ! !" He might have added that he was a member of the famous Literary Club founded by Dr. Johnson, a privy councillor, professor of ancient literature of the Royal Academy, honorary doctor of the University of Oxford, trustee of the British Museum, and, almost incidentally, the most profitable author on the list of the old established firm of Longmans, Green and Company. The crown of this impressive accumulation of public honors came in 1857, when the administration of Macaulay's old friend and colleague in Whig politics, Lord Palmerston, raised Macaulay to the peerage as Baron Macaulay of Rothley, the first such honor ever granted in England in recognition of literary achievement, and one which all agreed was eminently deserved.

Macaulay has now been dead for more than a century, and the extravagant public admiration that he was fortunate enough to receive well within his own lifetime has long since faded. He has not, as have a number of Victorian authors, passed into deep obscurity, but neither has he been granted any of the compensatory admiration that our generation has given to so many once-despised Victorians. He has never been exactly under a cloud, but neither has he been much attended to in the twentieth century. There is no question of restoring Macaulay to the position of unchallenged eminence that he once held—he is not a great enough artist for that. But the strong individuality, originality, and, not least, the amusing and readable qualities of his work, give it a continuing interest, certainly enough to justify a fresh look. He deserves this attention all the more because so much of the criticism written about him is stereotyped, a mere repetition of things that were being said of him in the generation after his death and which have never been reconsidered since. Macaulay himself had great confidence in his best writing and looked beyond the immediate popularity he enjoyed but knew to be transitory to the judgment of a remote posterity. It would be foolish to try to anticipate what that might be, but in the meantime a new collection designed to call attention to the range and variety of his work will suggest what Macaulay's claims are.

One reason for the comparative obscurity of Macaulay today is that he must be sought for not in one sort of work but in several, so that, unlike a poet or a novelist or a historian *tout pur*, he is difficult for us to classify. He had an active and important political career as well as one in literature; as a writer he was not confined to one form but ranged through literary and biographical essays, verse, and history, not to mention his official papers and his many speeches. He was one of that now almost extinct class, the man of letters, yet literature was never his whole life, nor did he ever depend on it for a living. Moreover, much of his effort went into forms no longer familiar or much appreciated: the long essays written for the *Edinburgh Review* are a very Victorian mode; narrative verse, as in the *Lays of Ancient Rome*, has dropped from favor; and Macaulay's speeches, of which he made scores and which are as genuinely literary as anything he ever wrote, are neglected with the general neglect of oratory.

Finally, his *History of England* fails of its full effect for the contradictory reasons that it is both a fragment and yet certainly too long for the common reader. A selection such as is offered in this anthology, by exhibiting within the covers of a single volume something of Macaulay's versatility, seems the best way to get at him.

Macaulay was the son of a London merchant who devoted much of his life to the great work, achieved in 1807, of abolishing the slave trade, and then to the abolition of slavery itself in the British dominions, an effort which at last succeeded in 1833. The father, Zachary Macaulay, was a notable man, energetic, intelligent, indefatigable, tough-minded and self-possessed; he was, like his fellow-workers in the antislavery cause, an Evangelical, a member of that section of the Church of England which turned away from the formal and rather anaemic Christianity of the eighteenth century to practice a Christianity urgent, insistent, fervent, and all-pervasive of the individual's life. Macaulay grew up in the strenuous religious atmosphere created by his father's zeal, where every thought and act were held as less than worthless unless sanctified to the Lord, and where the Christian's duty to improve both himself and those around him was paramount.

Macaulay himself rebelled, quietly but decisively, against the spiritual demands of the Evangelical life, but the influence nevertheless persisted, and some of the most distinctive things about Macaulay can be properly recognized as modified effects of his early religious experience. The habit of moral judgment on the subjects of his essays, for example, is probably to be referred to the Evangelical influences of his youth, and so also his mastery of the technique of biblical allusion and echo. More important, though, is the contribution of Evangelicalism, which itself inaugurated profound changes in the manners and morals of England, to Macaulay's sense that history, and particularly English history, revealed a pattern of progress. It would have been difficult for anyone given his experience to avoid the conclusion, for it was evident in the early nineteenth century that manners had improved, that literature had been purified, that public morality had been raised, that social concern was more general, that religion was more vitally received than in the generation before—

and much of this was no doubt the effect of Evangelical labors. At the same time, quite other forces were at work to suggest that England particularly and humanity generally were moving ahead in a way that reinforced the lesson taught by the confident Evangelicalism of Macaulay's youth. The point is important, for it means that the belief in progress which is one of the most obvious, if not the most fundamental, of Macaulay's opinions, was not simply the expression of his own self-confidence, but a consciousness widely and not unreasonably shared.

Macaulay was a more than remarkable child prodigy, revealing when barely beyond infancy an adult power of speaking, reading, and writing which only increased with his years. Zachary Macaulay hoped that his extraordinarily gifted son would grow up to enter the service of the Church, but he was too wise a man to insist upon his wishes, nor is there any evidence that Macaulay himself ever considered such a course. He was sent, in 1813, to a private school where he remained for five years and where he was very soon given great freedom to apply himself to the studies he liked best: classics, history, and the modern literatures of England, France, and Italy (he later added Spanish, German, Dutch, and Portuguese to his range). In 1818 he entered Trinity College, Cambridge, took his B.A. in 1822, and was elected fellow of Trinity in 1824. The six years that Macaulay spent in residence at Cambridge were golden years to him. He never applied himself to mathematics, which meant that he was ineligible for the highest academic honors of Cambridge, but he distinguished himself in classics, in writing verse, and in making speeches at the Cambridge Union. The prodigy who had hitherto been known only to the family circle and to his fellows at a small private school was soon regarded as the ablest man at the university and one marked out for certain distinction. Macaulay, in turn, was excited by his own success, and his imagination was stimulated especially by his winning a place for himself at Trinity, the largest and wealthiest of Cambridge colleges, whose graduates, as he was always pleased to recall, included Bacon, Newton, and Dryden. The mocking references to university tradition and privileges that he makes in his essay "The London University" were good for a polemical purpose, but they do not express what Macaulay really felt about Cambridge: a strong romantic attachment.

On leaving the university, Macaulay chose the law for his profession and was called to the bar in 1826. For the next four years he regularly attended the courts and went on the Northern Circuit, but he had hardly any business. The years that he spent as a briefless barrister are very sketchily documented and are not usually regarded as of much significance in his development; but they must have proven of vital importance to him when, in 1834, he went to India and, among other things, took on the awesome task of constructing an entire new penal code for British India.

Macaulay's years as an unemployed barrister were not idle. Already, in 1823, he had joined a group of Cambridge men in producing a miscellany called *Knight's Quarterly Magazine*, which ran for six numbers only. For this, Macaulay poured out a variety of sketches, essays, and songs which were quickly recognized as among the most lively writing of the day. Toward the end of 1824 he was invited to write for the *Edinburgh Review*, and thus began a connection maintained for the next twenty years. Until his *History of England* appeared, Macaulay's literary reputation rested mainly upon the articles he contributed to the *Edinburgh Review* with such success that the *Review* was known to sell or not to sell according to whether it did or did not contain an article from Macaulay.

The *Edinburgh Review*, the first of the great quarterlies of the nineteenth century, no longer exists; we have nothing quite like it now, and a little explanation is therefore useful in order to understand why Macaulay should have devoted so much of his best energies to writing for it. The *Edinburgh Review*, founded in 1802 by Sydney Smith, Francis Jeffrey, Henry Brougham, and others, had become the recognized spokesman for the Whig-liberal section of society on all public questions, matters of historical interpretation, and literature. Appearing once in every three months in numbers containing two hundred and fifty pages or more, it never had a large circulation by modern standards— only a few thousand—but it was read or looked at by everybody who counted, it paid well, and it attracted to it all the best writers among the class whose politics were acceptable. All contributions were anonymous (as they were in all English periodicals until the latter half of the nineteenth century), but the authors of articles of any éclat, such as Macaulay's invariably were, were pretty generally and quickly identified, and the tradition of collecting and republishing one's articles was established not very long after Macaulay began writing for the *Review*. As to the articles themselves, one must not be misled by the word *review*. The convention, strictly maintained, was that every article must be pegged to the title of some one or more books, which were ostensibly the subject of what followed; but beyond this the writer was free to proceed as he pleased. One of Macaulay's review articles, "History" (1828), after naming the title of a current book at the head of the page, never thereafter refers to it. With the freedom to say what he wanted to say on the subject suggested by the book nominally under review, the reviewer had also a generous measure of room in which to say it. Ten thousand words was an ordinary length, and some of Macaulay's essays— the longest is that on Bacon (1837)—are on the order of 70,000 to 80,000 words. These terms admirably suited Macaulay. With his keen and vigorous interest in the most diverse aspects of European history and literature, with his powerful memory making available to him any quantity of illustration and allusion, with his pleasure in argument and in the work of explanation, and with his gift for making the remote vivid and the obscure lucid, he was superbly equipped to write interesting and memorable articles, and he succeeded admirably. In his excellent *Life of Macaulay*, Sir George Otto Trevelyan says that on the publication of his first article, "Milton" (1825), Macaulay, like Byron, "awoke one morning and found himself famous." This needs a little modifying: his first article was not that on Milton, nor was his first fame even remotely like Byron's. But he certainly made a hit, and the impact grew stronger with each successive article— forty of them in all—until, in 1844, he ceased to write for the *Edinburgh Review* in order to devote himself to the *History of England*.

Macaulay's essays are usually divided according to their subjects into "historical" and "literary" classes: those on Mackintosh and Hastings are examples of the one; those on Restoration comedy and Johnson, of the other. But this division is very un-satisfactory. Macaulay's interest in literature was thoroughly his-torical; in the writings that he discusses, what they reveal of man-ners and morals, and the circumstances of time and place affecting their creation, were more attractive to him than the work of analyzing and commenting on their distinctive literary excel-lences. Indeed, though Macaulay *had* a theory of literature and has been duly included in René Wellek's magisterial survey of modern literary criticism, he himself knew that his gift did not lie in that direction. No one ever had a keener enjoyment of liter-ature, but in writing about it he dwelt most happily on the rela-tions between literature and the life of the times. A better division of his essays is that between the controversial and the descriptive. Those on the London University, on Sadler's Law of Population, and the series of attacks upon Utilitarian political theory belong to the first division. In the other are the many biographical and historical essays devoted to such subjects as Milton, Walpole, Frederic the Great, Pitt, and Warren Hastings. But again this division is misleading, for Macaulay is everywhere argumenta-tive, having always his own special view of the subject he chooses to set forth. Though the subjects of the essays range from Ma-chiavelli in the fifteenth century to the death of Lord Holland in 1840 and from India to Germany, by far the greater number deal with the seventeenth and eighteenth centuries. This was Macau-lay's chosen ground from the time of his first essays, as it was also the period which his *History of England* was to have covered. The essays as a group may be thought of as a series of related sketches preparatory to the *History*, though Macaulay certainly did not write them with that idea, and they stand up as inde-pendent works. To him they were recreations, giving him a chance to display the scenes and characters which he loved to dwell on in imagination. They must not be thought of as inde-pendent contributions to the research upon their subjects. Macau-lay himself thought so little of their permanent value that he long refused to reprint them and did so at last only because cheap American piracies (there was no international copyright then) were flooding into England.

Since they are such unmistakably distinctive productions, it ought to be easy to say what a Macaulay essay is and to enumerate the characteristics of his method and style; the object remains elusive, however. Macaulay himself thought that the distinguishing mark of his essays was their mixture of styles and tones, varying from grave to gay as the subject required. In an older day, when Macaulay was read as one of the standard authors for schools (a fate he would not have wished), much attention was given to the minute analysis of his style, especially to the varieties of figurative technique with which the essays abound. The curious student can easily find such exercises or, better, perform them for himself; they are useful for enhancing awareness of Macaulay's art, but they fail to convey any lively sense of Macaulay's quality. Here we will make only the general remark that Macaulay, though so often referred to as the most representative of Victorians, seems to express through his style a sensibility neither wholly Victorian nor wholly eighteenth century. He was steeped in the literature of the Augustan age to a degree that has probably never since been matched. He certainly looks back to the ideals of eighteenth-century prose in the balanced structure, the antithetical elements, and the epigrammatic character of his sentences. Their economy, too, is very unlike the verbose expression of so many Victorians who in literature as in architecture could not resist profusion and elaboration. But in common with the other prose writers of the nineteenth century Macaulay aimed at particularity rather than generality, the concrete rather than the abstract. So, when he has to tell in the essay on Johnson that Johnson as a boy read widely and beyond his years, he remembers an anecdote from Boswell and writes: "Once, while searching for some apples, he found a huge folio volume of Petrarch's work. The name excited his curiosity; and he eagerly devoured hundreds of pages." The general proposition is thus effectively developed by the specification of apples and a folio Petrarch. Allusiveness, the constant reference to names, places, books, historical events, and so on, which Macaulay supposes his reader will recognize, is one of his most familiar means of infusing particularity into his writing. The method is another instance of the mixture of eighteenth- and nineteenth-century qualities in his style, for it combines the Augustan attitude of writing for a community of educated and appreciative readers who will know what is meant and will have pleasure in recognizing the refer-

ence, with the liking of a later period for the definite and concrete. A passage in the journal kept by his admiring sister Margaret is worth quoting for its evidence of the importance that
Macaulay attached to the use of particulars, seeing in it the very
basis of his imaginative activity:

> I said that I was surprised at the great accuracy of his informa-
> tion, considering how desultory his reading had been. "My
> accuracy as to facts," he said, "I owe to a cause which many men
> would not confess. It is due to my love of castle-building. The
> past is in my mind soon constructed into a romance." He then
> went on to describe the way in which from his childhood his
> imagination had been filled by the study of history. "With a
> person of my turn," he said, "the minute touches are of as great
> interest, and perhaps greater, than the most important events.
> Spending so much time as I do in solitude, my mind would have
> rusted by gazing vacantly at the shop windows. As it is, I am no
> sooner in the streets than I am in Greece, in Rome, in the midst
> of the French Revolution. Precision in dates, the day or hour in
> which a man was born, or died, becomes absolutely necessary. A
> slight fact, a sentence, a word, are of importance in my romance.
> Pepys's Diary formed almost inexhaustible food for my fancy.
> I seem to know every inch of Whitehall. I go in at Hans Hol-
> bein's gate, and come out through the matted gallery. The con-
> versations which I compose between great people of the time are
> long, and sufficiently animated: in the style, if not with the
> merits, of Sir Walter Scott's. The old parts of London, which
> you are sometimes surprised at my knowing so well, those old
> gates and houses down by the river, have all played their part
> in my stories." He spoke, too, of the manner in which he used
> to wander about Paris, weaving tales of the Revolution, and he
> thought that he owed his command of language greatly to this
> habit. [Trevelyan, *Life,* 1: 183–84]

In 1830 Macaulay was brought into Parliament through the
patronage of the Whig magnate Lord Lansdowne, who had been
impressed by Macaulay's attacks on Utilitarian theory in the
Edinburgh Review. A new scene now opened before him, and at
an auspicious moment. The long phase of reaction and repression
in English politics created in response to the French Revolution
was, in 1830, beginning to break up. A Whig ministry, the first
in a generation, came in that year pledged to the reform of old

abuses. The great question was the reform of parliamentary representation—the object of the celebrated Reform Bill introduced in 1831—and in the struggles over this in the House of Commons, Macaulay, who took a leading part on the side of reform, instantly made a name for himself as an orator of the first rank. A selection from Macaulay's letters written at the time and reporting the progress of the Reform Bill communicates Macaulay's own excited sense of the crisis in descriptions that are as good as any he ever wrote.

For Macaulay, the Reform Bill, which gave parliamentary representation to hitherto unrepresented industrial towns and which enfranchised a substantial portion of the middle class, was more than merely a political measure. It was a historical necessity if England was to avoid revolution and bloodshed. History taught that the progress of civilization went hand in hand with the increase of wealth and the diffusion of knowledge. Political and constitutional arrangements had to adjust themselves to this process. By the time of the early nineteenth century, economic power had passed in a considerable degree to the middle classes. That must now be reflected, as it had not hitherto been, in the composition as well as in the election of the House of Commons. Landed property must share its power and privileges with commercial and industrial property.

If timely concessions of this sort were not granted by those in power, then the consequences were bound to bring violence and upheaval. That was the lesson taught by the English revolution of the seventeenth century and by the French Revolution of 1789, both constantly and vividly present in Macaulay's mind. What he feared most of all was that an excessively repressive attitude on the part of the aristocratic English ruling class would lead to the formation of an alliance between the middle and lower classes, led by a new and more dangerous species of Jacobin derived from disaffected members of the English middle classes.

That this contingency was the one of which Macaulay was most afraid should serve to delimit the extent of his reforming impulse. He was not a Radical. Indeed, his three articles against the Utilitarians (1829) which had helped to gain him his seat in Parliament on the Whig side had largely been an attack on the democratic tendencies of the Benthamites. He did not exclude the eventual participation of all male members of English society in the political process, but the prerequisite for this was education. Until the time of universal education had arrived—and Macaulay's estimate was that it was at least two generations away—the working class could not safely be entrusted with the vote.

Meanwhile, the working class could find consolation in the fact that, in spite of the birth pains of the industrial revolution, it was better off than ever before in history. Macaulay was not one of those who had any illusions about a golden age of the common man in preindustrial England. Nor did he feel—as he made clear in his essay on Southey's *Colloquies*—that the social and economic conditions of his own time called for the state to take over the sort of paternalistic responsibility for the welfare of the "lower orders" which had formerly been exercised by feudal landlords and the church. He may not have agreed with the political ideas of the Utilitarians, which advocated universal suffrage and democracy, but he agreed with their economic ideas, which derived from Adam Smith, Malthus, and Ricardo, and which called for a minimum of government intervention in the economic process. He was to change his mind on this subject and to lend both his vote and his voice in the House of Commons to the support of Fielden's Factory Act of 1847, which put a legal limit of ten hours a day on factory labor. But at the time of the Reform Bill debates, Macaulay's reformism was both middle class and laissez-faire. And his eloquent speeches in favor of reform were concerned with political rather than economic remedies.

Speechmaking was not new to Macaulay, for he had been the champion orator of the Cambridge Union for two years in his college days. But there is a deeper sense in which Macaulay, at a time when scores of able men sought to excel in the art, had long been prepared for success as a parliamentary orator. An essentially rhetorical quality pervades his writing from first to last, showing that the ends and means of the orator had always been part of his study. The short sentences, the repetitions, the accumulated illustrations reinforcing a point, the frequent rhetorical questions, the epigrammatic turn of sentences, the fondness for striking contrast and antithesis, the diction formal but tending toward rather than away from the colloquial—all are distinguishing points of style in both Macaulay's written and spoken prose. His enemies said that his speeches were spoken essays, but they might better have said that his essays were written speeches, always provided, of course, that the speaker is Macaulay. There are those who regret the strong rhetorical cast of Macaulay's writing—it is no doubt what Matthew Arnold had in mind when he complained that Macaulay's style had the fraudulent air of perpetually hitting the right nail on the head—and it is certainly a limitation. But what he manages to do within it! And if there is a universally agreed-upon praise of Macaulay's style, it is for its qualities of lucidity and energy, qualities directly dependent upon the rhetorical manner.

Following Macaulay's triumphs in the House of Commons, a grateful ministry appointed him to the Board of East Indian Commissioners, where he had a large part in preparing the bill for the renewal of the East India Company's charter. The British possessions in India were then, and until 1858 remained, under the direct administration of the private East India Company, so that the periodical revision of its charter constituted a major piece of imperial legislation. One of the provisions of the new charter act was for the appointment of a legal member to the newly-created Supreme Council of India, whose business it was to review and pass upon the constitutionality of the council's legislation. To this post, which carried a salary of £10,000 a year, Macaulay was appointed. He sailed for India in 1834, remained there three and a half years, and returned to England in 1838 with an independent fortune and entire freedom to follow his own interests.

Macaulay's Indian career was a continuation, in totally different circumstances, of his career as a reformer in English politics, the principle of which was faith in the useful effects of rational legislation and in the value of education. Apart from his routine work on the council, Macaulay quickly threw himself into two other enterprises—the composition of a penal code to replace the various competing systems then in force, and the establishment of English education in India for Indians. The first of these works can be properly appreciated only by the specialist, but it is perhaps the most impressive evidence that we have of the versatility of Macaulay's powers and of his confidence in them. For the second, Macaulay has left a minute by which the question of Indian education was determined for the next century and which, whatever objections may be made to its assumptions, is a model of Macaulay's skill in making a case on a point of great public importance.

In the years of what he called his Indian exile, Macaulay's ambitions underwent a change. More and more he came to prefer a life given to literature rather than to politics. He even thought for a time that on his return he would not reenter public life. Though he could not, in the event, resist the temptation, his political career after 1838 seems almost a distraction from the main object, the writing of the *History of England*, whose design had already occurred to him and of which more will be said later. Superficially, the years following his return to England seem to have been the most successful of Macaulay's public life. He was elected M.P. for Edinburgh in 1839 and was made a member of the cabinet as secretary-at-war in the same year. The Whigs went out in 1841, but on their return in 1846 Macaulay was again given a seat in the cabinet as paymaster-general. But when, in 1847, he was defeated at Edinburgh, he was glad to be free: "I think," he wrote to a friend, "that having been once manumitted, after the old fashion, by a slap in the face, I shall not take to bondage again." Five years later Macaulay enjoyed a triumph beyond that of Coriolanus when the citizens of Edinburgh begged him to stand and, without Macaulay's condescending to make a single statement during the election or even to appear in the city, overwhelmingly reelected him. But this gratifying event coincided with a heart attack from which Macaulay never fully recovered—"I became twenty years older in a week," he wrote to a sister. An active life in the House of Commons would have been impossible to him even had he wished it; he rarely attended the House, and when in 1856 he resigned his seat, he had made but three speeches in as many years. On receiving his peerage in 1857, Macaulay took his seat in the House of Lords, but he never spoke there.

In 1842 Macaulay published the *Lays of Ancient Rome*, sophisticated ballad-poetry designed to illustrate the sort of materials that, it was supposed, had been the basis of the traditional history of early Rome. Macaulay had no illusions about his claims as a poet, but a candid reader will allow that, though the genre is not of the highest order, the *Lays* are nevertheless very good examples of their kind.

From this time until his death Macaulay concentrated upon his magnum opus, the *History of England*, the idea of which was stirring in his mind at least as early as 1828 and which had taken definite form during his years in India. He began to write the *History* almost immediately upon his return to England, if not actually before; and though the writing was much interrupted, it soon became, as Macaulay said of it, "a work which is the business and the pleasure of my life."

The *History of England from the Accession of James II*, to give the work its full title, was ambitiously intended to cover the nearly 150 years between the Glorious Revolution of 1688 and the Reform Bill of 1832. It remains a fragment, but a fragment on a heroic scale. It is, moreover, dramatically complete through its presentation of the triumph of its hero, William III, and the overthrow of James II in the Revolution of 1688 and the decade of struggle that followed. The first two volumes of the *History* appeared at the end of 1848, were received with rapturous enthusiasm, and sold more copies than any such work had ever done. One of Macaulay's objects in writing the *History* had been to supersede the latest novel on the tables of young ladies (as Gibbon had boasted of doing in the century before); in this he completely succeeded.

What Macaulay set out to describe in the *History of England* was the process by which Crown and Parliament had been brought into harmony through the Revolution of 1688 and how this development had been completed by the harmony of Parliament and People created by the Reform Act of 1832, in the adoption of which he himself had had a prominent part. The great theme of this history, as Macaulay conceived it, was the "auspicious union of order and freedom" which was the unique possession of the English nation. By a happy coincidence, the first part of the *History* appeared in the year of European revolution. From the vantage point of a relatively tranquil England Macaulay was enabled to point the moral that England, by carrying out the peaceful and preserving revolutions of 1688 and 1832, was spared the violent upheavals convulsing the other great nations of Europe. This self-congratulatory view has created much offense among modern readers, who no longer share the assumptions of what are called the Whig historians, the school of historical writing whose great model is Macaulay. By Whig history is not meant history given to the indiscriminate praise of Whigs and their relatives. The term refers, rather, to the evident faith of such history in the reality of progress, and to the view which underlies that faith. This view may be defined as that which, taking the present as the measure of things, praises or blames the men and events of the past according to whether they do or do not lead toward the condition of the present. In this sense Macaulay's is certainly a Whig history.

But to confine one's comments on the *History*, as is sometimes done, purely to questions of its Whiggishness is both inadequate and unfair. It may indeed be the case that he makes of William, whom he had admired since his Trinity College days, too much of a marmoreal figure of pure virtue; and it may be that he sees James as too abject and foolish a villain. The argument about Macaulay's characters of Marlborough, Penn, and others still goes on, but concentrating upon such questions diverts us from a proper estimate of what Macaulay really achieved in the *History*. It is a remarkable achievement, for reasons that have nothing to do with the correctness of its judgments on points disputed between Whig and Tory.

The thoroughness and diligence of Macaulay's preparation for writing the *History* was unprecedented, at least among English historians. He had the advantage, of course, of his vast reading and of the memory that could recall anything that had once entered it. He did not, however, rely on what he knew already, prodigious though that was. He consulted the manuscript sources of the great public and university collections and enlisted his friends in the work of tracking down family archives—a tedious labor in the days before the Historical Manuscripts Commission had been thought of. He was the first to consult the records of Parliament, which had long lain undisturbed in the dust of the Jewel Tower. Although he had available to him the extensive collection of extracts from the archives of European countries made by his friend Sir James Mackintosh, he consulted the

French archives himself, and he learned Dutch in order to make use of the papers left by William III and his ministers. He made a point of visiting the scenes of his story—in Holland, Belgium, France, as well as such places closer to home as Sedgemoor, the Boyne, and Glencoe—to sharpen his sense of place. His use of every sort of literary source is notable. Ballads, broadsheets, newspapers, dramas, satirical verses, novels all contributed to the work of recreating the flesh and blood of the period.

As early as 1828, in his essay "History," Macaulay had argued that the ideal history ought not to be restricted to affairs of state but should cheerfully abandon the restraints of "dignity" in order to represent the commonplace realities of daily life as well. The examples that he had in mind were the historical novels of Sir Walter Scott, which Macaulay, in common with all of educated Europe and America, had read eagerly from the time of their first appearance in 1814. Scott's revelation of the denseness and richness of popular life, running on almost indifferent to political vicissitudes and yet determining them too, was, Macaulay felt, a lesson to the historian. He sought to apply it in his own *History*, especially in the famous third chapter, a survey of the state of society in 1685. We nowadays take for granted that history is something more than drums and trumpets, and we may therefore not fully appreciate Macaulay's originality in presenting a picture of the times. It is true that he had, as well as the example of Scott, some precedents in experiments of this kind made by a few eighteenth-century historians. Still, no historian before Macaulay had set out to convey the look and feel of an entire society at a certain point in its history. The method has of course been carried further since Macaulay wrote; but chapter 3 remains a tour de force for which a lifetime's immersion in the literature of the age was required. The chapter—in this it is representative of all Macaulay's narrative—is admirable for the way that it is organized as well as for its content. Part of the pleasure in reading it is in examining the steps by which we are led from the perimeter to the center of England and from high to low. The relations of part to part, the transitions connecting them, the logic of their sequence—these and the other means by which Macaulay makes a welter of miscellaneous material seem to fall effortlessly into place are well worth the reader's study.

As Macaulay wished to make history more inclusive, so he wished also to make it interesting. If he had a good story to tell, the historian was bound to try to tell it well. Chapter 9 of the *History of England*, the second part of which is included in this volume, can serve as a good illustration of Macaulay's mastery of narrative history, a form of historical writing whose difficulties tend to be greatly underrated in our own age of analysis. The story it tells is that of the landing of William of Orange in England in 1688 and of James II's flight in the face of his growing unpopularity and his desertion by increasing numbers of those powerful in church and state. The complex sequence of events, made more so by actual and rumored plots and counterplots, presents a considerable challenge to the historian's narrative skill.

Macaulay meets the challenge brilliantly. In the manner of a practised novelist, he switches back and forth between William's advancing forces in the West and James's court in London without ever losing the thread of the story. In the course of doing so he does not fail to underline the dramatic counterpoint between the Dutch prince and his royal father-in-law, forced to relinquish his throne to the invader: on the one hand, William— decisive, serene, energetic, skilled in dealing with subordinates and allies, not afraid to go his own way against well-meant advice when he felt the situation called for it, and on the other hand, James—insecure, uncertain, shifty, incapable of adopting the proper mode of dealing with either friend or foe. The narrative, cutting back and forth between palace and camp, is full of suspense, yet it unfolds in such a way as to suggest a providential design leading to an inevitable conclusion.

Within this general scheme, Macaulay enriches individual events, moments, and personalities with his unrivaled mastery of the telling detail and the meaningful allusion: the three large lanterns flaming on the stern of William's ship, the *Brill*; the citizens of Exeter gazing with wonder on the black faces, set off by embroidered turbans and white feathers, of the Guiana Negroes in the prince's army; the great organ of Exeter cathedral sounding a peal of triumph as William enters in military state; James, in the course of his flight, flinging the Great Seal into the Thames. Macaulay had a marvelous ear for the revealing lines of historically authentic dialogue, and some excellent examples appear in this chapter: thus James II to Bishop Lamplugh, "My Lord, you are a genuine old Cavalier"; William to his chaplain, Dr. Burnet, "Well, Doctor, what do you think of predestination now?"; and Charles II about James's dim son-in-law, nicknamed *Est-il possible*, "I have tried Prince George sober and I have tried him drunk; and, drunk or sober, there is nothing in him."

As did many of his great predecessors, from Thucydides on, Macaulay interspersed and enhanced his historical narrative with observations about human nature and psychology, whether in referring to "that gentle and temperate malice which inflicts the deepest wounds"; in characterizing revolutions as times during which, old habits of thought and action being violently broken, "novelties which at first sight inspire dread and disgust become in a few days familiar, endurable, attractive"; or whether in observing that "what could justly be called flattery when offered to the powerful is a debt of humanity to the fallen." Like so much of Victorian literature, Macaulay's *History* served as a repository of virtue and wisdom at the same time that it fulfilled its primary function of relating and judging the history of great events.

Judging did not merely mean making moral judgments— though Macaulay certainly never hesitated to do this. It also meant that the historian regarded as an important part of his duty to his readers the presentation of historical situations as they existed at moments of crisis in such a way that the various possibilities for action open to the major participants—whether groups or individuals—were clearly delineated, and then to weigh in the balance the actual course they pursued.

At least two examples of such judgments occur in the selection from the *History* in this volume. One concerns the advice given to James by Nottingham and Halifax, to grant an unlimited amnesty to all those who had taken up arms against him. Macaulay had no doubt that it was wrong for the King to show even the slightest hesitation in pardoning offenses which he was, after all, unable to punish. The other example concerns the policy to be adopted by William on the question whether he should make his designs on the English Crown explicit; he had to conciliate his supporters, consisting both of Whigs, who regarded passive obedience and indefeasible hereditary right as slavish superstitions, and of Tories, who had rallied to William because they saw the Church of England in peril but who "disclaimed with vehemence all thought of taking the crown from that anointed head which the ordinance of heaven and the fundamental laws of the realm had made sacred." Again, Macaulay, having fairly and lucidly set forth the views of the two parties, leaves the reader in no doubt that the proper course of action to be followed in this situation was the one in fact adopted by William: Not to seize the crown, but "to wait till, without any appearance of exertion or stratagem on his part, his secret wish should be accomplished by the force of circumstances, by the blunders of his opponents, and by the free choice of the Estates of the Realm." It is Macaulay's depiction and judgment of situations of this kind that has helped to gain him the plaudits of historians as temperamentally repelled by his self-confidence or his dogmatism or his political bias as Acton and Gardiner in the nineteenth century and Trevor-Roper in our own.

Macaulay's constant effort, the expression of his own fascination with the varied and exciting life of the past, is to make the dry bones of statistics and generalizations live, to make vivid by means of concrete and familiar images what would otherwise have stood in danger of remaining distant and dull. On the tenets of the Puritans, for example, he writes, "It was a sin to hang garlands on a Maypole, to drink a friend's health, to fly a hawk, to hunt a stag, to play at chess, to wear lovelocks, to put starch into a ruff, to touch the virginals, to read the *Faerie Queene*." He describes the profound submission and obedience of the Jesuit as persisting "whether he should live under the arctic circle or under the equator, whether he should pass his life in arranging gems and collating manuscripts at the Vatican or in persuading naked barbarians under the Southern Cross not to eat each other." And about the country squires hurrying to London early in 1690 to oppose the Corporation Bill, which they interpreted as a retroactive penal law against the entire Tory party, he writes, "A hundred knights and squires left their halls hung with mistletoe and holly, and their boards groaning with brawn and plum porridge, and rode up post to town, cursing the short days, the cold weather, the miry road, and the villainous Whigs."

These examples could be indefinitely multiplied, and their

visual and dramatic impact is obvious. What is worth noting is how often the historian's visual imagination is reinforced by what might be called his propulsive imagination. In other words, Macaulay has the knack of propelling inert facts into motion—an ability closely akin to his own powerful daydreaming and fantasy life in which he was able to propel *himself* into imaginary situations. It was this capacity which enabled Macaulay to propel the lord of the manor of the late seventeenth century to London, and to depict him there jostled by bullies, splashed by hackney coachmen, victimized by pickpockets and shopkeepers, and derided by fops; or to describe the effect on Englishmen of all ranks of the possible closing of hundreds of houses of entertainment and public resort:

> Men of fashion would have missed the chocolate house in Saint James's Street, and men of business the coffee pot, round which they were accustomed to smoke and talk politics, in Change Alley. Half the clubs would have been wandering in search of shelter. The traveler at nightfall would have found the inn where he had expected to sup and lodge deserted. The clown would have regretted the hedge alehouse, where he had been accustomed to take his pot on the bench before the door in summer, and at the chimney corner in winter.

His propulsive imagination enabled Macaulay to set in motion what for most other historians would have remained stationary puppets, to exploit to the full the dynamic potential of what in other hands would have been merely a static situation or social setting. It is this same propulsive imagination that helped to make Macaulay such a master of the art of transition—perhaps the most difficult task for the historian. After all, that art in its essence is nothing more than the orderly linkage of one paragraph or section of writing to the next, in a seemingly ineluctable progression, conceived in terms of the author's total vision and cemented by means of linguistic or logical association. In this way, Macaulay's particular gift of imagination supplemented effectively his concern with the technical structure of historical writing.

His imagination had its limits. Even a cursory reading of Macaulay suffices to show that he did not possess the all-embracing sympathy, the capacity for *Einfuehlung,* that would have enabled him to treat all persons, parties, and ideas in history with equal respect and understanding. This lack—which, by the way, as his "Epitaph on a Jacobite" shows, is not to be found in his poems—was due, in part, to the undoubted fact that Macaulay was a person of strong prejudices and, on occasion, of unfair bias. But, even discounting prejudice and *parti pris,* it was perhaps the particular quality of Macaulay's imagination itself which militated against the sort of all-inclusive sympathy he is justly accused of having lacked. As one reads the historian's letters and journals, one is struck again and again by his express intention to make his historical writing lively, amusing, and dramatic. Steeped from childhood in the English novel—to the point where he and his sisters would discuss household affairs and family gossip in the language of Mr. Woodhouse and Mrs. Elton—and an avid admirer of Scott's fictional historical reconstructions, Macaulay set himself the task of making his own *History* as vivid and as entertaining as the latest work of fiction. In this he succeeded. Yet the very harping on the necessity for making history lively, the self-conscious sense of literary artifice, and of what he himself called the need for purple patches, these traits— admirable as they are—may also have acted as impediments to the genuine historical imagination which is more concerned with the unvarnished truth than with enlivening it.

But the fact that Macaulay, like all other great historians, had limitations, should not stand in the way of our reading and enjoying his work today. Long after Macaulay's death the French critic and historian Taine wrote to an English friend:

> I read over again one or two of Macaulay's volumes every year. People now say in England that his talent is *merely rhetorical,* but that is not my opinion. To my mind, he is, as an historian, the greatest artist and the first writer of this century, being incomparable in explaining, setting forth, narrating, co-ordinating, passing from one topic to another and in varying his tone. I put on one side his opinions, his partisanship, his conclusions, all of which are subjects of controversy, and are secondary; but as regards his *art* he is in advance of every one else.

The praise is perhaps extravagant, but the judicious willingness to enjoy what is best in Macaulay is worth imitating.

A Note on Texts

The text of the essays reprinted in this volume of selections is that of their original publication in the *Edinburgh Review*. Macaulay revised the essays on Southey and Leigh Hunt when he reprinted them in volume form. Since, in revising, he often omitted the more highly colored or extreme statements, it has seemed to us that the text containing Macaulay's first, rapid expression of his mind is more interesting than the revised text of the essays, and we have therefore followed it. The essay on Johnson, which was never revised, is reprinted from Macaulay's *Miscellaneous Writings*, published by his friend Thomas Flower Ellis in 1860. The text of the verses reprinted in this volume is from the *Works*, 1866.

The selections from the *History of England* are from the edition of 1858. Macaulay took great pains with the text of the *History*, spending weeks of labor on the proofs of the many successive editions in an effort to transmit the *History* in as accurate a form as possible. This edition is in all essential respects Macaulay's last word.

The speeches are reprinted from the selection that Macaulay published in 1853. The speech on parliamentary reform is taken from a version corrected by Macaulay himself at the time; the others were revised by Macaulay in the summer of 1853 from the imperfect reports contained in Hansard's *Parliamentary Debates*.

The "Minute on Education" is reprinted from Sir George Otto Trevelyan's *The Competition Wallah*, second edition, 1866.

The letters are printed by permission of the Master and Fellows of Trinity College and by permission of the Pierpont Morgan Library.

Chronology

1800, October 25: Born at Rothley Temple, Leicestershire
1802–1818: Family reside at Clapham
1813–1818: At private school
1818: Enters Trinity College, Cambridge
1823: Begins contributing to *Knight's Quarterly Magazine*
1824: Elected fellow of Trinity College
1825: First contribution to the *Edinburgh Review*
1826: Called to the bar and joins the Northern Circuit
1830: Elected to the House of Commons for Calne
1831: Establishes reputation as orator with speeches on the Reform Bill
1832: Elected M.P. for Leeds
1834–1837: In India as legal member of the Supreme Council of India
1838 (October)–1839 (February): First trip to Italy
1839, March: Begins writing the *History of England*
1839, June: Elected M.P. for Edinburgh
1839, September: Appointed secretary-at-war in Lord Melbourne's cabinet
1841, July: Takes rooms in the Albany, where he remains for fifteen years
1841, August: Melbourne ministry resigns
1842, October: Publishes the *Lays of Ancient Rome*
1843: Publishes collected *Critical and Historical Essays*
1844: Last contribution to the *Edinburgh Review*

1846, July: Appointed paymaster-general in Lord John Russell's cabinet

1847, July: Defeated in election at Edinburgh; leaves public life

1848, December: First two volumes of *History of England* published

1852, July: Reelected for Edinburgh; suffers heart attack; in weak health thereafter

1853, July: Last speech in House of Commons

1855, December: Volumes 3 and 4 of *History of England* published

1856, January: Resigns seat in House of Commons

1856, May: Leaves the Albany for Holly Lodge, Kensington

1857, September: Raised to the peerage as Baron Macaulay of Rothley

1859, December 28: Dies

1860, January 9: Buried in Westminster Abbey

Bibliographical Note

Bibliography

There is no complete bibliography of Macaulay. The *New Cambridge Bibliography of English Literature* (Cambridge, 1969) is useful, as are the lists in Arthur Bryant, *Macaulay* (London, 1932), and W. H. French and G. D. Sanders, eds., *The Reader's Macaulay* (New York, [1936]).

Works by Macaulay

Collected Editions

The only collected edition is that edited by Macaulay's sister, Lady Trevelyan, *The Works of Lord Macaulay,* 8 vols. (London, 1866). This has been frequently reprinted, most attractively as the Albany Edition, 12 vols. (London, 1898). The edition is reasonably full but is not complete.

Essays

Critical and Historical Essays, Contributed to the Edinburgh Review, 3 vols. (London, 1843), is the first authorized edition. It was augmented in 1850 and 1853 but is not complete. An edition of Macaulay's essays is kept in print in the Everyman's

Library series. A reader wishing to survey all of Macaulay's essays for the *Edinburgh Review* must consult the full and accurate list in Walter E. Houghton, ed., *The Wellesley Index to Victorian Periodicals,* vol. 1 (Toronto, 1966).

History of England

The History of England from the Accession of James II, vols. 1–2 (1848 [dated 1849]); vols. 3–4 (1855); vol. 5 (1861). The fifth volume was posthumously published. Macaulay's final text of the first four volumes, which he revised with extreme care, is that in seven volumes (London, 1858). The illustrated edition by C. H. Firth, 6 vols. (London, 1913–15), is the most sumptuous.

Works about Macaulay

Biographies

Arnold, Frederick. *The Public Life of Lord Macaulay.* London, 1862.

Trevelyan, G. O. *The Life and Letters of Lord Macaulay.* 2 vols. London, 1876. By Macaulay's nephew; a charming and thoroughly readable book, it is one of the handful of first-rate biographies produced in the nineteenth century.

Stephen, Leslie. Life of Macaulay in the *Dictionary of National Biography.*

Bryant, Arthur. *Macaulay.* London, 1932. Derived from Trevelyan, it is both sympathetic and brief.

Beatty, Richmond Croom. *Lord Macaulay, Victorian Liberal.* Norman, Okla., 1938. The most recent full-length biography. Ostensibly based on new material, it is inaccurate and unoriginal.

General

I. Nineteenth Century Studies

Bagehot, Walter. "Thomas Babington Macaulay." In *Literary Studies,* vol. 2. London, 1879.

Gladstone, W. E. "Macaulay." In *Gleanings of Past Years,* vol. 2. London, 1879.

Morison, J. Cotter. *Macaulay.* English Men of Letters series. London, 1882.

Morley, John. "Macaulay." In *Critical Miscellanies,* vol. 1. London, 1877.

Paget, John. *The New Examen.* Edinburgh, 1861. Reprinted in Paget, *Paradoxes and Puzzles.* Edinburgh, 1874.

Stephen, Leslie. "Macaulay." In *Hours in a Library,* new ed., vol. 2. London, 1892.

Taine, H. A. *History of English Literature,* vol. 4. London, 1877.

II. Twentieth Century Studies

Clive, John. "Macaulay's Historical Imagination." *Review of English Literature* 1 (October 1960): 20–28.

Firth, C. H. *A Commentary on Macaulay's History of England.* London, 1938.

Geyl, Pieter. "Macaulay in His Essays." In *Debates with Historians.* Groningen, 1955. A hostile but judicious criticism by a distinguished Dutch historian.

Knowles, David. *Lord Macaulay, 1800–1859.* Cambridge, 1960. The text of a lecture delivered on the centennial of Macaulay's death.

Levine, George. "Macaulay: Progress and Retreat." In *The Boundaries of Fiction: Carlyle, Macaulay, Newman.* Princeton, 1968.

Madden, William A. "Macaulay's Style." In George Levine and William Madden, eds., *The Art of Victorian Prose.* New York, 1968.

Munby, A. N. L. *Macaulay's Library.* Glasgow, 1966.

Roberts, S. C. "Lord Macaulay: The Pre-eminent Victorian." In *An Eighteenth-century Gentleman and Other Essays.* Cambridge, 1930.

Stokes, Eric. *The English Utilitarians and India.* Oxford, 1959. A notable study of Macaulay's work in India.

Trevor-Roper, H. R. Introduction to Macaulay, *Critical and Historical Essays.* London, 1965.

————. Introduction to Macaulay, *The History of England.* The Great Historians series. New York, 1968.

Young, G. M. "Macaulay." In *Daylight and Champaign.* London, 1937. Reprinted in Young, *Victorian Essays.* Ed. W. D. Handcock. London, 1962.

I. Essays

The London University

The London University, or that part of it now known as University College, was organized in 1826 and held its first classes in October 1828. The object of the university was to make higher education available to qualified students without distinction as to religion. This put the new university in contrast to Oxford and Cambridge, whose degrees could be held only by members of the Church of England. This early effort to establish a school whose principle was toleration and whose instruction was wholly secular was carried out by a mixed company of Jews, Dissenters, Laodiceans, and Evangelical Protestants—among the latter Macaulay's father. It naturally encountered immediate hostility from orthodox churchmen and from defenders of the exclusive privileges of the established universities. Despite Macaulay's jealous affection for his own Trinity College, Cambridge, he could sincerely defend the new London University, for its principles were exactly his own: concern for the education of the rising middle class, the exclusion of religion from what to him was an essentially nonreligious activity, and reform in both administration and curriculum. Indeed, Macaulay's assertion that the university should teach only what its clientele freely chooses to learn has a very topical sound at a time when students are once again demanding just such a freedom.

"The London University" was never acknowledged by Macaulay and does not appear in any of the selections from his

Originally published in February 1826.

*essays that he authorized. It was nonetheless immediately and
widely attributed to him by people in a position to know. There
can be no reasonable doubt that it is his.*

Few things have ever appeared to us more inexplicable than
the cry which it has pleased those who arrogate to themselves
the exclusive praise of loyalty and orthodoxy, to raise against the
projected University of London. In most of those publications
which are distinguished by zeal for the Church and the Government, the scheme is never mentioned but with affected contempt,
or unaffected fury. The Academic pulpits have resounded with
invectives against it; and many even of the most liberal and enlightened members of the old foundations seem to contemplate
it with very uncomfortable feelings.

We were startled at this. For surely no undertaking of equal
importance was ever commenced in a manner more pacific and
conciliatory. If the management has fallen, in a great measure,
into the hands of persons whose political opinions are at variance
with those of the dominant party, this was not the cause, but
the effect of the jealousy which that party thought fit to entertain.
Oxford and Cambridge, to all appearance, had nothing to dread.
Hostilities were not declared. Even rivalry was disclaimed. The
new Institution did not aspire to participate in the privileges
which had been so long monopolized by those ancient corporations. It asked for no franchises, no lands, no advowsons. It did
not interfere with that mysterious scale of degrees on which good
churchmen look with as much veneration as the Patriarch on the
ladder up which he saw angels ascending. It did not ask permission to search houses without warrants, or to take books from
publishers without paying for them. There was to be no melo-
dramatic pageantry, no ancient ceremonial, no silver mace, no
gowns either black or red, no hoods either of fur or of satin,
no public orator to make speeches which nobody hears, no oaths
sworn only to be broken. Nobody thought of emulating the
cloisters, the organs, the painted glass, the withered mummies,
the busts of great men, and the pictures of naked women, which
attract visitors from every part of the Island to the banks of Isis
and Cam. The persons whose advantage was chiefly in view belonged to a class of which very few ever find their way to the

old colleges. The name of University was indeed assumed; and it has been said this gave offence. But we are confident that so ridiculous an objection can have been entertained by very few. It reminds us of the whimsical cruelty with which Mercury, in Plautus, knocks down poor Sosia for being so impudent as to have the same name with himself!

We know indeed that there are many to whom knowledge is hateful for its own sake,—owl-like beings, creatures of darkness, and rapine, and evil omen, who are sensible that their organs fit them only for the night,—and that, as soon as the day arises, they shall be pecked back to their nooks by those on whom they now prey with impunity. By the arts of those enemies of mankind, a large and influential party has been led to look with suspicion, if not with horror, on all schemes of education, and to doubt whether the ignorance of the people be not the best security for its virtue and repose.

We will not at present attack the principles of these persons, because we think that, even on those principles, they are bound to support the London University. If indeed it were possible to bring back, in all their ancient loveliness, the times of venerable absurdities and good old nuisances—if we could hope that gentlemen might again put their marks to deeds without blushing—that it might again be thought a miracle if any body in a parish could read, except the Vicar, or if the Vicar were to read any thing but the Service,—that all the literature of the multitude might again be comprised in a ballad or a prayer,—that the Bishop of Norwich might be burned for a heretic, and Sir Humphry Davy hanged for a conjuror,—that the Chancellor of the Exchequer might negotiate loans with Mr. Rothschild, by extracting one of his teeth daily till he brought him to terms,— then indeed the case would be different. But, alas! who can venture to anticipate such a millennium of stupidity? The zealots of ignorance will therefore do well to consider, whether, since the evils of knowledge cannot be altogether excluded, it may not be desirable to set them in array against each other. The best state of things, we will concede to them, would be that in which all men should be dunces together. That might be called the age of gold. The silver age would be that in which no man should be taught to spell, unless he could produce letters of ordination, or,

5

like a candidate for a German order of knighthood, prove his sixty-four quarters. Next in the scale would stand a community in which the higher and middling orders should be well educated, and the labouring people utterly uninformed. But the iron age would be that in which the lower classes should be rising in intelligence, while no corresponding improvement was taking place in the rank immediately above them.

England is in the last of these states. From one end of the country to the other the artisans, the draymen, the very ploughboys, are learning to read and write. Thousands of them attend lectures. Hundreds of thousands read newspapers. Whether this be a blessing or a curse, we are not now inquiring. But such is the fact. Education is spreading amongst the working people, and cannot be prevented from spreading amongst them. The change which has taken place in this respect within twenty years is prodigious. No person surely, will venture to say that information has increased in the same degree amongst those who constitute what may be called the lower part of the middling class,—farmers for instance, shopkeepers, or clerks in commercial houses.

If there be any truth in the principles held by the enemies of education, this is the most dangerous state in which a country can be placed. They maintain that knowledge renders the poor arrogant and discontented. It will hardly be disputed, we presume, that arrogance is the result, not of the absolute situation in which a man may be placed, but of the relation in which he stands to others. Where a whole society is equably rising in intelligence; where the distance between its different orders remains the same, though every order advances, that feeling is not likely to be excited. An individual is no more vain of his knowledge, because he participates in the universal improvement, than he is vain of his speed, because he is flying along with the earth and every thing upon it, at the rate of seventy thousand miles an hour. But if he feels that *he* is going forward, while those before him are standing still, the case is altered. If ever the diffusion of knowledge can be attended with the danger of which we hear so much, it is in England at the present moment. And this danger can be obviated in two ways only. Unteach the poor,—or teach those who may, by comparison, be called the rich. The former it is plainly impossible to do. And therefore, if those whom we are addressing be consistent, they will exert themselves to do the latter; and, by increasing the knowledge, increase also the power of an extensive and important class,—a class which is as deeply interested as the peerage or the hierarchy in the prosperity and tranquillity of the country; a class which, while it is too numerous to be corrupted by government, is too intelligent to be duped by demagogues, and which, though naturally hostile to oppression and profusion, is not likely to carry its zeal for reform to lengths inconsistent with the security of property and the maintenance of social order.

"But an University without religion!" softly expostulates the Quarterly Review.—"An University without religion!" roars John Bull, wedging in his pious horror between a slander and a double-entendre. And from pulpits and visitation-dinners and combination-rooms innumerable, the cry is echoed and reechoed, "An University without religion!"

This objection has really imposed on many excellent people, who have not adverted to the immense difference which exists between the new Institution and those foundations of which the members form a sort of family, living under the same roof, governed by the same regulations, compelled to eat at the same table, and to return to their apartments at the same hours. Have none of those who censure the London University on this account, daughters who are educated at home, and who are attended by different teachers? The music-master, a good Protestant, comes at twelve; the dancing-master, a French philosopher, at two; the Italian master, a believer in the blood of Saint Januarius, at three. The parents take upon themselves the office of instructing their child in religion. She hears the preachers whom they prefer, and reads the theological works which they put into her hands. Who can deny that this is the case in innumerable families? Who can point out any material difference between the situation in which this girl is placed, and that of a pupil at the new University? Why then is so crying an abuse suffered to exist without reprehension? Is there no Sacheverell to raise the old cry,—the Church is in danger,—that cry which was never uttered by any voice however feeble, or for any end however base, without being instantly caught up and repeated through all the dark and loathsome nooks where bigotry nestles with corruption? Where is the

7

charge of the Bishop and the sermon of the Chaplain, the tear of the Chancellor and the oath of the Heir-apparent, the speech of Mr. William Bankes and the pamphlet of Sir Harcourt Lees? What means the silence of those filthy and malignant baboons, whose favourite diversion is to grin and sputter at innocence and beauty through the grates of their spunging-houses? Why not attempt to blast the reputation of the poor ladies who are so irreligiously brought up? Why not search into all the secrets of their families? Why not enliven the Sunday breakfast-tables of priests and placemen with the elopements of their great-aunts and the bankruptcies of their second cousins?

Or, to make the parallel still clearer, take the case of a young man, a student, we will suppose, of surgery, resident in London. He wishes to become master of his profession, without neglecting other useful branches of knowledge. In the morning he attends Mr. M'Culloch's lecture on Political Economy. He then repairs to the Hospital, and hears Sir Astley Cooper explain the mode of reducing fractures. In the afternoon he joins one of the classes which Mr. Hamilton instructs in French or German. With regard to religious observances, he acts as he himself, or those under whose care he is, may think most advisable. Is there any thing objectionable in this? Is it not the most common case in the world? And in what does it differ from that of a young man at the London University? Our surgeon, it is true, will have to run over half London in search of his instructors; and the other will find all the lecture-rooms which he attends standing conveniently together, at the end of Gower Street. Is it in the local situation that the mischief lies? We have observed that, since Mr. Croker, in the last session of Parliament, declared himself ignorant of the site of Russell Square, the plan of forming an University in so inelegant a neighbourhood has excited much contempt amongst those estimable persons who think that the whole dignity of man consists in living within certain districts, wearing coats made by certain tailors, and eschewing certain meats and drinks. We should be sorry to think that the reports which any lying Mandeville from Bond Street may have circulated respecting that Terra Incognita, could seriously prejudice the new College. The Secretary of the Admiralty, however, has the remedy in his own hands. When Captain Franklin returns, as we trust he soon will, from his American expedition, he will, we hope, be sent to explore that other North-West passage which connects the city with the Regent's Park. It would then be found, that, though the natives generally belong to the same race with those Oriental barbarians whose irruptions have long been the terror of Hamilton Place and Grosvenor Square, they are, upon the whole, quiet and inoffensive; that, though they possess no architectural monument which can be compared to the Pavilion at Brighton, their habitations are neat and commodious; and that their language has many roots in common with that which is spoken in St. James's Street. One thing more we must mention, which will astonish some of our readers, as much as the discovery of the Syrian Christians of St. Thomas on the coast of Malabar. Our religion has been introduced by some Xavier or Augustin of former times into these tracts. Churches, with all their appurtenances of hassocks and organs, are to be found there; and even the tithe, that great *articulum stantis aut labantis ecclesiæ,* is by no means unknown.

The writer of the article on this subject in the last Number of the Quarterly Review severely censures the omission of religious instruction, in a place styling itself an University,—never perceiving that, with the inconsistency which belongs to error, he has already answered the objection. "A place of education," says he, "is the least of all proper to be made the arena of disputable and untried doctrine." He severely censures those academies in which "a perpetual vacillation of doctrine is observable, whether in morals, metaphysics, or religion, according to the frequency of change in the professional chair." Now, we venture to say, that these considerations, if they are worth anything at all, are decisive against any scheme of religious instruction in the London University. That University was intended to admit not only Christians of all persuasions, but even Jews. But suppose that it were to narrow its limits, to adopt the formularies of the Church of England, to require subscription, or the sacramental test, from every professor and from every pupil; still, we say, there would be more field for controversy, more danger of that vacillation of doctrine which seems to the Reviewer to be so great an evil, on subjects of theology, than on all other subjects together. Take a science which is still young, a

9

science of considerable intricacy, a science, we may add, which the passions and interests of men have rendered more intricate than it is in its own nature, the science of Political Economy. Who will deny, that, for one schism which is to be found among those who are engaged in that study, there are twenty on points of divinity, *within the Church of England?*

Is it not notorious that Arminians, who stand on the very frontier of Pelagianism, and Calvinists, whom a line scarcely discernible separates from Antinomianism, are to be found among those who eat the bread of the Establishment? Is it not notorious that predestination, final perseverance, the operation of grace, the efficacy of the sacraments, and a hundred other subjects which we could name, have been themes of violent disputes between eminent churchmen? The ethics of Christianity, as well as its theory, have been the theme of dispute. One party calls the other latitudinarian and worldly. The other retorts accusations of fanaticism and asceticism. The curate has been set against the rector, the dean against the bishop. There is scarcely a parish in England, into which the controversy has not found its way. There is scarcely an action of human life so trivial and familiar as not to be in some way or other affected by it. Whether it is proper to take in a Sunday newspaper, to shoot a partridge, to course a hare, to subscribe to a Bible Society, to dance, to play at whist, to read Tom Jones, to see Othello,—all these are questions on which the strongest difference of opinion exists between persons of high eminence in the hierarchy. The Quarterly Reviewer thinks it a very bad thing, that "the first object of a new professor should be to refute the fundamental positions of his predecessors." What would be the case if a High Churchman should succeed a Low Churchman, or a Low Churchman a High Churchman, in the chair of religion? And what possible security could the London University have against such an event? What security have Oxford or Cambridge now? In fact, all that we know of the state of religious parties at those places, fully bears out our statement. One of the most famous divines of our time, Dr. Marsh, Bishop of Peterborough, Margaret Professor of Theology at Cambridge, and author of eighty-seven of the most unanswerable questions that ever man propounded to his fellow men, published a very singular hypothesis respecting the origin of the Gospels. With the truth or falsehood of the hypothesis we have nothing to do. We have, however, heard another eminent Professor of the same University, high in the Church, condemn the theory as utterly unfounded, and of most dangerous consequence to the orthodox faith. Nay, the very pulpit of Saint Mary's has been "the arena of disputable and untried doctrine," as much as ever was the chair of any Scotch or German professor,—a fact, of which any person may easily satisfy himself, who will take the trouble to rescue from the hands of trunk-makers and pastry-cooks, a few of the sermons which have been preached there, and subsequently published. And if, in the course of his researches, he should happen to light on that which was preached by a very eminent scholar on a very remarkable occasion, the installation of the Duke of Gloucester, will see, that not only dispute, but something very like abuse, may take place between those whose office it is to instruct our young collegians in the doctrines and duties of Christianity.

"But," it is said, "would it not be shocking to expose the morals of young men to the contaminating influence of a great city, to all the fascinations of the Fives' Court and the gaming table, the tavern and the saloon?" Shocking, indeed, we grant, if it were possible to send them all to Oxford and Cambridge, those blessed spots where, to use the imagery of their own prize-poems, the Saturnian age still lingers, and where white-robed Innocence has left the print of her departing footsteps. There, we know, all the men are philosophers, and all the women vestals. There, simple and bloodless repasts support the body without distressing the mind. There, while the sluggish world is still sleeping, the ingenuous youth hasten to pour forth their fervent orisons in the chapel; and in the evening, elsewhere the season of riot and license, indulge themselves with a solitary walk beneath the venerable avenues, musing on the vanity of sensual pursuits, and the eternity and sublimity of virtue. But, alas! these blissful abodes of the Seven Cardinal Virtues are neither large enough nor cheap enough for those who stand in need of instruction. Many thousands of young men will live in London, whether an University be established there or not,—and that for this simple reason, that they cannot afford to live elsewhere. That they should be condemned to one misfortune because they labour under another, and debarred from knowledge because they are surrounded with temptations to vice, seems to be not a very rational or humane mode of proceeding.

To speak seriously, in comparing the dangers to which the morals of young men are exposed in London, with those which exist at the Universities, there is something to be said on both sides. The temptations of London may be greater. But with the temptation there is a way to escape. If the student live with his family, he will be under the influence of restraints more powerful, and, we will add, infinitely more salutary and respectable, than those which the best disciplined colleges can impose. Even if he be left completely to his own devices, he will still have within his reach two inestimable advantages, from which the students of Oxford and Cambridge are almost wholly excluded, the society of men older than himself, and of modest women.

There are no intimacies more valuable than those which a young man forms with one who is his senior by ten or twelve years. Those years do not destroy the sympathy and the sense of equality without which no cordiality can exist. Yet they strengthen the principles, and form the judgment. They make one of the parties a sensible adviser, and the other a docile listener. Such friendships it is almost impossible to form at College. Between the man of twenty and the man of thirty there is a great gulf, a distinction which cannot be mistaken, which is marked by the dress and by the seat, at prayers and at table. We do not believe that, of the young students at our ancient seats of learning, one in ten lives in confidence and familiarity with any member of the University who is a Master of Arts. When the members of the University are deducted, the society of Oxford and Cambridge is no more than that of an ordinary county town.

This state of things, it is clear, does more harm than all the exertions of Proctors and Proproctors can do good. The errors of young men are of a nature with which it is very difficult to deal. Slight punishments are inefficient; severe punishments generally and justly odious. The best course is to give them over to the arm of public opinion. To restrain them, it is necessary to make them discreditable. But how can they be made discreditable while the offenders associate only with those who are of the same age, who are exposed to the same temptations, and who are willing to grant the indulgence which they themselves may need? It is utterly impossible that a code of morality and honour, enacted by the young only, can be so severe against juvenile irregularities as that which is in force in general society, where manhood and age have the deciding voice, and where the partial inclinations of those whose passions are strong, and whose reason is weak, are withstood by those whom time and domestic life have sobered. The difference resembles that which would be found between laws passed by an assembly consisting solely of farmers, or solely of weavers, and those of a senate fairly representing every interest of the community.

A student in London, even though he may not live with his own relatives, will generally have it in his power to mix with respectable female society. This is not only a very pleasant thing, but it is one which, though it may not make him moral, is likely to make him decorous, and to preserve him from that brainless and heartless Yahooism, that disdain of the character of women, and that brutal indifference to their misery, which is the worst offence, and the severest punishment of the finished libertine. Many of the pupils will, in all probability, continue to reside with their parents or friends. We own that we can conceive no situation more agreeable or more salutary. One of the worst effects of College habits is that distaste for domestic life which they almost inevitably generate. The system is monastic; and it tends to produce the monastic selfishness, inattention to the convenience of others, and impatience of petty privations. We mean no reproach. It is utterly impossible that the most amiable man in the world can be accustomed to live for years independent of his neighbours, and to lay all his plans with a view only to himself, without becoming, in some degree, unfitted for a family. A course of education which should combine the enjoyments of a home with the excitements of a University, would be more likely than any other to form characters at once affectionate and manly. Home-bred boys, it is often said, are idle. The cause, we suspect, is the want of competitors. We no more believe that a young man at the London University would be made idle by the society of his mothers and sisters, than that the old German warriors, or the combatants in the tournaments of the middle ages, were made cowards by the presence of female spectators. On the contrary, we are convinced that his ambition would be at once animated and consecrated by daily intercourse with those who would be dearest to him, and most inclined to rejoice in his success.

The eulogists of the old Universities are fond of dwelling on the glorious associations connected with them. It has often been said that the young scholar is likely to catch a generous enthusiasm from looking upon spots ennobled by so many great names —that he can scarcely see the chair in which Bentley sat, the tree which Milton planted, the walls within which Wickliffe presided, the books illustrated by the autographs of famous men, the halls hung with their pictures, the chapels hallowed by their tombs, without aspiring to imitate those whom he admires. Far be it from us to speak with disrespect of such feelings. It is possible that the memorials of those who have asserted the freedom, and extended the empire of the mind, may produce a strong impression on a sensitive and ardent disposition. But these instances are rare. "Coram Lepidis male vivitur." Young academicians venture to get drunk within a few yards of the grave of Newton, and to commit solecisms, though the awful eye of Erasmus frowns upon them from the canvas. Some more homely sentiment, some more obvious association is necessary. For our part, when a young man is to be urged to persevering industry, and fortified against the seductions of pleasure, we would rather send him to the fireside of his own family, than to the abodes of philosophers who died centuries ago,—and to those kind familiar faces which are always anxious in his anxiety, and joyful in his success, than to the portrait of any writer that ever wore cap and gown.

The cry against the London University has been swelled by the voices of many really conscientious persons. Many have joined in it from the mere wanton love of mischief. But we believe that it has principally originated in the jealousy of those who are attached to Cambridge and Oxford, either by their interests, or by those feelings which men naturally entertain towards the place of their education, and which, when they do not interfere with schemes of public advantage, are entitled to respect. Many of these persons, we suspect, entertain a vague apprehension, scarcely avowed even to themselves, that some defects in the constitution of their favourite Academies will be rendered more glaring by the contrast which the system of this new College will exhibit.

That there are such defects, great and radical defects in the structure of the two Universities, we are strongly inclined to believe: and the jealousy which many of their members have expressed of the new Institution greatly strengthens our opinion. What those defects appear to us to be, we shall attempt to state with frankness, but, at the same time, we trust, with candour.

We are sensible that we have undertaken a dangerous task. There is perhaps no subject on which more people have made up their minds without knowing why. Whenever this is the case, discussion ends in scurrility, the last resource of the disputant who cannot answer, and who will not submit. The scurrility of those who are scurrilous on all occasions, and against all opponents, by nature and by habit, by taste and by trade, can excite only the mirth or the pity of a well regulated mind. But we neither possess, nor affect to possess, that degree of philosophy, which would render us indifferent to the pain and resentment of sincere and respectable persons, whose prejudices we are compelled to assail. It is not in the bitterness of party spirit, it is not in the wantonness of paradox and declamation, that we would put to hazard the good will of learned and estimable men. Such a sacrifice must be powerful, and nothing but a sense of public duty would lead us to make it. We would earnestly entreat the admirers of the two Universities to reflect on the importance of this subject, the advantages of calm investigation, and the folly of trusting, in an age like the present, to mere dogmatism and invective. If the system which they love and venerate rest upon just principles, the examination which we propose to institute, into the state of its foundations, can only serve to prove their solidity. If they be unsound, we will not permit ourselves to think, that intelligent and honourable men can wish to disguise a fact which, for the sake of this country, and of the whole human race, ought to be widely known. Let them, instead of reiterating assertions which leave the question exactly where they found it; instead of turning away from all argument, as if the subject were one on which doubt partook of the nature of sin; instead of attributing to selfishness or malevolence, that which may at worst be harmless error, join us in coolly studying so interesting and momentous a point.—As to this, however, they will please themselves. We speak to the English people. The public mind, if we are not deceived, is approaching to manhood. It has outgrown its swaddling bands, and thrown away its play-things. It can no longer be amused by a rattle, or laid asleep by a song, or awed by a fairy tale. At such a time, we cannot doubt that we shall obtain an impartial hearing.

Our objections to Oxford and Cambridge may be summed up in two words, their Wealth and their Privileges. Their prosperity does not depend on the public approbation. It would therefore be strange if they deserved the public approbation. Their revenues are immense. Their degrees are, in some professions, indispensable. Like manufacturers who enjoy a monopoly, they work at such an advantage, that they can venture to work ill.

Every person, we presume, will acknowledge that, to establish an academic system on immutable principles, would be the height of absurdity. Every year sees the empire of science enlarged by the acquisition of some new province, or improved by the construction of some easier road. Surely the change which daily takes place in the state of knowledge, ought to be accompanied by a corresponding change in the method of instruction. In many cases the rude and imperfect works of early speculators ought to give place to the more complete and luminous performances of those who succeed them. Even the comparative value of languages is subject to great fluctuations. The same tongue which at one period may be richer than any other in valuable works, may, some centuries after, be poorer than any. That, while such revolutions takes place, education ought to remain unchanged, is a proposition too absurd to be maintained for a moment.

If it be desirable that education should, by a gradual and constant change, adapt itself to the circumstances of every generation, how is this object to be secured? We answer—only by perfect freedom of competition. Under such a system, every possible exigence would be met. Whatever language, whatever art, whatever science, it might at any time be useful to know, *that* men would surely learn, and would as surely find instructors to teach. The professor who should persist in devoting his attention to branches of knowledge which had become useless, would soon be deserted by his pupils. There would be as much of every sort of information as would afford profit and pleasure to the possessor—and no more.

But the riches and the franchises of our Universities prevent this salutary rivalry from taking place. In its stead is introduced an unnatural system of premiums, prohibitions, and apprenticeships. Enormous bounties are lavished on particular acquirements; and, in consequence, there is among our youth a glut of Greek, Latin, and Mathematics, and a lamentable scarcity of every thing else.

We are by no means inclined to depreciate the studies which are encouraged at Oxford and Cambridge. We should reprobate with the same severity a system under which a like exclusive protection should be extended to French or Spanish, Chemistry or Mineralogy, Metaphysics or Political Economy. Some of these branches of knowledge are very important. But they may not always be equally important. Five hundred years hence, the Burmese language may contain the most valuable books in the world. Sciences, for which there is now no name, and of which the first rudiments are still undiscovered, may then be in the greatest demand. Our objection is to the principle. We abhor intellectual perpetuities. A chartered and endowed College, strong in its wealth and in its degrees, does not find it necessary to teach what is useful, because it can pay men to learn what is useless. Every fashion which was in vogue at the time of its foundation, enters into its constitution and partakes of its immortality. Its abuses savour of the realty, and its prejudices vest in mortmain, with its lands. In the present instance, the consequences are notorious. We every day see clever men of four and five-and-twenty, loaded with academical honours and rewards,—scholarships, fellowships, whole cabinets of medals, whole shelves of prize books,—enter into life with their education still to begin, unacquainted with the history, the literature, we might almost say, the language of their country, unacquainted with the first principles of the laws under which they live, unacquainted with the very rudiments of moral and political science! Who will deny that this is the state of things? Or who will venture to defend it?

This is no new complaint. Long before society had so far out-stripped the Colleges in the career of improvement as it has since done, the evil was noticed and traced to its true cause, by that great philosopher who most accurately mapped all the regions of science, and furnished the human intellect with its most complete Itinerary. "It is not to be forgotten," says Lord Bacon, "that the dedicating of foundations and donations to professory learning, hath not only had a malign influence upon the growth of sciences, but hath also been prejudicial to states and governments: For hence it proceedeth, that princes find a solitude in respect of able men to serve them in causes of state, *because there is no education collegiate which is* FREE, where such as were so disposed might give themselves to histories, modern languages, books of policy and civil discourse, and other like enablements unto causes of state."[1] The warmest admirers of the present system will hardly deny, that, if this was an evil in the sixteenth century, it must be a much greater evil in the nineteenth. The literature of Greece and Rome is now what it was then. That of every modern language has received considerable accessions. And surely, "books of policy and civil discourse" are as important to an English gentleman of the present day, as they could be to a subject of James the First.

We repeat, that we are not disparaging either the dead languages or the exact sciences. We only say, that if they are useful they will not need peculiar encouragement, and that, if they are useless, they ought not to receive it. Those who maintain that the present system is necessary to promote the study of classical and mathematical knowledge, are the persons who really depreciate those pursuits. They do in fact declare, by implication, that neither amusement nor profit is to be derived from them, and that no man has any motive to employ his time upon them, unless he expects that they may help him to a fellowship.

The utility of mathematical knowledge is felt in every part of the system of life, and acknowledged by every rational man. But does it therefore follow, that people ought to be paid to acquire it? A scarcity of persons capable of making almanacks and measuring land, is as little to be apprehended as a scarcity

1. Advancement of Learning, Book II.

of blacksmiths. In fact, very few of our academical mathematicians turn their knowledge to such practical purposes. There are many wranglers who have never touched a quadrant. What peculiar title then has the mere speculative knowledge of mathematical truth to such costly remuneration? The answer is well known. It makes men good reasoners: it habituates them to strict accuracy in drawing inferences. In this statement there is unquestionably some truth. A man who understands the nature of mathematical reasoning, the closest of all kinds of reasoning, is likely to reason better than another on points not mathematical, as a man who can dance generally walks better than a man who cannot. But no people walk so ill as dancing-masters; and no people reason so ill as mere mathematicians. They are accustomed to look only for one species of evidence; a species of evidence of which the transactions of life do not admit. When they come from certainties to probabilities, from a syllogism to a witness, their superiority is at an end. They resemble a man who, never having seen any object which was not either black or white, should be required to discriminate between two near shades of grey. Hence, on questions of religion, policy, or common life, we perpetually see these boasted demonstrators either extravagantly credulous, or extravagantly sceptical. That the science is a necessary ingredient in a liberal education, we admit. But it is only an ingredient, and an ingredient which is peculiarly dangerous, unless diluted by a large admixture of others. To encourage it by such rewards as are bestowed at Cambridge, is to make the occasional tonic of the mind its morning and evening nutriment.

The partisans of classical literature are both more numerous and more enthusiastic than the mathematicians; and the ignorant violence with which their cause has sometimes been assailed, has added to its popularity. On this subject we are sure that we are at least impartial judges. We feel the warmest admiration for the great remains of antiquity. We gratefully acknowledge the benefits which mankind has owed to them. But we would no more suffer a pernicious system to be protected by the reverence which is due to them, than we would show our reverence for a saint by erecting his shrine into a sanctuary for criminals.

An eloquent scholar has said, that ancient literature was the ark in which all the civilization of the world was preserved during the deluge of barbarism. We confess it. But we do not read that Noah thought himself bound to live in the ark after the deluge had subsided. When our ancestors first began to consider the study of the classics as the principal part of education, little or nothing worth reading was to be found in any modern language. Circumstances have confessedly changed. Is it not possible that a change of system may be desirable?

Our opinion of the Latin tongue will, we fear, be considered heretical. We cannot but think that its vocabulary is miserably poor, and its mechanism deficient both in power and precision. The want of a definite article, and of a distinction between the preterite and the aorist tenses, are two defects which are alone sufficient to place it below any other language with which we are acquainted. In its most flourishing era it was reproached with poverty of expression. Cicero, indeed, was induced, by his patriotic feelings, to deny the charge. But the perpetual recurrence of Greek words in his most hurried and familiar letters, and the frequent use which he is compelled to make of them, in spite of all his exertions to avoid them, in his philosophical works, fully prove that even this great master of the Latin tongue felt the evil which he laboured to conceal from others.

We do not think much better of the writers, as a body, than of the language. The literature of Rome was born old. All the signs of decrepitude were on it in the cradle. We look in vain for the sweet lisp and the graceful wildness of an infant dialect. We look in vain for a single great creative mind,—for a Homer or a Dante, a Shakespeare or a Cervantes. In their place we have a crowd of fourth-rate and fifth-rate authors, translators, and imitators without end. The rich heritage of Grecian philosophy and poetry was fatal to the Romans. They would have acquired more wealth, if they had succeeded to less. Instead of accumulating fresh intellectual treasures, they contented themselves with enjoying, disposing in new forms, or impairing by an injudicious management, those which they took by descent. Hence, in most of their works, there is scarcely any thing spontaneous and racy, scarcely any originality in the thoughts, scarcely any idiom in the style. Their poetry tastes of the hot-house. It is transplanted from Greece, with the earth of Pindus clinging round its roots. It is nursed in careful seclusion from the Italian air. The gardeners are often skilful; but the fruit is almost always sickly. One hardy and prickly shrub, of genuine Latin growth, must indeed be excepted. Satire was the only indigenous produce of Roman talent; and, in our judgment, by far the best.

We are often told the Latin language is more strictly grammatical than the English; and that it is, therefore, necessary to study it, in order to speak English with elegance and accuracy. This is one of those remarks, which are repeated till they pass into axioms, only because they have so little meaning, that no body thinks it worth while to refute them at their first appearance. If those who say that the Latin language is more strictly grammatical than the English, mean only that it is more regular, that there are fewer exceptions to its general laws of derivation, inflection, and construction, we grant it. This is, at least for the purposes of the orator and the poet, rather a defect than a merit; but be it merit or defect, it can in no possible way facilitate the acquisition of any other language. It would be about as reasonable to say, that the simplicity of the Code Napoleon renders the study of the laws of England easier than formerly. If it be meant, that the Latin language is formed in more strict accordance with the general principles of grammar than the English, that is to say, that the relations which words bear to each other are more strictly analogous to the relations between the ideas which they represent in Latin than in English, we venture to doubt the fact. We are quite sure, that not one in ten thousand of those who repeat the hackneyed remark on which we are commenting, have ever considered whether there be any principles of grammar whatever, anterior to positive enactment,—any solecism which is a *malum in se*, as distinct from a *malum prohibitum*. Or, if we suppose that there exist such principles, is not the circumstance, that a particular rule is found in one language and not in another, a sufficient proof that it is not one of those principles? That a man who knows Latin is likely to know English better than one who does not, we do not dispute. But this advantage is not peculiar to the study of Latin. Every language throws light on every other. There is not a single foreign tongue which will not suggest to a man of sense some new considerations respecting his own. We acknowledge, too, that the great body of our educated countrymen learn to grammaticise their English by means of their Latin. This however, proves, not the usefulness of their Latin, but the folly of their other instructors. Instead of being a vindication of the present system of education, it is high charge against it. A man who thinks the knowledge of Latin essential to the purity of English diction, either has never conversed with an accomplished woman, or does not deserve to have conversed with her. We are sure, that all persons who are in the habit of hearing public speaking must have observed, that the orators who are fondest of quoting Latin, are by no means the most scrupulous about marring their native tongue. We could mention several Members of Parliament, who never fail to usher in their scraps of Horace and Juvenal with half a dozen false concords.

The Latin language is principally valuable as an introduction to the Greek, the insignificant portico of a most chaste and majestic fabric. On this subject, our Confession of Faith will, we trust, be approved by the most orthodox scholar. We cannot refuse our admiration to that most wonderful and perfect machine of human thought, to the flexibility, the harmony, the gigantic power, the exquisite delicacy, the infinite wealth of words, the incomparable felicity of expression, in which are united the energy of the English, the neatness of the French, the sweet and infantine simplicity of the Tuscan. Of all dialects, it is the best fitted for the purposes both of science and of elegant literature. The philosophical vocabularies of ancient Rome, and of modern Europe, have been derived from that of Athens. Yet none of the imitations has ever approached the richness and precision of the original. It traces with ease distinctions so subtle, as to be lost in every other language. It draws lines where all the other instruments of the reason only make blots. Nor is it less distinguished by the facilities which it affords to the poet. There are pages even in the Greek Dictionaries over which it is impossible to glance without delight. Every word suggests some pleasant or striking image, which, wholly unconnected as it is with that which precedes or that which follows, gives the same sort of pleasure with that which we derive from reading the Adonais of poor Shelley, or from looking at those elegant, though unmeaning friezes, in which the eye wanders along a line of beautiful faces, graceful draperies, stags, chariots, altars, and garlands.

The literature is not unworthy of the language. It may boast of four poets of the very first order, Homer, Æschylus, Sophocles, and Aristophanes,—of Demosthenes, the greatest of orators—of Aristotle, who is perhaps entitled to the same rank among philosophers, and Plato, who, if not the most satisfactory of philosophers, is at least the most fascinating. These are the great names of Greece; and to these is to be added a long list of ingenious moralists, wits, and rhetoricians, of poets who, in the lower departments of their art, deserve the greatest praise, and of historians who, at least in the talent of narration, have never been equalled.

It was justly said by the Emperor Charles the Fifth, that to learn a new language was to acquire a new soul. He who is acquainted only with the writers of his native tongue, is in perpetual danger of confounding what is accidental with what is essential, and of supposing that tastes and habits of thought, which belong only to his own age and country, are inseparable from the nature of man. Initiated into foreign literature, he finds that principles of politics and morals, directly contrary to those which he has hitherto supposed to be unquestionable, because he never heard them questioned, have been held by large and enlightened communities; that feelings, which are so universal among his contemporaries, that he had supposed them instinctive, have been unknown to whole generations; that images, which have never failed to excite the ridicule of those among whom he has lived, have been thought sublime by millions. He thus loses that Chinese cast of mind, that stupid contempt for every thing beyond the wall of his celestial empire, which was the effect of his former ignorance. New associations take place among his ideas. He doubts where he formerly dogmatised. He tolerates where he formerly execrated. He ceases to confound that which is universal and eternal in human passions and opinions with that which is local and temporary. This is one of the most useful effects which results from studying the literature of other countries; and it is one which the remains of Greece, composed at a remote period, and in a state of society widely different from our own, are peculiarly calculated to produce.

But though we are sensible that great advantages may be

derived from the study of the Greek language, we think that they may be purchased at too high a price: And we think that seven or eight years of the life of a man who is to enter into active life at two or three-and-twenty, is too high a price. Those are bad economists who look only to the excellence of the article for which they are bargaining, and never ask about the cost. The cost, in the present instance, is too often the whole of that invaluable portion of time during which a fund of intellectual pleasure is to be stored up, and the foundations of wisdom and usefulness laid. No person doubts that much knowledge may be obtained from the Classics. It is equally certain that much gold may be found in Spain. But it by no means necessarily follows, that it is wise to work the Spanish mines, or to learn the ancient languages. Before the voyage of Columbus, Spain supplied all Europe with the precious metals. The discovery of America changed the state of things. New mines were found, from which gold could be procured in greater plenty, and with less labour. The old works were therefore abandoned— it being manifest those who persisted in laying out capital on them would be undersold and ruined. A new world of literature and science has also been discovered. New veins of intellectual wealth have been laid open. But a monstrous system of bounties and prohibitions compels us still to go on delving for a few glittering grains in the dark and laborious shaft of antiquity, instead of penetrating a district which would reward a less painful search with a more lucrative return. If, after the conquest of Peru, Spain had enacted that, in order to enable the old mines to maintain a competition against the new, a hundred pistoles should be given to every person who should extract an ounce of gold from them, the parallel would be complete.

We will admit that the Greek language is a more valuable language than the French, the Italian, or the Spanish. But whether it be more valuable than all the three together, may be doubted; and that all the three may be acquired in less than half the time in which it is possible to become thoroughly acquainted with the Greek, admits of no doubt at all. Nor does the evil end here. Not only do the modern dialects of the Continent receive less attention than they deserve, but our own tongue, second to that of Greece alone in force and copiousness, our own literature, second to none that ever existed, so rich in poetry, in eloquence, in philosophy, is unpardonably neglected. All the nineteen plays of Euripides are digested, from the first bubbling froth of the Hecuba to the last vapid dregs of the Electra; while our own sweet Fletcher, the second name of the modern drama, in spite of all the brilliancy of his wit, and all the luxury of his tenderness, is suffered to lie neglected. The Essay on the Human Understanding is abandoned for the Theotetus and the Phœdon. We have known the dates of all the petty skirmishes of the Peloponnesian war carefully transcribed and committed to memory, by a man who thought that Hyde and Clarendon were two different persons! That such a man has paid a dear price for his learning, will be admitted. But, it may be said, he has at least something to show for it. Unhappily he has sacrificed, in order to acquire it, the very things without which it was impossible for him to use it. He has acted like a man living in a small lodging, who, instead of spending his money in enlarging his apartments and fitting them up commodiously, should lay it all out on furniture fit only for Chatsworth or Belvoir. His little rooms are blocked up with bales of rich stuffs and heaps of gilded ornaments, which have cost more than he can afford, yet which he has no opportunity and no room to display. Elegant and precious in themselves, they are here utterly out of place; and their possessor finds that, at a ruinous expense, he has bought nothing but inconvenience and ridicule. Who has not seen men to whom ancient learning is an absolute curse, who have laboured only to accumulate what they cannot enjoy? They come forth into the world, expecting to find only a larger university. They find that they are surrounded by people who have not the least respect for the skill with which they detect etymologies, and twist corrupt Epodes into something like meaning. Classical knowledge is indeed valued by all intelligent men; but not such classical knowledge as theirs. To be prized by the public, it must be refined from its grosser particles, burnished into splendour, formed into graceful ornaments, or into current coin. Learning in the ore, learning with all the dross around it, is nothing to the common spectator. He prefers the cheapest tinsel; and leaves the rare and valuable clod, to the few who have the skill to detect its qualities, and the curiosity to prize them.

No man, we allow, can be said to have received a complete and liberal education, unless he have acquired a knowledge of the ancient languages. But not one gentleman in fifty can possibly receive what we should call a complete and liberal education. That term includes not only the ancient languages, but those of France, Italy, Germany, and Spain. It includes mathematics, the experimental sciences, and moral philosophy. An intimate acquaintance both with the profound and polite parts of English literature is indispensable. Few of those who are intended for professional or commercial life can find time for all these studies. It necessarily follows, that some portion of them must be given up: And the question is, what portion? We say, provide for the mind as you provide for the body,—first necessaries,—then conveniencies,—lastly luxuries. Under which of those heads do the Greek and Latin languages come? Surely under the last. Of all the pursuits which we have mentioned, they require the greatest sacrifice of time. He who can afford time for them, and for the others also, is perfectly right in acquiring them. He who cannot, will, if he is wise, be content to go without them. If a man is able to continue his studies till his twenty-eighth or thirtieth year, by all means let him learn Latin and Greek. If he must terminate them at one-and-twenty, we should in general advise him to be satisfied with the modern languages. If he is forced to enter into active life at fifteen or sixteen, we should think it best that he should confine himself almost entirely to his native tongue, and thoroughly imbue his mind with the spirit of its best writers. But no! The artificial restraints and encouragements which our academic system has introduced have altogether *reversed* this natural and salutary order of things. We deny ourselves what is indispensable, that we may procure what is superfluous. We act like a day-labourer who should stint himself in bread, that he might now and then treat himself with a pottle of January strawberries. Cicero tells us, in the Offices, a whimsical anecdote of Cato the Censor. Somebody asked him what was the best mode of employing capital. He said, To farm good pasture land. What the next? To farm middling pasture land. What next? To farm bad pasture land. Now the notions which prevail in England respecting classical learning seem to us very much to resemble those which the old Roman entertained with regard to his favourite method of cultivation. Is a young man able to spare the time necessary for passing through the University? Make him a good classical scholar! But a second, instead of residing at the University, must go into business when he leaves school. Make him then a tolerable classical scholar! A third has still less time for snatching up knowledge, and is destined for active employment while still a boy. Make him a bad classical scholar! If he does not become a Flaminius or a Buchanan, he may learn to write nonsense verses. If he does not get on to Horace, he may read the first book of Cæsar. If there is not time even for such a degree of improvement, he may at least be flogged through that immemorial vestibule of learning. "Quis docet? Who teacheth? Magister docet. The master teacheth." Would to heaven that he taught something better worth knowing!

All these evils are produced by the state of our Universities. Where they lead, those who prepare pupils for them, are forced to follow. Under a free system, the ancient languages would be less read, but quite as much enjoyed. We should not see so many lads who have a smattering of Latin and Greek, from which they derive no pleasure, and which, as soon as they are at liberty, they make all possible haste to forget. It must be owned, also, that there would be fewer young men really well acquainted with the ancient tongues. But there would be many more who had treasured up useful and agreeable information. Those who were compelled to bring their studies to an early close, would turn their attention to objects easily attainable. Those who enjoyed a longer space of literary leisure, would still exert themselves to acquire the classical languages. They would study them, not for any direct emolument which they would expect from the acquisition, but for their own intrinsic value. Their number would be smaller, no doubt, than that of present aspirants after classical honours. But they would not, like most of those aspirants, leave Homer and Demosthenes to gather dust on the shelves, as soon as the temporary purpose had been served. There would be fewer good scholars of twenty-five; but we believe that there would be quite as many of fifty.

Hitherto we have argued on the hypothesis most favourable to the Universities. We have supposed that the bounties which they offer to certain studies are fairly bestowed on those who excel. The fact however is, that they are in many cases appropriated to particular counties, parishes, or names. The effect of the former system is to encourage studies of secondary importance, at the expense of those which are entitled to preference. The effect of the latter is to encourage total idleness. It has been also asserted, that at some Colleges the distributors of fellowships and scholarships have allowed themselves to be influenced by party spirit, or personal animosity. On this point, however, we will not insist. We wish to expose the vices, not of individuals, but of the system. Indeed, in what we have hitherto written, we have generally had in our eye a College which exhibits that system in the most favourable light,—a College in which the evils which we have noticed are as much as possible alleviated by an enlightened and liberal administration,—a College not less distinguished by its opulence and splendour, than by the eminent talents of many of its members, by the freedom and impartiality of its elections, by the disposition which it has always shown to adopt improvements not inconsistent with its original constitution, and by the noble spirit with which it has supported the cause of civil and religious liberty.

We have hitherto reasoned as if all the students at our Universities learnt those things which the Universities profess to teach. But this, is, notoriously, not the fact—and the cause is evident. All who wish for degrees must reside at College; but only those who expect to obtain prizes and fellowships apply themselves with vigour to classical and mathematical pursuits. The great majority have no inducement whatever to exert themselves. They have no hope of obtaining the premium; and no value for the knowledge without the premium. For the acquisition of other kinds of knowledge the Universities afford no peculiar facilities. Hence proceeds the general idleness of collegians. Not one in ten, we venture to say, ever makes any considerable proficiency in those pursuits to which every thing else is sacrificed. A very large proportion carry away from the University less of ancient literature than they brought thither. It is quite absurd to attribute such a state of things to the indolence and levity of youth. Nothing like it is seen elsewhere. There are idle lads, no doubt, among those who walk the hospitals, who sit at the desks of bankers, and serve at the counters of tradesmen. But

what, after all, is the degree of *their* idleness, and what proportion do they bear to those who are active? Is it not the most common thing in the world, to see men, who have passed their time
at College in mere trifling, display the greatest energy as soon as
they enter on the business of life, and become profound lawyers,
skilful physicians, eminent writers? How can these things be explained, but by supposing that most of those who are compelled
to reside at the Universities have no motive to learn what is taught
there? Who ever employed a French master for four years without improving himself in French? The reason is plain. No man
employs such a master, but from a wish to become acquainted
with the language; and the same wish leads him to apply vigorously to it. Of those who go to our Universities, on the other
hand, a large proportion are attracted, not by their desire to learn
the things studied there, but by their wish to acquire certain
privileges, which residence confers alike on the idle and on the
diligent. Try the same experiment with the French language.
Erect the teachers of it into a corporation. Give them the power
of conferring degrees. Enact that no person who cannot produce
a certificate, attesting that he has been for a certain number of
years a student at this academy, shall be suffered to keep a shop;
and we will venture to predict, that there will soon be thousands,
who, after having wasted their money and their time in a formal attendance on lectures and examinations, will not understand the meaning of *Parlez-vous Français?*

It is the general course of those who patronize an abuse to
attribute to it every thing good which exists in spite of it. Thus,
the defenders of our Universities commonly take it for granted,
that we are indebted to them for all the talent which they have
not been able to destroy. It is usual, when their merits come
under discussion, to enumerate very pompously all the great men
whom they have produced; as if great men had not appeared
under every system of education. Great men were trained in the
schools of the Greek sophists and Arabian astrologers, of the
Jesuits and the Jansenists. There were great men when nothing
was taught but School Divinity and Canon Law; and there would
still be great men if nothing were taught but the fooleries of
Spurzheim and Swedenborg. A long list of eminent names is no
more a proof of the excellence of our Academic institutions,

than the commercial prosperity of the country is a proof of the utility of restrictions in trade. No financial regulations, however absurd and pernicious, can prevent a people amongst whom property is secure, and the motive to accumulate consequently strong, from becoming rich. The energy with which every individual struggles to advance, more than counteracts the retarding force, and carries him forward, though at a slower rate, than if he were left at liberty. It is the same with restrictions which prevent the intellect from taking the direction which existing circumstances point out. They do harm. But they cannot wholly prevent other causes from producing good. In a country in which public opinion is powerful, in which talents properly directed are sure to raise their professor to distinction, ardent and aspiring minds will surmount all the obstacles which may oppose their career. It is amongst persons who are engaged in public and professional life that genius is most likely to be developed. Of these a large portion is necessarily sent to our English Universities. It would, therefore, be wonderful if the Universities could not boast of many considerable men. Yet, after all, we are not sure whether, if we were to pass in review the Houses of Parliament and the English and Scottish Bar, the result of the investigation would be so favourable as is commonly supposed to Oxford and Cambridge. And of this we are sure, that many persons who, since they have risen to eminence, are perpetually cited as proofs of the beneficial tendency of English education, were at College never mentioned but as idle frivolous men, fond of desultory reading, and negligent of the studies of the place. It would be indelicate to name the living; but we may venture to speak more particularly of the dead. It is truly curious to observe the use which is made in such discussions as these, of names which we acknowledge to be glorious, but in which the Colleges have no reason to glory,—that of Bacon, who reprobated their fundamental constitution; of Dryden, who abjured his *Alma Mater*, and regretted that he had passed his youth under her care; of Locke, who was censured and expelled; of Milton, whose person was outraged at one University, and whose works were committed to the flames at the other!

That in particular cases an University education may have produced good effects, we do not dispute. But as to the great body of those who receive it, we have no hesitation in saying, that their minds permanently suffer from it. All the time which they can devote to the acquisition of speculative knowledge is wasted, and they have to enter into active life without it. They are compelled to plunge into the details of business, and are left to pick up general principles as they may. From all that we have seen and heard, we are inclined to suspect, in spite of all our patriotic prejudices, that the young men, we mean the very young men, of England, are not equal as a body to those of France, Germany, or Russia. They reason less justly, and the subjects with which they are chiefly conversant are less manly. As they grow older, they doubtless improve. Surrounded by a free people, enlightened by a free press, with the means of knowledge placed within their reach, and the rewards of exertion sparkling in their sight, it would indeed be strange if they did not in a great measure recover the superiority which they had lost. The finished men of England may, we allow, challenge a comparison with those of any nation. Yet our advantages are not so great that we can afford to sacrifice any of them. We do not proceed so rapidly, that we can prudently imitate the example of Lightfoot in the Nursery Tale, who never ran a race without tying his legs. The bad effects of our University system may be traced to the very last, in many eminent and respectable men. They have acquired great skill in business, they have laid up great stores of information. But something is still wanting. The superstructure is vast and splendid; but the foundations are unsound. It is evident that their knowledge is not systematized; that, however well they may argue on particular points, they have not that amplitude and intrepidity of intellect which it is the first object of education to produce. They hate abstract reasoning. The very name of theory is terrible to them. They seem to think that the use of experience is not to lead men to the knowledge of general principles, but to prevent them from ever thinking about general principles at all. They may play at bo-peep with truth; but they never get a full view of it in all its proportions. The cause we believe is, that they have passed those years during which the mind frequently acquires the character which it ever after retains, in studies, which, when exclusively pursued, have no tendency to strengthen or expand it.

31

From these radical defects of the old foundations the London University is free. It cannot cry up one study or cry down another. It has no means of bribing one man to learn what it is of no use to him to know, or of exacting a mock attendance from another who learns nothing at all. To be prosperous, it must be useful.

We would not be too sanguine. But there are signs of these times, and principles of human nature, to which we trust as firmly as ever any ancient astrologer trusted to the rules of his science. Judging from these, we will venture to cast the horoscope of the infant Institution. We predict, that the clamour by which it has been assailed will die away,—that it is destined to a long, a glorious, and a beneficent existence,—that, while the spirit of its system remains unchanged, the details will vary with the varying necessities and facilities of every age,—that it will be the model of many future establishments—that even those haughty foundations which now treat it with contempt, will in some degree feel its salutary influence,—and that the approbation of a great people, to whose wisdom, energy and virtue, its exertions will have largely contributed, will confer on it a dignity more imposing than any which it could derive from the most lucrative patronage, or the most splendid ceremonial.

Even those who think our hopes extravagant, must own that no positive harm has been even suggested as likely to result from this Institution. All the imputed sins of its founders are sins of omission. Whatever may be thought of them, it is surely better that something should be omitted, than that nothing should be done. The Universities it can injure in one way only—by surpassing them. This danger no sincere admirer of these bodies can apprehend. As for those who, believing that the project really tends to the good of the country, continue to throw obloquy upon it—and that there are such men we believe—to them we have nothing to say. We have no hope of converting them; no wish to revile them. Let them quibble, declaim, sneer, calumniate. Their punishment is to be what they are.

For us, our part has been deliberately chosen—and shall be manfully sustained. We entertain a firm conviction that the principles of liberty, as in government and trade, so also in education, are all-important to the happiness of mankind. To the triumph of those principles we look forward, not, we trust, with a fanatical confidence, but assuredly with a cheerful and steadfast hope. Their nature may be misunderstood. Their progress may be retarded. They may be maligned, derided, nay at times exploded, and apparently forgotten. But we do, in our souls, believe that they are strong with the strength, and quick with the vitality of truth; that when they fall, it is to rebound; that when they recede, it is to spring forward with greater elasticity; that when they seem to perish, there are the seeds of renovation in their very decay—and that their influence will continue to bless distant generations, when infamy itself shall have ceased to rescue from oblivion the arts and the names of those who have opposed them, the dupe, the dissembler, the bigot, the hireling—the buffoon and the sarcasm, the liar and the lie!

Southey's
Colloquies on Society

Macaulay's review of Southey's Colloquies, *completed just a few weeks before he received Lord Lansdowne's offer of a seat in Parliament, and sent off to the editor of the* Edinburgh Review *with a note that it was "too long, I fear, to meet your wishes, but as short as I could make it," is an excellent example of his polemical manner at its most vigorous. Many years later, Macaulay was to note in his journal that he had certainly not liked Robert Southey, and the aggressive, sarcastic tone of the essay confirms this. But the combative approach of the review was due to more than personal antipathy.*

Robert Southey (1774–1843) was a poet and man of letters who had initially welcomed the French Revolution with warm enthusiasm and then recanted his early views to the point of becoming one of the leading spokesmen for conservatism. His whole approach to the social problems of the day, as set forth in the Colloquies, *went against Macaulay's grain. His strictures against the deleterious consequences of industrialism for the quality of English life, his idealization of certain aspects of preindustrial society, his seeming ignorance of and disregard for the "laws" of classical economics—all this challenged some of Macaulay's most firmly held beliefs at the time and caused him to pour out the vials of his wrath.*

The essay shows two value systems in conflict: Southey's, rep-

Originally published in January 1830.

resenting a combination of political conservatism with a maximum of social responsibility; and Macaulay's, representing a combination of political liberalism with a maximum of reliance on individualism. A reading of the Colloquies *themselves shows that Southey was, in fact, not a pessimist. He too believed in progress. But unlike Macaulay, who at the time he wrote this essay agreed with the classical economists in seeing the dislocations caused by the Industrial Revolution as inevitable and not susceptible of correction by state intervention, Southey believed that those dislocations had their roots in society and could therefore be mitigated by the community.*

The twentieth-century reader's sympathies tend to be on Southey's side. But it is important to remember that while Macaulay's paean of praise for the "natural progress of society" was no doubt excessive, his arguments for the improvement, actual and potential, brought about by the Industrial Revolution in the general health and condition of the working classes, and against the roseate view of a golden age before machinery came on the scene, were by no means without foundation.

It would be scarcely possible for a man of Mr. Southey's talents and acquirements to write two volumes so large as those before us, which should be wholly destitute of information and amusement. Yet we do not remember to have read with so little satisfaction any equal quantity of matter, written by any man of real abilities. We have, for some time past, observed with great regret the strange infatuation which leads the Poet-laureate to abandon those departments of literature in which he might excel, and to lecture the public on sciences of which he has still the very alphabet to learn. He has now, we think, done his worst. The subject which he has at last undertaken to treat is one which demands all the highest intellectual and moral qualities of a philosophical statesman,—an understanding at once comprehensive and acute,—a heart at once upright and charitable. Mr. Southey brings to the task two faculties which were never, we believe, vouchsafed in measure so copious to any human being,—the faculty of believing without a reason, and the faculty of hating without a provocation.

It is, indeed, most extraordinary that a mind like Mr. Southey's,—a mind richly endowed in many respects by nature, and highly cultivated by study,—a mind which has exercised considerable influence on the most enlightened generation of the most enlightened people that ever existed—should be utterly destitute of the power of discerning truth from falsehood. Yet such is the fact. Government is to Mr. Southey one of the fine arts. He judges of a theory or a public measure, of a religion, a political party, a peace or a war, as men judge of a picture or a statue, by the effects produced on his imagination. A chain of associations is to him what a chain of reasoning is to other men; and what he calls his opinions, are in fact merely his tastes.

Part of this description might, perhaps, apply to a much greater man, Mr. Burke. But Mr. Burke, assuredly, possessed an understanding admirably fitted for the investigation of truth,—an understanding stronger than that of any statesman, active or speculative, of the eighteenth century,—stronger than every thing, except his own fierce and ungovernable sensibility. Hence, he generally chose his side like a fanatic, and defended it like a philosopher. His conduct, in the most important events of his life,—at the time of the impeachment of Hastings, for example, and at the time of the French Revolution,—seems to have been prompted by those feelings and motives, which Mr. Coleridge has so happily described:

> Stormy pity, and the cherish'd lure
> Of pomp, and proud precipitance of soul.

Hindostan, with its vast cities, its gorgeous pagodas, its infinite swarms of dusky population, its long-descended dynasties, its stately etiquette, excited in a mind so capacious, so imaginative, and so susceptible, the most intense interest. The peculiarities of the costume, of the manners, and of the laws, the very mystery which hung over the language and origin of the people, seized his imagination. To plead in Westminster Hall, in the name of the English people, at the bar of the English nobles, for great nations and kings separated from him by half the world, seemed to him the height of human glory. Again, it is not difficult to perceive, that his hostility to the French Revolution principally arose from the vexation which he felt, at having all his old political associations disturbed, at seeing the well-known boundary-marks of states obliterated, and the names and distinctions with which the history of Europe had been filled for ages, swept away. He felt like an antiquarian whose shield had been scoured, or a connoisseur, who found his Titian retouched. But however he came by an opinion, he had no sooner got it, than he did his best to make out a legitimate title to it. His reason, like a spirit in the service of an enchanter, though spell-bound, was still mighty. It did whatever work his passions and his imagination might impose. But it did that work, however arduous, with marvellous dexterity and vigour. His course was not determined by argument; but he could defend the wildest course by arguments more plausible, than those by which common men support opinions which they have adopted, after the fullest deliberation. Reason has scarcely ever displayed, even in those well-constituted minds of which she occupies the throne, so much power and energy as in the lowest offices of that imperial servitude.

Now, in the mind of Mr. Southey, reason has no place at all, as either leader or follower, as either sovereign or slave. He does not seem to know what an argument is. He never uses arguments himself. He never troubles himself to answer the arguments of his opponents. It has never occurred to him, that a man ought to be able to give some better account of the way in which he has arrived at his opinions than merely that it is his will and pleasure to hold them,—that there is a difference between assertion and demonstration,—that a rumour does not always prove a fact,—that a fact does not always prove a theory, —that two contradictory propositions cannot be undeniable truths,—that to beg the question, is not the way to settle it,—or that when an objection is raised, it ought to be met with something more convincing, than "scoundrel" and "blockhead."

It would be absurd to read the works of such a writer for political instruction. The utmost that can be expected from any system promulgated by him is that it may be splendid and affecting,—that it may suggest sublime and pleasing images. His scheme of philosophy is a mere day-dream, a poetical creation, like the Domdaniel caverns, the Swerga, or Padalon; and indeed, it bears no inconsiderable resemblance to those gorgeous visions. Like them, it has something of invention, grandeur, and brilliancy. But like them, it is grotesque and extravagant, and perpetually violates that conventional probability which is essential to the effect even of works of art.

The warmest admirers of Mr. Southey will scarcely, we think, deny that his success has almost always borne an inverse proportion to the degree in which his undertakings have required a logical head. His poems, taken in the mass, stand far higher than his prose works. The Laureate Odes, indeed, among which the Vision of Judgment must be classed, are, for the most part, worse than Pye's, and as bad as Cibber's; nor do we think him generally happy in short pieces. But his longer poems, though full of faults, are nevertheless very extraordinary productions. We doubt greatly whether they will be read fifty years hence,— but that if they are read, they will be admired, we have no doubt whatever.

But though in general we prefer Mr. Southey's poetry to his prose, we must make one exception. The Life of Nelson is, beyond all doubt, the most perfect and the most delightful of his works. The fact is, as his poems most abundantly prove, that he is by no means so skilful in designing, as in filling up. It was therefore an advantage to him to be furnished with an outline of characters and events, and to have no other task to perform than that of touching the cold sketch into life. No writer, perhaps, ever lived, whose talents so precisely qualified him to write the history of the great naval warrior. There were no fine riddles of the human heart to read—no theories to found—no hidden causes to develop—no remote consequences to predict. The character of the hero lay on the surface. The exploits were brilliant and picturesque. The necessity of adhering to the real course of events saved Mr. Southey from those faults which deform the original plan of almost every one of his poems, and which even his innumerable beauties of detail scarcely redeem. The subject did not require the exercise of those reasoning powers the want of which is the blemish of his prose. It would not be easy to find in all literary history, an instance of a more exact hit between wind and water. John Wesley, and the Peninsular War, were subjects of a very different kind,—subjects which required all the qualities of a philosophic historian. In Mr. Southey's works on these subjects, he has, on the whole, failed. Yet there are charming specimens of the art of narration in both of them. The Life of Wesley will probably live. Defective as it is, it contains the only popular account of a most remarkable moral revolution, and of a man whose eloquence and logical acuteness might have rendered him eminent in literature, whose genius for government was not inferior to that of Richelieu, and who, whatever his errors may have been, devoted all his powers, in defiance of obloquy and derision, to what he sincerely considered as the highest good of his species. The History of the Peninsular War is already dead:—indeed, the second volume was dead-born. The glory of producing an imperishable record of that great conflict seems to be reserved for Colonel Napier.

The Book of the Church contains some stories very prettily told. The rest is mere rubbish. The adventure was manifestly one which could be achieved only by a profound thinker, and in which even a profound thinker might have failed, unless his passions had been kept under strict control. In all those works in which Mr. Southey has completely abandoned narration, and undertaken to argue moral and political questions, his failure has been complete and ignominious. On such occasions, his writings are rescued from utter contempt and derision solely by the beauty and purity of the English. We find, we confess, so great a charm in Mr. Southey's style, that, even when he writes nonsense, we generally read it with pleasure, except indeed when he tries to be droll. A more insufferable jester never existed. He very often attempts to be humorous, and yet we do not remember a single occasion on which he has succeeded farther than to be quaintly and flippantly dull. In one of his works, he tells us that Bishop Sprat was very properly so called, inasmuch as he was a very small poet. And in the book now before us, he cannot quote Francis Bugg without a remark on his unsavoury name. A man might talk folly like this by his own fireside; but that any human being, after having made such a joke, should write it down, and copy it out, and transmit it to the printer, and correct the proof-sheets, and send it forth into the world, is enough to make us ashamed of our species.

The extraordinary bitterness of spirit which Mr. Southey manifests towards his opponents is, no doubt, in a great measure to be attributed to the manner in which he forms his opinions. Differences of taste, it has often been remarked, produce greater exasperation than differences on points of science. But this is not all. A peculiar austerity marks almost all Mr. Southey's judgments of men and actions. We are far from blaming him for fixing on a high standard of morals, and for applying that standard to every case. But rigour ought to be accompanied by discernment, and of discernment Mr. Southey seems to be utterly destitute. His mode of judging is monkish; it is exactly what we should expect from a stern old Benedictine, who had been preserved from many ordinary frailties by the restraints of his situation. No man out of a cloister ever wrote about love, for example, so coldly and at the same time so grossly. His descriptions of it are just what we should hear from a recluse, who knew the passion only from the details of the confessional. Almost all his heroes make love either like seraphim or like cattle. He seems to have no notion of any thing between the Platonic passion of the Glendoveer, who gazes with rapture on his mistress's leprosy, and the brutal appetite of Arvalan and Roderick. In Roderick, indeed, the two characters are united. He is first all clay, and then all spirit; he goes forth a Tarquin, and comes back too ethereal to be married. The only love-scene, as far as we can recollect, in Madoc, consists of the delicate attentions which a savage, who has drunk too much of the Prince's metheglin, offers to Goervyl. It would be the labour of a week to find, in all the vast mass of Mr. Southey's poetry, a single passage indicating any sympathy with those feelings which have consecrated the shades of Vaucluse and the rocks of Meillerie.

Indeed, if we except some very pleasing images of paternal tenderness and filial duty, there is scarcely any thing soft or humane in Mr. Southey's poetry. What theologians call the spiritual sins are his cardinal virtues—hatred, pride, and the insatiable thirst of vengeance. These passions he disguises under the name of duties; he purifies them from the alloy of vulgar interests; he ennobles them by uniting them with energy, fortitude, and a severe sanctity of manners, and then, holds them up to the admiration of mankind. This is the spirit of Thalaba, of Ladurlad, of Adosinda, of Roderick after his regeneration. It is the spirit which, in all his writings, Mr. Southey appears to affect. "I do well to be angry," seems to be the predominant feeling of his mind. Almost the only mark of charity which he vouchsafes to his opponents is to pray for their conversion, and this he does in terms not unlike those in which we can imagine a Portuguese priest interceding with Heaven for a Jew, delivered over to the secular arm after a relapse.

We have always heard, and fully believe, that Mr. Southey is a very amiable and humane man; nor do we intend to apply to him personally any of the remarks which we have made on the spirit of his writings. Such are the caprices of human nature. Even Uncle Toby troubled himself very little about the French grenadiers who fell on the glacis of Namur. And when Mr. Southey takes up his pen, he changes his nature as much as Captain Shandy when he girt on his sword. The only opponents to whom he gives quarter are those in whom he finds something of his own character reflected. He seems to have an instinctive antipathy for calm, moderate men—for men who shun extremes and who render reasons. He has treated Mr. Owen of Lanark, for example, with infinitely more respect than he has shown to Mr. Hallam or to Dr. Lingard; and this for no reason that we can discover, except that Mr. Owen is more unreasonably and hopelessly in the wrong than any speculator of our time.

Mr. Southey's political system is just what we might expect from a man who regards politics, not as a matter of science, but as a matter of taste and feeling. All his schemes of government have been inconsistent with themselves. In his youth he was a republican; yet, as he tells us in his preface to these Colloquies, he was even then opposed to the Catholic claims. He is now a violent Ultra-Tory. Yet while he maintains, with vehemence approaching to ferocity, all the sterner and harsher parts of the Ultra-Tory theory of government, the baser and dirtier part of that theory disgusts him. Exclusion, persecution, severe punishments for libellers and demagogues, proscriptions, massacres, civil war, if necessary, rather than any concession to a discontented people,—these are the measures which he seems inclined to recommend. A severe and gloomy tyranny—crushing opposition—silencing remonstrance—drilling the minds of the people into unreasoning obedience,—has in it something of grandeur which delights his imagination. But there is nothing fine in the shabby tricks and jobs of office. And Mr. Southey, accordingly, has no toleration for them. When a democrat, he did not perceive that his system led logically, and would have led practically, to the removal of religious distinctions. He now commits a similar error. He renounces the abject and paltry part of the creed of his party, without perceiving that it is also an essential part of that creed. He would have tyranny and purity together; though the most superficial observation might have shown him that there can be no tyranny without corruption.

It is high time, however, that we should proceed to the consideration of the work, which is our more immediate subject, and which, indeed, illustrates in almost every page our general remarks on Mr. Southey's writings. In the preface, we are informed that the author, notwithstanding some statements to the contrary, was always opposed to the Catholic Claims. We fully believe this; both because we are sure that Mr. Southey is incapable of publishing a deliberate falsehood, and because his averment is in itself probable. It is exactly what we should have expected that, even in his wildest paroxysms of democratic enthusiasm, Mr. Southey would have felt no wish to see a simple remedy applied to a great practical evil; that the only measure which all the great statesmen of two generations have agreed with each other in supporting, would be the only measure which Mr. Southey would have agreed with himself in opposing. He has passed from one extreme of political opinion to another, as Satan in Milton went round the globe, contriving constantly to "ride with darkness." Wherever the thickest shadow of the night may at any moment chance to fall, there is Mr. Southey. It is not every body who could have so dexterously avoided blundering on the daylight in the course of a journey to the Antipodes.

Mr. Southey has not been fortunate in the plan of any of his fictitious narratives. But he has never failed so conspicuously, as in the work before us; except, indeed, in the wretched Vision of Judgment. In November 1817, it seems, the Laureate was sitting over his newspaper, and meditating about the death of the Princess Charlotte. An elderly person, of very dignified aspect, makes his appearance, announces himself as a stranger from a distant country, and apologises very politely for not having provided himself with letters of introduction. Mr. Southey supposes his visitor to be some American gentleman, who has come to see the lakes and the lake-poets, and accordingly proceeds to perform, with that grace which only long experience can give, all the duties which authors owe to starers. He assures his guest that some of the most agreeable visits which he has received have been from Americans, and that he knows men among them whose talents and virtues would do honour to any country. In passing, we may observe, to the honour of Mr. Southey, that, though he evidently has no liking for the American institutions, he never speaks of the people of the United States with that pitiful affectation of contempt by which some members of his party have done more than wars or tariffs can do to excite mutual enmity between two communities formed for mutual friendship. Great as the faults of his mind are, paltry spite like this has no place in it. Indeed, it is scarcely conceivable that a man of his sensibility and his imagination should look without pleasure and national pride on the vigorous and splendid youth of a great people, whose veins are filled with our blood, whose minds are nourished with our literature, and on whom is entailed the rich inheritance of our civilisation, our freedom, and our glory.

But we must return to Mr. Southey's study at Keswick. The visitor informs the hospitable poet that he is not an American, but a spirit. Mr. Southey, with more frankness than civility, tells him that he is a very queer one. The stranger holds out his hand. It has neither weight nor substance. Mr. Southey upon this becomes more serious; his hair stands on end; and he adjures the spectre to tell him what he is, and why he comes. The ghost turns out to be Sir Thomas More. The traces of martyrdom, it seems, are worn in the other world, as stars and ribbands are worn in this. Sir Thomas shows the poet a red streak round his neck, brighter than a ruby, and informs him that Cranmer wears a suit of flames in paradise,—the right hand glove, we suppose, of peculiar brilliancy.

Sir Thomas pays but a short visit on this occasion, but promises to cultivate the new acquaintance which he has formed, and, after begging that his visit may be kept secret from Mrs. Southey, vanishes into air.

The rest of the book consists of conversations between Mr. Southey and the spirit about trade, currency, Catholic emancipation, periodical literature, female nunneries, butchers, snuff, book-stalls, and a hundred other subjects. Mr. Southey very hospitably takes an opportunity to lionize the ghost round the lakes, and directs his attention to the most beautiful points of view. Why a spirit was to be evoked for the purpose of talking over such matters, and seeing such sights—why the vicar of the parish, a blue-stocking from London, or an American, such as Mr. Southey supposed his aerial visitor to be, might not have done as well—we are unable to conceive. Sir Thomas tells Mr. Southey nothing about future events, and indeed absolutely disclaims the gift of prescience. He has learned to talk modern English: he has read all the new publications, and loves a jest as well as when he jested with the executioner, though we cannot say that the quality of his wit has materially improved in Paradise. His powers of reasoning, too, are by no means in as great vigour as when he sate on the woolsack; and though he boasts that he is "divested of all those passions which cloud the intellects and warp the understandings of men," we think him—we must confess—far less stoical than formerly. As to revelations, he tells Mr. Southey at the outset to expect none from him. The Laureate expresses some doubts, which assuredly will not raise him in the opinion of our modern millennarians, as to the divine authority of the Apocalypse. But the ghost preserves an impenetrable silence. As far as we remember, only one hint about the employments of disembodied spirits escapes him. He encourages Mr. Southey to hope that there is a Paradise Press, at which all the valuable publications of Mr. Murray and Mr. Colburn are reprinted as regularly as at Philadelphia; and delicately insinuates, that Thalaba and the Curse of Kehama are among the number. What a contrast does this absurd fiction present to those charming narratives which Plato and Cicero prefixed to their dialogues! What cost in machinery, yet what poverty of effect! A ghost brought in to say what any man might have said! The glorified spirit of a great statesman and philosopher dawdling, like a bilious old Nabob at a watering-place, over quarterly reviews and novels—dropping in to pay long calls—making excursions in search of the picturesque! The scene of St. George and St. Denys in the Pucelle is hardly more ridiculous. We know what Voltaire meant. Nobody, however, can suppose that Mr. Southey means to make game of the mysteries of a higher state of existence. The fact is, that in the work before us, in the Vision of Judgment, and in some of his other pieces, his mode of treating the most solemn subjects differs from that of open scoffers only as the extravagant representations of sacred persons and things in some grotesque Italian paintings differ from the caricatures which Carlile exposes in the front of his shop. We interpret the particular act by the general character. What in the window of a convicted blasphemer we call blasphemous, we call only absurd and ill-judged in an altar-piece.

We now come to the conversations which pass between Mr. Southey and Sir Thomas More, or rather between two Southeys, equally eloquent, equally angry, equally unreasonable, and equally given to talking about what they do not understand. Perhaps we could not select a better instance of the spirit which pervades the whole book than the discussion touching butchers. These persons are represented as castaways, as men whose employment hebetates the faculties and hardens the heart;—not that the poet has any scruples about the use of animal food. He acknowledges that it is for the good of the animals themselves that men should feed upon them. "Nevertheless," says he, "I cannot but acknowledge, like good old John Fox, that the sight of a slaughter-house or shambles, if it does not disturb this clear conviction, excites in me uneasiness and pain, as well as loathing. And that they produce a worse effect upon the persons employed in them, is a fact acknowledged by that law or custom which excludes such persons from sitting on juries upon cases of life and death."

This is a fair specimen of Mr. Southey's mode of looking at all moral questions. Here is a body of men engaged in an employment, which, by his own account, is beneficial, not only to mankind, but to the very creatures on whom we feed. Yet he represents them as men who are necessarily reprobates—as men who must necessarily be reprobates, even in the most improved state of society—even, to use his own phrase, in a Christian Utopia. And what reasons are given for a judgment so directly opposed to every principle of sound and manly morality? Merely this, that he cannot abide the sight of their apparatus—that, from certain peculiar associations, he is affected with disgust when he passes by their shops. He gives, indeed, another reason; a certain law or custom, which never existed but in the imaginations of old

women, and which, if it had existed, would have proved just
as much against butchers as the ancient prejudice against the
practice of taking interest for money, proves against the merchants of England. Is a surgeon a castaway? We believe that
nurses, when they instruct children in that venerable law or
custom which Mr. Southey so highly approves, generally join the
surgeon to the butcher. A dissecting-room would, we should
think, affect the nerves of most people as much as a butcher's
shambles. But the most amusing circumstance is, that Mr.
Southey, who detests a butcher, should look with special favour
on a soldier. He seems highly to approve of the sentiment of
General Meadows, who swore that a grenadier was the highest
character in this world or in the next; and assures us, that a virtuous soldier is placed in the situation which most tends to his
improvement, and will most promote his eternal interests. Human blood, indeed, is by no means an object of so much loathing
to Mr. Southey, as the hides and paunches of cattle. In 1814, he
poured forth poetical maledictions on all who talked of peace
with Buonaparte. He went over the field of Waterloo,—a field,
beneath which twenty thousand of the stoutest hearts that ever
beat are mouldering,—and came back in an ecstasy, which he
mistook for poetical inspiration. In most of his poems,—particularly in his best poem, Roderic,—and in most of his prose
works, particularly in The History of the Peninsular War, he
shows a delight in snuffing up carnage, which would not have
misbecome a Scandinavian bard, but which sometimes seems to
harmonize ill with the Christian morality. We do not, however,
blame Mr. Southey for exulting, even a little ferociously, in the
brave deeds of his countrymen, or for finding something "comely
and reviving" in the bloody vengeance inflicted by an oppressed
people on its oppressors. Now, surely, if we find that a man
whose business is to kill Frenchmen may be humane, we may
hope that means may be found to render a man humane whose
business is to kill sheep. If the brutalizing effect of such scenes
as the storm of St. Sebastian may be counteracted, we may hope
that in a Christian Utopia, some minds might be proof against
the kennels and dressers of Aldgate. Mr. Southey's feeling, however, is easily explained. A butcher's knife is by no means so

elegant as a sabre, and a calf does not bleed with half the grace of a poor wounded hussar.

It is in the same manner that Mr. Southey appears to have formed his opinion of the manufacturing system. There is nothing which he hates so bitterly. It is, according to him, a system more tyrannical than that of the feudal ages,—a system of actual servitude,—a system which destroys the bodies and degrades the minds of those who are engaged in it. He expresses a hope that the competition of other nations may drive us out of the field; that our foreign trade may decline, and that we may thus enjoy a restoration of national sanity and strength. But he seems to think that the extermination of the whole manufacturing population would be a blessing, if the evil could be removed in no other way.

Mr. Southey does not bring forward a single fact in support of these views, and, as it seems to us, there are facts which lead to a very different conclusion. In the first place, the poor-rate is very decidedly lower in the manufacturing than in the agricultural districts. If Mr. Southey will look over the Parliamentary returns on this subject, he will find that the amount of parish relief required by the labourers in the different counties of England, is almost exactly in inverse proportion to the degree in which the manufacturing system has been introduced into those counties. The returns for the years ending in March 1825, and in March 1828, are now before us. In the former year, we find the poor-rate highest in Sussex,—about 20s. to every inhabitant. Then come Buckinghamshire, Essex, Suffolk, Bedfordshire, Huntingdonshire, Kent, and Norfolk. In all these the rate is above 15s. a-head. We will not go through the whole. Even in Westmoreland, and the North Riding of Yorkshire, the rate is at more than 8s. In Cumberland and Monmouthshire, the most fortunate of all the agricultural districts, it is at 6s. But in the West Riding of Yorkshire, it is as low as 5s.; and when we come to Lancashire, we find it at 4s.,—one-fifth of what it is in Sussex. The returns of the year ending in March 1828, are a little, and but a little, more unfavourable to the manufacturing districts. Lancashire, even in that season of distress, required a smaller poor-rate than any other district, and little more than one-fourth of the poor-rate raised in Sussex. Cumberland alone, of the agricultural districts, was as well off as the West Riding of Yorkshire. These facts seem to indicate that the manufacturer is both in a more comfortable and in a less dependent situation than the agricultural labourer.

As to the effect of the manufacturing system on the bodily health, we must beg leave to estimate it by a standard far too low and vulgar for a mind so imaginative as that of Mr. Southey —the proportion of births and deaths. We know that, during the growth of this atrocious system—this new misery,—(we use the phrases of Mr. Southey,)—this new enormity—this birth of a portentous age—this pest, which no man can approve whose heart is not seared, or whose understanding has not been darkened—there has been a great diminution of mortality—and that this diminution has been greater in the manufacturing towns than anywhere else. The mortality still is, as it always was, greater in towns than in the country. But the difference has diminished in an extraordinary degree. There is the best reason to believe, that the annual mortality of Manchester, about the middle of the last century, was one in twenty-eight. It is now reckoned at one in forty-five. In Glasgow and Leeds a similar improvement has taken place. Nay, the rate of mortality in those three great capitals of the manufacturing districts, is now considerably less than it was fifty years ago over England and Wales taken together—open country and all. We might with some plausibility maintain, that the people live longer because they are better fed, better lodged, better clothed, and better attended in sickness; and that these improvements are owing to that increase of national wealth which the manufacturing system has produced.

Much more might be said on this subject. But to what end? It is not from bills of mortality and statistical tables that Mr. Southey has learned his political creed. He cannot stoop to study the history of the system which he abuses—to strike the balance between the good and evil which it has produced—to compare district with district, or generation with generation. We will give his own reason for his opinion—the only reason which he gives for it—in his own words:

We remained awhile in silence, looking upon the assemblage of dwellings below. Here, and in the adjoining hamlet of Millbeck, the effects of manufactures and of agriculture may be seen and compared. The old cottages are such as the poet and the painter equally delight in beholding. Substantially built of the native stone without mortar, dirtied with no white lime, and their long, low roofs covered with slate, if they had been raised by the magic of some indigenous Amphion's music, the materials could not have adjusted themselves more beautifully in accord with the surrounding scene; and time has still further harmonized them with weather-stains, lichens, and moss, short grasses, and short fern, and stone-plants of various kinds. The ornamented chimneys, round or square, less adorned than those which, like little turrets, crest the houses of the Portuguese peasantry; and yet not less happily suited to their place, the hedge of clipt box beneath the windows, the rose-bushes beside the door, the little patch of flower-ground, with its tall hollyocks in front; the garden beside, the bee-hives, and the orchard with its bank of daffodils and snow-drops, the earliest and the profusest in these parts, indicate in the owners some portion of ease and leisure, some regard to neatness and comfort, some sense of natural, and innocent, and healthful enjoyment. The new cottages of the manufacturers are upon the manufacturing pattern—naked, and in a row.

How is it, said I, that every thing which is connected with manufactures presents such features of unqualified deformity? From the largest of Mammon's temples down to the poorest hovel in which his helotry are stalled, these edifices have all one character. Time will not mellow them; nature will neither clothe nor conceal them; and they will remain always as offensive to the eye as to the mind.

Here is wisdom. Here are the principles on which nations are to be governed. Rose-bushes and poor-rates, rather than steam-engines and independence. Mortality and cottages with weather-stains, rather than health and long life with edifices which time cannot mellow. We are told, that our age has invented atrocities beyond the imagination of our fathers; that society has been brought into a state, compared with which extermination would be a blessing;—and all because the dwellings of cotton-spinners are naked and rectangular. Mr. Southey has found out a way, he tells us, in which the effects of manufactures and agriculture may be compared. And what is this way? To stand on a hill, to look at a cottage and a manufactory, and to see which is the prettier. Does Mr. Southey think that the body of the English peasantry live, or ever lived, in substantial and ornamented cottages, with box-hedges, flower-gardens, bee-hives, and orchards? If not, what is his parallel worth? We despise those *filosofastri,* who think that they serve the cause of science by depreciating literature and the fine arts. But if any thing could excuse their narrowness of mind, it would be such a book as this. It is not strange that when one enthusiast makes the picturesque the test of political good, another should feel inclined to prescribe altogether the pleasures of taste and imagination.

Thus it is that Mr. Southey reasons about matters with which he thinks himself perfectly conversant. We cannot, therefore, be surprised to find that he commits extraordinary blunders when he writes on points of which he acknowledges himself to be ignorant. He confesses that he is not versed in political economy —that he has neither liking nor aptitude for it; and he then proceeds to read the public a lecture concerning it which fully bears out his confession.

"All wealth," says Sir Thomas More, "in former times was tangible. It consisted in land, money, or chattels, which were either of real or conventional value."

Montesinos, as Mr. Southey somewhat affectedly calls himself, answers:

"Jewels, for example, and pictures, as in Holland,—where indeed at one time tulip bulbs answered the same purpose."

"That bubble," says Sir Thomas, "was one of those contagious insanities to which communities are subject. All wealth was real, till the extent of commerce rendered a paper currency necessary; which differed from precious stones and pictures in this important point, that there was no limit to its production."

"We regard it," says Montesinos, "as the representative of real wealth; and, therefore, limited always to the amount of what it represents."

"Pursue that notion," answers the ghost, "and you will be in the dark presently. Your provincial bank-notes, which constitute almost wholly the circulating medium of certain districts, pass current to-day. To-morrow, tidings may come that the house which issued them has stopt payment, and what do they represent then? You will find them the shadow of a shade."

We scarcely know at which end to begin to disentangle this knot of absurdities. We might ask, why it should be a greater proof of insanity in men to set a high value on rare tulips than on rare stones, which are neither more useful nor more beautiful? We might ask, how it can be said that there is no limit to the production of paper-money, when a man is hanged if he issues any in the name of another, and is forced to cash what he issues in his own? But Mr. Southey's error lies deeper still. "All wealth," says he, "was tangible and real till paper currency was introduced." Now, was there ever, since men emerged from a state of utter barbarism, an age in which there were no debts? Is not a debt, while the solvency of the debtor is undoubted, always reckoned as part of the wealth of the creditor? Yet is it tangible and real wealth? Does it cease to be wealth, because there is the security of a written acknowledgment for it? And what else is paper currency? Did Mr. Southey ever read a bank-note? If he did, he would see that it is a written acknowledgment of a debt, and a promise to pay that debt. The promise may be violated—the debt may remain unpaid—those to whom it was due may suffer: but this is a risk not confined to cases of paper currency—it is a risk inseparable from the relation of debtor and creditor. Every man who sells goods for any thing but ready money, runs the risk of finding that what he considered as part of his wealth one day is nothing at all the next day. Mr. Southey refers to the picture-galleries of Holland. The pictures were undoubtedly real and tangible possessions. But surely it might happen, that a burgomaster might owe a picture-dealer a thousand guilders for a Teniers. What in this case corresponds to our paper money is not the picture, which is tangible, but the claim of the picture-dealer on his customer for the price of the picture, which is not tangible. Now, would not the picture-dealer consider this claim as part of his wealth? Would not a tradesman who knew of it give credit to the picture-dealer the more readily on account of it? The burgomaster might be ruined. If so, would not those consequences follow which, as Mr. Southey tells us, were never heard of till paper money came into use? Yesterday this claim was worth a thousand guilders. To-day what is it? The shadow of a shade.

It is true, that the more readily claims of this sort are transferred from hand to hand, the more extensive will be the injury produced by a single failure. The laws of all nations sanction, in certain cases, the transfer of rights not yet reduced into possession. Mr. Southey would scarcely wish, we should think, that all indorsements of bills and notes should be declared invalid. Yet even if this were done, the transfer of claims would imperceptibly take place to a very great extent. When the baker trusts the butcher, for example, he is in fact, though not in form, trusting the butcher's customers. A man who owes large bills to tradesmen and fails to pay them, almost always produces distress through a very wide circle of people whom he never dealt with.

In short, what Mr. Southey takes for a difference in kind, is only a difference of form and degree. In every society men have claims on the property of others. In every society there is a possibility that some debtors may not be able to fulfil their obligations. In every society, therefore, there is wealth which is not tangible, and which may become the shadow of a shade.

Mr. Southey then proceeds to a dissertation on the national debt, which he considers in a new and most consolatory light, as a clear addition to the income of the country.

"You can understand," says Sir Thomas, "that it constitutes a great part of the national wealth."

"So large a part," answers Montesinos, "that the interest amounted, during the prosperous time of agriculture, to as much as the rental of all the land in Great Britain; and at present to the rental of all lands, all houses, and all other fixed property put together."

The Ghost and the Laureate agree that it is very desirable that there should be so secure and advantageous a deposit for wealth as the funds afford. Sir Thomas then proceeds:

"Another and far more momentous benefit must not be overlooked; the expenditure of an annual interest, equalling, as you have stated, the present rental of all fixed property."

"That expenditure," quoth Montesinos, "gives employment to half the industry in the kingdom, and feeds half the mouths.

Take, indeed, the weight of the national debt from this great and complicated social machine, and the wheels must stop."

From this passage we should have been inclined to think, that Mr. Southey supposes the dividends to be a free-gift periodically sent down from heaven to the fundholders, as quails and manna were sent to the Israelites; were it not that he has vouchafed, in the following question and answer, to give the public some information which, we believe, was very little needed.

"Whence comes the interest?" says Sir Thomas.

"It is raised," answers Montesinos, "by taxation."

Now, has Mr. Southey ever considered what would be done with this sum if it were not paid as interest to the national creditor? If he would think over this matter for a short time, we suspect that the "momentous benefit" of which he talks would appear to him to shrink strangely in amount. A fundholder, we will suppose, spends an income of five hundred pounds a-year, and his ten nearest neighbours pay fifty pounds each to the tax-gatherer, for the purpose of discharging the interest of the national debt. If the debt were wiped out—a measure, be it understood, which we by no means recommend—the fundholder would cease to spend his five hundred pounds a-year. He would no longer give employment to industry, or put food into the mouths of labourers. This Mr. Southey thinks a fearful evil. But is there no mitigating circumstance? Each of his ten neighbours has fifty pounds more than formerly. Each of them will, as it seems to our feeble understandings, employ more industry, and feed more mouths, than formerly. The sum is exactly the same. It is in different hands. But on what grounds does Mr. Southey call upon us to believe that it is in the hands of men who will spend less liberally or less judiciously? He seems to think, that nobody but a fundholder can employ the poor; that if a tax is remitted, those who formerly used to pay it proceed immediately to dig holes in the earth, and bury the sum which the government had been accustomed to take; that no money can set industry in motion till it has been taken by the tax-gatherer out of one man's pocket and put into another man's. We really wish that Mr. Southey would try to prove this principle, which is indeed the foundation of his whole theory of finance; for we think it right to hint to him, that our hard-hearted and unimaginative generation will expect some more satisfactory reason than the only one with which he has yet favoured it,—a similitude touching evaporation and dew.

Both the theory and the illustration, indeed, are old friends of ours. In every season of distress which we can remember, Mr. Southey has been proclaiming that it is not from economy, but from increased taxation, that the country must expect relief; and he still, we find, places the undoubting faith of a political Diafoirus, in his

Resaignare, repurgare, et reclysterizare.

"A people," he tells us, "may be too rich, but a government cannot be so."

"A state," says he, "cannot have more wealth at its command than may be employed for the general good, a liberal expenditure in national works being one of the surest means for promoting national prosperity; and the benefit being still more obvious, of an expenditure directed to the purposes of national improvement. But a people may be too rich."

We fully admit, that a state cannot have at its command more wealth than *may be* employed for the general good. But neither can individuals, or bodies of individuals, have at their command more wealth than *may be* employed for the general good. If there be no limit to the sum which may be usefully laid out in public works and national improvement, then wealth, whether in the hands of private men or of the government, *may* always, if the possessors choose to spend it usefully, be usefully spent. The only ground, therefore, on which Mr. Southey can possibly maintain that a government cannot be too rich, but that a people may be too rich, must be this, that governments are more likely to spend their money on good objects than private individuals.

But what is useful expenditure? "A liberal expenditure in national works," says Mr. Southey, "is one of the surest means for promoting national prosperity." What does he mean by national prosperity? Does he mean wealth of the state? If so, his reasoning runs thus:—The more wealth a state has the better; for the more wealth a state has, the more wealth it will have.

54

This is surely something like that fallacy, which is ungallantly termed a lady's reason. If by national prosperity he means the wealth of the people, of how gross a contradiction is he guilty. A people, he tells us, may be too rich—a government cannot— for a government can employ its riches in making the people richer. The wealth of the people is to be taken from them, because they have too much, and laid out in works which will yield them more.

We are really at a loss to determine whether Mr. Southey's reason for recommending large taxation is that it will make the people rich, or that it will make them poor. But we are sure, that if his object is to make them rich, he takes the wrong course. There are two or three principles respecting public works, which, as an experience of vast extent proves, may be trusted in almost every case.

It scarcely ever happens, that any private man, or body of men, will invest property in a canal, a tunnel, or a bridge, but from an expectation that the outlay will be profitable to them. No work of this sort can be profitable to private speculators, unless the public be willing to pay for the use of it. The public will not pay of their own accord for what yields no profit or convenience to them. There is thus a direct and obvious connexion between the motive which induces individuals to undertake such a work, and the utility of the work.

Can we find any such connexion in the case of a public work executed by a government? If it is useful, are the individuals who rule the country richer? If it is useless, are they poorer? A public man may be solicitous for his credit: but is not he likely to gain more credit by an useless display of ostentatious architecture in a great town, than by the best road or the best canal in some remote province? The fame of public works is a much less certain test of their utility, than the amount of toll collected at them. In a corrupt age, there will be direct embezzlement. In the purest age, there will be abundance of jobbing. Never were the statesmen of any country more sensitive to public opinion, and more spotless in pecuniary transactions, than those who have of late governed England. Yet we have only to look at the buildings recently erected in London for a proof of our rule. In a bad age, the fate of the public is to be robbed. In a good age, it is much milder—merely to have the dearest and the worst of every thing.

Buildings for state purposes the state must erect. And here we think that, in general, the state ought to stop. We firmly believe, that five hundred thousand pounds subscribed by individuals for rail-roads or canals would produce more advantage to the public than five millions voted by Parliament for the same purpose. There are certain old saws about the master's eye and about every body's business, in which we place very great faith.

There is, we have said, no consistency in Mr. Southey's political system. But if there be in it any leading principle, if there be any one error which diverges more widely and variously than any other, it is that of which his theory about national works is a ramification. He conceives that the business of the magistrate is, not merely to see that the persons and property of the people are secure from attack, but that he ought to be a perfect jack-of-all-trades,—architect, engineer, schoolmaster, merchant, theologian,—a Lady Bountiful in every parish,—a Paul Pry in every house, spying, eaves-dropping, relieving, admonishing, spending our money for us, and choosing our opinions for us. His principle is, if we understand it rightly, that no man can do any thing so well for himself, as his rulers, be they who they may, can do it for him; that a government approaches nearer and nearer to perfection, in proportion as it interferes more and more with the habits and notions of individuals.

He seems to be fully convinced, that it is in the power of government to relieve the distresses under which the lower orders labour. Nay, he considers doubt on this subject as impious. We cannot refrain from quoting his argument on this subject. It is a perfect jewel of logic.

> "Many thousands in your metropolis," says Sir Thomas More, "rise every morning without knowing how they are to subsist during the day; as many of them, where they are to lay their heads at night. All men, even the vicious themselves, know that wickedness leads to misery; but many, even among the good and the wise, have yet to learn that misery is almost as often the cause of wickedness."
>
> "There are many," says Montesinos, "who know this, but

believe that it is not in the power of human institutions to prevent this misery. They see the effect, but regard the causes as inseparable from the condition of human nature."

"As surely as God is good," replies Sir Thomas, "so surely there is no such thing as necessary evil. For, by the religious mind, sickness, and pain, and death, are not to be accounted evils."

Now, if sickness, pain, and death, are not evils, we cannot understand why it should be an evil that thousands should rise without knowing how they are to subsist. The only evil of hunger is, that it produces first pain, then sickness, and finally death. If it did not produce these it would be no calamity. If these are not evils, it is no calamity. We cannot conceive why it should be a greater impeachment of the Divine goodness, that some men should not be able to find food to eat, than that others should have stomachs which derive no nourishment from food when they have eaten it. Whatever physical effects want produces may also be produced by disease. Whatever salutary effects disease may produce, may also be produced by want. If poverty makes men thieves, disease and pain often sour the temper and contract the heart.

We will propose a very plain dilemma: Either physical pain is an evil, or it is not an evil. If it is an evil, then there is necessary evil in the universe: If it is not, why should the poor be delivered from it?

Mr. Southey entertains as exaggerated a notion of the wisdom of governments as of their power. He speaks with the greatest disgust of the respect now paid to public opinion. That opinion is, according to him, to be distrusted and dreaded; its usurpation ought to be vigorously resisted; and the practice of yielding to it is likely to ruin the country. To maintain police is, according to him, only one of the ends of government. Its duties are patriarchal and paternal. It ought to consider the moral discipline of the people as its first object, to establish a religion, to train the whole community in that religion, and to consider all dissenters as its own enemies.

"Nothing," says Sir Thomas, "is more certain, than that religion is the basis upon which civil government rests; that from religion power derives its authority, laws their efficacy, and both their zeal and sanction; and it is necessary that this religion be established as for the security of the state, and for the welfare of the people, who would otherwise be moved to and fro with every wind of doctrine. A state is secure in proportion as the people are attached to its institutions; it is, therefore, the first and plainest rule of sound policy, that the people be trained up in the way they should go. The state that neglects this prepares its own destruction; and they who train them in any other way are undermining it. Nothing in abstract science can be more certain than these positions are."

"All of which," answers Montesinos, "are nevertheless denied by our professors of the arts Babblative and Scribblative; some in the audacity of evil designs, and others in the glorious assurance of impenetrable ignorance."

The greater part of the two volumes before us is merely an amplification of these absurd paragraphs. What does Mr. Southey mean by saying, that religion is demonstrably the basis of civil government? He cannot surely mean that men have no motives except those derived from religion for establishing and supporting civil government, that no temporal advantage is derived from civil government, that man would experience no temporal inconvenience from living in a state of anarchy? If he allows, as we think he must allow, that it is for the good of mankind in this world to have civil government, and that the great majority of mankind have always thought it for their good in this world to have civil government, we then have a basis for government quite distinct from religion. It is true, that the Christian religion sanctions government, as it sanctions every thing which promotes the happiness and virtue of our species. But we are at a loss to conceive in what sense religion can be said to be the basis of government, in which it is not also the basis of the practices of eating, drinking, and lighting fires in cold weather. Nothing in history is more certain than that government has existed, has received some obedience and given some protection, in times in which it derived no support from religion,—in times in which there was no religion that influenced the hearts and lives of men. It was not from dread of Tartarus, or belief in the Elysian fields, that an Athenian wished to have some institutions which might keep Orestes from filching his cloak, or Midias from breaking his head. "It is from religion," says Mr. Southey, "that power derives its authority, and laws their efficacy." From what religion does our power over the Hindoos derive its authority, or the law in virtue of which we hang Brahmins its efficacy? For thousands of years civil government has existed in almost every corner of the world,—in ages of priestcraft,—in ages of fanaticism,—in ages of Epicurean indifference,—in ages of enlightened piety. However pure or impure the faith of the people might be, whether they adored a beneficent or a malignant power, whether they thought the soul mortal or immortal, they have, as soon as they ceased to be absolute savages, found out their need of civil government, and instituted it accordingly. It is as universal as the practice of cookery. Yet, it is as certain, says Mr. Southey, as any thing in abstract science, that government is founded on religion. We should like to know what notion Mr. Southey has of the demonstrations of abstract science. But a vague one, we suspect.

The proof proceeds. As religion is the basis of government, and as the state is secure in proportion as the people are attached to its institutions, it is therefore, says Mr. Southey, the first rule of policy, that the government should train the people in the way in which they should go; and it is plain, that those who train them in any other way, are undermining the state.

Now it does not appear to us to be the first object that people should always believe in the established religion, and be attached to the established government. A religion may be false. A government may be oppressive. And whatever support government gives to false religions, or religion to oppressive governments, we consider as a clear evil.

The maxim, that governments ought to train the people in the way in which they should go, sounds well. But is there any reason for believing that a government is more likely to lead the people in the right way, than the people to fall into the right way of themselves? Have there not been governments which were blind leaders of the blind? Are there not still such governments? Can it be laid down as a general rule that the movement of political and religious truth is rather downwards from the government to the people, than upwards from the people to the government? These are questions which it is of importance to have clearly resolved. Mr. Southey declaims against public opinion, which is now, he tells us, usurping supreme power. Formerly, according to him, the laws governed; now public opinion governs. What are laws but expressions of the opinion of some class which has power over the rest of the community? By what was the world ever governed, but by the opinion of some person or persons? By what else can it ever be governed? What are all systems, religious, political, or scientific, but opinions resting on evidence more or less satisfactory? The question is not between human opinion, and some higher and more certain mode of arriving at truth, but between opinion and opinion, —between the opinion of one man and another, or of one class and another, or of one generation and another. Public opinion is not infallible; but can Mr. Southey construct any institutions which shall secure to us the guidance of an infallible opinion? Can Mr. Southey select any family,—any profession—any class, in short, distinguished by any plain badge from the rest of the community, whose opinion is more likely to be just than this much-abused public opinion? Would he choose the peers, for example? Or the two hundred tallest men in the country? Or the poor Knights of Windsor? Or children who are born with cawls, seventh sons of seventh sons? We cannot suppose that he would recommend popular election; for that is merely an appeal to public opinion. And to say that society ought to be governed by the opinion of the wisest and best, though true, is useless. Whose opinion is to decide, who are the wisest and best?

Mr. Southey and many other respectable people seem to think that when they have once proved the moral and religious training of the people to be a most important object, it follows, of course, that it is an object which the government ought to pursue. They forget that we have to consider, not merely the goodness of the end, but also the fitness of the means. Neither in the natural nor in the political body have all members the same office. There is surely no contradiction in saying that a certain section of the community may be quite competent to protect the persons and property of the rest, yet quite unfit to direct our opinions, or to superintend our private habits.

So strong is the interest of a ruler, to protect his subjects against all depredations and outrages except his own,—so clear and simple are the means by which this end is to be effected, that men are probably better off under the worst governments in the world, than they would be in a state of anarchy. Even when the appointment of magistrates has been left to chance, as in the Italian Republics, things have gone on better than they would have done, if there had been no magistrates at all, and every man had done what seemed right in his own eyes. But we see no reason for thinking that the opinions of the magistrate are more likely to be right than those of any other man. None of the modes by which rulers are appointed,—popular election, the accident of the lot, or the accident of birth,—afford, as far as we can perceive, much security for their being wiser than any of their neighbours. The chance of their being wiser than all their neighbours together is still smaller. Now we cannot conceive how it can be laid down, that it is the duty and the right of one class to direct the opinions of another, unless it can be proved that the former class is more likely to form just opinions than the latter.

The duties of government would be, as Mr. Southey says that they are, paternal, if a government were necessarily as much superior in wisdom to a people, as the most foolish father, for a time, is to the most intelligent child, and if a government loved a people as fathers generally love their children. But there is no reason to believe, that a government will either have the paternal warmth of affection or the paternal superiority of intellect. Mr. Southey might as well say, that the duties of the shoemaker are paternal, and that it is an usurpation in any man not of the craft to say that his shoes are bad, and to insist on having better. The division of labour would be no blessing, if those by whom a thing is done were to pay no attention to the opinion of those for whom it is done. The shoemaker, in the Relapse, tells Lord Foppington, that his lordship is mistaken in supposing that his shoe pinches. "It does not pinch—it cannot pinch—I know my business—and I never made a better shoe." This is the way in which Mr. Southey would have a government treat a people who usurp the privilege of thinking. Nay, the shoemaker of Vanbrugh has the advantage in the comparison. He contented himself with regulating his customer's shoes, about which he knew something, and did not presume to dictate about the coat and hat. But Mr. Southey would have the rulers of a country prescribe opinions to the people, not only about politics, but about matters concerning which a government has no peculiar sources of information,—concerning which any man in the streets may know as much, and think as justly, as a king,—religion and morals.

Men are never so likely to settle a question rightly, as when they discuss it freely. A government can interfere in discussion, only by making it less free than it would otherwise be. Men are most likely to form just opinions, when they have no other wish than to know the truth, and are exempt from all influence, either of hope or fear. Government, as government, can bring nothing but the influence of hopes and fears to support its doctrines. It carries on controversy, not with reasons, but with threats and bribes. If it employs reasons, it does so not in virtue of any powers which belong to it as a government. Thus, instead of a contest between argument and argument, we have a contest between argument and force. Instead of a contest in which truth, from the natural constitution of the human mind, has a decided advantage over falsehood, we have a contest, in which truth can be victorious only by accident.

And what, after all, is the security which this training gives to governments? Mr. Southey would scarcely recommend, that discussion should be more effectually shackled, that public opinion should be more strictly disciplined into conformity with established institutions, than in Spain and Italy. Yet we know that the restraints which exist in Spain and Italy have not prevented atheism from spreading among the educated classes, and especially among those whose office it is to minister at the altars of God. All our readers know how, at the time of the French Revolution, priest after priest came forward to declare that his doctrine, his ministry, his whole life, had been a lie,—a mummery during which he could scarcely compose his countenance sufficiently to carry on the imposture. This was the case of a false, or at least a grossly corrupted religion. Let us take, then, the case of all others the most favourable to Mr. Southey's argument. Let us take that form of religion, which he holds to be the purest, the system of the Arminian part of the Church of England. Let us take the form of government which he most admires and regrets, the government of England in the time of

Charles the First. Would he wish to see a closer connexion between church and state than then existed? Would he wish for
more powerful ecclesiastical tribunals? for a more zealous king?
for a more active primate? Would he wish to see a more complete
monopoly of public instruction given to the Established Church?
Could any government do more to train the people in the way in
which he would have them go? And in what did all this training
end? The Report of the State of the Province of Canterbury, delivered by Laud to his Master at the close of 1639, represents
the Church of England as in the highest and most palmy state.
So effectually had the government pursued that policy which Mr.
Southey wishes to see revived, that there was scarcely the least
appearance of dissent. Most of the bishops stated that all was well
among their flocks. Seven or eight persons in the diocese of
Peterborough had seemed refractory to the church, but had made
ample submission. In Norfolk and Suffolk all whom there had
been reason to suspect had made profession of conformity, and
appeared to observe it strictly. It is confessed that there was a
little difficulty in bringing some of the vulgar in Suffolk to take
the sacrament at the rails in the chancel. This was the only
open instance of non-conformity which the vigilant eye of Laud
could find in all the dioceses of his twenty-one suffragans, on
the very eve of a revolution, in which primate and church, and
monarch and monarchy, were to perish together.

At which time would Mr. Southey pronounce the constitution
more secure; in 1639, when Laud presented this Report to
Charles, or now, when thousands of meetings openly collect millions of dissenters, when designs against the tithes are openly
avowed, when books attacking not only the Establishment, but
the first principles of Christianity, are openly sold in the streets?
The signs of discontent, he tells us, are stronger in England
now than in France when the States-General met; and hence
he would have us infer that a revolution like that of France may
be at hand. Does he not know that the danger of states is to be
estimated, not by what breaks out of the public mind, but by
what stays in it? Can he conceive any thing more terrible than
the situation of a government which rules without apprehension
over a people of hypocrites,—which is flattered by the press, and
cursed in the inner chambers—which exults in the attachment

and obedience of its subjects, and knows not that those subjects are leagued against it in a free-masonry of hatred, the sign of which is every day conveyed in the glance of ten thousand eyes, the pressure of ten thousand hands, and the tone of ten thousand voices? Profound and ingenious policy! Instead of curing the disease to remove those symptoms by which alone its nature can be known! To leave the serpent his deadly sting, and deprive him only of his warning rattle!

When the people whom Charles had so assiduously trained in the good way had rewarded his paternal care by cutting off his head, a new kind of training came into fashion. Another government arose, which, like the former, considered religion as its surest basis, and the religious discipline of the people as its first duty. Sanguinary laws were enacted against libertinism; profane pictures were burned; drapery was put on indecorous statues; the theatres were shut up; fast-days were numerous; and the Parliament resolved that no person should be admitted into any public employment, unless the House should be first satisfied of his vital godliness. We know what was the end of this training. We know that it ended in impiety, in filthy and heartless sensuality, in the dissolution of all ties of honour and morality. We know that at this very day scriptural phrases, scriptural names, perhaps some scriptural doctrines, excite disgust and ridicule, solely because they are associated with the austerity of that period.

Thus has the experiment of training the people in established forms of religion been twice tried in England on a large scale; once by Charles and Laud, and once by the Puritans. The High Tories of our time still entertain many of the feelings and opinions of Charles and Laud, though in a mitigated form; nor is it difficult to see that the heirs of the Puritans are still amongst us. It would be desirable that each of these parties should remember how little advantage or honour it formerly derived from the closest alliance with power,—that it fell by the support of rulers, and rose by their opposition,—that of the two systems, that in which the people were at any time being drilled, was always at that time the unpopular system,—that the training of the High Church ended in the reign of the Puritans, and the training of the Puritans in the reign of the harlots.

This was quite natural. Nothing is so galling and detestable to a people not broken in from the birth, as a paternal, or, in other words, a meddling government,—a government which tells them what to read, and say, and eat, and drink, and wear. Our fathers could not bear it two hundred years ago; and we are not more patient than they. Mr. Southey thinks that the yoke of the church is dropping off, because it is loose. We feel convinced that it is borne only because it is easy, and that, in the instant in which an attempt is made to tighten it, it will be flung away. It will be neither the first nor the strongest yoke that has been broken asunder and trampled under foot in the day of the vengeance of England.

How far Mr. Southey would have the government carry its measures for training the people in the doctrines of the church, we are unable to discover. In one passage Sir Thomas More asks with great vehemence,

> Is it possible that your laws should suffer the unbelievers to exist as a party?
> Vetitum est adeo sceleris nihil?

Montesinos answers.

> They avow themselves in defiance of the laws. The fashionable doctrine which the press at this time maintains is, that this is a matter in which the laws ought not to interfere, every man having a right, both to form what opinion he pleases upon religious subjects, and to promulgate that opinion.

It is clear, therefore, that Mr. Southey would not give full and perfect toleration to infidelity. In another passage, however, he observes, with some truth, though too sweepingly, that

> any degree of intolerance short of that full extent which the Papal Church exercises where it has the power, acts upon the opinions which it is intended to suppress, like pruning upon vigorous plants; they grow the stronger for it.

These two passages, put together, would lead us to the conclusion that, in Mr. Southey's opinion, the utmost severity ever employed by the Roman Catholic Church in the days of its greatest power ought to be employed against unbelievers in England; in plain words, that Carlile and his shopmen ought to be burned in Smithfield, and that every person who, when called upon, should decline to make a solemn profession of Christianity, ought to suffer the same fate. We do not, however, believe that Mr. Southey would recommend such a course, though his language would, in the case of any other writer, justify us in supposing this to be his meaning. His opinions form no system at all. He never sees, at one glance, more of a question than will furnish matter for one flowing and well-turned sentence; so that it would be the height of unfairness to charge him personally with holding a doctrine, merely because that doctrine is deducible, though by the closest and most accurate reasoning, from the premises which he has laid down. We are, therefore, left completely in the dark as to Mr. Southey's opinions about toleration. Immediately after censuring the government for not punishing infidels, he proceeds to discuss the question of the Catholic disabilities— now, thank God, removed—and defends them on the ground that the Catholic doctrines tend to persecution, and that the Catholics persecuted when they had power.

"They must persecute," says he, "if they believe their own creed, for conscience-sake; and if they do not believe it, they must persecute for policy; because it is only by intolerance that so corrupt and injurious a system can be upheld."

That unbelievers should not be persecuted, is an instance of national depravity at which the glorified spirits stand aghast. Yet a sect of Christians is to be excluded from power, because those who formerly held the same opinions were guilty of persecution. We have said that we do not very well know what Mr. Southey's opinion about toleration is. But, on the whole, we take it to be this, that everybody is to tolerate him, and that he is to tolerate nobody.

We will not be deterred by any fear of misrepresentation from expressing our hearty approbation of the mild, wise, and eminently Christian manner, in which the Church and the Government have lately acted with respect to blasphemous publications. We praise them for not having thought it necessary to encircle a religion pure, merciful, and philosophical,—a religion to the evidences of which the highest intellects have yielded,—with the defences of a false and bloody superstition. The ark of God was never taken till it was surrounded by the arms of earthly defenders. In captivity, its sanctity was sufficient to vindicate it from insult, and to lay the hostile fiend prostrate on the threshold of his own temple. The real security of Christianity is to be found in its benevolent morality, in its exquisite adaptation to the human heart, in the facility with which its scheme accommodates itself to the capacity of every human intellect, in the consolation which it bears to the house of mourning, in the light with which it brightens the great mystery of the grave. To such a system it can bring no addition of dignity or of strength, that it is part and parcel of the common law. It is not now for the first time left to rely on the force of its own evidences, and the attractions of its own beauty. Its sublime theology confounded the Grecian schools in the fair conflict of reason with reason. The bravest and wisest of the Cæsars found their arms and their policy unavailing when opposed to the weapons that were not carnal, and the kingdom that was not of this world. The victory which Porphyry and Diocletian failed to gain, is not, to all appearance, reserved for any of those who have in this age directed their attacks against the last restraint of the powerful, and the last hope of the wretched. The whole history of the Christian Religion shows, that she is in far greater danger of being corrupted by the alliance of power, than of being crushed by its opposition. Those who thrust temporal sovereignty upon her, treat her as their prototypes treated her author. They bow the knee, and spit upon her; they cry Hail! and smite her on the cheek; they put a sceptre into her hand, but it is a fragile reed; they crown her, but it is with thorns; they cover with purple the wounds which their own hands have inflicted on her; and inscribe magnificent titles over the cross on which they have fixed her to perish in ignominy and pain.

The general view which Mr. Southey takes of the prospects of society is very gloomy; but we comfort ourselves with the consideration that Mr. Southey is no prophet. He foretold, we remember, on the very eve of the abolition of the Test and Corporation Acts, that these hateful laws were immortal, and that pious minds would long be gratified by seeing the most solemn religious rite of the Church profaned, for the purpose of upholding her political supremacy. In the book before us, he says that Catholics cannot possibly be admitted into Parliament until those whom Johnson called "the bottomless Whigs," come into power. While the book was in the press, the prophecy was falsified, and a Tory of the Tories, Mr. Southey's own favourite hero, won and wore that noblest wreath, *"Ob cives servatos."*

The signs of the times, Mr. Southey tells us, are very threatening. His fears for the country would decidedly preponderate over his hopes, but for his firm reliance on the mercy of God. Now, as we know that God has once suffered the civilised world to be overrun by savages, and the Christian religion to be corrupted by doctrines which made it, for some ages, almost as bad as Paganism, we cannot think it inconsistent with his attributes that similar calamities should again befall mankind.

We look, however, on the state of the world, and of this kingdom in particular, with much greater satisfaction, and with better hopes. Mr. Southey speaks with contempt of those who think the savage state happier than the social. On this subject, he says, Rousseau never imposed on him even in his youth. But he conceives that a community which has advanced a little way in civilisation is happier than one which has made greater progress. The Britons in the time of Cæsar were happier, he suspects, than the English of the nineteenth century. On the whole, he selects the generation which preceded the Reformation as that in which the people of this country were better off than at any time before or since.

This opinion rests on nothing, as far as we can see, except his own individual associations. He is a man of letters; and a life destitute of literary pleasures seems insipid to him. He abhors the spirit of the present generation, the severity of its studies, the boldness of its enquiries, and the disdain with which it regards some old prejudices by which his own mind is held in bondage. He dislikes an utterly unenlightened age; he dislikes an investigating and reforming age. The first twenty years of the sixteenth century would have exactly suited him. They furnished just the quantity of intellectual excitement which he requires. The learned few read and wrote largely. A scholar was held in high estimation; but the rabble did not presume to think; and even the most enquiring and independent of the educated classes paid more reverence to authority, and less to reason, than is usual in our time. This is a state of things in which Mr. Southey would have found himself quite comfortable; and, accordingly, he pronounces it the happiest state of things ever known in the world.

The savages were wretched, says Mr. Southey; but the people in the time of Sir Thomas More were happier than either they or we. Now, we think it quite certain that we have the advantage over the contemporaries of Sir Thomas More, in every point in which they had any advantage over savages.

Mr. Southey does not even pretend to maintain that the people in the sixteenth century were better lodged or clothed than at present. He seems to admit that in these respects there has been some little improvement. It is indeed a matter about which scarcely any doubt can exist in the most perverse mind, that the improvements of machinery have lowered the price of manufactured articles, and have brought within the reach of the poorest some conveniencies which Sir Thomas More or his master could not have obtained at any price.

The labouring classes, however, were, according to Mr. Southey, better fed three hundred years ago than at present. We believe that he is completely in error on this point. The condition of servants in noble and wealthy families, and of scholars at the Universities, must surely have been better in those times than that of common day-labourers; and we are sure that it was not better than that of our workhouse paupers. From the household book of the Northumberland family, we find that in one of the greatest establishments of the kingdom the servants lived almost entirely on salt meat, without any bread at all. A more unwholesome diet can scarcely be conceived. In the reign of Edward the Sixth, the state of the students at Cambridge is described to us, on the very best authority, as most wretched. Many of them dined on pottage made of a farthing's worth of beef with a little salt and oatmeal, and literally nothing else. This account we have from a contemporary master of St. Johns. Our parish poor now eat wheaten bread. In the sixteenth century the labourer was glad to get barley, and was often forced to content himself with poorer fare. In Harrison's introduction to Holinshed we have an account of the state of our working population in the "golden days," as Mr. Southey calls them, of good Queen Bess. "The gentilitie," says he, "commonly provide themselves sufficiently of wheat for their own tables, whylest their household and poore neighbours in some shires are inforced to content themselves with rice or barleie; yea, and in time of dearth, many with bread made eyther of beanes, peason, or otes, or of altogether, and some acornes among. I will not say that this extremity is oft so well to be seen in time of plentie as of dearth; but if I should I could easily bring my trial: for albeit there be much more grounde eared nowe almost in everye place then hath beene of late yeares, yet such a price of corne continueth in eache towne and markete, without any just cause, that the artificer and poore labouring man is not able to reach unto it, but is driven to content himself with horse-corne; I mean beanes, peason, otes, tares, and lintelles." We should like to see what the effect would be of putting any parish in England now on allowance of "horse-corne." The helotry of Mammon are not, in our day, so easily enforced to content themselves as the peasantry of that happy period, as Mr. Southey considers it, which elapsed between the fall of the feudal and the rise of the commercial tyranny.

"The people," says Mr. Southey, "are worse fed than when they were fishers." And yet in another place he complains that they will not eat fish. "They have contracted," says he, "I know not how, some obstinate prejudice against a kind of food at once wholesome and delicate, and everywhere to be obtained cheaply and in abundance, were the demand for it as general as it ought to be." It is true that the lower orders have an obstinate prejudice against fish. But hunger has no such obstinate prejudices. If what was formerly a common diet is now eaten only in times of severe pressure, the inference is plain. The people must be fed with what they at least think better food than that of their ancestors.

The advice and medicine which the poorest labourer can now obtain, in disease or after an accident, is far superior to what Henry the Eighth could have commanded. Scarcely any part of the country is out of the reach of practitioners, who are probably not so far inferior to Sir Henry Halford as they are superior to Sir Anthony Denny. That there has been a great improvement in this respect Mr. Southey allows. Indeed he could not well have denied it. "But," says he, "the evils for which these sciences are the palliative, have increased since the time of the Druids, in a proportion that heavily overweighs the benefit of improved therapeutics." We know nothing either of the diseases or the remedies of the Druids. But we are quite sure that the improvement of medicine has far more than kept pace with the increase of disease during the last three centuries. This is proved by the best possible evidence. The term of human life is decidedly longer in England than in any former age, respecting which we possess any information on which we can rely. All the rants in the world about picturesque cottages and temples of Mammon will not shake this argument. No test of the state of society can be named so decisive as that which is furnished by bills of mortality. That the lives of the people of this country have been gradually lengthening during the course of several generations, is as certain as any fact in statistics, and that the lives of men should become longer and longer, while their physical condition, during life, is becoming worse and worse, is utterly incredible.

Let our readers think over these circumstances. Let them take into the account the sweating sickness and the plague. Let them take into the account that fearful disease which first made its appearance in the generation to which Mr. Southey assigns the palm of felicity, and raged through Europe with a fury at which the physician stood aghast, and before which the people were swept away by thousands. Let them consider the state of the northern counties, constantly the scene of robberies, rapes, massacres, and conflagrations. Let them add to all this the fact that seventy-two thousand persons suffered death by the hands of the executioner during the reign of Henry the Eighth, and judge between the nineteenth and the sixteenth century.

We do not say that the lower orders in England do not suffer severe hardships. But, in spite of Mr. Southey's assertions, and in spite of the assertions of a class of politicians, who, differing from Mr. Southey in every other point, agree with him in this, we are inclined to doubt whether they really suffer greater physical distress than the labouring classes of the most flourishing countries of the Continent.

It will scarcely be maintained that the lazzaroni who sleep under the porticos of Naples, or the beggars who besiege the convents of Spain, are in a happier situation than the English commonalty. The distress which has lately been experienced in the northern part of Germany, one of the best governed and most prosperous districts of Europe, surpasses, if we have been correctly informed, any thing which has of late years been known among us. In Norway and Sweden the peasantry are constantly compelled to mix bark with their bread, and even this expedient has not always preserved whole families and neighbourhoods from perishing together of famine. An experiment has lately been tried in the kingdom of the Netherlands, which has been cited to prove the possibility of establishing agricultural colonies on the waste-lands of England; but which proves to our minds nothing so clearly as this, that the rate of subsistence to which the labouring classes are reduced in the Netherlands is miserably low, and very far inferior to that of the English paupers. No distress which the people here have endured for centuries, approaches to that which has been felt by the French in our own time. The beginning of the year 1817 was a time of great distress in this island. But the state of the lowest classes here was luxury compared with that of the people of France. We find in Magendie's *Journal de Physiologie Expérimentale*, a paper on a point of physiology connected with the distress of that season. It appears that the inhabitants of six departments, Aix, Jura, Doubs, Haute Saone, Vosges, and Saone et Loire, were reduced first to oatmeal and potatoes, and at last to nettles, bean-stalks, and other kinds of herbage fit only for cattle; that when the next harvest enabled them to eat barley-bread, many of them died from intemperate indulgence in what they thought an exquisite repast; and that a dropsy of a peculiar description was produced by the hard fare of the year. Dead bodies were found on the roads and in the fields. A single surgeon dissected six of these, and found the stomach shrunk, and filled with the unwholesome aliments which hunger had driven men to share with beasts. Such extremity of distress as this is never heard of in England, or even in Ireland. We are, on the whole, inclined to think, though we would speak with diffidence on a point on which it would be rash to pronounce a positive judgment without a much longer and closer investigation than we have bestowed upon it, that the labouring classes of this island, though they have their grievances and distresses, some produced by their own improvidence, some by the errors of their rulers, are on the whole better off as to physical comforts, than the inhabitants of any equally extensive district of the old world. On this very account, suffering is more acutely felt and more loudly bewailed here than elsewhere. We must take into the account the liberty of discussion, and the strong interest which the opponents of a ministry always have to exaggerate the extent of the public disasters. There are many parts of Europe in which the people quietly endure distress that here would shake the foundations of the state,—in which the inhabitants of a whole province turn out to eat grass with less clamour than one Spitalfields weaver would make here, if the overseers were to put him on barley-bread. In those new countries in which a civilized population has at its command a boundless extent of the richest soil, the condition of the labourer is probably happier than in any society which has lasted for many centuries. But in the old world we must confess ourselves unable to find any satisfactory record of any great nation, past or present, in which the working classes have been in a more comfortable situation than in England during the last thirty years. When this island was thinly peopled, it was barbarous. There was little capital; and that little was insecure. It is now the richest and the most highly civilized spot in the world; but the population is dense. Thus we have never known that golden age, which the lower orders in the United States are now enjoying. We have never known an age of liberty, of order, and of education, an age in which the mechanical sciences were carried to a great height, yet in which the people were not sufficiently numerous to cultivate even the most fertile valleys. But, when we compare our own condition with that of our ancestors, we think it clear that the advantages arising from the progress of civilisation have far more than counterbalanced the disadvantages arising from the progress of population. While our numbers have increased tenfold, our wealth has increased a hundred fold. Though there are so many more people to share the wealth now existing in the country than there were in the sixteenth century, it seems certain, that a greater share falls to almost every individual, than fell to the share of any of the corresponding class in the sixteenth century. The King keeps a more splendid court. The establishments of the nobles are more magnificent. The esquires are richer, the merchants are richer, the shopkeepers are richer. The serving-man, the artisan, and the husbandman, have a more copious and palatable supply of food, better clothing, and better furniture. This is no reason for tolerating abuses, or for neglecting any means of ameliorating the condition of our poorer countrymen. But it is a reason against telling them, as some of our philosophers are constantly telling them, that they are the most wretched people who ever existed on the face of the earth.

We have already adverted to Mr. Southey's amusing doctrine about national wealth. A state, says he, cannot be too rich; but a people may be too rich. His reason for thinking this, is extremely curious.

> A people may be too rich, because it is the tendency of the commercial, and more especially, of the manufacturing system, to collect wealth rather than to diffuse it. Where wealth is necessarily employed in any of the speculations of trade, its increase is in proportion to its amount. Great capitalists become like pikes in a fish-pond, who devour the weaker fish; and it is but too certain, that the poverty of one part of the people seems to increase in the same ratio as the riches of another. There are examples of this in history. In Portugal, when the high tide of wealth flowed in from the conquests in Africa and the East, the effect of that great influx was not more visible in the augmented splendour of the court, and the luxury of the higher ranks, than in the distress of the people.

Mr. Southey's instance is not a very fortunate one. The wealth which did so little for the Portuguese was not the fruit, either of manufactures or of commerce carried on by private individuals. It was the wealth, not of the people, but of the government and its creatures, of those who, as Mr. Southey thinks, can never be too rich. The fact is, that Mr. Southey's proposition is opposed to all history, and to the phenomena which surround us on every side. England is the richest country in Europe, the most commercial, and the most manufacturing. Russia and Poland are the poorest countries in Europe. They have scarcely any trade, and none but the rudest manufactures. Is wealth more diffused in Russia and Poland than in England? There are individuals in Russia and Poland, whose incomes are probably equal to those of our richest countrymen. It may be doubted, whether there are not, in those countries, as many fortunes of eighty thousand a-year, as here. But are there as many fortunes of five thousand a-year, or of one thousand a-year? There are parishes in England, which contain more people of between five hundred and three thousand pounds a-year, than could be found in all the dominions of the Emperor Nicholas. The neat and commodious houses which have been built in London and its vicinity, for people of this class, within the last thirty years, would of themselves form a city larger than the capitals of some European kingdoms. And this is the state of society in which the great proprietors have devoured the smaller!

The cure which Mr. Southey thinks that he has discovered is worthy of the sagacity which he has shown in detecting the evil. The calamities arising from the collection of wealth in the hands of a few capitalists are to be remedied by collecting it in the hands of one great capitalist, who has no conceivable motive to use it better than other capitalists,—the all-devouring state.

It is not strange that, differing so widely from Mr. Southey as to the past progress of society, we should differ from him also as to its probable destiny. He thinks, that to all outward appearance, the country is hastening to destruction; but he relies firmly on the goodness of God. We do not see either the piety, or the rationality, of thus confidently expecting that the Supreme Being will interfere to disturb the common succession of causes and effects. We, too, rely on his goodness,—on his goodness as manifested, not in extraordinary interpositions, but in those general laws which it has pleased him to establish in the physical and in the moral world. We rely on the natural tendency of the human intellect to truth, and on the natural tendency of society to improvement. We know no well-authenticated instance of a people which has decidedly retrograded in civilisation and prosperity, except from the influence of violent and terrible calamities,— such as those which laid the Roman Empire in ruins, or those which, about the beginning of the sixteenth century, desolated Italy. We know of no country which, at the end of fifty years of peace and tolerably good government, has been less prosperous than at the beginning of that period. The political importance of a state may decline, as the balance of power is disturbed by the introduction of new forces. Thus the influence of Holland and of Spain is much diminished. But are Holland and Spain poorer than formerly? We doubt it. Other countries have outrun them.

But we suspect that they have been positively, though not relatively, advancing. We suspect that Holland is richer than when she sent her navies up the Thames,—that Spain is richer than when a French king was brought captive to the footstool of Charles the Fifth.

History is full of the signs of this natural progress of society. We see in almost every part of the annals of mankind how the industry of individuals, struggling up against wars, taxes, famines, conflagrations, mischievous prohibitions, and more mischievous protections, creates faster than governments can squander, and repairs whatever invaders can destroy. We see the capital of nations increasing, and all the arts of life approaching nearer and nearer to perfection, in spite of the grossest corruption and the wildest profusion on the part of rulers.

The present moment is one of great distress. But how small will that distress appear when we think over the history of the last forty years;—a war, compared with which, all other wars sink into insignificance;—taxation, such as the most heavily taxed people of former times could not have conceived;—a debt larger than all the public debts that ever existed in the world added together;—the food of the people studiously rendered dear;—the currency imprudently debased, and imprudently restored. Yet is the country poorer than in 1790? We fully believe that, in spite of all the misgovernment of her rulers, she has been almost constantly becoming richer and richer. Now and then there has been a stoppage, now and then a short retrogression; but as to the general tendency there can be no doubt. A single breaker may recede, but the tide is evidently coming in.

If we were to prophesy that in the year 1930, a population of fifty millions, better fed, clad, and lodged than the English of our time, will cover these islands,—that Sussex and Huntingdonshire will be wealthier than the wealthiest parts of the West-Riding of Yorkshire now are,—that cultivation, rich as that of a flower-garden, will be carried up to the very tops of Ben Nevis and Helvellyn,—that machines, constructed on principles yet undiscovered, will be in every house,—that there will be no highways but rail-roads, no travelling but by steam,—that our debt, vast as it seems to us, will appear to our great-grandchildren a trifling encumbrance, which might easily be paid off in a year or two,—many people would think us insane. We prophesy nothing; but this we say—If any person had told the Parliament which met in perplexity and terror after the crash in 1720, that in 1830 the wealth of England would surpass all their wildest dreams—that the annual revenue would equal the principal of that debt which they considered as an intolerable burden—that for one man of £10,000 then living, there would be five men of £50,000; that London would be twice as large and twice as populous, and that nevertheless the mortality would have diminished to one-half what it then was,—that the post-office would bring more into the exchequer than the excise and customs had brought in together under Charles II,—that stagecoaches would run from London to York in twenty-four hours—that men would sail without wind, and would be beginning to ride without horses—our ancestors would have given as much credit to the prediction as they gave to Gulliver's Travels. Yet the prediction would have been true; and they would have perceived that it was not altogether absurd, if they had considered that the country was then raising every year a sum which would have purchased the fee-simple of the revenue of the Plantagenets—ten times what supported the government of Elizabeth—three times what, in the time of Oliver Cromwell, had been thought intolerably oppressive. To almost all men the state of things under which they have been used to live seems to be the necessary state of things. We have heard it said, that five per cent is the natural interest of money, that twelve is the natural number of a jury, that forty shillings is the natural qualification of a county voter. Hence it is, that though, in every age, every body knows that up to his own time progressive improvement has been taking place, nobody seems to reckon on any improvement during the next generation. We cannot absolutely prove that those are in error who tell us that society has reached a turning point—that we have seen our best days. But so said all who came before us, and with just as much apparent reason. "A million a-year will beggar us," said the patriots of 1640. "Two millions a-year will grind the country to powder," was the cry in 1660. "Six millions a-year, and a debt of fifty millions!" exclaimed Swift—"the high allies have been the ruin of us." "A hundred and forty millions of debt!" said Junius—"well may we say that we owe Lord Chatham more than we shall ever pay, if we owe him such a load as this." "Two hundred and forty millions of debt!" cried all the statesmen of 1783 in chorus—"what abilities, or what economy on the part of a minister, can save a country so burdened?" We know that if, since 1783, no fresh debt had been incurred, the increased resources of the country would have enabled us to defray that burden, at which Pitt, Fox, and Burke stood aghast—to defray it over and over again, and that with much lighter taxation than what we have actually borne. On what principle is it, that when we see nothing but improvement behind us, we are to expect nothing but deterioration before us?

It is not by the intermeddling of Mr. Southey's idol—the omniscient and omnipotent State—but by the prudence and energy of the people, that England has hitherto been carried forward in civilisation; and it is to the same prudence and the same energy that we now look with comfort and good hope. Our rulers will best promote the improvement of the people by strictly confining themselves to their own legitimate duties—by leaving capital to find its most lucrative course, commodities their fair price, industry and intelligence their natural reward, idleness and folly their natural punishment—by maintaining peace, by defending property, by diminishing the price of law, and by observing strict economy in every part of the state. Let the Government do this—the People will assuredly do the rest.

Comic Dramatists
of the Restoration

Restoration comedy—that is, English stage comedy in the period roughly from 1660 to 1700—was rarely produced in Macaulay's day, so that the criticism and defense of its morality was an academic rather than a public question. The publication of an edition of these comedies by the veteran poet, essayist, and liberal journalist Leigh Hunt (for whom a few years later Macaulay was instrumental in obtaining a government pension) gave Macaulay a double opportunity: first, to make a favorite point about the improvement over the last century in the morality of literature, one of the evidences for his belief in the reality of general social progress; and second, to provide in the sketches of Wycherley and Congreve examples of the rapid and vivid biographical narratives in which he excelled.

Much of Macaulay's criticism is determined by the defense of Restoration comedy made by Charles Lamb in his essay "On the Artificial Comedy of the Last Century" (1822), which asserted the absolutely conventional character of this literature, inhabiting a realm having "no reference whatever to the world that is." The problem of literature as historical evidence is not one easily solved; Macaulay, however, is certain that, such as these plays were, so was the society that produced them. The conviction is at least partly owing to Macaulay's susceptible imagination which found in the light literature of an age materials even more con-

Originally published in January 1841.

vincing for history than the most austere documents. As to Macaulay's condemnation of the immorality of Restoration comedy, it should be noted that it is not simply a matter of the Victorian revulsion from "indecency" but a protest against the "inhuman spirit" of this literature at its worst, which, like pornography, treats men and women merely as various functions.

We have a kindness for Mr. Leigh Hunt. We form our judgment of him, indeed, only from events of universal notoriety—from his own works, and from the works of other writers, who have generally abused him in the most rancorous manner. But, unless we are greatly mistaken, he is a very clever, a very honest, and a very good-natured man. We can clearly discern, together with many merits, many serious faults both in his writings and in his conduct. But we really think that there is hardly a man living whose merits have been so grudgingly allowed, and whose faults have been so cruelly expiated.

In some respects, Mr. Leigh Hunt is excellently qualified for the task which he has now undertaken. His style, in spite of its mannerism—nay, partly by reason of its mannerism—is well suited for light, garrulous, desultory *ana*, half critical half biographical. We do not always agree with his literary judgments; but we find in him what is very rare in our time—the power of justly appreciating and heartily enjoying good things of very different kinds. He can adore Shakspeare and Spenser without denying poetical genius to the author of "Alexander's Feast"; or fine observation, rich fancy, and exquisite humour to him who imagined "Will Honeycomb" and "Sir Roger de Coverley." He has paid particular attention to the history of the English drama, from the age of Elizabeth down to our own time, and has every right to be heard with respect on that subject.

The plays to which he now acts as introducer are, with few exceptions, such as, in the opinion of many very respectable people, ought not to be reprinted. In this opinion we can by no means concur. We cannot wish that any work or class of works which has exercised a great influence on the human mind, and which illustrates the character of an important epoch in letters, politics, and morals, should disappear from the world. If we err in this matter, we err with the gravest men and bodies of men in the empire, and especially with the Church of England, and with the great schools of learning which are connected with her. The whole liberal education of our countrymen is conducted on the principle, that no book which is valuable, either by reason of the excellence of its style, or by reason of the light which it throws on the history, polity, and manners of nations, should be withheld from the student on account of its impurity. The Athenian Comedies, in which there are scarcely a hundred lines together without some passage of which Rochester would have been ashamed, have been reprinted at the Pitt Press and the Clarendon Press, under the direction of syndics and delegates appointed by the Universities; and have been illustrated with notes by reverend, very reverend, and right reverend commentators. Every year the most distinguished young men in the kingdom are examined by bishops and professors of divinity in the *Lysistrata* of Aristophanes, and the Sixth Satire of Juvenal. There is certainly something a little ludicrous in the idea of a conclave of venerable fathers of the church rewarding a lad for his intimate acquaintance with writings, compared with which the loosest tale in Prior is modest. But for our own part we have no doubt that the great societies which direct the education of the English gentry, have herein judged wisely. It is unquestionable that an extensive acquaintance with ancient literature enlarges and enriches the mind. It is unquestionable that a man whose mind has been thus enlarged and enriched, is likely to be far more useful to the state and to the church, than one who is unskilled, or little skilled in classical learning. On the other hand, we find it difficult to believe that, in a world so full of temptation as this, any gentleman, whose life would have been virtuous if he had not read Aristophanes and Juvenal, will be made vicious by reading them. A man who, exposed to all the influences of such a state of society as that in which we live, is yet afraid of exposing himself to the influences of a few Greek or Latin verses, acts, we think, much like the felon who begged the sheriffs to let him have an umbrella held over his head from the door of Newgate to the gallows, because it was a drizzling morning, and he was apt to take cold.

The virtue which the world wants is a healthful virtue, not a valetudinarian virtue—a virtue which can expose itself to the risks inseparable from all spirited exertion—not a virtue which keeps out of the common air for fear of infection, and eschews the common food as too stimulating. It would be indeed absurd to attempt to keep men from acquiring those qualifications which fit them to play their part in life with honour to themselves and advantage to their country, for the sake of preserving a delicacy which cannot be preserved—a delicacy which a walk from Westminster to the Temple is sufficient to destroy.

But we should be justly chargeable with gross inconsistency, if, while we defend the policy which invites the youth of our country to study such writers as Theocritus and Catullus, we were to set up a cry against a new edition of the "Country Wife," or the "Way of the World." The immoral English writers of the seventeenth century are indeed much less excusable than those of Greece and Rome. But the worst English writings of the seventeenth century are decent, compared with much that has been bequeathed to us by Greece and Rome. Plato, we have little doubt, was a much better man than Sir George Etherege. But Plato has written things at which Sir George Etherege would have shuddered. Buckhurst and Sedley, even in those wild orgies at the Cock in Bow Street, for which they were pelted by the rabble and fined by the Court of King's Bench, would never have dared to hold such discourse as passed between Socrates and Phædrus on that fine summer day, under the plane-tree, while the fountain warbled at their feet, and the cicadas chirped overhead. If it be, as we think it is, desirable that an English gentleman should be well informed touching the government and the manners of little commonwealths, which both in place and time are far removed from us—whose independence has been more than two thousand years extinguished, whose language has not been spoken for ages, and whose ancient magnificence is attested only by a few broken columns and friezes—much more must it be desirable that he should be intimately acquainted with the history of the public mind of his own country; and with the causes, the nature, and the extent of those revolutions of opinion and feeling, which, during the last two centuries, have alternately raised and depressed the standard of our national morality. And knowledge of this sort is to be very sparingly gleaned from Parliamentary debates, from state papers, and from the works of grave historians. It must either not be acquired at all, or it must be acquired by the perusal of the light literature which has at various periods been fashionable. We are therefore by no means disposed to condemn this publication, though we certainly cannot recommend the handsome volume[1] before us as an appropriate Christmas present for young ladies.

We have said that we think the present publication perfectly justifiable. But we can by no means agree with Mr. Leigh Hunt, who seems to hold that there is little or no ground for the charge of immorality so often brought against the literature of the Restoration. We do not blame him for not bringing to the judgment-seat the merciless rigour of Lord Angelo; but we really think that such flagitious and impudent offenders as those who are now at the bar, deserved at least the gentle rebuke of Escalus. Mr. Leigh Hunt treats the whole matter a little too much in the easy style of Lucio, and perhaps his exceeding lenity disposes us to be somewhat too severe.

And yet, it is not easy to be too severe. For, in truth, this part of our literature is a disgrace to our language and our national character. It is clever, indeed, and very entertaining; but it is, in the most emphatic sense of the words, "earthly, sensual, devilish." Its indecency, though perpetually such as is condemned, not less by the rules of good taste than by those of morality, is not, in our opinion, so disgraceful a fault as its singularly inhuman spirit. We have here Belial, not as when he inspired Ovid and Ariosto, "graceful and humane," but with the iron eye and cruel sneer of Mephistopheles. We find ourselves in a world, in which the ladies are like very profligate, impudent, and unfeeling men, and in which the men are too bad for any place but Pandæmonium or Norfolk Island. We are surrounded by foreheads of bronze, hearts like the nether millstone, and tongues set on fire of hell.

Dryden defended or excused his own offences, and those of his contemporaries, by pleading the example of the earlier English dramatists; and Mr. Leigh Hunt seems to think that there is force

---

1. Mr. Moxon, its publisher, is well entitled to commendation and support for having, by a series of corresponding Reprints, (comprising the works of the elder Dramatists,)—executed in a compendious but very comely form, and accompanied with useful prolegomena—put it in the power of any one desirous of such an acquisition, to procure, at a comparatively small cost, the noblest Dramatic Library in the world.

in the plea. We altogether differ from this opinion. The crime charged is not mere coarseness of expression. The terms which are delicate in one age, become gross in the next. The diction of the English version of the Pentateuch, is sometimes such as Addison would not have ventured to imitate; and Addison, the standard of purity in his own age, used many phrases which are now proscribed. Whether a thing shall be designated by a plain noun-substantive, or by a circumlocution, is mere matter of fashion. Morality is not at all interested in the question. But morality is deeply interested in this—that what is immoral shall not be presented to the imagination of the young and susceptible in constant connexion with what is attractive. For every person who has observed the operation of the law of association in his own mind, and in the minds of others, knows, that whatever is constantly presented to the imagination in connexion with what is attractive, will commonly itself become attractive. There is undoubtedly a great deal of indelicate writing in Fletcher and Massinger; and more than might be wished even in Ben Jonson and Shakspeare, who are comparatively pure. But it is impossible to trace in their plays any systematic attempt to associate vice with those things which men value most and desire most, and virtue with every thing ridiculous and degrading. And such a systematic attempt we find in the whole dramatic literature of the generation which followed the return of Charles the Second. We will take, as an instance of what we mean, a single subject of the highest importance to the happiness of mankind—conjugal fidelity. We can at present hardly call to mind a single English play, written before the civil war, in which the character of a seducer of married women is represented in a favourable light. We remember many plays in which such persons are baffled, exposed, covered with derision, and insulted by triumphant husbands. Such is the fate of Falstaff, with all his wit and knowledge of the world. Such is the fate of Brisac in Fletcher's "Elder Brother"—and of Ricardo and Ubaldo, in Massinger's "Picture." Sometimes, as in the "Fatal Dowery," and "Love's Cruelty," the outraged honour of families is repaired by a bloody revenge. If now and then the lover is represented as an accomplished man, and the husband as a person of weak or odious character, this only makes the triumph of female virtue the more signal; as in Jonson's Celia and Mrs.

Fitzdottrel, and in Fletcher's Maria. In general, we will venture to say, that the dramatists of the age of Elizabeth and James the First, either treat the breach of the marriage-vow as a serious crime—or, if they treat it as a matter for laughter, turn the laugh against the gallant.

On the contrary, during the forty years which followed the Restoration, the whole body of the dramatists invariably represent adultery—we do not say as a peccadillo—we do not say as an error which the violence of passion may excuse—but as the calling of a fine gentleman—as a grace without which his character would be imperfect. It is as essential to his breeding and to his place in society that he should make love to the wives of his neighbours, as that he should know French, or that he should have a sword at his side. In all this there is no passion, and scarcely any thing that can be called preference. The hero intrigues, just as he wears a wig; because, if he did not, he would be a queer fellow, a city prig, perhaps a Puritan. All the agreeable qualities are always given to the gallant. All the contempt and aversion are the portion of the unfortunate husband. Take Dryden for example; and compare Woodall with Brainsick, or Lorenzo with Gomez. Take Wycherley, and compare Horner with Pinchwife. Take Vanbrugh, and compare Constant with Sir John Brute. Take Farquhar, and compare Archer with Squire Sullen. Take Congreve, and compare Bellmour with Fondlewife, Careless with Sir Paul Plyant, or Scandal with Foresight. In all these cases, and in many more which might be named, the dramatist evidently does his best to make the person who commits the injury graceful, sensible, and spirited; and the person who suffers it a fool or a tyrant, or both.

Mr. Charles Lamb, indeed, attempted to set up a defence for this way of writing. The dramatists of the latter part of the seventeenth century are not, according to him, to be tried by the standard of morality which exists, and ought to exist in real life. Their world is a conventional world. Their heroes and heroines belong, not to England, not to Christendom, but to an Utopia of gallantry, to a Fairyland, where the Bible and Burns's Justice are unknown—where a prank which on this earth would be rewarded with the pillory, is merely matter for a peal of elvish laughter. A real Horner, a real Careless would, it is admitted, be exceedingly bad men. But to predicate morality or immorality of the Horner of Wycherley, and the Careless of Congreve, is as absurd as it would be to arraign a sleeper for his dreams. They belong "to the regions of pure comedy, where no cold moral reigns—when we are amongst them we are amongst a chaotic people. We are not to judge them by our usages. No reverend institutions are insulted by their proceedings, for they have none among them. No peace of families is violated, for no family ties exist among them. There is neither right nor wrong—gratitude or its opposite—claim or duty—paternity or sonship."

This is, we believe, a fair summary of Mr. Lamb's doctrine. We are sure that we do not wish to represent him unfairly. For we admire his genius; we love the kind nature which appears in all his writings; and we cherish his memory as much as if we had known him personally. But we must plainly say that his argument, though ingenious, is altogether sophistical.

Of course we perfectly understand that it is possible for a writer to create a conventional world in which things forbidden by the Decalogue and the Statute Book shall be lawful, and yet that the exhibition may be harmless, or even edifying. For example, we suppose that the most austere critics would not accuse Fenelon of impiety and immorality, on account of his Telemachus and his Dialogues of the Dead. In Telemachus and the Dialogues of the Dead, we have a false religion, and consequently a morality which is in some points incorrect. We have a right and a wrong, differing from the right and the wrong of real life. It is represented as the first duty of men to pay honour to Jove and Minerva. Philocles, who employs his leisure in making graven images of these deities, is extolled for his piety in a way which contrasts singularly with the expressions of Isaiah on the same subject. The dead are judged by Minos, and rewarded with lasting happiness for actions which Fenelon would have been the first to pronounce splendid sins. The same may be said of Mr. Southey's Mahommedan and Hindoo heroes and heroines. In Thalaba, to speak in derogation of the Arabian impostor is blasphemy —to drink wine is a crime—to perform ablutions, and to pay honour to the holy cities, are works of merit. In the Curse of Kehama, Kailyal is commended for her devotion to the statue of Mariataly, the goddess of the poor. But certainly no person will accuse Mr. Southey of having promoted or intended to promote either Islamism or Brahminism.

It is easy to see why the conventional worlds of Fenelon and Mr. Southey are unobjectionable. In the first place, they are utterly unlike the real world in which we live. The state of society, the laws even of the physical world, are so different from those with which we are familiar, that we cannot be shocked at finding the morality also very different. But in truth, the morality of these conventional worlds differs from the morality of the real world, only in points where there is no danger that the real world will ever go wrong. The generosity and docility of Telemachus, the fortitude, the modesty, and filial tenderness of Kailyal, are virtues of all ages and nations. And there was very little danger that the Dauphin would worship Minerva, or that an English damsel would dance with a bucket on her head before the statue of Mariataly.

The case is widely different with what Mr. Charles Lamb calls the conventional world of Wycherley and Congreve. Here the costume, the manners, the topics of conversation are those of the real town, and of the passing day. The hero is in all superficial accomplishments exactly the fine gentleman, whom every youth in the pit would gladly resemble. The heroine is the fine lady, whom every youth in the pit would gladly marry. The scene is laid in some place which is as well known to the audience as their own houses, in St. James's Park, or Hyde Park, or Westminster Hall. The lawyer bustles about with his bag, between the Common Pleas and the Exchequer. The Peer calls for his carriage to go to the House of Lords on a private bill. A hundred little touches are employed to make the fictitious world appear like the actual world. And the immorality is of a sort which never can be out of date, and which all the force of religion, law, and public opinion united can but imperfectly restrain.

In the name of art, as well as in the name of virtue, we protest against the principle that the world of pure comedy is one into which no moral enters. If comedy be an imitation, under whatever conventions, of real life, how is it possible that it can have no reference to the great rule which directs life, and to feelings which are called forth by every incident of life?

87

If what Mr. Charles Lamb says were correct, the inference would be, that these dramatists did not in the least understand the very first principles of their craft. Pure landscape painting into which no light or shade enters, pure portrait painting into which no expression enters, are phrases less at variance with sound criticism, than pure comedy into which no moral enters.

But it is not the fact, that the world of these dramatists is a world into which no moral enters. Morality constantly enters into that world, a sound morality, and an unsound morality; the sound morality to be insulted, derided, associated with every thing mean and hateful; the unsound morality to be set off to every advantage, and inculcated by all methods, direct and indirect. It is not the fact, that none of the inhabitants of this conventional world feel reverence for sacred institutions, and family ties. Fondlewife, Pinchwife, every person in short of narrow understanding, and disgusting manners, expresses that reverence strongly. The heroes and heroines too, have a moral code of their own, an exceedingly bad one; but not, as Mr. Charles Lamb seems to think, a code existing only in the imagination of dramatists. It is, on the contrary, a code actually received, and obeyed by great numbers of people. We need not go to Utopia or Fairyland to find them. They are near at hand. Every night some of them play at the "hells" in the Quadrant, and others pace the Piazza in Covent-Garden. Without flying to Nephelococcygia, or to the Court of Queen Mab, we can meet with sharpers, bullies, hard-hearted impudent debauchees, and women worthy of such paramours. The morality of the "Country Wife" and the "Old Bachelor," is the morality, not, as Mr. Charles Lamb maintains, of an unreal world, but of a world which is a great deal too real. It is the morality, not of a chaotic people, but of low town-rakes, and of those ladies whom the newspapers call "dashing Cyprians." And the question is simply, whether a man of genius, who constantly and systematically endeavours to make this sort of character attractive, by uniting it with beauty, grace, dignity, spirit, a high social position, popularity, literature, wit, taste, knowledge of the world, brilliant success in every undertaking, does or does not make an ill use of his powers. We own that we are unable to understand how this question can be answered in any way but one.

It must, indeed, be acknowledged, in justice to the writers of whom we have spoken thus severely, that they were, to a great extent, the creatures of their age. And if it be asked why that age encouraged immorality which no other age would have tolerated, we have no hesitation in answering that this great depravation of the national taste was the effect of the prevalence of Puritanism under the Commonwealth.

To punish public outrages on morals and religion is unquestionably within the competence of rulers. But when a government, not content with requiring decency, requires sanctity, it oversteps the bounds which mark its proper functions. And it may be laid down as a universal rule, that a government which attempts more than it ought will perform less. A lawgiver who, in order to protect distressed borrowers, limits the rate of interest, either makes it impossible for the objects of his care to borrow at all, or places them at the mercy of the worst class of usurers. A lawgiver who, from tenderness for labouring men, fixes the hours of their work and the amount of their wages, is certain to make them far more wretched than he found them. And so a government which, not content with repressing scandalous excesses, demands from its subjects fervent and austere piety, will soon discover that, while attempting to render an impossible service to the cause of virtue, it has in truth only promoted vice.

For what are the means by which a government can effect its ends? Two only, rewards and punishments;—powerful means, indeed, for influencing the exterior act, but altogether impotent for the purpose of touching the heart. A public functionary who is told that he will be advanced if he is a devout Catholic, and turned out of his place if he is not, will probably go to mass every morning, exclude meat from his table on Fridays, shrive himself regularly, and perhaps let his superiors know that he wears a hair shirt next his skin. Under a Puritan government, a person who is apprised that piety is essential to thriving in the world, will be strict in the observance of the Sunday, or, as he will call it, Sabbath, and will avoid a theatre as if it were plague-stricken. Such a show of religion as this, the hope of gain and the fear of loss will produce, at a week's notice, in any abundance which a government may require. But under this show, sensuality, ambition, avarice, and hatred retain unimpaired power; and the seeming convert has only added to the vices of a man of the world all the still darker vices which are engendered by the constant practice of dissimulation. The truth cannot be long concealed. The public discovers that the grave persons who are proposed to it as patterns, are more utterly destitute of moral principle and of moral sensibility than avowed libertines. It sees that these Pharisees are further removed from real goodness than publicans and harlots. And, as usual, it rushes to the extreme opposite to that which it quits. It considers a high religious profession as a sure mark of meanness and depravity. On the very first day on which the restraint of fear is taken away, and on which men can venture to say what they feel, a frightful peal of blasphemy and ribaldry proclaims that the short-sighted policy which aimed at making a nation of saints has made a nation of scoffers.

It was thus in France about the beginning of the eighteenth century. Louis the Fourteenth in his old age became religious, and determined that his subjects should be religious too—shrugged his shoulders and knitted his brows if he observed at his levee or near his dinner-table any gentleman who neglected the duties enjoined by the church—and rewarded piety with blue ribands, invitations to Marli, governments, pensions, and regiments. Forthwith Versailles became, in every thing but dress, a convent. The pulpits and confessionals were surrounded by swords and embroidery. The marshals of France were much in prayer; and there was hardly one among the dukes and peers who did not carry good little books in his pocket, fast during Lent, and communicate at Easter. Madame de Maintenon, who had a great share in the blessed work, boasted that devotion had become quite the fashion. A fashion indeed it was; and like a fashion it passed away. No sooner had the old king been carried to St. Denis, than the whole court unmasked. Every man hastened to indemnify himself, by the excess of licentiousness and impudence, for years of mortification. The same persons who, a few months before, with meek voices and demure looks, had consulted divines about the state of their souls, now surrounded the midnight table, where, amidst the bounding of champagne corks, a drunken prince, enthroned between Dubois and Madame de Parabère, hiccoughed out atheistical arguments and obscene jests. The early part of the reign of Louis the Fourteenth had been a time of license; but the most dissolute men of that generation would have blushed at the orgies of the Regency.

It was the same with our fathers in the time of the Great Civil War. We are by no means unmindful of the great debt which mankind owes to the Puritans of that time, the deliverers of England, the founders of the great American Commonwealths. But in the day of their power they committed one great fault, which left deep and lasting traces in the national character and manners. They mistook the end and overrated the force of government. They determined not merely to protect religion and public morals from insult—an object for which the civil sword, in discreet hands, may be beneficially employed—but to make the people committed to their rule truly devout. Yet if they had only reflected on events which they had themselves witnessed, and in which they had themselves borne a great part, they would have seen what was likely to be the result of their enterprise. They had lived under a government which, during a long course of years, did all that could be done, by lavish bounty and by rigorous punishment, to enforce conformity to the doctrine and discipline of the Church of England. No person suspected of hostility to that church had the smallest chance of obtaining favour at the court of Charles. Avowed dissent was punished by imprisonment, by ignominious exposure, by cruel mutilations, and by ruinous fines. And the event had been, that the Church had fallen, and had, in its fall, dragged down with it a monarchy which had stood six hundred years. The Puritan might have learned, if from nothing else, yet from his own recent victory, that governments which attempt things beyond their reach are likely not merely to fail, but to produce an effect directly the opposite of that which they contemplate as desirable.

All this was overlooked. The saints were to inherit the earth. The theatres were closed. The fine arts were placed under absurd restraints. Vices which had never before been even misdemeanors were made capital felonies. And it was solemnly resolved by Parliament, "that no person shall be employed but such as the

House shall be satisfied of his real godliness." The pious assembly had a Bible lying on the table for reference. If they had consulted it they might have learned that the wheat and the tares grow together inseparably, and must either be spared together, or rooted up together. To know whether a man was really godly was impossible. But it was easy to know whether he had a plain dress, lank hair, no starch in his linen, no gay furniture in his house; whether he talked through his nose, and showed the whites of his eyes; whether he named his children Assurance, Tribulation, or Maher-shalal-hash-baz—whether he avoided Spring Garden when in town, and abstained from hunting and hawking when in the country—whether he expounded hard scriptures to his troop of dragoons, and talked in a committee of ways and means about seeking the Lord. These were tests which could easily be applied. The misfortune was, that they were tests which proved nothing. Such as they were, they were employed by the dominant party. And the consequence was, that a crowd of impostors, in every walk of life, began to mimic and to caricature what were then regarded as the outward signs of sanctity. The nation was not duped. The restraints of that gloomy time were such as would have been impatiently borne, if imposed by men who were universally believed to be saints. Those restraints became altogether insupportable when they were known to be kept up for the profit of hypocrites. It is quite certain that, even if the Royal Family had never returned—even if Richard Cromwell or Henry Cromwell had been at the head of the administration—there would have been a great relaxation of manners. Before the Revolution many signs indicated that a period of license was at hand. The Restoration crushed for a time the Puritan party, and placed supreme power in the hands of a libertine. The political counter-revolution assisted the moral counter-revolution, and was in turn assisted by it. A period of wild and desperate dissoluteness followed. Even in remote manor-houses and hamlets the change was in some degree felt; but in London the outbreak of debauchery was appalling. And in London the places most deeply infected were the Palace, the quarters inhabited by the aristocracy, and the Inns of Court. It was on the support of these parts of the town that the playhouses depended. The character of the drama became conformed to the character of its patrons. The comic poet was the mouthpiece of the most deeply corrupted part of a corrupted society. And in the plays before us, we find distilled and condensed, the essential spirit of the fashionable world during the Anti-puritan reaction.

The Puritan had affected formality; the comic poet laughed at decorum. The Puritan had frowned at innocent diversions; the comic poet took under his patronage the most flagitious excesses. The Puritan had canted; the comic poet blasphemed. The Puritan had made an affair of gallantry felony, without benefit of clergy; the comic poet represented it as an honourable distinction. The Puritan spoke with disdain of the low standard of popular morality; his life was regulated by a far more rigid code; his virtue was sustained by motives unknown to men of the world. Unhappily it had been amply proved in many cases, and might well be suspected in many more, that these high pretensions were unfounded. Accordingly, the fashionable circles, and the comic poets who were the spokesmen of those circles, took up the notion that all professions of piety and integrity were to be construed by the rule of contrary; that it might well be doubted whether there was such a thing as virtue in the world; but that, at all events, a person who affected to be better than his neighbours was sure to be a knave.

In the old drama there had been much that was reprehensible. But whoever compares even the least decorous plays of Fletcher with those contained in the volume before us, will see how much the profligacy which follows a period of overstrained austerity, goes beyond the profligacy which precedes such a period. The nation resembled the demoniac in the New Testament. The Puritans boasted that the unclean spirit was cast out. The house was empty, swept, and garnished, and for a time the expelled tenant wandered through dry places seeking rest and finding none. But the force of the exorcism was spent. The fiend returned to his abode; and returned not alone. He took to him seven other spirits more wicked than himself. They entered in, and dwelt together: and the second possession was worse than the first.

We will now, as far as our limits will permit, pass in review

93

the writers to whom Mr. Leigh Hunt has introduced us. Of the four, Wycherley stands, we think, last in literary merit, but first in order of time, and first, beyond all doubt, in immorality.

William Wycherley was born in 1640. He was the son of a Shropshire gentleman of old family, and of what was then accounted a good estate. The property was estimated at £600 a-year, a fortune which, among the fortunes of that time, probably ranked as a fortune of £2000 a-year would rank in our days.

William was an infant when the civil war broke out; and, while he was still in his rudiments, a presbyterian hierarchy and a republican government were established on the ruins of the ancient church and throne. Old Mr. Wycherley was attached to the royal cause, and was not disposed to entrust the education of his heir to the solemn Puritans who now ruled the universities and public schools. Accordingly, the young gentleman was sent at fifteen to France. He resided some time in the neighbourhood of the Duke of Montausier, chief of one of the noblest races of Touraine. The duke's wife, a daughter of the house of Rambouillet, was a finished specimen of those talents and accomplishments for which her house was celebrated. The young foreigner was introduced to the splendid circle which surrounded the duchess, and there he appears to have learned some good and some evil. In a few years he returned to this country a fine gentleman and a Papist. His conversion, it may safely be affirmed, was the effect, not of any strong impression on his understanding or feelings, but partly of intercourse with an agreeable society in which the Church of Rome was the fashion; and partly of that aversion to Calvinistic austerities, which was then almost universal among young Englishmen of parts and spirit, and which, at one time, seemed likely to make one half of them Catholics, and the other half Atheists.

But the Restoration came. The universities were again in loyal hands; and there was reason to hope that there would be again a national church fit for a gentleman. Wycherley became a member of Queen's College, Oxford, and abjured the errors of the Church of Rome. The somewhat equivocal glory of turning,

94

for a short time, a very good-for-nothing Papist into a very good-for-nothing Protestant is ascribed to Bishop Barlow.

Wycherley left Oxford without taking a degree, and entered at the Temple, where he lived gaily for some years, observing the humours of the town, enjoying its pleasures, and picking up just as much law as was necessary to make the character of a petti-fogging attorney, or of a litigious client entertaining in a comedy.

From an early age he had been in the habit of amusing himself by writing. Some wretched lines of his on the Restoration are still extant. Had he devoted himself to the making of verses, he would have been nearly as far below Tate and Blackmore as Tate and Blackmore are below Dryden. His only chance for renown would have been, that he might have occupied a niche, in a satire, between Flecknoe and Settle. There was, however, another kind of composition in which his talents and acquire-ments qualified him to succeed; and to that he judiciously be-took himself.

In his old age he used to say, that he wrote "Love in a Wood" at nineteen, the "Gentleman Dancing-Master" at twenty-one, the "Plain Dealer" at twenty-five, and the "Country Wife" at one or two and thirty. We are incredulous, we own, as to the truth of this story. Nothing that we know of Wycherley leads us to think him incapable of sacrificing truth to vanity. And his mem-ory in the decline of his life played him such strange tricks, that we might question the correctness of his assertion, without throw-ing any imputation on his veracity. It is certain that none of his plays was acted till 1672, when he gave "Love in a Wood" to the public. It seems improbable that he should resolve, on so important an occasion as that of a first appearance before the world, to run his chance with a feeble piece, written before his talents were ripe, before his style was formed, before he had looked abroad into the world; and this when he had actually in his desk two highly-finished plays, the fruit of his matured powers. When we look minutely at the pieces themselves, we find in every part of them reason to suspect the accuracy of Wycherley's statement. In the first scene of "Love in a Wood," to go no further, we find many passages which he could not have written when he was nineteen. There is an allusion to gentlemen's periwigs, which first came into fashion in 1663; an allusion to guineas, which were first struck in 1663; an allusion to the vests which Charles ordered to be worn at court in 1666; an allusion to the fire of 1666; and several allusions to political and ecclesiastical affairs which must be assigned to times later than the year of the Restoration—to times when the government and the city were opposed to each other, and when the Presbyterian ministers had been driven from the parish churches to the conventicles. But it is needless to dwell on particular expressions. The whole air and spirit of the piece belong to a period subsequent to that mentioned by Wycherley. As to the "Plain Dealer," which is said to have been written when he was twenty-five, it contains one scene unquestionably written after 1675, several which are later than 1668, and scarcely a line which can have been composed before the end of 1666.

Whatever may have been the age at which Wycherley composed his plays, it is certain that he did not bring them before the public till he was upwards of thirty. In 1672, "Love in a Wood" was acted with more success than it deserved, and this event produced a great change in the fortunes of the author. The Duchess of Cleveland cast her eyes upon him, and was pleased with his appearance. This abandoned woman, not content with her complaisant husband, and her royal keeper, lavished her fondness on a crowd of paramours of all ranks, from dukes to rope-dancers. In the time of the commonwealth, she commenced her career of gallantry; and terminated it under Anne, by marrying, when a great-grandmother, that worthless fop, Beau Fielding. It is not strange that she should have regarded Wycherley with favour. His figure was commanding, his countenance strikingly handsome, his look and deportment full of grace and dignity. He had, as Pope said long after, "the true nobleman look"; the look which seems to indicate superiority, and a not unbecoming consciousness of superiority. His hair indeed, as he says in one of his poems, was prematurely grey. But in that age of periwigs, this misfortune was of little importance. The Duchess admired him, and proceeded to make love to him, after the fashion of the coarse-minded and shameless circle to which she belonged. In the Ring, when the crowd of beauties and fine gentlemen was thickest, she put her head out of her coach-window, and bawled to him—"Sir, you are a rascal; you are a villain"; and, if she is not belied, added another phrase of abuse which we will not quote, but of which we may say, that it might most justly have been applied to her own children. Wycherley called on her grace the next day, and with great humility begged to know in what way he had been so unfortunate as to disoblige her. Thus began an intimacy from which the poet probably expected wealth and honours. Nor were such expectations unreasonable. A handsome young fellow about the court, known by the name of Jack Churchill, was, about the same time, so lucky as to become the object of a short-lived fancy of the Duchess. She had presented him with £4500; the price, in all probability, of some title or some pardon. The prudent youth had lent the money on high interest, and on landed security; and this judicious investment was the beginning of the most splendid private fortune in Europe. Wycherley was not so lucky. The partiality with which the great lady regarded him, was indeed the talk of the whole town; and sixty years later, old men who remembered those days, told Voltaire that she often stole from the court to her lover's chambers in the Temple, disguised like a country girl, with a straw-hat on her head, pattens on her feet, and a basket in her hand. The poet was indeed too happy and proud to be discreet. He dedicated to the Duchess the play which had led to their acquaintance, and in the dedication expressed himself in terms which could not but confirm the reports which had gone abroad. But at Whitehall such an affair was regarded in no serious light. The lady was not afraid to bring Wycherley to court, and to introduce him to a splendid society, with which, as far as appears, he had never before mixed. The easy king, who allowed to his mistresses the same liberty which he claimed for himself, was pleased with the conversation and manners of his new rival. So high did Wycherley stand in the royal favour, that once, when he was confined by a fever to his lodgings in Bow Street, Charles, who, with all his faults, was certainly a man of a social and affable disposition, called on him, sat by his bed, advised him to try change of air, and gave him a handsome sum of money to defray the expense of the journey. Buckingham, then master of the horse, and one of that infamous ministry known by the name of the Cabal, had been one of the

Duchess's innumerable paramours. He at first showed some symptoms of jealousy; but soon, after his fashion, veered round from anger to fondness, and gave Wycherley a commission in his own regiment, and a place in the royal household.

It would be unjust to Wycherley's memory not to mention here the only good action, as far as we know, of his whole life. He is said to have made great exertions to obtain the patronage of Buckingham for the illustrious author of "Hudibras," who was now sinking into an obscure grave, neglected by a nation proud of his genius, and by a court which he had served too well. His Grace consented to see poor Butler; and an appointment was made. But unhappily two pretty women passed by; the volatile Duke ran after them; the opportunity was lost, and could never be regained.

The second Dutch war, the most disgraceful war in the whole history of England, was now raging. It was not in that age considered as by any means necessary that a naval officer should receive a professional education. Young men of rank, who were hardly able to keep their feet in a breeze, served on board of the king's ships, sometimes with commissions, and sometimes as volunteers. Mulgrave, Dorset, Rochester, and many others, left the playhouses and the Mall for hammocks and salt pork; and, ignorant as they were of the rudiments of naval service, showed at least, on the day of battle, the courage which is seldom wanting in an English gentleman. All good judges of maritime affairs, complained that, under this system, the ships were grossly mismanaged; and that the tarpaulins contracted the vices, without acquiring the graces, of the court. But on this subject, as on every other, the government of Charles was deaf to all remonstrances, where the interests or whims of favourites were concerned. Wycherley did not choose to be out of the fashion. He embarked, was present at a battle, and celebrated it, on his return, in a copy of verses too bad for the bellman.[2]

---

2. Mr. Leigh Hunt supposes that the battle at which Wycherley was present, was that which the Duke of York gained over Opdam, in 1665. We believe that it was one of the battles between Rupert and De Ruyter, in 1673.

The point is of no importance; and there can scarcely be said to be any evidence either way. We offer, however, to Mr. Leigh Hunt's consideration, three arguments—of no great weight certainly—yet such as ought, we think, to prevail in the absence of better. First, it is not very likely that a young Tem-

About the same time, he brought on the stage his second piece, the "Gentleman Dancing-Master." The biographer says nothing, as far as we remember, about the fate of this play. There is, however, reason to believe, that, though certainly far superior to "Love in a Wood," it was not equally successful. It was first tried at the west end of the town, and, as the poet confessed, "would scarce do there." It was then performed in Salisbury Court, but, as it should seem, with no better event. For, in the prologue to the "Country Wife," Wycherley described himself as "the late so baffled scribbler."

In 1675, the "Country Wife" was performed with brilliant success, which, in a literary point of view, was not wholly unmerited. For, though one of the most profligate and heartless of human compositions, it is the elaborate production of a mind, not indeed rich, original, or imaginative, but ingenious, observant, quick to seize hints, and patient of the toil of polishing.

The "Plain Dealer," equally immoral and equally well written, appeared in 1677. At first this piece pleased the people less than the critics; but after a time its unquestionable merits, and the zealous support of Lord Dorset, whose influence in literary and fashionable society was unbounded, established it in the public favour.

The fortune of Wycherley was now in the zenith, and began to decline. A long life was still before him. But it was destined to be filled with nothing but shame and wretchedness, domestic dissensions, literary failures, and pecuniary embarrassments.

The king, who was looking about for an accomplished man to conduct the education of his natural son, the young Duke of Richmond, at length fixed on Wycherley. The poet, exulting in his good luck, went down to amuse himself at Tunbridge; looked into a bookseller's shop on the Pantiles, and to his great delight, heard a handsome woman ask for the "Plain Dealer,"

---

plar, quite unknown in the world—and Wycherley was such in 1665—should have quitted his chambers to go to sea. On the other hand, it would have been in the regular course of things, that, when a courtier and an equerry, he should offer his services. Secondly, his verses appear to have been written after a drawn battle, like those of 1673, and not after a complete victory, like that of 1665. Thirdly, in the epilogue to the "Gentleman Dancing-Master," written in 1673, he says, that "all gentlemen must pack to sea"; an expression which makes it probable that he did not himself mean to stay behind.

which had just been published. He made acquaintance with the lady, who proved to be the Countess of Drogheda, a gay young widow, with an ample jointure. She was charmed with his person and his wit; and, after a short flirtation, agreed to become his wife. Wycherley seems to have been apprehensive that this connexion might not suit well with the king's plans respecting the Duke of Richmond. He accordingly prevailed on the lady to consent to a private marriage. All came out. Charles thought the conduct of Wycherley both disrespectful and disingenuous. Other causes probably assisted to alienate the sovereign from the subject who had lately been so highly favoured. Buckingham was now in opposition, and had been committed to the Tower; not, as Mr. Leigh Hunt supposes, on a charge of treason, but by an order of the House of Lords for some expressions which he had used in debate. Wycherley wrote some bad lines in praise of his imprisoned patron, which, if they came to the knowledge of the king, would certainly have made his majesty very angry. The favour of the court was completely withdrawn from the poet. An amiable woman, with a large fortune, might indeed have been an ample compensation for the loss. But Lady Drogheda was ill-tempered, imperious, and extravagantly jealous. She had herself been a maid of honour at Whitehall. She well knew in what estimation conjugal fidelity was held among the fine gentlemen there; and watched her town husband as assiduously as Mr. Pinchwife watched his country wife. The unfortunate wit was, indeed, allowed to meet his friends at a tavern opposite to his own house. But on such occasions the windows were always open, in order that her ladyship, who was posted on the other side of the street, might be satisfied that no woman was of the party.

The death of Lady Drogheda released the unfortunate poet from this distress; but a series of disasters, in rapid succession, broke down his health, his spirits, and his fortune. His wife meant to leave him a good property, and left him only a lawsuit. His father could not or would not assist him. He was at length thrown into the Fleet, and languished there during seven years, utterly forgotten, as it should seem, by the gay and lively circle of which he had been a distinguished ornament. In the extremity of his distress he implored the publisher who had been enriched by the sale of his works, to lend him twenty pounds, and was refused. His comedies, however, still kept possession of the stage, and drew great audiences, which troubled themselves little about the situation of the author. At length, James the Second, who had now succeeded to the throne, happened to go to the theatre on an evening when the "Plain Dealer" was acted. He was pleased by the performance, and touched by the fate of the writer, whom he probably remembered as one of the gayest and handsomest of his brother's courtiers. The King determined to pay Wycherley's debts, and to settle on the unfortunate poet a pension of £200 a-year. This munificence, on the part of a prince who was little in the habit of rewarding literary merit, and whose whole soul was devoted to the interests of his church, raises in us a surmise which Mr. Leigh Hunt will, we fear, pronounce very uncharitable. We cannot help suspecting that it was at this time that Wycherley returned to the communion of the Church of Rome. That he did return to the communion of the Church of Rome is certain. The date of his reconversion, as far as we know, has never been mentioned by any biographer. We believe that, if we place it at this time, we do no injustice to the character either of Wycherley or James.

Not long after, old Mr. Wycherley died; and his son, now past the middle of life, came to the family estate. Still, however, he was not at his ease. His embarrassments were great: his property was strictly tied up; and he was on very bad terms with the heir-at-law. He appears to have led, during a long course of years, that most wretched life, the life of an old boy about town. Expensive tastes with little money, and licentious appetites with declining vigour, were the just penance for his early irregularities. A severe illness had produced a singular effect on his intellect. His memory played him pranks stranger than almost any that are to be found in the history of that strange faculty. It seemed to be at once preternaturally strong and preternaturally weak. If a book was read to him before he went to bed, he would wake the next morning with his mind full of the thoughts and expressions which he had heard over night; and he would write them down, without in the least suspecting that they were not his own. In his verses the same ideas, and even the same words came over and over again several times in a short composition. His fine person bore the marks of age, sickness, and sorrow; and he mourned for his departed beauty with an effeminate regret. He could not look without a sigh at the portrait which Lely had painted of him when he was only twenty-eight; and often murmured, *Quantum mutatus ab illo.* He was still nervously anxious about his literary reputation; and, not content with the fame which he still possessed as a dramatist, was determined to be renowned as a satirist and an amatory poet. In 1704, after twenty-seven years of silence, he again appeared as an author. He put forth a large folio of miscellaneous verses, which, we believe, has never been reprinted. Some of these pieces had probably circulated through the town in manuscript. For, before the volume appeared, the critics at the coffee-houses very confidently predicted that it would be utterly worthless; and were in consequence bitterly reviled by the poet in an ill-written, foolish, and egotistical preface. The book amply vindicated the most unfavourable prophecies that had been hazarded. The style and versification are beneath criticism; the morals are those of Rochester. For Rochester, indeed, there was some excuse. When his offences against decorum were committed, he was a very young man, misled by a prevailing fashion. Wycherley was sixty-four. He had long outlived the times when libertinism was regarded as essential to the character of a wit and a gentleman. Most of the rising poets, like Addison, John Philips, and Rowe, were studious of decency. We can hardly conceive any thing more miserable than the figure which the ribald old man makes in the midst of so many sober and well-conducted youths.

In the very year in which this bulky volume of obscene doggerel was published, Wycherley formed an acquaintance of a very singular kind. A little, pale, crooked, sickly, bright-eyed urchin, just turned of sixteen, had written some copies of verses, in which discerning judges could detect the promise of future eminence. There was, indeed, as yet nothing very striking or original in the conceptions of the young poet. But he was already skilled in the art of metrical composition. His diction and his music were not those of the great old masters; but that which his ablest contemporaries were labouring to do, he already did best. His style was not richly poetical; but it was always neat, compact, and pointed. His verse wanted variety of pause, of swell, and of cadence; but it never grated on the ear by a harsh turn, or disappointed it by a feeble close. The youth was already free of the company of wits, and was greatly elated at being introduced to the author of the "Plain Dealer" and the "Country Wife."

It is curious to trace the history of the intercourse which took place between Wycherley and Pope—between the representative of the age that was going out, and the representative of the age that was coming in—between the friend of Rochester and Buckingham, and the friend of Lyttelton and Mansfield. At first the boy was enchanted by the kindness and condescension of his new friend, haunted his door, and followed him about like a spaniel, from coffee-house to coffee-house. Letters full of affection, humility, and fulsome flattery were interchanged between the friends. But the first ardour of affection could not last. Pope, though at no time scrupulously delicate in his writings, or fastidious as to the morals of his associates, was shocked by the indecency of a rake who, at seventy, was still the representative of the monstrous profligacy of the Restoration. As he grew older, as his mind expanded and his fame rose, he appreciated both himself and Wycherley more justly. He felt a well-founded contempt for the old gentleman's verses, and was at no great pains to conceal his opinion. Wycherley, on the other hand, though blinded by self-love to the imperfections of what he called his poetry, could not but see that there was an immense difference between his young companion's rhymes and his own. He was divided between two feelings. He wished to have the assistance of so skilful a hand to polish his lines; and yet he shrank from the humiliation of being beholden for literary assistance to a lad who might have been his grandson. Pope was willing to give assistance; but was by no means disposed to give assistance and flattery too. He took the trouble to retouch whole reams of feeble stumbling verses, and inserted many vigorous lines, which the least skilful reader will distinguish in an instant. But he thought that by these services he acquired a right to express himself in terms which would not, under ordinary circumstances, become a youth when addressing a man of four times his age. In one letter, he tells Wycherley that "the worst pieces are such as, to render them very good, would require almost the en-

tire new writing of them." In another, he gives the following
account of his corrections:

> Though the whole be as short again as at first, there is not one
> thought omitted but what is a repetition of something in your
> first volume, or in this very paper; and the versification through-
> out is, I believe, such as nobody can be shocked at. The repeated
> permission you give me of dealing freely with you, will, I hope,
> excuse what I have done; for, if I have not spared you when I
> thought severity would do you a kindness, I have not mangled
> you where I thought there was no absolute need of amputation.

Wycherley continued to return thanks for all this hacking and
hewing; which was, indeed, of inestimable service to his compositions. But by degrees his thanks began to sound very like reproaches. In private, he is said to have described Pope as a person
who could not cut out a suit, but who had some skill in turning
old coats. In his letters to Pope, while he acknowledged that the
versification of his poems had been greatly improved, he spoke
of the whole art of versification with scorn, and sneered at those
who preferred sound to sense. Pope revenged himself for this
outbreak of spleen by return of post. He had in his hands a volume of Wycherley's rhymes, and he wrote to say that this volume
was so full of faults that he could not correct it without completely defacing the manuscript. "I am," he said, "equally afraid
of sparing you, and of offending you by too impudent a correction." This was more than flesh and blood could bear: Wycherley
reclaimed his papers, in a letter in which resentment shows itself
plainly through the thin disguise of civility. Pope, glad to be rid
of a troublesome and inglorious task, sent back the deposit; and,
by way of a parting courtesy, advised the old man to turn his
poetry into prose, and assured him that the public would like
his thoughts much better without his versification. Thus ended
this memorable correspondence.

Wycherley lived some years after the termination of the
strange friendship which we have described. The last scene of
his life was, perhaps, the most scandalous. Ten days before his
death, at seventy-five, he married a young girl, merely in order
to injure his nephew—an act which proves that neither years,
nor adversity, nor what he called his philosophy, nor either of the
religions which he had at different times professed, had taught

him the rudiments of morality. He died in December 1715, and lies in the vault under the church of St. Paul in Covent-Garden.

His bride soon after married a Captain Shrimpton, who thus became possessed of a large collection of manuscripts. These were sold to a bookseller. They were so full of erasures and interlineations that no printer could decipher them. It was necessary to call in the aid of a professed critic; and Theobald, the editor of Shakspeare, and the hero of the first Dunciad, was employed to ascertain the true reading. In this way a volume of miscellanies in verse and prose was got up for the market. The collection derives all its value from the traces of Pope's hand, which are every where discernible.

Of the moral character of Wycherley it can hardly be necessary for us to say more. His fame as a writer rests wholly on his comedies, and chiefly on the last two. Even as a comic writer, he was neither of the best school, nor highest in his school. He was in truth a worse Congreve. His chief merit, like Congreve, lies in the style of his dialogue. But the wit which lights up the "Plain Dealer" and the "Country Wife" is pale and flickering, when compared with the gorgeous blaze which dazzles us almost to blindness in "Love for Love" and the "Way of the World." Like Congreve—and, indeed, even more than Congreve— Wycherley is ready to sacrifice dramatic propriety to the liveliness of his dialogue. The poet speaks out of the mouths of all his dunces and coxcombs, and makes them describe themselves with a good sense and acuteness which puts them on a level with the wits and heroes. We will give two instances, the first which occur to us, from the "Country Wife." There are to be found in the world fools who find the society of old friends insipid, and who are always running after new companions. Such a character is a fair subject for comedy. But nothing can be more absurd than to introduce a man of this sort saying to his comrade—"I can deny you nothing; for though I have known thee a great while, never go if I do not love thee as well as a new acquaintance." That town-wits, again, have always been rather a heartless class, is true. But none of them, we will answer for it, ever said to a young lady to whom he was making love—"We wits rail and make love often but to show our parts: as we have no affections, so we have no malice."

Wycherley's plays are said to have been the produce of long and patient labour. The epithet of "slow" was early given to him by Rochester, and was frequently repeated. In truth, his mind, unless we are greatly mistaken, was naturally a very meagre soil, and was forced only by great labour and outlay to bear fruit, which, after all, was not of the highest flavour. He has scarcely more claim to originality than Terence. It is not too much to say, that there is hardly any thing of the least value in his plays, of which the hint is not to be found elsewhere. The best scenes in the "Gentleman Dancing-Master," were suggested by Calderon's *Maestro de Danzar,* not by any means one of the happiest comedies of the great Castilian poet. The "Country Wife" is borrowed from the *Ecole des Maris* and the *Ecole des Femmes.* The groundwork of the "Plain Dealer" is taken from the *Misanthrope* of Molière. One whole scene is almost translated from the *Critique de l'Ecole des Femmes;* Fidelia is Shakspeare's Viola stolen, and marred in the stealing; and the Widow Blackacre, beyond comparison Wycherley's best comic character, is the Countess in Racine's *Plaideurs,* talking the jargon of English instead of that of French chicane.

The only thing original about Wycherley—the only thing which he could furnish from his own mind in inexhaustible abundance—was profligacy. It is curious to observe how every thing that he touched, however pure and noble, took in an instant the colour of his own mind. Compare the *Ecole des Femmes* with the "Country Wife." Agnes is a simple and amiable girl, whose heart is indeed full of love, but of love sanctioned by honour, morality, and religion. Her natural talents are great. They have been hidden, and, as it might appear, destroyed by an education elaborately bad. But they are called forth into full energy by a virtuous passion. Her lover, while he adores her beauty, is too honest a man to abuse the confiding tenderness of a creature so charming and inexperienced. Wycherley takes this plot into his hands; and forthwith this sweet and graceful courtship becomes a licentious intrigue of the lowest and least sentimental kind, between an impudent London rake and the idiot wife of a country squire. We will not go into details. In truth, Wycherley's indecency is protected against the critics as a skunk is protected against the hunters. It is safe, because it is too filthy to handle, and too noisome even to approach.

It is the same with the "Plain Dealer." How careful has Shakspeare been in "Twelfth Night," to preserve the dignity and delicacy of Viola, under her disguise! Even when wearing a page's doublet and hose, she is never mixed up with any transaction which the most fastidious mind could regard as leaving a stain on her. She is employed by the Duke on an embassy of love to Olivia; but on an embassy of the most honourable kind. Wycherley borrows Viola—and Viola forthwith becomes a pander of the basest sort. But the character of Manly is the best illustration of our meaning. Molière exhibited in his misanthrope a pure and noble mind, which had been sorely vexed by the sight of perfidy and malevolence, disguised under the forms of politeness. As every extreme naturally generates its contrary, Alceste adopts a standard of good and evil directly opposed to that of the society which surrounds him. Courtesy seems to him a vice; and those stern virtues which are neglected by the fops and coquettes of Paris, become too exclusively the objects of his veneration. He is often to blame; he is often ridiculous; but he is always a good man; and the feeling which he inspires is regret that a person so estimable should be so unamiable. Wycherley borrowed Alceste, and turned him—we quote the words of so lenient a critic as Mr. Leigh Hunt—into "a ferocious sensualist, who believed himself as great a rascal as he thought every body else." The surliness of Molière's hero is copied and caricatured. But the most nauseous libertinism, and the most dastardly fraud, are substituted for the purity and integrity of the original. And, to make the whole complete, Wycherley does not seem to have been aware that he was not drawing the portrait of an eminently honest man. So depraved was his moral taste, that, while he firmly believed he was producing a picture of virtue too exalted for the commerce of this world, he was really delineating the greatest rascal that is to be found, even in his own writings.

We pass a very severe censure on Wycherley, when we say that it is a relief to turn from him to Congreve. Congreve's writings, indeed, are by no means pure, nor was he, as far as we are able to judge, a warm-hearted or high-minded man. Yet, in coming to him, we feel that the worst is over—that we are one remove further from the Restoration—that we are past the Nadir of national taste and morality.

William Congreve was born in 1670,[3] at Bardsey, in the neighbourhood of Leeds. His father, a younger son of a very ancient Staffordshire family, had distinguished himself among the cavaliers in the civil war, was set down after the Restoration for the Order of the Royal Oak, and subsequently settled in Ireland, under the patronage of the Earl of Burlington.

Congreve passed his childhood and youth in Ireland. He was sent to school at Kilkenny, and thence went to the University of Dublin. His learning does great honour to his instructors. From his writings it appears, not only that he was well acquainted with Latin literature, but that his knowledge of the Greek poets was such as was not, in his time, common even in a college.

When he had completed his academical studies, he was sent to London to study the law, and was entered of the Middle Temple. He troubled himself, however, very little about pleading or conveyancing; and gave himself up to literature and society. Two kinds of ambition early took possession of his mind, and often pulled it in opposite directions. He was conscious of great fertility of thought, and power of ingenious combination. His lively conversation, his polished manners, and his highly respectable connexions, had obtained for him ready access to the best company. He longed to be a great writer. He longed to be a man of fashion. Either object was within his reach. But could he secure both? Was there not something vulgar in letters —something inconsistent with the easy apathetic graces of a man of the mode? Was it aristocratical to be confounded with creatures who lived in the cocklofts of Grub Street, to bargain with publishers, to hurry printers' devils, to squabble with managers, to be applauded or hissed by pit, boxes, and galleries? Could he forego the renown of being the first wit of his age? Could he attain that renown without sullying what he valued quite as much—his character for gentility? The history of his life is the history of a conflict between these two impulses. In his youth the desire of literary fame had the mastery; but soon the

3. Mr. Leigh Hunt says 1669. But the Old Style has misled him.

meaner ambition overpowered the higher, and obtained supreme domination over his mind.

His first work, a novel of no great value, he published under the assumed name of "Cleophil." His second was the "Old Bachelor," acted in 1693, a play inferior indeed to his other comedies, but, in its own line, inferior to them alone. The plot is equally destitute of interest and of probability. The characters are either not distinguishable, or are distinguished only by peculiarities of the most glaring kind. But the dialogue is resplendent with wit and eloquence—which indeed are so abundant that the fools come in for an ample share—and yet preserves a certain colloquial air, a certain indescribable ease, of which Wycherley had given no example, and which Sheridan in vain attempted to imitate. The author, divided between pride and shame—pride at having written a good play, and shame at having done an ungentlemanlike thing—pretended that he had merely scribbled a few scenes for his own amusement, and affected to yield unwillingly to the importunities of those who pressed him to try his fortune on the stage. The "Old Bachelor" was seen in manuscript by Dryden; one of whose best qualities was a hearty and generous admiration for the talents of others. He declared that he had never seen such a first play; and lent his services to bring it into a form fit for representation. Nothing was wanting to the success of the piece. It was so cast as to bring into play all the comic talent, and to exhibit on the boards in one view all the beauty, which Drury-Lane Theatre, then the only theatre in London, could assemble. The result was a complete triumph; and the author was gratified with rewards more substantial than the applauses of the pit. Montagu, then a lord of the treasury, immediately gave him a place, and, in a short time, added the reversion of another place of much greater value, which, however, did not become vacant till many years had elapsed.

In 1694, Congreve brought out the "Double-Dealer," a comedy in which all the powers which had produced the "Old Bachelor" show themselves, matured by time and improved by exercise. But the audience was shocked by the characters of Maskwell and Lady Touchwood. And, indeed, there is something strangely revolting in the way in which a group that seems to belong to the house of Laius or of Pelops, is intro-

duced into the midst of the Brisks, Froths, Carelesses, and Ply-
ants. The play was unfavourably received. Yet, if the praise of
distinguished men could compensate an author for the disap-
probation of the multitude, Congreve had no reason to repine.
Dryden, in one of the most ingenious, magnificent, and pathetic
pieces that he ever wrote, extolled the author of the "Double-
Dealer" in terms which now appear extravagantly hyperbolical.
Till Congreve came forth—so ran this exquisite flattery—the
superiority of the poets who preceded the civil wars was acknowledged.

> Theirs was the giant race before the flood.

Since the return of the Royal house, much art and ability had
been exerted, but the old masters had been still unrivalled.

> Our builders were with want of genius curst,
> The second temple was not like the first.

At length a writer had arisen who, just emerging from boyhood,
had surpassed the authors of the "Knight of the Burning Pestle"
and the "Silent Woman," and who had only one rival left to
contend with.

> Heaven, that but once was prodigal before,
> To Shakspeare gave as much, he could not give him more.

Some lines near the end of the poem are singularly graceful and
touching, and sank deep into the heart of Congreve.

> Already am I worn with cares and age,
> And just abandoning the ungrateful stage;
> But you, whom every Muse and Grace adorn,
> Whom I foresee to better fortune born,
> Be kind to my remains; and, oh, defend
> Against your judgment your departed friend;
> Let not the insulting foe my fame pursue,
> But guard those laurels which descend to you.

The crowd as usual gradually came over to the opinion of the
men of note; and the "Double-Dealer" was before long quite as
much admired, though perhaps never so much liked, as the "Old
Bachelor."

In 1695 appeared "Love for Love," superior both in wit and in scenic effect to either of the preceding plays. It was performed at a new theatre which Betterton and some other actors, disgusted by the treatment which they received in Drury-Lane, had just opened in a tennis-court near Lincoln's Inn. Scarcely any comedy within the memory of the oldest man had been equally successful. The actors were so elated that they gave Congreve a share in their theatre, and he promised in return to furnish them with a play every year, if his health would permit. Two years passed, however, before he produced the "Mourning Bride," a play which, paltry as it is when compared, we do not say with Lear or Macbeth, but with the best dramas of Massinger and Ford, stands very high among the tragedies of the age in which it was written. To find any thing so good we must go twelve years back to "Venice Preserved," or six years forward to the "Fair Penitent." The noble passage which Johnson, both in writing and in conversation, extolled above any other in the English drama, has suffered greatly in the public estimation from the extravagance of his praise. Had he contented himself with saying that it was finer than any thing in the tragedies of Dryden, Otway, Lee, Rowe, Southern, Hughes, and Addison—than any thing, in short, that had been written for the stage since the days of Charles the First—he would not have been in the wrong.

The success of the "Mourning Bride" was even greater than that of "Love for Love." Congreve was now allowed to be the first tragic, as well as the first comic dramatist of his time; and all this at twenty-seven. We believe that no English writer except Lord Byron has, at so early an age, stood so high in the estimation of his contemporaries.

At this time took place an event which deserves, in our opinion, a very different sort of notice from that which has been bestowed on it by Mr. Leigh Hunt. The nation had now nearly recovered from the demoralizing effect of the Puritan austerity. The gloomy follies of the reign of the Saints were but faintly remembered. The evils produced by profaneness and debauchery were recent and glaring. The Court, since the Revolution, had ceased to patronise licentiousness. Mary was strictly pious; and the vices of the cold, stern, and silent William, were not obtruded on the public eye. Discountenanced by the government, and falling in the favour of the people, the profligacy of the Restoration still maintained its ground in some parts of society. Its strongholds were the places where men of wit and fashion congregated, and above all, the theatres. At this conjuncture arose a great reformer, whom, widely as we differ from him in many important points, we can never mention without respect.

Jeremy Collier was a clergyman of the Church of England, bred at Cambridge. His talents and attainments were such as might have been expected to raise him to the highest honours of his profession. He had an extensive knowledge of books, and yet he had mingled with polite society, and is said not to have wanted either grace or vivacity in conversation. There were few branches of literature to which he had not paid some attention. But ecclesiastical antiquity was his favourite study. In religious opinions he belonged to that section of the Church of England which lies furthest from Geneva and nearest to Rome. His notions touching Episcopal government, holy orders, the efficacy of the sacraments, the authority of the Fathers, the guilt of schism, the importance of vestments, ceremonies, and solemn days, differed little from those which are now held by Dr. Pusey and Mr. Newman. Towards the close of his life, indeed, Collier took some steps which brought him still nearer to Popery—mixed water with the wine in the Eucharist, made the sign of the cross in confirmation, employed oil in the visitation of the sick, and offered up prayers for the dead. His politics were of a piece with his divinity. He was a Tory of the highest sort, such as in the cant of that age was called a Tantivy. Not even the tyranny of James, not even the persecution of the bishops and the spoliation of the universities, could shake that steady loyalty. While the Convention was sitting, Collier wrote with vehemence in defence of the fugitive king, and was in consequence arrested. But his dauntless spirit was not to be so tamed. He refused to take the oaths, renounced all his preferment, and, in a succession of pamphlets written with much violence and with some ability, attempted to excite the nation against its new masters. In 1692, he was again arrested on suspicion of having been concerned in a treasonable plot. So unbending were his principles that his friends could hardly persuade him to let them bail him; and he afterwards expressed his remorse for having been induced thus to acknowledge, by implication, the authority of an usurping government. He was soon in trouble again. Sir John Friend and Sir William Parkins were tried and convicted of high treason for planning the murder of King William. Collier administered spiritual consolation to them, attended them to Tyburn, and just before the executioner laid his hands on their heads, and by the authority which he derived from Christ, solemnly absolved them. This scene gave indescribable scandal. Tories joined with Whigs in blaming the conduct of the daring priest. There are, it was said, some acts which fall under the definition of treason into which a good man may, in troubled times, be led even by his virtues. It may be necessary for the protection of society to punish such a man. But even in punishing him we consider him as legally rather than morally guilty, and hope that his honest error, though it cannot be pardoned here, will not be counted to him for sin hereafter. But such was not the case of Collier's penitents. They were concerned in a plot for waylaying and butchering, in an hour of security, one who, whether he were or were not their king, was at all events their fellow-creature. Whether the Jacobite theory about the rights of governments, and the duties of subjects, were or were not well founded, assassination must always be considered as a great crime. It is condemned even by the maxims of worldly honour and morality. Much more must it be an object of abhorrence to the pure Spouse of Christ. The Church cannot surely, without the saddest and most mournful forebodings, see one of her children who has been guilty of this great wickedness, pass into eternity without any sign of repentance. That these traitors had given any sign of repentance was not alleged. It might be that they had privately declared their contrition; and, if so, the minister of religion might be justified in privately assuring them of the Divine forgiveness. But a public remission ought to have been preceded by a public atonement. The regret of these men, if expressed at all, had been expressed in secret. The hands of Collier had been laid on them in the presence of thousands. The inference which his enemies drew from his conduct was, that he did not consider the conspiracy against the life of William as sinful. But this inference he very vehemently, and, we doubt not, very sincerely denied.

The storm raged. The bishops put forth a solemn censure of

the absolution. The Attorney-General brought the matter before the Court of King's Bench. Collier had now made up his mind not to give bail for his appearance before any court which derived its authority from the usurper. He accordingly absconded, and was outlawed. He survived these events about thirty years. The prosecution was not pressed, and he was soon suffered to resume his literary pursuits in quiet. At a later period, many attempts were made to shake his perverse integrity by offers of wealth and dignity, but in vain. When he died, towards the end of the reign of George I, he was still under the ban of the law.

We shall not be suspected of regarding either the politics or the theology of Collier with partiality; but we believe him to have been as honest and courageous a man as ever lived. We will go further, and say that, though passionate and often wrong-headed, he was a singularly fair controversialist—candid, generous, too high-spirited to take mean advantages even in the most exciting disputes, and pure from all taint of personal malevolence. It must also be admitted that his opinions on ecclesiastical and political affairs, though in themselves absurd and pernicious, eminently qualified him to be the reformer of our lighter literature. The libertinism of the press and of the stage, was, as we have said, the effect of a reaction against the puritan strictness. Profligacy was, like the oak leaf on the twenty-ninth of May, the badge of a cavalier and a high-churchman. Decency was associated with conventicles and calves' head. Grave prelates were too much disposed to wink at the excesses of a body of zealous and able allies, who covered Roundheads and Presbyterians with ridicule. If a Whig raised his voice against the impiety and licentiousness of the fashionable writers, his mouth was instantly stopped by the retort—You are one of those who groan at a light quotation from Scripture, and raise estates out of the plunder of the Church,—who shudder at a *double entendre*, and chop off the heads of kings. A Baxter, a Burnet, even a Tillotson, would have done little to purify our literature. But when a man, fanatical in the cause of episcopacy, and actually under outlawry for his attachment to hereditary right, came forward as the champion of decency, the battle was already half won.

In 1698, Collier published his "Short View of the Profaneness and Immorality of the English Stage," a book which threw the whole literary world into commotion, but which is now much less read than it deserves. The faults of the work, indeed, are neither few nor small. The dissertations on the Greek and Latin drama do not at all help the argument; and, whatever may have been thought of them by the generation which fancied that Christ Church had refuted Bentley, are such as, in the present day, a scholar of very humble pretensions may venture to pronounce boyish, or rather babyish. The censures are not sufficiently discriminating. The authors whom Collier accused had been guilty of such gross sins against decency, that he was certain to weaken, instead of strengthening his case, by introducing into his charge against them any matter about which there could be the smallest dispute. He was, however, so injudicious as to place among the outrageous offences, which he justly arraigned, some things which are really quite innocent; and some slight instances of levity which, though not perhaps strictly correct, could easily be paralleled from the works of writers who had rendered great services to morality and religion. Thus he blames Congreve, the number and gravity of whose real transgressions made it quite unnecessary to tax him with any that were not real, for using the words "martyr" and "inspiration" in a light sense; as if an archbishop might not say that a speech was inspired by claret, or that an alderman was a martyr to the gout. Sometimes, again, Collier does not sufficiently distinguish between the dramatist and the persons of the drama. Thus he blames Vanbrugh for putting into Lord Foppington's mouth some raillery on the Church service; though it is obvious that Vanbrugh could not better express reverence than by making Lord Foppington express contempt. There is also throughout the "Short View" too strong a display of professional feeling. Collier is not content with claiming for his order an immunity from insult and indiscriminate scurrility; he will not allow that, in any case, any word or act of a divine can be a proper subject for ridicule. Nor does he confine this benefit of clergy to the ministers of the Established Church; he extends the privilege to Catholic priests, and, what in him is more surprising, to Dissenting preachers. This, however, is a mere trifle. Imauns, Brahmins, priests of Jupiter, priests of Baal, are all to be held sacred. Dryden is blamed for making the Mufti in "Don Sebastian" talk nonsense. Lee is called to a severe account for his incivility to Tiresias. But the most curious passage is that in which Collier resents some uncivil reflections thrown by Cassandra, in "Cleomenes," on the calf Apis and his hierophants. The words, "grass-eating, foddered god,"—words which really are much in the style of several passages in the Old Testament, give as much offence to this Christian divine as they could have given to the priests at Memphis.

But, when all these deductions have been made, great merit must be allowed to this work. There is hardly any book of that time from which it would be possible to select specimens of writing so excellent and so various. To compare Collier with Pascal would indeed be absurd. Yet we hardly know where, except in the "Provincial Letters," we can find mirth so harmoniously and becomingly blended with solemnity as in the "Short View." In truth, all the modes of ridicule, from broad fun to polished and antithetical sarcasm, were at Collier's command. On the other hand, he was complete master of the rhetoric of honest indignation. We scarcely know any volume which contains so many bursts of that peculiar eloquence which comes from the heart, and goes to the heart. Indeed, the spirit of the book is truly heroic. In order fairly to appreciate it, we must remember the situation in which the writer stood. He was under the frown of power. His name was already a mark for the invectives of one half of the writers of the age; when, in the cause of good taste, good sense, and good morals, he gave battle to the other half. Strong as his political prejudices were, he seems on this occasion to have entirely laid them aside. He has forgotten that he is a Jacobite, and remembers only that he is a citizen and a Christian. Some of his sharpest censures are directed against poetry which had been hailed with delight by the Tory party, and had inflicted a deep wound on the Whigs. It is really inspiriting to see how gallantly the solitary outlaw advances to attack enemies, formidable separately, and, it might have been thought, irresistible when combined—distributes his swashing blows right and left among Wycherley, Congreve, and Vanbrugh—treads the wretched D'Urfey down in the dirt beneath his feet—and strikes with all his strength full at the towering crest of Dryden.

The effect produced by the "Short View" was immense. The nation was on the side of Collier. But it could not be doubted that, in the great host which he had defied, some champion would be found to lift the gauntlet. The general belief was, that Dryden would take the field; and all the wits anticipated a sharp contest between two well-paired combatants. The great poet had been singled out in the most marked manner. It was well known that he was deeply hurt, that much smaller provocations had formerly roused him to violent resentment, and that there was no literary weapon, offensive or defensive, of which he was not master. But his conscience smote him; he stood abashed, like the fallen archangel at the rebuke of Zephon,

> And felt how awful goodness is, and saw
> Virtue in her shape how lovely; saw and pined
> His loss.

At a later period he mentioned the "Short View" in the preface to his "Fables." He complained, with some asperity, of the harshness with which he had been treated, and urged some matters in mitigation. But, on the whole, he frankly acknowledged that he had been justly reproved. "If," said he, "Mr. Collier be my enemy, let him triumph. If he be my friend, as I have given him no personal occasion to be otherwise, he will be glad of my repentance."

It would have been wise in Congreve to follow his master's example. He was precisely in that situation in which it is madness to attempt a vindication; for his guilt was so clear, that no address or eloquence could obtain an acquittal. On the other hand, there were, in his case, many extenuating circumstances, which, if he had acknowledged his error, and promised amendment, would have procured his pardon. The most rigid censor could not but make great allowances for the faults into which so young a man had been seduced by evil example, by the luxuriance of a vigorous fancy, and by the inebriating effect of popular applause. The esteem, as well as the admiration, of the public was still within his reach. He might easily have effaced all memory of his transgressions, and have shared with Addison the glory of showing that the most brilliant wit may be the ally of virtue. But in any case, prudence should have restrained him from encountering Collier. The nonjuror was a man thoroughly fitted by nature, education, and habit, for polemical dispute.

Congreve's mind, though one of no common fertility and vigour, was of a different class. No man understood so well the art of polishing epigrams and repartees into the clearest effulgence, and setting them tastefully in easy and familiar dialogue. In this sort of jewellery he attained to a mastery unprecedented and inimitable. But he was altogether rude in the art of controversy, and he had a cause to defend which scarcely any art could have rendered victorious.

The event was such as might have been foreseen. Congreve's answer was a complete failure. He was angry, obscure, and dull. Even the Green Room and Will's Coffee-House were compelled to acknowledge, that in wit the parson had a decided advantage over the poet. Not only was Congreve unable to make any show of a case where he was in the wrong, but he succeeded in putting himself completely in the wrong where he was in the right. Collier had taxed him with profaneness for calling a clergyman Mr. Prig, and for introducing a coachman named Jehu, in allusion to the King of Israel, who was known at a distance by his furious driving. Had there been nothing worse in the "Old Bachelor" and "Double Dealer," Congreve might pass for as pure a writer as Cowper himself; who in poems revised by so austere a censor as John Newton, calls a fox-hunting squire Nimrod, and gives to a chaplain the disrespectful name of Smug. Congreve might with good effect have appealed to the public whether it might not be fairly presumed that, when such frivolous charges were made, there were no very serious charges to make. Instead of doing this, he pretended that he meant no allusion to the Bible by the name of Jehu, and no reflection by the name of Prig. Strange that a man of such parts should, in order to defend himself against imputations which nobody could regard as important, tell untruths which it was certain that nobody would believe.

One of the pleas which Congreve set up for himself and his brethren was, that, though they might be guilty of a little levity here and there, they were careful to inculcate a moral, packed close into two or three lines, at the end of every play. Had the fact been as he stated it, the defence would be worth very little. For no man acquainted with human nature could think that a sententious couplet would undo all the mischief that five profligate acts had done. But it would have been wise in Congreve to have looked again at his own comedies before he used this argument. Collier did so; and found that the moral of the "Old Bachelor"—the grave apophthegm which is to be a set-off against all the libertinism of the piece—is contained in the following triplet:—

> What rugged ways attend the noon of life!
> Our sun declines, and with what anxious strife,
> What pain, we tug that galling load—a wife.

" 'Love for Love,' " says Collier, "may have a somewhat better farewell, but it would do a man little service should he remember it to his dying day:"

> The miracle to-day is, that we find
> A lover true, not that a woman's kind.

Collier's reply was severe and triumphant. One of his repartees we will quote, not as a favourable specimen of his manner, but because it was called forth by Congreve's characteristic affectation. The poet spoke of the "Old Bachelor" as a trifle to which he attached no value, and which had become public by a sort of accident. "I wrote it," he said, "to amuse myself in a slow recovery from a fit of sickness."—"What his disease was," replied Collier, "I am not to enquire: but it must be a very ill one to be worse than the remedy."

All that Congreve gained by coming forward on this occasion was, that he completely deprived himself of the excuse which he might with justice have pleaded for his early offences. "Why," asked Collier, "should the man laugh at the mischief of the boy, and make the disorders of his nonage his own, by an after approbation?"

Congreve was not Collier's only opponent. Vanbrugh, Dennis, and Settle took the field. And, from a passage in a contemporary satire, we are inclined to think that among the answers to the "Short View" was one written, or supposed to be written, by Wycherley. The victory remained with Collier. A great and rapid reform in all the departments of our lighter literature was the effect of his labours. A new race of wits and poets arose, who generally treated with reverence the great ties which bind society together; and whose very indecencies were decent when compared with those of the school which flourished during the last forty years of the seventeenth century.

This controversy probably prevented Congreve from fulfilling the engagements into which he had entered with the actors. It was not till 1700 that he produced the "Way of the World," the most deeply meditated, and the most brilliantly written, of all his works. It wants, perhaps, the constant movement, the effervescence of animal spirits, which we find in "Love for Love." But the hysterical rants of Lady Wishfort, the meeting of Witwould and his brother, the country knight's courtship and his subsequent revel, and above all, the chase and surrender of Milamant, are superior to any thing that is to be found in the whole range of English comedy from the civil war downwards. It is quite inexplicable to us that this play should have failed on the stage. Yet so it was; and the author, already sore with the wounds which Collier had inflicted, was galled past endurance by this new stroke. He resolved never again to expose himself to the rudeness of a tasteless audience, and took leave of the theatre for ever.

He lived twenty-eight years longer, without adding to the high literary reputation which he had attained. He read much while he retained his eyesight, and now and then wrote a short essay, or an idle tale in verse; but appears never to have planned any considerable work. The miscellaneous pieces which he published in 1710, are of little value, and have long been forgotten.

The stock of fame which he had acquired by his comedies was sufficient, assisted by the graces of his manner and conversation, to secure for him a high place in the estimation of the world. During the winter, he lived among the most distinguished and agreeable people in London. His summers were passed at the splendid country-seats of ministers and peers. Literary envy, and political faction, which in that age respected nothing else, respected his repose. He professed to be one of the party of which his patron Montagu, now Lord Halifax, was the head. But he had civil words and small good offices for men of every shade of opinion. And men of every shade of opinion spoke well of him in return.

His means were for a long time scanty. The place which he

had in possession, barely enabled him to live with comfort. And when the Tories came into power, some thought that he would lose even this moderate provision. But Harley, who was by no means disposed to adopt the exterminating policy of the October club, and who, with all his faults of understanding and temper, had a sincere kindness for men of genius, re-assured the anxious poet by quoting very gracefully and happily the lines of Virgil,

Non obtusa adeo gestamus pectora Pœni,
Nec tam aversus equos Tyria sol jungit ab urbe.

The indulgence with which Congreve was treated by the Tories, was not purchased by any concession on his part which could justly offend the Whigs. It was his rare good fortune to share the triumph of his friends without having shared their pro-scription. When the House of Hanover came to the throne, his fortunes began to flourish. The reversion to which he had been nominated twenty years before, fell in. He was made secretary to the Island of Jamaica; and his whole income amounted to £1200 a-year—a fortune which, for a single man, was in that age, not only easy, but splendid. He continued, however, to practise the frugality which he had learned when he could scarcely spare, as Swift tells us, a shilling to pay the chairman who carried him to Lord Halifax's. Though he had nobody to save for, he laid up at least as much as he spent.

The infirmities of age came early upon him. His habits had been intemperate; he suffered much from gout; and when con-fined to his chamber, had no longer the solace of literature. Blindness, the most cruel misfortune that can befall the lonely student, made his books useless to him. He was thrown on society for all his amusement, and, in society, his good breeding and vivacity made him always welcome.

By the rising men of letters he was considered not as a rival, but as a classic. He had left their arena; he never measured his strength with them; and he was always loud in applause of their exertions. They could, therefore, entertain no jealousy of him; and thought no more of detracting from his fame than of carping at the great men who had been lying a hundred years in Poets' Corner. Even the inmates of Grub Street, even the heroes of the Dunciad, were for once just to living merit. There can be no stronger illustration of the estimation in which Congreve was held, than the fact that Pope's "Iliad," a work which appeared with more splendid auspices than any other in our language, was dedicated to him. There was not a Duke in the kingdom who would not have been proud of such a compliment. Dr. Johnson expresses great admiration for the independence of spirit which Pope showed on this occasion, and some surprise at his choice. "He passed over peers and statesmen to inscribe his 'Iliad' to Congreve, with a magnanimity of which the praise had been complete, had his friend's virtue been equal to his wit. Why he was chosen for so great an honour, it is not now possible to know." It is certainly impossible to know; yet we think, it is possible to guess. The translation of the "Iliad" had been zealously befriended by men of all political opinions. The poet who at an early age had been raised to affluence by the emulous liberality of Whigs and Tories, could not with propriety inscribe to a chief of either party, a work which had been munificently patronised by both. It was necessary to find some person who was at once eminent and neutral. It was therefore necessary to pass over peers and statesmen. Congreve had a high name in letters. He had a high name in aristocratic circles. He lived on terms of civility with men of all parties. By a courtesy paid him, neither the ministers nor the leaders of the opposition could be offended.

The singular affectation which had from the first been characteristic of Congreve, grew stronger and stronger as he advanced in life. At last it became disagreeable to him to hear his own comedies praised. Voltaire, whose soul was burned up by the raging desire for literary renown, was half puzzled half disgusted by what he saw, during his visit to England, of this extraordinary whim. Congreve disclaimed the character of a poet —declared that his plays were trifles produced in an idle hour, and begged that Voltaire would consider him merely as a gentleman. "If you had been merely a gentleman," said Voltaire, "I should not have come to see you."

Congreve was not a man of warm affections. Domestic ties he had none; and in the temporary connexions which he formed with a succession of beauties from the green-room, his heart does not appear to have been at all interested. Of all his attachments that to Mrs. Bracegirdle lasted the longest, and was the most celebrated. This charming actress, who was, during many years, the idol of all London; whose face caused the fatal broil in which Mountfort fell, and for which Lord Mohun was tried by the peers; and to whom the Earl of Scarsdale was said to have made honourable addresses, had conducted herself, in very trying circumstances, with extraordinary discretion. Congreve at length became her confidential friend. They constantly rode out together, and dined together. Some people said that she was his mistress, and others that she would soon be his wife. He was at last drawn away from her by the influence of a wealthier and haughtier beauty. Henrietta, daughter of the great Marlborough, and wife of the Earl of Godolphin, had, on her father's death, succeeded to his dukedom, and to the greater part of his immense property. Her husband was an insignificant man, of whom Lord Chesterfield said, that he came to the House of Peers only to sleep, and that he might as well sleep on the right as on the left of the woolsack. Between the Duchess and Congreve sprung up a most eccentric friendship. He had a seat every day at her table, and assisted in the direction of her concerts. That malignant old hag, the Dowager Duchess Sarah, who had quarrelled with her daughter, as she had quarrelled with every body else, affected to suspect that there was something wrong. But the world in general appears to have thought that a great lady might, without any imputation on her character, pay attention to a man of eminent genius, who was nearly sixty years old, who was still older in appearance and in constitution, who was confined to his chair by gout, and was unable to read from blindness.

In the summer of 1728, Congreve was ordered to try the Bath waters. During his excursion he was overturned in his chariot, and received some severe internal injury, from which he never recovered. He came back to London in a dangerous state, complained constantly of a pain in his side, and continued to sink, till in the following January he expired.

He left £10,000, saved out of the emoluments of his lucrative places. Johnson says that this money ought to have gone to the Congreve family, which was then in great distress. Doctor Young and Mr. Leigh Hunt, two gentlemen who seldom agree with each other, but with whom, on this occasion, we are happy to agree, think that it ought to have gone to Mrs. Bracegirdle. Congreve bequeathed £200 to Mrs. Bracegirdle, and an equal sum to a certain Mrs. Jellat; but the bulk of his accumulations went to the Duchess of Marlborough, in whose immense wealth such a legacy was as a drop in the bucket. It might have raised the fallen fortunes of a Staffordshire squire—it might have enabled a retired actress to enjoy every comfort, and, in her sense, every luxury—but it was not sufficient to defray the Duchess's establishment for two months.

The great lady buried her friend with a pomp seldom seen at the funerals of poets. The corpse lay in state under the ancient roof of the Jerusalem Chamber, and was interred in Westminster Abbey. The pall was borne by the Duke of Bridgewater, Lord Cobham, the Earl of Wilmington, who had been Speaker, and who was afterwards First Lord of the Treasury, and other men of high consideration. Her Grace laid out her friend's bequest in a superb diamond necklace, which she wore in honour of him; and, if report is to be believed, showed her regard in ways much more extraordinary. It is said that she had a statue of him in ivory, which moved by clockwork, and was placed daily at her table; that she had a wax doll made in imitation of him, and that the feet of this doll were regularly blistered and anointed by the doctors, as poor Congreve's feet had been when he suffered from the gout. A monument was erected to the poet in Westminster Abbey, with an inscription written by the Duchess; and Lord Cobham honoured him with a cenotaph, which seems to us, though that is a bold word, the ugliest and most absurd of the buildings at Stowe.

We have said that Wycherley was a worse Congreve. There was, indeed, a remarkable analogy between the writings and lives of these two men. Both were gentlemen liberally educated. Both led town lives, and knew human nature only as it appears between Hyde Park and the Tower. Both were men of wit. Neither had much imagination. Both at an early age produced lively and profligate comedies. Both retired from the field while still in early manhood, and owed to their youthful achievements in literature the consideration which they enjoyed in later life. Both, after they had ceased to write for the stage, published volumes of miscellanies, which did little credit either to their talents or to their morals. Both, during their declining years, hung loose upon society; and both, in their last moments, made eccentric and unjustifiable dispositions respecting their estates.

But in every point Congreve maintained his superiority to Wycherley. Wycherley had wit; but the wit of Congreve far outshines that of every comic writer, except Sheridan, who has arisen within the last two centuries. Congreve had not, in a large measure, the poetical faculty; but compared with Wycherley he might be called a great poet. Wycherley had some knowledge of books; but Congreve was a man of real learning. Congreve's offences against decorum, though highly culpable, were not so gross as those of Wycherley; nor did Congreve, like Wycherley, exhibit to the world the deplorable spectacle of a licentious dotage. Congreve died in the enjoyment of high consideration; Wycherley forgotten or despised. Congreve's will was absurd and capricious; but Wycherley's last actions appeared to have been prompted by obdurate malignity.

Here, at least for the present, we must stop. Vanbrugh and Farquhar are not men to be hastily dismissed, and we have not left ourselves space to do them justice.

Samuel Johnson

The Johnson of Boswell's Life had been a lifelong favorite of Macaulay, who thought that he knew the subject as minutely and intimately as any man of his own time. He had written a famous —or notorious—review of an edition of Boswell by his political enemy John Wilson Croker in 1831 which was distorted by his hostility to Croker and his uncurbed tendency to paradox. This second essay on Johnson, twenty-five years after the first, was written for love, as an unpaid contribution to the eighth edition of the Encyclopaedia Britannica, published by his friend Adam Black. Matthew Arnold, who reprinted the article in 1878 as the introduction to his selection from Johnson's Lives of the Poets, called it the most admirable example of literary biography in English; he also appealed to it as evidence for his interesting remark that "Macaulay himself belonged, in many respects, to the eighteenth century." Although it is still printed, in slightly modified form, in current editions of the Encyclopaedia Britannica, it would not now be regarded as a model of an encyclopaedia article; it assumes rather too much information about Johnson and his times, the sort of information that Macaulay was prone to regard as what "every schoolboy knows"; and it is indistinct about names and dates. But it cannot be bettered as an instance of what Macaulay could do when writing out of the full resources of his own mind and animated simply by his affection

Originally published in December 1856.

*for the subject. The essay was written from April to June 1856,
during an interval of rest from the writing of the* History of
England *enforced on Macaulay by his move from his old chambers in the Albany, Piccadilly, to his last home, Holly Lodge,
Kensington, when his books were packed up and unavailable to
him. The volume of the* Encyclopaedia Britannica *containing the
article was published at the end of 1856.*

Samuel Johnson, one of the most eminent English writers of the
eighteenth century, was the son of Michael Johnson, who was,
at the beginning of that century, a magistrate of Lichfield, and a
bookseller of great note in the midland counties. Michael's abilities and attainments seem to have been considerable. He was so
well acquainted with the contents of the volumes which he exposed to sale, that the country rectors of Staffordshire and
Worcestershire thought him an oracle on points of learning.
Between him and the clergy, indeed, there was a strong religious
and political sympathy. He was a zealous churchman, and, though
he had qualified himself for municipal office by taking the oaths
to the sovereigns in possession, was to the last a Jacobite in
heart. At his house, a house which is still pointed out to every
traveller who visits Lichfield, Samuel was born on the 18th of
September 1709. In the child, the physical, intellectual, and
moral peculiarities which afterwards distinguished the man were
plainly discernible; great muscular strength accompanied by
much awkwardness and many infirmities; great quickness of
parts, with a morbid propensity to sloth and procrastination; a
kind and generous heart, with a gloomy and irritable temper.
He had inherited from his ancestors a scrofulous taint, which it
was beyond the power of medicine to remove. His parents were
weak enough to believe that the royal touch was a specific for
this malady. In his third year he was taken up to London, in-
spected by the court surgeon, prayed over by the court chaplains,
and stroked and presented with a piece of gold by Queen Anne.
One of his earliest recollections was that of a stately lady in a
diamond stomacher and a long black hood. Her hand was applied
in vain. The boy's features, which were originally noble and
not irregular, were distorted by his malady. His cheeks were
deeply scarred. He lost for a time the sight of one eye; and he

saw but very imperfectly with the other. But the force of his mind overcame every impediment. Indolent as he was, he acquired knowledge with such ease and rapidity that at every school to which he was sent he was soon the best scholar. From sixteen to eighteen he resided at home, and was left to his own devices. He learned much at this time, though his studies were without guidance and without plan. He ransacked his father's shelves, dipped into a multitude of books, read what was interesting, and passed over what was dull. An ordinary lad would have acquired little or no useful knowledge in such a way: but much that was dull to ordinary lads was interesting to Samuel. He read little Greek; for his proficiency in that language was not such that he could take much pleasure in the masters of Attic poetry and eloquence. But he had left school a good Latinist; and he soon acquired, in the large and miscellaneous library of which he now had the command, an extensive knowledge of Latin literature. That Augustan delicacy of taste which is the boast of the great public schools of England he never possessed. But he was early familiar with some classical writers who were quite unknown to the best scholars in the sixth form at Eton. He was peculiarly attracted by the works of the great restorers of learning. Once, while searching for some apples, he found a huge folio volume of Petrarch's works. The name excited his curiosity; and he eagerly devoured hundreds of pages. Indeed, the diction and versification of his own Latin compositions show that he had paid at least as much attention to modern copies from the antique as to the original models.

While he was thus irregularly educating himself, his family was sinking into hopeless poverty. Old Michael Johnson was much better qualified to pore upon books, and to talk about them, than to trade in them. His business declined; his debts increased; it was with difficulty that the daily expenses of his household were defrayed. It was out of his power to support his son at either university: but a wealthy neighbour offered assistance; and, in reliance on promises which proved to be of very little value, Samuel was entered at Pembroke College, Oxford. When the young scholar presented himself to the rulers of that society, they were amazed not more by his ungainly figure and eccentric manners than by the quantity of extensive and curious information which he had picked up during many months of desultory but not unprofitable study. On the first day of his residence he surprised his teachers by quoting Macrobius; and one of the most learned among them declared that he had never known a freshman of equal attainments.

At Oxford, Johnson resided during about three years. He was poor, even to raggedness; and his appearance excited a mirth and a pity which were equally intolerable to his haughty spirit. He was driven from the quadrangle of Christ Church by the sneering looks which the members of that aristocratical society cast at the holes in his shoes. Some charitable person placed a new pair at his door; but he spurned them away in a fury. Distress made him, not servile, but reckless and ungovernable. No opulent gentleman commoner, panting for one-and-twenty, could have treated the academical authorities with more gross disrespect. The needy scholar was generally to be seen under the gate of Pembroke, a gate now adorned with his effigy, haranguing a circle of lads, over whom, in spite of his tattered gown and dirty linen, his wit and audacity gave him an undisputed ascendency. In every mutiny against the discipline of the college he was the ringleader. Much was pardoned, however, to a youth so highly distinguished by abilities and acquirements. He had early made himself known by turning Pope's Messiah into Latin verse. The style and rhythm, indeed, were not exactly Virgilian; but the translation found many admirers, and was read with pleasure by Pope himself.

The time drew near at which Johnson would, in the ordinary course of things, have become a Bachelor of Arts: but he was at the end of his resources. Those promises of support on which he had relied had not been kept. His family could do nothing for him. His debts to Oxford tradesmen were small indeed, yet larger than he could pay. In the autumn of 1731, he was under the necessity of quitting the university without a degree. In the following winter his father died. The old man left but a pittance; and of that pittance almost the whole was appropriated to the support of his widow. The property to which Samuel succeeded amounted to no more than twenty pounds.

His life, during the thirty years which followed, was one hard struggle with poverty. The misery of that struggle needed no aggravation, but was aggravated by the sufferings of an unsound body and an unsound mind. Before the young man left the university, his hereditary malady had broken forth in a singularly cruel form. He had become an incurable hypochondriac. He said long after that he had been mad all his life, or at least not perfectly sane; and, in truth, eccentricities less strange than his have often been thought grounds sufficient for absolving felons, and for setting aside wills. His grimaces, his gestures, his mutterings, sometimes diverted and sometimes terrified people who did not know him. At a dinner table he would, in a fit of absence, stoop down and twitch off a lady's shoe. He would amaze a drawing room by suddenly ejaculating a clause of the Lord's Prayer. He would conceive an unintelligible aversion to a particular alley, and perform a great circuit rather than see the hateful place. He would set his heart on touching every post in the streets through which he walked. If by any chance he missed a post, he would go back a hundred yards and repair the omission. Under the influence of his disease, his senses became morbidly torpid, and his imagination morbidly active. At one time he would stand poring on the town clock without being able to tell the hour. At another, he would distinctly hear his mother, who was many miles off, calling him by his name. But this was not the worst. A deep melancholy took possession of him, and gave a dark tinge to all his views of human nature and of human destiny. Such wretchedness as he endured has driven many men to shoot themselves or drown themselves. But he was under no temptation to commit suicide. He was sick of life; but he was afraid of death; and he shuddered at every sight or sound which reminded him of the inevitable hour. In religion he found but little comfort during his long and frequent fits of dejection; for his religion partook of his own character. The light from heaven shone on him indeed, but not in a direct line, or with its own pure splendour. The rays had to struggle through a disturbing medium; they reached him refracted, dulled and discoloured by the thick gloom which had settled on his soul; and, though they might be sufficiently clear to guide him, were too dim to cheer him.

With such infirmities of body and of mind, this celebrated man was left, at two-and-twenty, to fight his way through the world. He remained during about five years in the midland counties. At Lichfield, his birth-place and his early home, he had inherited some friends and acquired others. He was kindly noticed by Henry Hervey, a gay officer of noble family, who happened to be quartered there. Gilbert Walmesley, registrar of the ecclesiastical court of the diocese, a man of distinguished parts, learning, and knowledge of the world, did himself honour by patronising the young adventurer, whose repulsive person, unpolished manners and squalid garb moved many of the petty aristocracy of the neighbourhood to laughter or to disgust. At Lichfield, however, Johnson could find no way of earning a livelihood. He became usher of a grammar school in Leicestershire; he resided as a humble companion in the house of a country gentleman; but a life of dependence was insupportable to his haughty spirit. He repaired to Birmingham, and there earned a few guineas by literary drudgery. In that town he printed a translation, little noticed at the time, and long forgotten, of a Latin book about Abyssinia. He then put forth proposals for publishing by subscription the poems of Politian, with notes containing a history of modern Latin verse: but subscriptions did not come in; and the volume never appeared.

While leading this vagrant and miserable life, Johnson fell in love. The object of his passion was Mrs. Elizabeth Porter, a widow who had children as old as himself. To ordinary spectators, the lady appeared to be a short, fat, coarse woman, painted half an inch thick, dressed in gaudy colours, and fond of exhibiting provincial airs and graces which were not exactly those of the Queensberrys and Lepels. To Johnson, however, whose passions were strong, whose eyesight was too weak to distinguish ceruse from natural bloom, and who had seldom or never been in the same room with a woman of real fashion, his Titty, as he called her, was the most beautiful, graceful and accomplished of her sex. That his admiration was unfeigned cannot be doubted; for she was as poor as himself. She accepted, with a readiness which did her little honour, the addresses of a suitor who might have been her son. The marriage, however, in spite of occasional wranglings, proved happier than might have been expected. The lover continued to be under the illusions of the wedding-day till the lady died in her sixty-fourth year. On her monument he placed an inscription extolling the charms of her person and of her manners; and, when, long after her decease, he had occasion to mention her, he exclaimed, with a tenderness half ludicrous, half pathetic, "Pretty creature!"

His marriage made it necessary for him to exert himself more strenuously than he had hitherto done. He took a house in the neighbourhood of his native town, and advertised for pupils. But eighteen months passed away; and only three pupils came to his academy. Indeed, his appearance was so strange, and his temper so violent, that his schoolroom must have resembled an ogre's den. Nor was the tawdry painted grandmother whom he called his Titty well qualified to make provision for the comfort of young gentlemen. David Garrick, who was one of the pupils, used, many years later, to throw the best company of London into convulsions of laughter by mimicking the endearments of this extraordinary pair.

At length Johnson, in the twenty-eighth year of his age, determined to seek his fortune in the capital as a literary adventurer. He set out with a few guineas, three acts of the tragedy of Irene in manuscript, and two or three letters of introduction from his friend Walmesley.

Never, since literature became a calling in England, had it been a less gainful calling than at the time when Johnson took up his residence in London. In the preceding generation a writer of eminent merit was sure to be munificently rewarded by the government. The least that he could expect was a pension or a sinecure place; and, if he showed any aptitude for politics, he might hope to be a member of Parliament, a lord of the treasury, an ambassador, a secretary of state. It would be easy, on the other hand, to name several writers of the nineteenth century of whom the least successful has received forty thousand pounds from the booksellers. But Johnson entered on his vocation in the most dreary part of the dreary interval which separated two ages of prosperity. Literature had ceased to flourish under the patronage of the great, and had not begun to flourish under the patronage of the public. One man of letters, indeed, Pope, had acquired by his pen what was then considered as a handsome fortune, and lived on a footing of equality with nobles and ministers of state. But this was a solitary exception. Even an author whose reputation was established, and whose works were popular, such an author as Thomson, whose Seasons were in every library, such an author as Fielding, whose Pasquin had had a greater run than any drama since The Beggar's Opera, was sometimes glad to obtain, by pawning his best coat, the means of dining on tripe at a cookshop underground, where he could wipe his hands, after his greasy meal, on the back of a Newfoundland dog. It is easy, therefore, to imagine what humiliations and privations must have awaited the novice who had still to earn a name. One of the publishers to whom Johnson applied for employment measured with a scornful eye that athletic though uncouth frame, and exclaimed, "You had better get a porter's knot, and carry trunks." Nor was the advice bad; for a porter was likely to be as plentifully fed, and as comfortably lodged, as a poet.

Some time appears to have elapsed before Johnson was able to form any literary connection from which he could expect more than bread for the day which was passing over him. He never forgot the generosity with which Hervey, who was now residing in London, relieved his wants during this time of trial. "Harry Hervey," said the old philosopher many years later, "was a vicious man; but he was very kind to me. If you call a dog Hervey I shall love him." At Hervey's table Johnson sometimes enjoyed feasts which were made more agreeable by contrast. But in general he dined, and thought that he dined well, on sixpenny worth of meat, and a pennyworth of bread, at an alehouse near Drury Lane.

The effect of the privations and sufferings which he endured at this time was discernible to the last in his temper and his deportment. His manners had never been courtly. They now became almost savage. Being frequently under the necessity of wearing shabby coats and dirty shirts, he became a confirmed sloven. Being often very hungry when he sat down to his meals, he contracted a habit of eating with ravenous greediness. Even to the end of his life, and even at the tables of the great, the sight of food affected him as it affects wild beasts and birds of prey. His taste in cookery, formed in subterranean ordinaries and alamode beefshops, was far from delicate. Whenever he was so fortunate as to have near him a hare that had been kept too long, or a meat pie made with rancid butter, he gorged himself with such violence that his veins swelled, and the moisture broke out on his forehead. The affronts which his poverty emboldened stupid and low-minded men to offer to him would have broken a mean spirit into sycophancy, but made him rude even to ferocity. Unhappily the insolence which, while it was defensive, was pardonable, and in some sense respectable, accompanied him into societies where he was treated with courtesy and kindness. He was repeatedly provoked into striking those who had taken liberties with him. All the sufferers, however, were wise enough to abstain from talking about their beatings, except Osborne, the most rapacious and brutal of booksellers, who proclaimed everywhere that he had been knocked down by the huge fellow whom he had hired to puff the Harleian Library.

About a year after Johnson had begun to reside in London, he was fortunate enough to obtain regular employment from Cave, an enterprising and intelligent bookseller, who was proprietor and editor of the "Gentleman's Magazine." That journal, just entering on the ninth year of its long existence, was the only periodical work in the kingdom which then had what would now be called a large circulation. It was, indeed, the chief source of parliamentary intelligence. It was not then safe, even during a recess, to publish an account of the proceedings of either House without some disguise. Cave, however, ventured to entertain his readers with what he called "Reports of the Debates of the Senate of Lilliput." France was Blefuscu; London was Mildendo; pounds were sprugs; the Duke of Newcastle was the Nardac secretary of State; Lord Hardwicke was the Hurgo Hickrad; and William Pulteney was Wingul Pulnub. To write the speeches was, during several years, the business of Johnson. He was generally furnished with notes, meagre indeed, and inaccurate, of what had been said; but sometimes he had to find arguments and eloquence both for the ministry and for the opposition. He was himself a Tory, not from rational conviction—for his serious opinion was that one form of government was just as good or as bad as another—but from mere passion, such as inflamed the Capulets against the Montagues, or the Blues of the Roman circus against the Greens. In his infancy he had heard so much talk about the villainies of the Whigs, and the dangers of the Church, that he had become a furious partisan when he could scarcely speak. Before he was three he had insisted on being taken to hear Sacheverell preach at Lichfield Cathedral, and had listened to the sermon with as much respect, and probably with as much intelligence, as any Staffordshire squire in the congregation. The work which had been begun in the nursery had been completed by the university. Oxford, when Johnson resided there, was the most Jacobitical place in England; and Pembroke was one of the most Jacobitical colleges in Oxford. The prejudices which he brought up to London were scarcely less absurd than those of his own Tom Tempest. Charles II and James II were two of the best kings that ever reigned. Laud, a poor creature who never did, said, or wrote anything indicating more than the ordinary capacity of an old woman, was a prodigy of parts and learning over whose tomb Art and Genius still continued to weep. Hampden deserved no more honourable name than that of "the zealot of rebellion." Even the ship money, condemned not less decidedly by Falkland and Clarendon than by the bitterest Roundheads, Johnson would not pronounce to have been an unconstitutional impost. Under a government, the mildest that had ever been known in the world—under a government which allowed to the people an unprecedented liberty of speech and action—he fancied that he was a slave; he assailed the ministry with obloquy which refuted itself, and regretted the lost freedom and happiness of those golden days in which a writer who had taken but one-tenth part of the license allowed to him would have been pilloried, mangled with the shears, whipped at the cart's tail, and flung into a noisome dungeon to die. He hated dissenters and stock-jobbers, the excise and the army, septennial parliaments, and continental connections. He long had an aversion to the Scotch, an aversion of which he could not remember the commencement, but which, he owned, had probably originated in his abhorrence of the conduct of the nation during the Great Rebellion. It is easy to guess in what manner debates on great party questions were likely to be reported by a man whose judgment was so much disordered by party spirit. A show of fairness was indeed necessary to the prosperity of the Magazine. But Johnson long afterwards owned that, though he had saved appearances, he had taken care that the Whig dogs should not have the best of it; and, in fact, every passage which has lived, every passage which bears the marks of his higher faculties, is put into the mouth of some member of the opposition.

A few weeks after Johnson had entered on these obscure labours, he published a work which at once placed him high among the writers of his age. It is probable that what he had suffered during his first year in London had often reminded him of some parts of that noble poem in which Juvenal had described the misery and degradation of a needy man of letters, lodged among the pigeons' nests in the tottering garrets which overhung the streets of Rome. Pope's admirable imitations of Horace's Satires and Epistles had recently appeared, were in every hand, and were by many readers thought superior to the originals. What Pope had done for Horace, Johnson aspired to do for Juvenal. The enterprise was bold, and yet judicious. For between Johnson and Juvenal there was much in common, much more certainly than between Pope and Horace.

Johnson's London appeared without his name in May 1738. He received only ten guineas for this stately and vigorous poem: but the sale was rapid, and the success complete. A second edition was required within a week. Those small critics who are always desirous to lower established reputations ran about proclaiming that the anonymous satirist was superior to Pope in Pope's own peculiar department of literature. It ought to be remembered, to the honour of Pope, that he joined heartily in the applause with which the appearance of a rival genius was welcomed. He made inquiries about the author of London. Such a man, he said, could not long be concealed. The name was soon discovered; and Pope, with great kindness, exerted himself to obtain an academical degree and the mastership of a grammar school for the poor young poet. The attempt failed; and Johnson remained a bookseller's hack.

It does not appear that these two men, the most eminent writer of the generation which was going out, and the most eminent writer of the generation which was coming in, ever saw each other. They lived in very different circles, one surrounded by dukes and earls, the other by starving pamphleteers and indexmakers. Among Johnson's associates at this time may be mentioned Boyse, who, when his shirts were pledged, scrawled Latin verses sitting up in bed with his arms through two holes in his blanket, who composed very respectable sacred poetry when he was sober, and who was at last run over by a hackney coach when he was drunk; Hoole, surnamed the metaphysical tailor, who, instead of attending to his measures, used to trace geometrical diagrams on the board where he sate cross-legged; and the penitent impostor, George Psalmanazar, who, after poring all day, in a humble lodging, on the folios of Jewish rabbis and Christian fathers, indulged himself at night with literary and theological conversation at an alehouse in the city. But the most remarkable of the persons with whom at this time Johnson consorted was Richard Savage, an earl's son, a shoemaker's apprentice, who had seen life in all its forms, who had feasted among blue ribands in Saint James's Square, and had lain with fifty pounds' weight of irons on his legs in the condemned ward of Newgate. This man had, after many vicissitudes of fortune, sunk at last into abject and hopeless poverty. His pen had failed him. His patrons had been taken away by death, or estranged by the riotous profusion with which he squandered their bounty, and the ungrateful insolence with which he rejected their advice. He now lived by begging. He dined on venison and champagne whenever he had been so fortunate as to borrow a guinea. If his questing had been unsuccessful, he appeased the rage of hunger with some scraps of broken meat, and lay down to rest under the Piazza of Covent Garden in warm weather, and, in cold weather, as near as he could get to the furnace of a glass house. Yet, in his misery, he was still an agreeable companion. He had an inexhaustible store of anecdotes about that gay and brilliant world from which he was now an outcast. He had observed the great men of both parties in hours of careless relaxation, had seen the leaders of opposition without the mask of patriotism, and had heard the prime minister roar with laughter and tell stories not over decent. During some months Savage lived in the closest familiarity with Johnson; and then the friends parted, not without tears. Johnson remained in London to drudge for Cave. Savage went to the West of England, lived there as he had lived everywhere, and, in 1743 died, penniless and heart-broken, in Bristol gaol.

Soon after his death, while the public curiosity was strongly excited about his extraordinary character, and his not less extraordinary adventures, a life of him appeared widely different from the catchpenny lives of eminent men which were then a staple article of manufacture in Grub Street. The style was indeed deficient in ease and variety; and the writer was evidently too partial to the Latin element of our language. But the little work, with all its faults, was a masterpiece. No finer specimen of literary biography existed in any language, living or dead; and a discerning critic might have confidently predicted that the author was destined to be the founder of a new school of English eloquence.

The Life of Savage was anonymous; but it was well known in literary circles that Johnson was the writer. During the three years which followed, he produced no important work; but he was not, and indeed could not be, idle. The fame of his abilities and learning continued to grow. Warburton pronounced him a man of parts and genius; and the praise of Warburton was then no light thing. Such was Johnson's reputation that, in 1747, several eminent booksellers combined to employ him in the arduous work of preparing a Dictionary of the English Language, in two folio volumes. The sum which they agreed to pay him was only fifteen hundred guineas; and out of this sum he had to pay several poor men of letters who assisted him in the humbler parts of his task.

The prospectus of the Dictionary he addressed to the Earl of Chesterfield. Chesterfield had long been celebrated for the politeness of his manners, the brilliancy of his wit, and the delicacy of his taste. He was acknowledged to be the finest speaker in the House of Lords. He had recently governed Ireland, at a momentous conjuncture, with eminent firmness, wisdom, and humanity; and he had since become Secretary of State. He received Johnson's homage with the most winning affability, and requited it with a few guineas, bestowed doubtless in a very graceful manner, but was by no means desirous to see all his carpets blackened with the London mud, and his soups and wines thrown to right and left over the gowns of fine ladies and the waistcoats of fine gentlemen, by an absent, awkward scholar, who gave strange starts and uttered strange growls, who dressed like a scarecrow, and ate like a cormorant. During some time Johnson continued to call on his patron, but, after being repeatedly told by the porter that his lordship was not at home, took the hint, and ceased to present himself at the inhospitable door.

Johnson had flattered himself that he should have completed his Dictionary by the end of 1750; but it was not till 1755 that he at length gave his huge volumes to the world. During the seven years which he passed in the drudgery of penning definitions and marking quotations for transcription, he sought for relaxation in literary labour of a more agreeable kind. In 1749 he published the Vanity of Human Wishes, an excellent imitation of the Tenth Satire of Juvenal. It is in truth not easy to say whether the palm belongs to the ancient or to the modern poet. The couplets in which the fall of Wolsey is described, though lofty and sonorous, are feeble when compared with the wonderful lines which bring before us all Rome in tumult on the day of the fall of Sejanus, the laurels on the doorposts, the white bull stalking towards the Capitol, the statues rolling down from their pedestals, the flatterers of the disgraced minister running to see him dragged with a hook through the streets, and to have a kick at his carcase before it is hurled into the Tiber. It must be owned too that in the concluding passage the Christian moralist has not made the most of his advantages, and has fallen decidedly short of the sublimity of his Pagan model. On the other hand, Juvenal's Hannibal must yield to Johnson's Charles; and Johnson's vigorous and pathetic enumeration of the miseries of a literary life must be allowed to be superior to Juvenal's lamentation over the fate of Demosthenes and Cicero.

For the copyright of the Vanity of Human Wishes Johnson received only fifteen guineas.

A few days after the publication of this poem, his tragedy, begun many years before, was brought on the stage. His pupil, David Garrick, had, in 1741, made his appearance on a humble stage in Goodman's Fields, had at once risen to the first place among actors, and was now, after several years of almost uninterrupted success, manager of Drury Lane Theatre. The relation between him and his old preceptor was of a very singular kind. They repelled each other strongly, and yet attracted each other strongly. Nature had made them of very different clay; and circumstances had fully brought out the natural peculiarities of both. Sudden prosperity had turned Garrick's head. Continued adversity had soured Johnson's temper. Johnson saw with more envy than became so great a man the villa, the plate, the china, the Brussels carpet, which the little mimic had got by repeating, with grimaces and gesticulations, what wiser men had written; and the exquisitely sensitive vanity of Garrick was galled by the thought that, while all the rest of the world was applauding him, he could obtain from one morose cynic, whose opinion it was impossible to despise, scarcely any compliment not acidulated with scorn. Yet the two Lichfield men had so many early recollections in common, and sympathised with each other on so many points on which they sympathised with nobody else in the vast population of the capital, that, though the master was often provoked by the monkeylike impertinence of the pupil, and the pupil by the bearish rudeness of the master, they remained friends till they were parted by death. Garrick now brought Irene out, with alterations sufficient to displease the author, yet not sufficient to make the piece pleasing to the audience. The public, however, listened with little emotion, but with much civility, to five acts of monotonous declamation. After nine representations the play was withdrawn. It is, indeed, altogether unsuited to the stage, and, even when perused in the closet, will be found hardly worthy of the author. He had not the slightest notion of what blank verse should be. A change in the last syllable of every other line would make the versification of the Vanity of Human Wishes closely resemble the versification of Irene. The poet, however, cleared, by his benefit nights, and by the sale of the copyright of his tragedy, about three hundred pounds, then a great sum in his estimation.

About a year after the representation of Irene, he began to publish a series of short essays on morals, manners, and literature. This species of composition had been brought into fashion by the success of the Tatler, and by the still more brilliant success of the Spectator. A crowd of small writers had vainly attempted to rival Addison. The Lay Monastery, the Censor, the Freethinker, the Plain Dealer, the Champion, and other works of the same kind, had had their short day. None of them had obtained a permanent place in our literature; and they are now to be found only in the libraries of the curious. At length Johnson undertook the adventure in which so many aspirants had failed. In the thirty-sixth year after the appearance of the last number of the Spectator appeared the first number of the Rambler. From March 1750 to March 1752, this paper continued to come out every Tuesday and Saturday.

From the first the Rambler was enthusiastically admired by a few eminent men. Richardson, when only five numbers had appeared, pronounced it equal, if not superior, to the Spectator. Young and Hartley expressed their approbation not less warmly. Bubb Dodington, among whose many faults indifference to the claims of genius and learning cannot be reckoned, solicited the acquaintance of the writer. In consequence probably of the good offices of Dodington, who was then the confidential adviser of Prince Frederic, two of his Royal Highness's gentlemen carried a gracious message to the printing office, and ordered seven copies for Leicester House. But these overtures seem to have been very coldly received. Johnson had had enough of the patronage of the great to last him all his life, and was not disposed to haunt any other door as he had haunted the door of Chesterfield.

By the public the Rambler was at first very coldly received. Though the price of a number was only twopence, the sale did not amount to five hundred. The profits were therefore very small. But as soon as the flying leaves were collected and reprinted they became popular. The author lived to see thirteen thousand copies spread over England alone. Separate editions were published for the Scotch and Irish markets. A large party pronounced the style perfect, so absolutely perfect that in some essays it would be impossible for the writer himself to alter a single word for the better. Another party, not less numerous, vehemently accused him of having corrupted the purity of the English tongue. The best critics admitted that his diction was too monotonous, too obviously artificial, and now and then turgid even to absurdity. But they did justice to the acuteness of his observations on morals and manners, to the constant precision and frequent brilliancy of his language, to the weighty and magnificent eloquence of many serious passages, and to the solemn yet pleasing humour of some of the lighter papers. On the question of precedence between Addison and Johnson, a question which, seventy years ago, was much disputed, posterity has pronounced a decision from which there is no appeal. Sir Roger, his chaplain and his butler, Will Wimble and Will Honeycomb, the Vision of Mirza, the Journal of the Retired Citizen, the Everlasting Club, the Dunmow Flitch, the Loves of Hilpah and Shalum, the Visit to the Exchange, and the Visit to the Abbey, are known to everybody. But many men and women, even of highly cultivated minds, are unacquainted with Squire Bluster and Mrs. Busy, Quisquilius and Venustulus, the Allegory of Wit and Learning, the Chronicle of the Revolutions of a Garret, and the sad fate of Aningait and Ajut.

The last Rambler was written in a sad and gloomy hour. Mrs. Johnson had been given over by the physicians. Three days later she died. She left her husband almost broken-hearted. Many people had been surprised to see a man of his genius and learning stooping to every drudgery, and denying himself almost every comfort, for the purpose of supplying a silly, affected old woman with superfluities, which she accepted with but little gratitude. But all his affection had been concentrated on her. He had neither brother nor sister, neither son nor daughter. To him she was beautiful as the Gunnings, and witty as Lady Mary. Her opinion of his writings was more important to him than the voice of the pit of Drury Lane Theatre or the judgment of the Monthly Review. The chief support which had sustained him through the most arduous labour of his life was the hope that she would enjoy the fame and the profit which he anticipated from his Dictionary. She was gone; and in that vast labyrinth of streets, peopled by eight hundred thousand human beings, he was alone. Yet it was necessary for him to set himself, as he expressed it, doggedly to work. After three more laborious years, the Dictionary was at length complete.

It had been generally supposed that this great work would be dedicated to the eloquent and accomplished nobleman to whom the prospectus had been addressed. He well knew the value of such a compliment; and therefore, when the day of publication drew near, he exerted himself to soothe, by a show of zealous and at the same time of delicate and judicious kindness, the pride which he had so cruelly wounded. Since the Ramblers had ceased to appear, the town had been entertained by a journal called The World, to which many men of high rank

and fashion contributed. In two successive numbers of The
World, the Dictionary was, to use the modern phrase, puffed with
wonderful skill. The writings of Johnson were warmly praised.
It was proposed that he should be invested with the authority
of a Dictator, nay, of a Pope, over our language, and that his
decisions about the meaning and the spelling of words should
be received as final. His two folios, it was said, would of course
be bought by everybody who could afford to buy them. It was
soon known that these papers were written by Chesterfield. But
the just resentment of Johnson was not to be so appeased. In
a letter written with singular energy and dignity of thought and
language, he repelled the tardy advances of his patron. The
Dictionary came forth without a dedication. In the preface the
author truly declared that he owed nothing to the great, and
described the difficulties with which he had been left to struggle
so forcibly and pathetically that the ablest and most malevolent
of all the enemies of his fame, Horne Tooke, never could read
that passage without tears.

The public, on this occasion, did Johnson full justice, and
something more than justice. The best lexicographer may well
be content if his productions are received by the world with
cold esteem. But Johnson's Dictionary was hailed with an enthusiasm such as no similar work has ever excited. It was indeed the
first dictionary which could be read with pleasure. The definitions
show so much acuteness of thought and command of language,
and the passages quoted from poets, divines and philosophers
are so skilfully selected, that a leisure hour may always be very
agreeably spent in turning over the pages. The faults of the book
resolve themselves, for the most part, into one great fault. Johnson was a wretched etymologist. He knew little or nothing of
any Teutonic language except English, which indeed, as he
wrote it, was scarcely a Teutonic language; and thus he was
absolutely at the mercy of Junius and Skinner.

The Dictionary, though it raised Johnson's fame, added nothing to his pecuniary means. The fifteen hundred guineas which
the booksellers had agreed to pay him had been advanced and
spent before the last sheets issued from the press. It is painful
to relate that, twice in the course of the year which followed
the publication of this great work, he was arrested and carried to

spunging-houses, and that he was twice indebted for his liberty to his excellent friend Richardson. It was still necessary for the man who had been formally saluted by the highest authority as Dictator of the English language to supply his wants by constant toil. He abridged his Dictionary. He proposed to bring out an edition of Shakspeare by subscription; and many subscribers sent in their names, and laid down their money; but he soon found the task so little to his taste that he turned to more attractive employments. He contributed many papers to a new monthly journal, which was called the Literary Magazine. Few of these papers have much interest; but among them was the very best thing that he ever wrote, a masterpiece both of reasoning and of satirical pleasantry, the review of Jenyns's Inquiry into the Nature and Origin of Evil.

In the spring of 1758 Johnson put forth the first of a series of essays, entitled The Idler. During two years these essays continued to appear weekly. They were eagerly read, widely circulated, and, indeed, impudently pirated, while they were still in the original form, and had a large sale when collected into volumes. The Idler may be described as a second part of the Rambler, somewhat livelier and somewhat weaker than the first part.

While Johnson was busied with his Idlers, his mother, who had accomplished her ninetieth year, died at Lichfield. It was long since he had seen her; but he had not failed to contribute largely, out of his small means, to her comfort. In order to defray the charges of her funeral, and to pay some debts which she had left, he wrote a little book in a single week, and sent off the sheets to the press without reading them over. A hundred pounds were paid him for the copyright; and the purchasers had great cause to be pleased with their bargain; for the book was Rasselas.

The success of Rasselas was great, though such ladies as Miss Lydia Languish must have been grievously disappointed when they found that the new volume from the circulating library was little more than a dissertation on the author's favourite theme, the Vanity of Human Wishes; that the Prince of Abyssinia was without a mistress, and the Princess without a lover; and that the story set the hero and the heroine down exactly where it had taken them up. The style was the subject of much eager controversy. The Monthly Review and the Critical Review took different sides. Many readers pronounced the writer a pompous pedant, who would never use a word of two syllables where it was possible to use a word of six, and who could not make a waiting woman relate her adventures without balancing every noun with another noun, and every epithet with another epithet. Another party, not less zealous, cited with delight numerous passages in which weighty meaning was expressed with accuracy and illustrated with splendour. And both the censure and the praise were merited.

About the plan of Rasselas little was said by the critics; and yet the faults of the plan might seem to invite severe criticism. Johnson has frequently blamed Shakspeare for neglecting the proprieties of time and place, and for ascribing to one age or nation the manners and opinions of another. Yet Shakspeare has not sinned in this way more grievously than Johnson. Rasselas and Imlac, Nekayah and Pekuah, are evidently meant to be Abyssinians of the eighteenth century: for the Europe which Imlac describes is the Europe of the eighteenth century; and the inmates of the Happy Valley talk familiarly of that law of gravitation which Newton discovered, and which was not fully received even at Cambridge till the eighteenth century. What a real company of Abyssinians would have been may be learned from Bruce's Travels. But Johnson, not content with turning filthy savages, ignorant of their letters, and gorged with raw steaks cut from living cows, into philosophers as eloquent and enlightened as himself or his friend Burke, and into ladies as highly accomplished as Mrs. Lennox or Mrs. Sheridan, transferred the whole domestic system of England to Egypt. Into a land of harems, a land of polygamy, a land where women are married without ever being seen, he introduced the flirtations and jealousies of our ballrooms. In a land where there is boundless liberty of divorce, wedlock is described as the indissoluble compact. "A youth and maiden meeting by chance, or brought together by artifice, exchange glances, reciprocate civilities, go home, and dream of each other. Such," says Rasselas, "is the common process of marriage." Such it may have been, and may still be, in London, but assuredly not at Cairo. A writer who was guilty of such improprieties had little right to blame the poet who made Hector quote Aristotle, and represented Julio Romano as flourishing in the days of the oracle of Delphi.

By such exertions as have been described, Johnson supported himself till the year 1762. In that year a great change in his circumstances took place. He had from a child been an enemy of the reigning dynasty. His Jacobite prejudices had been exhibited with little disguise both in his works and in his conversation. Even in his massy and elaborate Dictionary, he had, with a strange want of taste and judgment, inserted bitter and contumelious reflections on the Whig party. The excise, which was a favourite resource of Whig financiers, he had designated as a hateful tax. He had railed against the commissioners of excise in language so coarse that they had seriously thought of prosecuting him. He had with difficulty been prevented from holding up the Lord Privy Seal by name as an example of the meaning of the word "renegade." A pension he had defined as pay given to a state hireling to betray his country; a pensioner as a slave of state hired by a stipend to obey a master. It seemed unlikely that the author of these definitions would himself be pensioned. But that was a time of wonders. George the Third had ascended the throne; and had, in the course of a few months, disgusted many of the old friends and conciliated many of the old enemies of his house. The city was becoming mutinous. Oxford was becoming loyal. Cavendishes and Bentincks were murmuring. Somersets and Wyndhams were hastening to kiss hands. The head of the treasury was now Lord Bute, who was a Tory, and could have no objection to Johnson's Toryism. Bute wished to be thought a patron of men of letters; and Johnson was one of the most eminent and one of the most needy men of letters in Europe. A pension of three hundred a year was graciously offered, and with very little hesitation accepted.

This event produced a change in Johnson's whole way of life. For the first time since his boyhood he no longer felt the daily goad urging him to the daily toil. He was at liberty, after thirty years of anxiety and drudgery, to indulge his constitutional indolence, to lie in bed till two in the afternoon, and to sit up talking till four in the morning, without fearing either the printer's devil or the sheriff's officer.

One laborious task indeed he had bound himself to perform. He had received large subscriptions for his promised edition of Shakspeare; he had lived on those subscriptions during some years; and he could not without disgrace omit to perform his part of the contract. His friends repeatedly exhorted him to make an effort; and he repeatedly resolved to do so. But, notwithstanding their exhortations and his resolutions, month followed month, year followed year, and nothing was done. He prayed fervently against his idleness; he determined, as often as he received the sacrament, that he would no longer doze away and trifle away his time; but the spell under which he lay resisted prayer and sacrament. His private notes at this time are made up of self-reproaches. "My indolence," he wrote on Easter eve in 1764, "has sunk into grosser sluggishness. A kind of strange oblivion has overspread me, so that I know not what has become of the last year." Easter 1765 came, and found him still in the same state, "My time," he wrote, "has been unprofitably spent, and seems as a dream that has left nothing behind. My memory grows confused, and I know not how the days pass over me." Happily for his honour, the charm which held him captive was at length broken by no gentle or friendly hand. He had been weak enough to pay serious attention to a story about a ghost which haunted a house in Cock Lane, and had actually gone himself, with some of his friends, at one in the morning, to St. John's Church, Clerkenwell, in the hope of receiving a communication from the perturbed spirit. But the spirit, though adjured with all solemnity, remained obstinately silent; and it soon appeared that a naughty girl of eleven had been amusing herself by making fools of so many philosophers. Churchill, who, confident in his powers, drunk with popularity, and burning with party spirit, was looking for some man of established fame and Tory politics to insult, celebrated the Cock Lane Ghost in three cantos, nicknamed Johnson Pomposo, asked where the book was which had been so long promised and so liberally paid for, and directly accused the great moralist of cheating. This terrible word proved effectual; and in October 1765 appeared, after a delay of nine years, the new edition of Shakspeare.

This publication saved Johnson's character for honesty, but added nothing to the fame of his abilities and learning. The preface, though it contains some good passages, is not in his best manner. The most valuable notes are those in which he had an opportunity of showing how attentively he had during many years observed human life and human nature. The best specimen is the note on the character of Polonius. Nothing so good is to be found even in Wilhelm Meister's admirable examination of Hamlet. But here praise must end. It would be difficult to name a more slovenly, a more worthless, edition of any great classic. The reader may turn over play after play without finding one happy conjectural emendation, or one ingenious and satisfactory explanation of a passage which had baffled preceding commentators. Johnson had, in his Prospectus, told the world that he was peculiarly fitted for the task which he had undertaken, because he had, as a lexicographer, been under the necessity of taking a wider view of the English language than any of his predecessors. That his knowledge of our literature was extensive is indisputable. But, unfortunately, he had altogether neglected that very part of our literature with which it is especially desirable that an editor of Shakspeare should be conversant. It is dangerous to assert a negative. Yet little will be risked by the assertion, that in the two folio volumes of the English Dictionary there is not a single passage quoted from any dramatist of the Elizabethan age, except Shakspeare and Ben. Even from Ben the quotations are few. Johnson might easily, in a few months, have made himself well acquainted with every old play that was extant. But it never seems to have occurred to him that this was a necessary preparation for the work which he had undertaken. He would doubtless have admitted that it would be the height of absurdity in a man who was not familiar with the works of Æschylus and Euripides to publish an edition of Sophocles. Yet he ventured to publish an edition of Shakspeare, without having ever in his life, as far as can be discovered, read a single scene of Massinger, Ford, Decker, Webster, Marlow, Beaumont, or Fletcher. His detractors were noisy and scurrilous. Those who most loved and honoured him had little to say in praise of the manner in which he had discharged the duty of a commentator. He had, however, acquitted himself of a debt which had long lain heavy on his conscience; and he sank back into the repose from which the sting of satire had roused him. He long continued to live upon the fame which he had already won. He was honoured by the University of Oxford with a Doctor's degree, by the Royal Academy with a professorship, and by the King with an interview, in which his Majesty most graciously expressed a hope that so excellent a writer would not cease to write. In the interval, however, between 1765 and 1775 Johnson published only two or three political tracts, the longest of which he could have produced in forty-eight hours, if he had worked as he worked on the Life of Savage and on Rasselas.

But, though his pen was now idle, his tongue was active. The influence exercised by his conversation, directly upon those with whom he lived, and indirectly on the whole literary world, was altogether without a parallel. His colloquial talents were indeed of the highest order. He had strong sense, quick discernment, wit, humour, immense knowledge of literature and of life, and an infinite store of curious anecdotes. As respected style, he spoke far better than he wrote. Every sentence which dropped from his lips was as correct in structure as the most nicely balanced period of the Rambler. But in his talk there were no pompous triads, and little more than a fair proportion of words in *osity* and *ation*. All was simplicity, ease, and vigour. He uttered his short, weighty, and pointed sentences with a power of voice, and a justness and energy of emphasis, of which the effect was rather increased than diminished by the rollings of his huge form, and by the asthmatic gaspings and puffings in which the peals of his eloquence generally ended. Nor did the laziness which made him unwilling to sit down to his desk prevent him from giving instruction or entertainment orally. To discuss questions of taste, of learning, of casuistry, in language so exact and so forcible that it might have been printed without the alteration of a word, was to him no exertion but a pleasure. He loved, as he said, to fold his legs and have his talk out. He was ready to bestow the overflowings of his full mind on anybody who would start a subject, on a fellow-passenger in a stage coach, or on the person who sate at the same table with him in an eating house. But his conversation was nowhere so brilliant and striking as when he was surrounded by a few friends, whose abilities and knowledge enabled them, as he once expressed it, to send him back every ball that he threw. Some of these, in 1764, formed themselves into a club, which gradually became a formidable power in the commonwealth of letters. The verdicts pronounced by this conclave on new books were speedily known over all London, and were sufficient to sell off a whole edition in a day, or to condemn the sheets to the service of the trunk-maker and the pastry-cook. Nor shall we think this strange when we consider what great and various talents and acquirements met in the little fraternity. Goldsmith was the representative of poetry and light literature, Reynolds of the arts, Burke of political eloquence and political philosophy. There, too, were Gibbon, the greatest historian, and Jones, the greatest linguist, of the age. Garrick brought to the meetings his inexhaustible pleasantry, his incomparable mimicry, and his consummate knowledge of stage effect. Among the most constant attendants were two high-born and high-bred gentlemen, closely bound together by friendship, but of widely different characters and habits; Bennet Langton, distinguished by his skill in Greek literature, by the orthodoxy of his opinions, and by the sanctity of his life; and Topham Beauclerk, renowned for his amours, his knowledge of the gay world, his fastidious taste, and his sarcastic wit. To predominate over such a society was not easy. Yet even over such a society Johnson predominated. Burke might indeed have disputed the supremacy to which others were under the necessity of submitting. But Burke, though not generally a very patient listener, was content to take the second part when Johnson was present; and the club itself, consisting of so many eminent men, is to this day popularly designated as Johnson's Club.

Among the members of this celebrated body was one to whom it has owed the greater part of its celebrity, yet who was regarded with little respect by his brethren, and had not without difficulty obtained a seat among them. This was James Boswell, a young Scotch lawyer, heir to an honourable name and a fair estate. That he was a coxcomb, and a bore, weak, vain, pushing, curious, garrulous, was obvious to all who were acquainted with him. That he could not reason, that he had no wit, no humour, no eloquence, is apparent from his writings. And yet his writings are read beyond the Mississippi, and under the Southern Cross, and are likely to be read as long as the English exists, either as a living or as a dead language. Nature had made him a slave and an idolater. His mind resembled those creepers which the botanists call parasites, and which can subsist only by clinging round the stems and imbibing the juices of stronger plants. He must have fastened himself on somebody. He might have fastened himself on Wilkes, and have become the fiercest patriot in the Bill of Rights Society. He might have fastened himself on Whitfield, and have become the loudest field preacher among the Calvinistic Methodists. In a happy hour he fastened himself on Johnson. The pair might seem ill matched. For Johnson had early been prejudiced against Boswell's country. To a man of Johnson's strong understanding and irritable temper, the silly egotism and adulation of Boswell must have been as teasing as the constant buzz of a fly. Johnson hated to be questioned; and Boswell was eternally catechising him on all kinds of subjects, and sometimes propounded such questions as "What would you do, sir, if you were locked up in a tower with a baby?" Johnson was a water-drinker; and Boswell was a wine-bibber, and indeed little better than a habitual sot. It was impossible that there should be perfect harmony between two such companions. Indeed, the great man was sometimes provoked into fits of passion in which he said things which the small man, during a few hours, seriously resented. Every quarrel, however, was soon made up. During twenty years the disciple continued to worship the master: the master continued to scold the disciple, to sneer at him, and to love him. The two friends ordinarily resided at a great distance from each other. Boswell practised in the Parliament House of Edinburgh, and could pay only occasional visits to London. During those visits his chief business was to watch Johnson, to discover all Johnson's habits, to turn the conversation to subjects about which Johnson was likely to say something remarkable, and to fill quarto note books with minutes of what Johnson had said. In this way were gathered the materials out of which was afterwards constructed the most interesting biographical work in the world.

Soon after the club began to exist, Johnson formed a connection less important indeed to his fame, but much more important to his happiness, than his connection with Boswell. Henry Thrale, one of the most opulent brewers in the kingdom, a man of sound and cultivated understanding, rigid principles, and liberal spirit, was married to one of those clever, kind-hearted, engaging, vain, pert young women, who are perpetually doing or saying what is not exactly right, but who, do or say what they may, are always agreeable. In 1765 the Thrales became acquainted with Johnson; and the acquaintance ripened fast into friendship. They were astonished and delighted by the brilliancy of his conversation. They were flattered by finding that a man so widely celebrated preferred their house to any other in London. Even the peculiarities which seemed to unfit him for civilised society, his gesticulations, his rollings, his puffings, his mutterings, the strange way in which he put on his clothes, the ravenous eagerness with which he devoured his dinner, his fits of melancholy, his fits of anger, his frequent rudeness, his occasional ferocity, increased the interest which his new associates took in him. For these things were the cruel marks left behind by a life which had been one long conflict with disease and with adversity. In a vulgar hack writer such oddities would have excited only disgust. But in a man of genius, learning, and virtue their effect was to add pity to admiration and esteem. Johnson soon had an apartment at the brewery in Southwark, and a still more pleasant apartment at the villa of his friends on Streatham Common. A large part of every year he passed in those abodes, abodes which must have seemed magnificent and luxurious indeed, when compared with the dens in which he had generally been lodged. But his chief pleasures were derived from what the astronomer of his Abyssinian tale called "the endearing elegance of female friendship." Mrs. Thrale rallied him, soothed him, coaxed him, and, if she sometimes provoked him by her flippancy, made ample amends by listening to his reproofs with angelic sweetness of temper. When he was diseased in body and in mind, she was the most tender of nurses. No comfort that wealth could purchase, no contrivance that womanly ingenuity, set to work by womanly compassion, could devise, was wanting to his sick room. He requited her kindness by an affection pure as the affection of a father, yet delicately tinged with a gallantry, which, though awkward, must have been more flattering than the attentions of a crowd of the fools who gloried in the names, now obsolete, of Buck and Maccaroni. It should seem that a full half of Johnson's life, during about sixteen years, was passed under

the roof of the Thrales. He accompanied the family sometimes
to Bath, and sometimes to Brighton, once to Wales, and once
to Paris. But he had at the same time a house in one of the
narrow and gloomy courts on the north of Fleet Street. In the
garrets was his library, a large and miscellaneous collection of
books, falling to pieces and begrimed with dust. On a lower floor
he sometimes, but very rarely, regaled a friend with a plain
dinner, a veal pie, or a leg of lamb and spinage, and a rice pud-
ding. Nor was the dwelling uninhabited during his long absences.
It was the home of the most extraordinary assemblage of inmates
that ever was brought together. At the head of the establishment
Johnson had placed an old lady named Williams, whose chief
recommendations were her blindness and her poverty. But, in
spite of her murmurs and reproaches, he gave an asylum to another lady who was as poor as herself, Mrs. Desmoulins, whose
family he had known many years before in Staffordshire. Room
was found for the daughter of Mrs. Desmoulins, and for another
destitute damsel, who was generally addressed as Miss Car-
michael, but whom her generous host called Polly. An old quack
doctor named Levett, who bled and dosed coal-heavers and hackney coachmen, and received for fees crusts of bread, bits of
bacon, glasses of gin, and sometimes a little copper, completed
this strange menagerie. All these poor creatures were at constant war with each other, and with Johnson's negro servant
Frank. Sometimes, indeed, they transferred their hostilities
from the servant to the master, complained that a better table
was not kept for them, and railed or maundered till their bene-
factor was glad to make his escape to Streatham, or to the Mitre
Tavern. And yet he, who was generally the haughtiest and most
irritable of mankind, who was but too prompt to resent anything
which looked like a slight on the part of a purse-proud bookseller, or of a noble and powerful patron, bore patiently from
mendicants, who, but for his bounty, must have gone to the
workhouse, insults more provoking than those for which he had
knocked down Osborne and bidden defiance to Chesterfield.
Year after year Mrs. Williams and Mrs. Desmoulins, Polly and
Levett, continued to torment him and to live upon him.

The course of life which has been described was interrupted
in Johnson's sixty-fourth year by an important event. He had

early read an account of the Hebrides, and had been much interested by learning that there was so near him a land peopled
by a race which was still as rude and simple as in the middle ages.
A wish to become intimately acquainted with a state of society so
utterly unlike all that he had ever seen frequently crossed his
mind. But it is not probable that his curiosity would have over-
come his habitual sluggishness, and his love of the smoke, the
mud, and the cries of London, had not Boswell importuned him
to attempt the adventure, and offered to be his squire. At length,
in August 1773, Johnson crossed the Highland line, and plunged
courageously into what was then considered, by most Englishmen, as a dreary and perilous wilderness. After wandering about
two months through the Celtic region, sometimes in rude boats
which did not protect him from the rain, and sometimes on small
shaggy ponies which could hardly bear his weight, he returned
to his old haunts with a mind full of new images and new theories. During the following year he employed himself in record-
ing his adventures. About the beginning of 1775, his Journey
to the Hebrides was published, and was, during some weeks,
the chief subject of conversation in all circles in which any
attention was paid to literature. The book is still read with
pleasure. The narrative is entertaining; the speculations, whether
sound or unsound, are always ingenious; and the style, though too
stiff and pompous, is somewhat easier and more graceful than
that of his early writings. His prejudice against the Scotch had at
length become little more than matter of jest; and whatever
remained of the old feeling had been effectually removed by the
kind and respectful hospitality with which he had been received
in every part of Scotland. It was, of course, not to be expected
that an Oxonian Tory should praise the Presbyterian polity and
ritual, or that an eye accustomed to the hedgerows and parks of
England should not be struck by the bareness of Berwickshire
and East Lothian. But even in censure Johnson's tone is not un-
friendly. The most enlightened Scotchmen, with Lord Mansfield
at their head, were well pleased. But some foolish and ignorant
Scotchmen were moved to anger by a little unpalatable truth
which was mingled with much eulogy, and assailed him whom
they chose to consider as the enemy of their country with libels
much more dishonourable to their country than anything that

he had ever said or written. They published paragraphs in the newpapers, articles in the magazines, sixpenny pamphlets, five shilling books. One scribbler abused Johnson for being bleareyed; another for being a pensioner; a third informed the world that one of the Doctor's uncles had been convicted of felony in Scotland, and had found that there was in that country one tree capable of supporting the weight of an Englishman. Macpherson, whose Fingal had been proved in the Journey to be an impudent forgery, threatened to take vengeance with a cane. The only effect of this threat was that Johnson reiterated the charge of forgery in the most contemptuous terms, and walked about, during some time, with a cudgel, which, if the impostor had not been too wise to encounter it, would assuredly have descended upon him, to borrow the sublime language of his own epic poem, "like a hammer on the red son of the furnace."

Of other assailants Johnson took no notice whatever. He had early resolved never to be drawn into controversy; and he adhered to his resolution with a steadfastness which is the more extraordinary, because he was, both intellectually and morally, of the stuff of which controversialists are made. In conversation, he was a singularly eager, acute, and pertinacious disputant. When at a loss for good reasons, he had recourse to sophistry; and, when heated by altercation, he made unsparing use of sarcasm and invective. But, when he took his pen in his hand, his whole character seemed to be changed. A hundred bad writers misrepresented him and reviled him; but not one of the hundred could boast of having been thought by him worthy of a refutation, or even of a retort. The Kenricks, Campbells, MacNicols, and Hendersons, did their best to annoy him, in the hope that he would give them importance by answering them. But the reader will in vain search his works for any allusion to Kenrick or Campbell, to MacNicol or Henderson. One Scotchman, bent on vindicating the fame of Scotch learning, defied him to the combat in a detestable Latin hexameter.

Maxime, si tu vis, cupio contendere tecum.

But Johnson took no notice of the challenge. He had learned, both from his own observation and from literary history, in which he was deeply read, that the place of books in the public estimation is fixed, not by what is written about them, but by what is written in them; and that an author whose works are likely to live is very unwise if he stoops to wrangle with detractors whose works are certain to die. He always maintained that fame was a shuttlecock which could be kept up only by being beaten back, as well as beaten forward, and which would soon fall if there were only one battledore. No saying was oftener in his mouth than that fine apophthegm of Bentley, that no man was ever written down but by himself.

Unhappily, a few months after the appearance of the Journey to the Hebrides, Johnson did what none of his envious assailants could have done, and to a certain extent succeeded in writing himself down. The disputes between England and her American colonies had reached a point at which no amicable adjustment was possible. Civil war was evidently impending; and the ministers seem to have thought that the eloquence of Johnson might with advantage be employed to inflame the nation against the opposition here, and against the rebels beyond the Atlantic. He had already written two or three tracts in defence of the foreign and domestic policy of the government; and those tracts, though hardly worthy of him, were much superior to the crowd of pamphlets which lay on the counters of Almon and Stockdale. But his Taxation No Tyranny was a pitiable failure. The very title was a silly phrase, which can have been recommended to his choice by nothing but a jingling alliteration which he ought to have despised. The arguments were such as boys use in debating societies. The pleasantry was as awkward as the gambols of a hippopotamus. Even Boswell was forced to own that, in this unfortunate piece, he could detect no trace of his master's powers. The general opinion was that the strong faculties which had produced the Dictionary and the Rambler were beginning to feel the effect of time and of disease, and that the old man would best consult his credit by writing no more.

But this was a great mistake. Johnson had failed, not because his mind was less vigorous than when he wrote Rasselas in the evenings of a week, but because he had foolishly chosen, or suffered others to choose for him, a subject such as he would at no time have been competent to treat. He was in no sense a statesman. He never willingly read or thought or talked about affairs of state. He loved biography, literary history, the history of manners; but political history was positively distasteful to him. The question at issue between the colonies and the mother country was a question about which he had really nothing to say. He failed, therefore, as the greatest men must fail when they attempt to do that for which they are unfit; as Burke would have failed if Burke had tried to write comedies like those of Sheridan; as Reynolds would have failed if Reynolds had tried to paint landscapes like those of Wilson. Happily, Johnson soon had an opportunity of proving most signally that his failure was not to be ascribed to intellectual decay.

On Easter Eve 1777, some persons, deputed by a meeting which consisted of forty of the first booksellers in London, called upon him. Though he had some scruples about doing business at that season, he received his visitors with much civility. They came to inform him that a new edition of the English poets, from Cowley downwards, was in contemplation, and to ask him to furnish short biographical prefaces. He readily undertook the task, a task for which he was pre-eminently qualified. His knowledge of the literary history of England since the Restoration was unrivalled. That knowledge he had derived partly from books, and partly from sources which had long been closed; from old Grub Street traditions; from the talk of forgotten poetasters and pamphleteers who had long been lying in parish vaults; from the recollections of such men as Gilbert Walmesley, who had conversed with the wits of Button; Cibber, who had multilated the plays of two generations of dramatists; Orrery, who had been admitted to the society of Swift; and Savage, who had rendered services of no very honourable kind to Pope. The biographer therefore sate down to his task with a mind full of matter. He had at first intended to give only a paragraph to every minor poet, and only four or five pages to the greatest name. But the flood of anecdote and criticism overflowed the narrow channel. The work, which was originally meant to consist only of a few sheets, swelled into ten volumes, small volumes, it is true, and not closely printed. The first four appeared in 1779, the remaining six in 1781.

The Lives of the Poets are, on the whole, the best of Johnson's works. The narratives are as entertaining as any novel. The remarks on life and on human nature are eminently shrewd and profound. The criticisms are often excellent, and, even when grossly and provokingly unjust, well deserve to be studied. For, however erroneous they may be, they are never silly. They are the judgments of a mind trammelled by prejudice and deficient in sensibility, but vigorous and acute. They therefore generally contain a portion of valuable truth which deserves to be separated from the alloy; and, at the very worst, they mean something, a praise to which much of what is called criticism in our time has no pretensions.

Savage's Life Johnson reprinted nearly as it had appeared in 1744. Whoever, after reading that life, will turn to the other lives will be struck by the difference of style. Since Johnson had been at ease in his circumstances he had written little and had talked much. When, therefore, he, after the lapse of years, resumed his pen, the mannerism which he had contracted while he was in the constant habit of elaborate composition was less perceptible than formerly; and his diction frequently had a colloquial ease which it had formerly wanted. The improvement may be discerned by a skilful critic in the Journey to the Hebrides, and in the Lives of the Poets is so obvious that it cannot escape the notice of the most careless reader.

Among the lives the best are perhaps those of Cowley, Dryden, and Pope. The very worst is, beyond all doubt, that of Gray.

This great work at once became popular. There was, indeed, much just and much unjust censure: but even those who were loudest in blame were attracted by the book in spite of themselves. Malone computed the gains of the publishers at five or six thousand pounds. But the writer was very poorly remunerated. Intending at first to write very short prefaces, he had stipulated for only two hundred guineas. The booksellers, when they saw how far his performance had surpassed his promise, added only another hundred. Indeed, Johnson, though he did not despise, or affect to despise, money, and though his strong sense and long experience ought to have qualified him to protect his own interests, seems to have been singularly unskillful and unlucky in his literary bargains. He was generally reputed the first English writer of his time. Yet several writers of his time sold their copyrights for sums such as he never ventured to ask. To give a single instance, Robertson received four thousand five hundred pounds for the History of Charles V; and it is no disrespect to the memory of Robertson to say that the History of Charles V is both a less valuable and a less amusing book than the Lives of the Poets.

Johnson was now in his seventy-second year. The infirmities of age were coming fast upon him. That inevitable event of which he never thought without horror was brought near to him; and his whole life was darkened by the shadow of death. He had often to pay the cruel price of longevity. Every year he lost what could never be replaced. The strange dependents to whom he had given shelter, and to whom, in spite of their faults, he was strongly attached by habit, dropped off one by one; and, in the silence of his home, he regretted even the noise of their scolding matches. The kind and generous Thrale was no more; and it would have been well if his wife had been laid beside him. But she survived to be the laughing-stock of those who had envied her, and to draw from the eyes of the old man who had loved her beyond anything in the world tears far more bitter than he would have shed over her grave. With some estimable and many agreeable qualities, she was not made to be independent. The control of a mind more steadfast than her own was necessary to her respectability. While she was restrained by her husband, a man of sense and firmness, indulgent to her taste in trifles, but always the undisputed master of his house, her worst offences had been impertinent jokes, white lies, and short fits of pettishness ending in sunny good humour. But he was gone; and she was left an opulent widow of forty, with strong sensibility, volatile fancy, and slender judgment. She soon fell in love with a music-master from Brescia, in whom nobody but herself could discover anything to admire. Her pride, and perhaps some better feelings, struggled hard against this degrading passion. But the struggle irritated her nerves, soured her temper, and at length endangered her health. Conscious that her choice was one which Johnson could not approve, she became desirous to escape from his inspection. Her manner towards him changed. She was sometimes cold and sometimes petulant. She did not conceal her joy when he left Streatham; she never pressed him to return; and, if he came unbidden, she received him in a manner which convinced him that he was no longer a welcome guest. He took the very intelligible hints which she gave. He read, for the last time, a chapter of the Greek Testament in the library which had been formed by himself. In a solemn and tender prayer he commended the house and its inmates to the Divine protection, and, with emotions which choked his voice and convulsed his powerful frame, left for ever that beloved home for the gloomy and desolate house behind Fleet Street, where the few and evil days which still remained to him were to run out. Here, in June 1783, he had a paralytic stroke, from which, however, he recovered, and which does not appear to have at all impaired his intellectual faculties. But other maladies came thick upon him. His asthma tormented him day and night. Dropsical symptoms made their appearance. While sinking under a complication of diseases, he heard that the woman whose friendship had been the chief happiness of sixteen years of his life had married an Italian fiddler; that all London was crying shame upon her; and that the newspapers and magazines were filled with allusions to the Ephesian matron, and the two pictures in Hamlet. He vehemently said that he would try to forget her existence. He never uttered her name. Every memorial of her which met his eye he flung into the fire. She meanwhile fled from the laughter and hisses of her countrymen and countrywomen to a land where she was unknown, hastened across Mount Cenis, and learned, while passing a merry Christmas of concerts and lemonade parties at Milan, that the great man with whose name hers is inseparably associated had ceased to exist.

He had, in spite of much mental and much bodily affliction, clung vehemently to life. The feeling described in that fine but gloomy paper which closes the series of his Idlers seemed to grow stronger in him as his last hour drew near. He fancied that he should be able to draw his breath more easily in a southern climate, and would probably have set out for Rome and Naples, but for his fear of the expense of the journey. That expense, indeed, he had the means of defraying; for he had laid up about two thousand pounds, the fruit of labours which had made the fortune of several publishers. But he was unwilling to break in upon this hoard; and he seems to have wished even to keep its existence a secret. Some of his friends hoped that the government might be induced to increase his pension to six hundred pounds a year: but this hope was disappointed; and he resolved to stand one English winter more. That winter was his last. His legs grew weaker; his breath grew shorter; the fatal water gathered fast, in spite of incisions which he, courageous against pain, but timid against death, urged his surgeons to make deeper and deeper. Though the tender care which had mitigated his sufferings during months of sickness at Streatham was withdrawn, he was not left desolate. The ablest physicians and surgeons attended him, and refused to accept fees from him. Burke parted from him with deep emotion. Windham sate much in the sick-room, arranged the pillows, and sent his own servant to watch a night by the bed. Frances Burney, whom the old man had cherished with fatherly kindness, stood weeping at the door; while Langton, whose piety eminently qualified him to be an adviser and comforter at such a time, received the last pressure of his friend's hand within. When at length the moment, dreaded through so many years, came close, the dark cloud passed away from Johnson's mind. His temper became unusually patient and gentle; he ceased to think with terror of death, and of that which lies beyond death; and he spoke much of the mercy of God, and of the propitiation of Christ. In this serene frame of mind he died on the 13th of December, 1784. He was laid, a week later, in Westminster Abbey, among the eminent men of whom he had been the historian,—Cowley and Denham, Dryden and Congreve, Gay, Prior, and Addison.

Since his death the popularity of his works—the Lives of the Poets, and, perhaps, the Vanity of Human Wishes, excepted—has greatly diminished. His Dictionary has been altered by editors till it can scarcely be called his. An allusion to his Rambler or his Idler is not readily apprehended in literary circles. The fame even of Rasselas has grown somewhat dim. But, though the celebrity of the writings may have declined, the celebrity of the writer, strange to say, is as great as ever. Boswell's book has done for him more than the best of his own books could do. The memory of other authors is kept alive by their works. But the memory of Johnson keeps many of his works alive. The old philosopher is still among us in the brown coat with the metal buttons and the shirt which ought to be at wash, blinking, puffing, rolling his head, drumming with his fingers, tearing his meat like a tiger, and swallowing his tea in oceans. No human being who has been more than seventy years in the grave is so well known to us. And it is but just to say that our intimate acquaintance with what he would himself have called the anfractuosities of his intellect and of his temper serves only to strengthen our conviction that he was both a great and a good man.

II. Speeches

Parliamentary Reform

On 1 March 1831 Lord John Russell, on behalf of the Whig government, moved for leave to bring the first Reform Bill in the House of Commons. The bill sought to take both members of Parliament away from sixty boroughs of less than two thousand inhabitants, and one member each from forty-seven boroughs with populations from two thousand to four thousand. The seats thus made available were to be redistributed, with seven large English towns (including Manchester and Birmingham) and four districts in London given two members each for the first time. The borough franchise was henceforth to belong uniformly to all householders rated annually at ten pounds or more.

Recent scholarship has severely questioned the time-honored assumption that this was a measure for the exclusive benefit of the middle class. The aristocracy certainly held its own. But there can be no doubt about the fact that the manufacturing interests and the middle class gained from the Reform Act of 1832. That the governing classes were ultimately prepared to make concessions was certainly due, in part, to their fear of revolution—especially of a revolution carried out, as in 1789 in France, by an alliance between the "middling" and "lower" orders. Macaulay's first speech on the Reform Bill, delivered the day after the bill was introduced, played on such fears. But it did more than that.

Delivered March 2, 1831.

It tried to bring home the Burkean lesson of "Reform, that you may preserve."

Many years later, Macaulay called the day on which he delivered this speech an epoch in his own life as well as in that of the nation. Friend and foe rushed to congratulate him. The Speaker sent for him and told him that in all his long experience he had never seen the House of Commons in a comparable state of excitement. Sir James Mackintosh thought the speech one of the finest ever spoken in Parliament. Sir Robert Peel remarked that parts of it were as beautiful as anything he had ever heard or read. It reminded him, he said, of the old times. Macaulay spoke on several other occasions during the long struggles over the Reform Bill, which finally became law in the summer of 1832.

It is a circumstance, Sir, of happy augury for the motion before the House, that almost all those who have opposed it have declared themselves hostile on principle to Parliamentary Reform. Two Members, I think, have confessed that, though they disapprove of the plan now submitted to us, they are forced to admit the necessity of a change in the Representative system. Yet even those gentlemen have used, as far as I have observed, no arguments which would not apply as strongly to the most moderate change as to that which has been proposed by His Majesty's Government. I say, Sir, that I consider this as a circumstance of happy augury. For what I feared was, not the opposition of those who are averse to all Reform, but the disunion of reformers. I knew that, during three months, every reformer had been employed in conjecturing what the plan of the Government would be. I knew that every reformer had imagined in his own mind a scheme differing doubtless in some points from that which my noble friend, the Paymaster of the Forces, has developed. I felt therefore great apprehension that one person would be dissatisfied with one part of the bill, that another person would be dissatisfied with another part, and that thus our whole strength would be wasted in internal dissensions. That apprehension is now at an end. I have seen with delight the perfect concord which prevails among all who deserve the name of reformers in this House; and I trust that I may consider it as an omen of the concord which will prevail among reformers throughout the country. I will not, Sir, at present express any opinion as to the details of the bill; but, having during the last twenty-four hours given the most diligent consideration to its general principles, I have no hesitation in pronouncing it a wise, noble, and comprehensive measure, skilfully framed for the healing of great distempers, for the securing at once of the public liberties and of the public repose, and for the reconciling and knitting together of all the orders of the State.

The honorable Baronet who has just sate down,[1] has told us, that the Ministers have attempted to unite two inconsistent principles in one abortive measure. Those were his very words. He thinks, if I understand him rightly, that we ought either to leave the representative system such at it is, or to make it perfectly symmetrical. I think, Sir, that the Ministers would have acted unwisely if they had taken either course. Their principle is plain, rational, and consistent. It is this, to admit the middle class to a large and direct share in the representation, without any violent shock to the institutions of our country. I understand those cheers: but surely the gentlemen who utter them will allow that the change which will be made in our institutions by this bill is far less violent than that which, according to the honorable Baronet, ought to be made if we make any Reform at all. I praise the Ministers for not attempting, at the present time, to make the representation uniform. I praise them for not effacing the old distinction between the towns and the counties, and for not assigning Members to districts, according to the American practice, by the Rule of Three. The Government has, in my opinion, done all that was necessary for the removing of a great practical evil, and no more than was necessary.

I consider this, Sir, as a practical question. I rest my opinion on no general theory of government. I distrust all general theories of government. I will not positively say, that there is any form of polity which may not, in some conceivable circumstances, be the best possible. I believe that there are societies in which every man may safely be admitted to vote. Gentlemen may cheer, but such is my opinion. I say, Sir, that there are countries in which the condition of the labouring classes is such that they may safely be

1. Sir John Walsh.

intrusted with the right of electing Members of the Legislature. If the labourers of England were in that state in which I, from my soul, wish to see them, if employment were always plentiful, wages always high, food always cheap, if a large family were considered not as an encumbrance but as a blessing, the principal objections to Universal Suffrage would, I think, be removed. Universal Suffrage exists in the United States without producing any very frightful consequences; and I do not believe, that the people of those States, or of any part of the world, are in any good quality naturally superior to our own countrymen. But, unhappily, the labouring classes in England, and in all old countries, are occasionally in a state of great distress. Some of the causes of this distress are, I fear, beyond the control of the Government. We know what effect distress produces, even on people more intelligent than the great body of the labouring classes can possibly be. We know that it makes even wise men irritable, unreasonable, credulous, eager for immediate relief, heedless of remote consequences. There is no quackery in medicine, religion, or politics, which may not impose even on a powerful mind, when that mind has been disordered by pain or fear. It is therefore no reflection on the poorer class of Englishmen, who are not, and who cannot in the nature of things be, highly educated, to say that distress produces on them its natural effects, those effects which it would produce on the Americans, or on any other people, that it blinds their judgment, that it inflames their passions, that it makes them prone to believe those who flatter them, and to distrust those who would serve them. For the sake, therefore, of the whole society, for the sake of the labouring classes themselves, I hold it to be clearly expedient that, in a country like this, the right of suffrage should depend on a pecuniary qualification.

But, Sir, every argument which would induce me to oppose Universal Suffrage, induces me to support the plan which is now before us. I am opposed to Universal Suffrage, because I think that it would produce a destructive revolution. I support this plan, because I am sure that it is our best security against a revolution. The noble Paymaster of the Forces hinted, delicately indeed and remotely, at this subject. He spoke of the danger of disappointing the expectations of the nation; and for this he was charged with threatening the House. Sir, in the year 1817, the late Lord Londonderry proposed a suspension of the Habeas Corpus Act. On that occasion he told the House that, unless the measures which he recommended were adopted, the public peace could not be preserved. Was he accused of threatening the House? Again, in the year 1819, he proposed the laws known by the name of the Six Acts. He then told the House that, unless the executive power were reinforced, all the institutions of the country would be overturned by popular violence. Was he then accused of threatening the House? Will any gentleman say that it is parliamentary and decorous to urge the danger arising from popular discontent as an argument for severity; but that it is unparliamentary and indecorous to urge that same danger as an argument for conciliation? I, Sir, do entertain great apprehension for the fate of my country. I do in my conscience believe that, unless the plan proposed, or some similar plan, be speedily adopted, great and terrible calamities will befal us. Entertaining this opinion, I think myself bound to state it, not as a threat, but as a reason. I support this bill because it will improve our institutions; but I support it also because it tends to preserve them. That we may exclude those whom it is necessary to exclude, we must admit those whom it may be safe to admit. At present we oppose the schemes of revolutionists with only one half, with only one quarter of our proper force. We say, and we say justly, that it is not by mere numbers, but by property and intelligence, that the nation ought to be governed. Yet, saying this, we exclude from all share in the government great masses of property and intelligence, great numbers of those who are most interested in preserving tranquillity, and who know best how to preserve it. We do more. We drive over to the side of revolution those whom we shut out from power. Is this a time when the cause of law and order can spare one of its natural allies?

My noble friend, the Paymaster of the Forces, happily described the effect which some parts of our representative system would produce on the mind of a foreigner, who had heard much of our freedom and greatness. If, Sir, I wished to make such a foreigner clearly understand what I consider as the great defects of our system, I would conduct him through that immense city which lies to the north of Great Russell Street and Oxford Street, a city superior in size and in population to the capitals of many mighty kingdoms; and probably superior in opulence, intelligence, and general respectability, to any city in the world. I would conduct him through that interminable succession of streets and squares, all consisting of well built and well furnished houses. I would make him observe the brilliancy of the shops, and the crowd of well appointed equipages. I would show him that magnificent circle of palaces which surrounds the Regent's Park. I would tell him, that the rental of this district was far greater than that of the whole kingdom of Scotland, at the time of the Union. And then I would tell him, that this was an unrepresented district. It is needless to give any more instances. It is needless to speak of Manchester, Birmingham, Leeds, Sheffield, with no representation, or of Edinburgh and Glasgow with a mock representation. If a property tax were now imposed on the principle that no person who had less than a hundred and fifty pounds a year should contribute, I should not be surprised to find that one half in number and value of the contributors had no votes at all; and it would, beyond all doubt, be found that one fiftieth part in number and value of the contributors had a larger share of the representation than the other forty-nine fiftieths. This is not government by property. It is government by certain detached portions and fragments of property, selected from the rest, and preferred to the rest, on no rational principle whatever.

To say that such a system is ancient is no defence. My honorable friend, the Member for the University of Oxford[2] challenges us to show, that the Constitution was ever better than it is. Sir, we are legislators, not antiquaries. The question for us is, not whether the Constitution was better formerly, but whether we can make it better now. In fact, however, the system was not in ancient times by any means so absurd as it is in our age. One noble Lord[3] has to-night told us that the town of Aldborough, which he represents, was not larger in the time of Edward the First than it is at present. The line of its walls, he assures us, may still be traced. It is now built up to that line. He argues, therefore, that as the founders of our representative institutions gave Members to Aldborough when it was as small as it now is, those who

2. Sir Robert Harry Inglis.
3. Lord Stormont.

would disfranchise it on account of its smallness have no right to say that they are recurring to the original principle of our representative institutions. But does the noble Lord remember the change which has taken place in the country during the last five centuries? Does he remember how much England has grown in population, while Aldborough has been standing still? Does he consider, that in the time of Edward the First the kingdom did not contain two millions of inhabitants? It now contains nearly fourteen millions. A hamlet of the present day would have been a town of some importance in the time of our early Parliaments. Aldborough may be absolutely as considerable a place as ever. But compared with the kingdom, it is much less considerable, by the noble Lord's own showing, than when it first elected burgesses. My honorable friend, the Member for the University of Oxford, has collected numerous instances of the tyranny which the kings and nobles anciently exercised, both over this House and over the electors. It is not strange that, in times when nothing was held sacred, the rights of the people, and of the representatives of the people, should not have been held sacred. The proceedings which my honorable friend has mentioned, no more prove that, by the ancient constitution of the realm, this House ought to be a tool of the king and of the aristocracy, than the Benevolences and the Shipmoney prove their own legality, or than those unjustifiable arrests, which took place long after the ratification of the great Charter, and even after the Petition of Right, prove that the subject was not anciently entitled to his personal liberty. We talk of the wisdom of our ancestors: and in one respect at least they were wiser than we. They legislated for their own times. They looked at the England which was before them. They did not think it necessary to give twice as many Members to York as they gave to London, because York had been the capital of Britain in the time of Constantius Chlorus; and they would have been amazed indeed if they had foreseen, that a city of more than a hundred thousand inhabitants would be left without Representatives in the nineteenth century, merely because it stood on ground which, in the thirteenth century, had been occupied by a few huts. They framed a representative system, which, though not without defects and irregularities, was well adapted to the state of England in their time. But a great revolution took place. The character of the old corporations changed. New forms of property came into existence. New portions of society rose into importance. There were in our rural districts rich cultivators, who were not freeholders. There were in our capital rich traders, who were not liverymen. Towns shrank into villages. Villages swelled into cities larger than the London of the Plantagenets. Unhappily, while the natural growth of society went on, the artificial polity continued unchanged. The ancient form of the representation remained; and precisely because the form remained, the spirit departed. Then came that pressure almost to bursting, the new wine in the old bottles, the new society under the old institutions. It is now time for us to pay a decent, a rational, a manly reverence to our ancestors, not by superstitiously adhering to what they, in other circumstances, did, but by doing what they, in our circumstances, would have done. All history is full of revolutions, produced by causes similar to those which are now operating in England. A portion of the community which had been of no account expands and becomes strong. It demands a place in the system, suited, not to its former weakness, but to its present power. If this is granted, all is well. If this is refused, then comes the struggle between the young energy of one class and the ancient privileges of another. Such was the struggle between the Plebeians and the Patricians of Rome. Such was the struggle of the Italian allies for admission to the full rights of Roman citizens. Such was the struggle of our North American colonies against the mother country. Such was the struggle which the Third Estate of France maintained against the aristocracy of birth. Such was the struggle which the Roman Catholics of Ireland maintained against the aristocracy of creed. Such is the struggle which the free people of colour in Jamaica are now maintaining against the aristocracy of skin. Such, finally, is the struggle which the middle classes in England are maintaining against an aristocracy of mere locality, against an aristocracy the principle of which is to invest a hundred drunken potwallopers in one place, or the owner of a ruined hovel in another, with powers which are withheld from cities renowned to the furthest ends of the earth, for the marvels of their wealth and of their industry.

But these great cities, says my honorable friend, the Member for the University of Oxford, are virtually, though not directly, represented. Are not the wishes of Manchester, he asks, as much consulted as those of any town which sends Members to Parliament? Now, Sir, I do not understand how a power which is salutary when exercised virtually can be noxious when exercised directly. If the wishes of Manchester have as much weight with us as they would have under a system which should give Representatives to Manchester, how can there be any danger in giving Representatives to Manchester? A virtual Representative is, I presume, a man who acts as a direct Representative would act: for surely it would be absurd to say that a man virtually represents the people of Manchester, who is in the habit of saying No, when a man directly representing the people of Manchester would say Aye. The utmost that can be expected from virtual Representation is that it may be as good as direct Representation. If so, why not grant direct Representation to places which, as every body allows, ought, by some process or other, to be represented?

If it be said that there is an evil in change as change, I answer that there is also an evil in discontent as discontent. This, indeed, is the strongest part of our case. It is said that the system works well. I deny it. I deny that a system works well, which the people regard with aversion. We may say here, that it is a good system and a perfect system. But if any man were to say so to any six hundred and fifty-eight respectable farmers or shopkeepers, chosen by lot in any part of England, he would be hooted down, and laughed to scorn. Are these the feelings with which any part of the government ought to be regarded? Above all, are these the feelings with which the popular branch of the legislature ought to be regarded? It is almost as essential to the utility of a House of Commons, that it should possess the confidence of the people, as that it should deserve that confidence. Unfortunately, that which is in theory the popular part of our government, is in practice the unpopular part. Who wishes to dethrone the King? Who wishes to turn the Lords out of their House? Here and there a crazy radical, whom the boys in the street point at as he walks along. Who wishes to alter the constitution of this House? The whole people. It is natural that it should be so. The House of Commons is, in the language of Mr. Burke, a check, not on the people, but for the people. While that check is efficient, there is no reason to fear that the King or the nobles will oppress the people. But if that check requires checking, how is it to be checked? If the salt shall lose its savour, wherewith shall we season it? The distrust with which the nation regards this House may be unjust. But what then? Can you remove that distrust? That it exists cannot be denied. That it is an evil cannot be denied. That is is an increasing evil cannot be denied. One gentleman tells us that it has been produced by the late events in France and Belgium; another, that it is the effect of seditious works which have lately been published. If this feeling be of origin so recent, I have read history to little purpose. Sir, this alarming discontent is not the growth of a day or of a year. If there be any symptoms by which it is possible to distinguish the chronic diseases of the body politic from its passing inflammations, all those symptoms exist in the present case. The taint has been gradually becoming more extensive and more malignant, through the whole lifetime of two generations. We have tried anodynes. We have tried cruel operations. What are we to try now? Who flatters himself that he can turn this feeling back? Does there remain any argument which escaped the comprehensive intellect of Mr. Burke, or the subtlety of Mr. Windham? Does there remain any species of coercion which was not tried by Mr. Pitt and by Lord Londonderry? We have had laws. We have had blood. New treasons have been created. The Press has been shackled. The Habeas Corpus Act has been suspended. Public meetings have been prohibited. The event has proved that these expedients were mere palliatives. You are at the end of your palliatives. The evil remains. It is more formidable than ever. What is to be done?

Under such circumstances, a great plan of reconciliation, prepared by the Ministers of the Crown, has been brought before us in a manner which gives additional lustre to a noble name, inseparably associated during two centuries with the dearest liberties of the English people. I will not say, that this plan is in all its details precisely such as I might wish it to be; but it is founded on a great and a sound principle. It takes away a vast power from a few. It distributes that power through the great mass of the middle order. Every man, therefore, who thinks as I think is bound to stand firmly by Ministers who are resolved to stand or fall with this measure. Were I one of them, I would sooner, infinitely sooner, fall with such a measure than stand by any other means that ever supported a Cabinet.

My honorable friend, the Member for the University of Oxford, tells us, that if we pass this law, England will soon be a republic. The reformed House of Commons will, according to him, before it has sate ten years, depose the King, and expel the Lords from their House. Sir, if my honorable friend could prove this, he would have succeeded in bringing an argument for democracy, infinitely stronger than any that is to be found in the works of Paine. My honorable friend's proposition is in fact this; that our monarchical and aristocratical institutions have no hold on the public mind of England; that these institutions are regarded with aversion by a decided majority of the middle class. This, Sir, I say, is plainly deducible from his proposition; for he tells us that the Representatives of the middle class will inevitably abolish royalty and nobility within ten years: and there is surely no reason to think that the Representatives of the middle class will be more inclined to a democratic revolution than their constituents. Now, Sir, if I were convinced that the great body of the middle class in England look with aversion on monarchy and aristocracy, I should be forced, much against my will, to come to this conclusion, that monarchical and aristocratical institutions are unsuited to my country. Monarchy and aristocracy, valuable and useful as I think them, are still valuable and useful as means, and not as ends. The end of government is the happiness of the people: and I do not conceive that, in a country like this, the happiness of the people can be promoted by a form of government in which the middle classes place no confidence, and which exists only because the middle classes have no organ by which to make their sentiments known. But, Sir, I am fully convinced that the middle classes sincerely wish to uphold the Royal prerogatives and the constitutional rights of the Peers. What facts does my honorable friend produce in support of his opinion? One fact only; and that a fact which has absolutely nothing to do with the question. The effect of this Reform, he tells us, would be to make the House of Commons allpowerful. It was allpowerful once before, in the beginning of 1649. Then it cut off the head of the King, and abolished the House of Peers. Therefore, if it again has the supreme power, it will act in the same manner.

Now, Sir, it was not the House of Commons that cut off the head of Charles the First; nor was the House of Commons then all-powerful. It had been greatly reduced in numbers by successive expulsions. It was under the absolute dominion of the army. A majority of the House was willing to take the terms offered by the King. The soldiers turned out the majority; and the minority, not a sixth part of the whole House, passed those votes of which my honorable friend speaks, votes of which the middle classes disapproved then, and of which they disapprove still.

My honorable friend, and almost all the gentlemen who have taken the same side with him in this Debate, have dwelt much on the utility of close and rotten boroughs. It is by means of such boroughs, they tell us, that the ablest men have been introduced into Parliament. It is true that many distinguished persons have represented places of this description. But, Sir, we must judge of a form of government by its general tendency, not by happy accidents. Every form of government has its happy accidents. Despotism has its happy accidents. Yet we are not disposed to abolish all constitutional checks, to place an absolute master over us, and to take our chance whether he may be a Caligula or a Marcus Aurelius. In whatever way the House of Commons may be chosen, some able men will be chosen in that way who would not be chosen in any other way. If there were a law that the hundred tallest men in England should be Members of Parliament, there would probably be some able men among those who would come into the House by virtue of this law. If the hundred persons whose names stand first in the alphabetical list of the Court Guide were made Members of Parliament, there would probably be able men among them. We read in ancient history, that a very able king was elected by the neighing of his horse: but we shall scarcely, I think, adopt this mode of election. In one of the most celebrated republics of antiquity, Athens, Senators and Magistrates were chosen by lot; and sometimes the lot fell fortunately. Once, for example, Socrates was in office. A cruel and unjust proposition was made by a demagogue. Socrates resisted it at the hazard of his own life. There is no event in Grecian history more interesting than that memorable resistance. Yet who would have officers appointed by lot, because the accident of the lot may have given to a great and good man a power which he would probably never have attained in any other way? We must judge, as I said, by the general tendency of a system. No person can doubt that a House of Commons, chosen freely by the middle classes, will contain many very able men. I do not say, that precisely the same able men who would find their way into the present House of Commons will find their way into the reformed House: but that is not the question. No particular man is necessary to the State. We may depend on it that, if we provide the country with popular institutions, those institutions will provide it with great men.

There is another objection, which, I think, was first raised by the honorable and learned Member for Newport.[4] He tells us that the elective franchise is property; that to take it away from a man who has not been judicially convicted of malpractices is robbery; that no crime is proved against the voters in the close boroughs; that no crime is even imputed to them in the preamble of the bill; and that therefore to disfranchise them without compensation would be an act of revolutionary tyranny. The honorable and learned gentleman has compared the conduct of the present Ministers to that of those odious tools of power, who, towards the close of the reign of Charles the Second, seized the charters of the Whig Corporations. Now, there was another precedent, which I wonder that he did not recollect, both because it is much more nearly in point than that to which he referred, and because my noble friend, the Paymaster of the Forces, had previously alluded to it. If the elective franchise is property, if to disfranchise voters without a crime proved, or a compensation given, be robbery, was there ever such an act of robbery as the disfranchising of the Irish forty shilling freeholders? Was any pecuniary compensation given to them? Is it declared in the preamble of the bill which took away their franchise, that they had been convicted of any offence? Was any judicial inquiry instituted into their conduct? Were they even accused of any crime? Or if you say that it was a crime in the electors of Clare to vote for the honorable and learned gentleman who now represents the county of Waterford, was a Protestant freeholder in Louth to be punished for the crime of a Catholic freeholder in Clare? If the principle of the honorable and learned Member for Newport be

4. Mr. Horace Twiss.

sound, the franchise of the Irish peasant was property. That franchise the Ministers under whom the honorable and learned Member held office did not scruple to take away. Will he accuse those Ministers of robbery? If not, how can he bring such an accusation against their successors?

Every gentleman, I think, who has spoken from the other side of the House, has alluded to the opinions which some of His Majesty's Ministers formerly entertained on the subject of Reform. It would be officious in me, Sir, to undertake the defence of gentlemen who are so well able to defend themselves. I will only say that, in my opinion, the country will not think worse either of their capacity or of their patriotism, because they have shown that they can profit by experience, because they have learned to see the folly of delaying inevitable changes. There are others who ought to have learned the same lesson. I say, Sir, that there are those who, I should have thought, must have had enough to last them all their lives of that humiliation which follows obstinate and boastful resistance to changes rendered necessary by the progress of society, and by the development of the human mind. Is it possible that those persons can wish again to occupy a position which can neither be defended nor surrendered with honour? I well remember, Sir, a certain evening in the month of May, 1827. I had not then the honor of a seat in this House; but I was an attentive observer of its proceedings. The right honorable Baronet opposite,[5] of whom personally I desire to speak with that high respect which I feel for his talents and his character, but of whose public conduct I must speak with the sincerity required by my public duty, was then, as he is now, out of office. He had just resigned the seals of the Home Department, because he conceived that the recent ministerial arrangements had been too favourable to the Catholic claims. He rose to ask whether it was the intention of the new Cabinet to repeal the Test and Corporation Acts, and to reform the Parliament. He bound up, I well remember, those two questions together; and he declared that, if the Ministers should either attempt to repeal the Test and Corporation Acts, or bring forward a measure of Parliamentary Reform, he should think it his duty to oppose them to

5. Sir Robert Peel.

the utmost. Since that declaration was made four years have elapsed; and what is now the state of the three questions which then chiefly agitated the minds of men? What is become of the Test and Corporation Acts? They are repealed. By whom? By the right honorable Baronet. What has become of the Catholic disabilities? They are removed. By whom? By the right honorable Baronet. The question of Parliamentary Reform is still behind. But signs, of which it is impossible to misconceive the import, do most clearly indicate that, unless that question also be speedily settled, property, and order, and all the institutions of this great monarchy, will be exposed to fearful peril. Is it possible that gentlemen long versed in high political affairs cannot read these signs? Is it possible that they can really believe that the Representative system of England, such as it now is, will last till the year 1860? If not, for what would they have us wait? Would they have us wait merely that we may show to all the world how little we have profited by our own recent experience? Would they have us wait, that we may once again hit the exact point where we can neither refuse with authority, nor concede with grace? Would they have us wait, that the numbers of the discontented party may become larger, its demands higher, its feelings more acrimonious, its organisation more complete? Would they have us wait till the whole tragicomedy of 1827 has been acted over again; till they have been brought into office by a cry of "No Reform," to be reformers, as they were once before brought into office by a cry of "No Popery," to be emancipators? Have they obliterated from their minds—gladly, perhaps, would some among them obliterate from their minds—the transactions of that year? And have they forgotten all the transactions of the succeeding year? Have they forgotten how the spirit of liberty in Ireland, debarred from its natural outlet, found a vent by forbidden passages? Have they forgotten how we were forced to indulge the Catholics in all the licence of rebels, merely because we chose to withhold from them the liberties of subjects? Do they wait for associations more formidable than that of the Corn Exchange, for contributions larger than the Rent, for agitators more violent than those who, three years ago, divided with the King and the Parliament the sovereignty of Ireland? Do they wait for that last and most dreadful paroxysm of popular rage, for that last and most cruel test of military fidelity? Let them wait, if their past experience shall induce them to think that any high honor or any exquisite pleasure is to be obtained by a policy like this. Let them wait, if this strange and fearful infatuation be indeed upon them, that they should not see with their eyes, or hear with their ears, or understand with their heart. But let us know our interest and our duty better. Turn where we may, within, around, the voice of great events is proclaiming to us, Reform, that you may preserve. Now, therefore, while every thing at home and abroad forebodes ruin to those who persist in a hopeless struggle against the spirit of the age, now, while the crash of the proudest throne of the continent is still resounding in our ears, now, while the roof of a British palace affords an ignominious shelter to the exiled heir of forty kings, now, while we see on every side ancient institutions subverted, and great societies dissolved, now, while the heart of England is still sound, now, while old feelings and old associations retain a power and a charm which may too soon pass away, now, in this your accepted time, now, in this your day of salvation, take counsel, not of prejudice, not of party spirit, not of the ignominious pride of a fatal consistency, but of history, of reason, of the ages which are past, of the signs of this most portentous time. Pronounce in a manner worthy of the expectation with which this great debate has been anticipated, and of the long remembrance which it will leave behind. Renew the youth of the State. Save property, divided against itself. Save the multitude, endangered by its own ungovernable passions. Save the aristocracy, endangered by its own unpopular power. Save the greatest, and fairest, and most highly civilised community that ever existed, from calamities which may in a few days sweep away all the rich heritage of so many ages of wisdom and glory. The danger is terrible. The time is short. If this bill should be rejected, I pray to God that none of those who concur in rejecting it may ever remember their votes with unavailing remorse, amidst the wreck of laws, the confusion of ranks, the spoliation of property, and the dissolution of social order.

Jewish Disabilities

The law that all holders of civil office and members of Parliament must take an oath on their faith as Christians meant that English Jews were excluded from public office. After Dissenters and Roman Catholics were admitted to full civil rights in 1828 and 1829, it seemed to most liberal politicans, Macaulay among them, that the full enfranchisement of the Jews must speedily follow. A bill for that purpose was introduced in 1830 and provided the occasion for Macaulay's first speech in the House of Commons (5 April 1830). Though it was then defeated, Macaulay still felt that it must soon pass into law. "The Jews," he wrote in 1831, "cannot, I imagine, be kept out of parliament longer." When the question came before Parliament again in 1833, Macaulay made his second speech on it, that printed here. The cause was again lost, however, through the resistance of conservative churchmen such as Sir Robert Inglis ("the Member for the University of Oxford"), to whose speech Macaulay's is a reply. The Jews did not succeed in entering Parliament until 1858, when Baron Lionel de Rothschild took his seat as M.P. for the City of London.

I recollect, and my honorable friend the Member for the University of Oxford will recollect, that, when this subject was discussed three years ago, it was remarked, by one whom we both loved and whom we both regret, that the strength of the case

Delivered April 17, 1833.

of the Jews was a serious inconvenience to their advocate, for that it was hardly possible to make a speech for them without wearying the audience by repeating truths which were universally admitted. If Sir James Mackintosh felt this difficulty when the question was first brought forward in this House, I may well despair of being able now to offer any arguments which have a pretence to novelty.

My honorable friend, the Member for the University of Oxford, began his speech by declaring that he had no intention of calling in question the principles of religious liberty. He utterly disclaims persecution, that is to say, persecution as defined by himself. It would, in his opinion, be persecution to hang a Jew, or to flay him, or to draw his teeth, or to imprison him, or to fine him; for every man who conducts himself peaceably has a right to his life and his limbs, to his personal liberty and his property. But it is not persecution, says my honorable friend, to exclude any individual or any class from office; for nobody has a right to office: in every country official appointments must be subject to such regulations as the supreme authority may choose to make; nor can any such regulations be reasonably complained of by any member of the society as unjust. He who obtains an office obtains it, not as matter of right, but as matter of favour. He who does not obtain an office is not wronged; he is only in that situation in which the vast majority of every community must necessarily be. There are in the United Kingdom five and twenty million Christians without places; and, if they do not complain, why should five and twenty thousand Jews complain of being in the same case? In this way my honorable friend has convinced himself that, as it would be most absurd in him and me to say that we are wronged because we are not Secretaries of State, so it is most absurd in the Jews to say that they are wronged because they are, as a people, excluded from public employment.

Now, surely my honorable friend cannot have considered to what conclusions his reasoning leads. Those conclusions are so monstrous that he would, I am certain, shrink from them. Does he really mean that it would not be wrong in the legislature to enact that no man should be a judge unless he weighed twelve stone, or that no man should sit in parliament unless he were six feet high? We are about to bring in a bill for the government of India. Suppose that we were to insert in that bill a clause providing that no graduate of the University of Oxford should be Governor General or Governor of any Presidency, would not my honorable friend cry out against such a clause as most unjust to the learned body which he represents? And would he think himself sufficiently answered by being told, in his own words, that the appointment to office is a mere matter of favour, and that to exclude an individual or a class from office is no injury? Surely, on consideration, he must admit that official appointments ought not to be subject to regulations purely arbitrary, to regulations for which no reason can be given but mere caprice, and that those who would exclude any class from public employment are bound to show some special reason for the exclusion.

My honorable friend has appealed to us as Christians. Let me then ask him how he understands that great commandment which comprises the law and the prophets. Can we be said to do unto others as we would that they should do unto us if we wantonly inflict on them even the smallest pain? As Christians, surely we are bound to consider, first, whether, by excluding the Jews from all public trust, we give them pain; and, secondly, whether it be necessary to give them that pain in order to avert some greater evil. That by excluding them from public trust we inflict pain on them my honorable friend will not dispute. As a Christian, therefore, he is bound to relieve them from that pain, unless he can show, what I am sure he has not yet shown, that it is necessary to the general good that they should continue to suffer.

But where, he says, are you to stop, if once you admit into the House of Commons people who deny the authority of the Gospels? Will you let in a Mussulman? Will you let in a Parsee? Will you let in a Hindoo, who worships a lump of stone with seven heads? I will answer my honorable friend's question by another. Where does he mean to stop? Is he ready to roast unbelievers at slow fires? If not, let him tell us why: and I will engage to prove that his reason is just as decisive against the intolerance which he thinks a duty as against the intolerance which he thinks a crime. Once admit that we are bound to inflict pain on a man because he is not of our religion; and where are you to stop? Why stop at the point fixed by my honorable friend rather than at the point fixed by the honorable Member for Oldham,[1] who would make the Jews incapable of holding land? And why stop at the point fixed by the honorable Member for Oldham rather than at the point which would have been fixed by a Spanish Inquisitor of the sixteenth century? When once you enter on a course of persecution, I defy you to find any reason for making a halt till you have reached the extreme point. When my honorable friend tells us that he will allow the Jews to possess property to any amount, but that he will not allow them to possess the smallest political power, he holds contradictory language. Property is power. The honorable Member for Oldham reasons better than my honorable friend. The honorable Member for Oldham sees very clearly that it is impossible to deprive a man of political power if you suffer him to be the proprietor of half a county, and therefore very consistently proposes to confiscate the landed estates of the Jews. But even the honorable Member for Oldham does not go far enough. He has not proposed to confiscate the personal property of the Jews. Yet it is perfectly certain that any Jew who has a million may easily make himself very important in the state. By such steps we pass from official power to landed property, and from landed property to personal property, and from property to liberty, and from liberty to life. In truth, those persecutors who use the rack and the stake have much to say for themselves. They are convinced that their end is good; and it must be admitted that they employ means which are not unlikely to attain the end. Religious dissent has repeatedly been put down by sanguinary persecution. In that way the Albigenses were put down. In that way Protestantism was suppressed in Spain and Italy, so that it has never since reared its head. But I defy any body to produce an instance in which disabilities such as we are now considering have produced any other effect than that of making the sufferers angry and obstinate. My honorable friend should either persecute to some purpose, or not persecute at all. He dislikes the word persecution, I know. He will not admit that the Jews are persecuted. And yet I am confident that he would rather be sent to the King's Bench Prison for three months, or

1. Mr. Cobbett.

be fined a hundred pounds, than be subject to the disabilities under which the Jews lie. How can he then say that to impose such disabilities is not persecution, and that to fine and imprison is persecution? All his reasoning consists in drawing arbitrary lines. What he does not wish to inflict he calls persecution. What he does wish to inflict he will not call persecution. What he takes from the Jews he· calls political power. What he is too good-natured to take from the Jews he will not call political power. The Jew must not sit in parliament: but he may be the proprietor of all the ten pound houses in a borough. He may have more fifty pound tenants than any peer in the kingdom. He may give the voters treats to please their palates, and hire bands of gipsies to break their heads, as if he were a Christian and a Marquess. All the rest of this system is of a piece. The Jew may be a jury-man, but not a judge. He may decide issues of fact, but not issues of law. He may give a hundred thousand pounds damages; but he may not in the most trivial case grant a new trial. He may rule the money market: he may influence the exchanges: he may be summoned to congresses of Emperors and Kings. Great potentates, instead of negotiating a loan with him by tying him in a chair and pulling out his grinders, may treat with him as with a great potentate, and may postpone the declaring of war or the signing of a treaty till they have conferred with him. All this is as it should be: but he must not be a Privy Councillor. He must not be called Right Honorable, for that is political power. And who is it that we are trying to cheat in this way? Even Omniscience. Yes, Sir; we have been gravely told that the Jews are under the divine displeasure, and that if we give them polit-ical power God will visit us in judgment. Do we then think that God cannot distinguish between substance and form? Does not He know that, while we withhold from the Jews the sem-blance and name of political power, we suffer them to possess the substance? The plain truth is that my honorable friend is drawn in one direction by his opinions, and in a directly opposite direction by his excellent heart. He halts between two opinions. He tries to make a compromise between principles which admit of no compromise. He goes a certain way in intolerance. Then he stops, without being able to give a reason for stopping. But I know the reason. It is his humanity. Those who formerly dragged

185

the Jew at a horse's tail, and singed his beard with blazing furze-bushes, were much worse men than my honorable friend; but they were more consistent than he.

It has been said that it would be monstrous to see a Jew judge try a man for blasphemy. In my opinion it is monstrous to see any judge try a man for blasphemy under the present law. But, if the law on that subject were in a sound state, I do not see why a conscientious Jew might not try a blasphemer. Every man, I think, ought to be at liberty to discuss the evidences of religion; but no man ought to be at liberty to force on the unwilling ears and eyes of others sounds and sights which must cause annoyance and irritation. The distinction is clear. I think it wrong to punish a man for selling Paine's Age of Reason in a back shop to those who choose to buy, or for delivering a Deistical lecture in a private room to those who choose to listen. But if a man exhibits at a window in the Strand a hideous caricature of that which is an object of awe and adoration to nine hundred and ninety-nine out of every thousand of the people who pass up and down that great thoroughfare; if a man, in a place of public resort, applies opprobrious epithets to names held in reverence by all Christians; such a man ought, in my opinion, to be severely punished, not for differing from us in opinion, but for committing a nuisance which gives us pain and disgust. He is no more entitled to outrage our feelings by obtruding his impiety on us, and to say that he is exercising his right of discussion, than to establish a yard for butchering horses close to our houses and to say that he is exercising his right of property, or to run naked up and down the public streets and to say that he is exercising his right of locomotion. He has a right of discussion, no doubt, as he has a right of property and a right of locomotion. But he must use all his rights so as not to infringe the rights of others.

These, Sir, are the principles on which I would frame the law of blasphemy; and, if the law were so framed, I am at a loss to understand why a Jew might not enforce it as well as a Christian. I am not a Roman Catholic; but if I were a judge at Malta, I should have no scruple about punishing a bigoted Protestant who should burn the Pope in effigy before the eyes of thousands of Roman Catholics. I am not a Mussulman; but if I were a judge in India, I should have no scruple about punishing a Christian who should pollute a mosque. Why, then, should I doubt that a Jew, raised by his ability, learning, and integrity to the judicial bench, would deal properly with any person who, in a Christian country, should insult the Christian religion?

But, says my honorable friend, it has been prophesied that the Jews are to be wanderers on the face of the earth, and that they are not to mix on terms of equality with the people of the countries in which they sojourn. Now, Sir, I am confident that I can demonstrate that this is not the sense of any prophecy which is part of Holy Writ. For it is an undoubted fact that, in the United States of America, Jewish citizens do possess all the privileges possessed by Christian citizens. Therefore, if the prophecies mean that the Jews never shall, during their wanderings, be admitted by other nations to equal participation of political rights, the prophecies are false. But the prophecies are certainly not false. Therefore their meaning cannot be that which is attributed to them by my honorable friend.

Another objection which has been made to this motion is that the Jews look forward to the coming of a great deliverer, to their return to Palestine, to the rebuilding of their temple, to the revival of their ancient worship, and that therefore they will always consider England, not their country, but merely as their place of exile. But, surely, Sir, it would be the grossest ignorance of human nature to imagine that the anticipation of an event which is to happen at some time altogether indefinite, of an event which has been vainly expected during many centuries, of an event which even those who confidently expect that it will happen do not confidently expect that they or their children or their grandchildren will see, can ever occupy the minds of men to such a degree as to make them regardless of what is near and present and certain. Indeed Christians, as well as Jews, believe that the existing order of things will come to an end. Many Christians believe that Jesus will visibly reign on earth during a thousand years. Expositors of prophecy have gone so far as to fix the year when the Millennial period is to commence. The prevailing opinion is, I think, in favour of the year 1866; but, according to some commentators, the time is close at hand. Are we to exclude all millennarians from parliament and office, on the ground that they are impatiently looking forward to the miraculous monarchy which is to supersede the present dynasty and the present constitution of England, and that therefore they cannot be heartily loyal to King William?

In one important point, Sir, my honorable friend, the Member for the University of Oxford, must acknowledge that the Jewish religion is of all erroneous religions the least mischievous. There is not the slightest chance that the Jewish religion will spread. The Jew does not wish to make proselytes. He may be said to reject them. He thinks it almost culpable in one who does not belong to his race to presume to belong to his religion. It is therefore not strange that a conversion from Christianity to Judaism should be a rarer occurrence than a total eclipse of the sun. There was one distinguished convert in the last century, Lord George Gordon; and the history of his conversion deserves to be remembered. For if ever there was a proselyte of whom a proselytising sect would have been proud, it was Lord George; not only because he was a man of high birth and rank; not only because he had been a member of the legislature; but also because he had been distinguished by the intolerance, nay, the ferocity, of his zeal for his own form of Christianity. But was he allured into the Synagogue? Was he even welcomed to it? No, Sir; he was coldly and reluctantly permitted to share the reproach and suffering of the chosen people; but he was sternly shut out from their privileges. He underwent the painful rite which their law enjoins. But when, on his deathbed, he begged hard to be buried among them according to their ceremonial, he was told that his request could not be granted. I understand that cry of "Hear." It reminds me that one of the arguments against this motion is that the Jews are an unsocial people, that they draw close to each other, and stand aloof from strangers. Really, Sir, it is amusing to compare the manner in which the question of Catholic emancipation was argued formerly by some gentlemen with the manner in which the question of Jew emancipation is argued by the same gentlemen now. When the question was about Catholic emancipation, the cry was, "See how restless, how versatile, how encroaching, how insinuating, is the spirit of the Church of Rome. See how her priests compass earth and sea to make one proselyte, how indefatigably they toil, how attentively they study the weak and strong parts of every character, how skilfully they employ literature, arts, sciences, as engines for the propagation of their faith. You find them in every region and under every disguise, collating manuscripts in the Bodleian, fixing telescopes in the Observatory of Pekin, teaching the use of the plough and the spinning wheel to the savages of Paraguay. Will you give power to the members of a Church so busy, so aggressive, so insatiable?" Well, now the question is about people who never try to seduce any stranger to join them, and who do not wish any body to be of their faith who is not also of their blood. And now you exclaim, "Will you give power to the members of a sect which remains sullenly apart from other sects, which does not invite, nay, which hardly even admits, neophytes?" The truth is, that bigotry will never want a pretence. Whatever the sect be which it is proposed to tolerate, the peculiarities of that sect will, for the time, be pronounced by intolerant men to be the most odious and dangerous that can be conceived. As to the Jews, that they are unsocial as respects religion is true; and so much the better: for surely, as Christians, we cannot wish that they should bestir themselves to pervert us from our own faith. But that the Jews would be unsocial members of the civil community, if the civil community did its duty by them, has never been proved. My right honorable friend who made the motion which we are discussing has produced a great body of evidence to show that they have been grossly misrepresented; and that evidence has not been refuted by my honorable friend the Member for the University of Oxford. But what if it were true that the Jews are unsocial? What if it were true that they do not regard England as their country? Would not the treatment which they have undergone explain and excuse their antipathy to the society in which they live? Has not similar antipathy often been felt by persecuted Christians to the society which persecuted them? While the bloody code of Elizabeth was enforced against the English Roman Catholics, what was the patriotism of Roman Catholics? Oliver Cromwell said that in his time they were Espaniolised. At a later period it might have been said that they were Gallicised. It was the same with the Calvinists. What more deadly enemies had France in the days of Lewis the Fourteenth than the persecuted Huguenots? But would any rational man infer from these facts that either the Roman Catholic as such, or the Calvinist as such, is incapable of loving the land of his birth? If England were now invaded by Roman Catholics, how many English Roman Catholics would go over to the invader? If France were now attacked by a Protestant enemy, how many French Protestants would lend him help? Why not try what effect would be produced on the Jews by that tolerant policy which has made the English Roman Catholic a good Englishman, and the French Calvinist a good Frenchman?

Another charge has been brought against the Jews, not by my honorable friend the Member for the University of Oxford, —he has too much learning and too much good feeling to make such a charge,—but by the honorable Member for Oldham, who has, I am sorry to see, quitted his place. The honorable Member for Oldham tells us that the Jews are naturally a mean race, a sordid race, a moneygetting race; that they are averse to all honorable callings; that they neither sow nor reap; that they have neither flocks nor herds; that usury is the only pursuit for which they are fit; that they are destitute of all elevated and amiable sentiments. Such, Sir, has in every age been the reasoning of bigots. They never fail to plead in justification of persecution the vices which persecution has engendered. England has been to the Jews less than half a country; and we revile them because they do not feel for England more than a half patriotism. We treat them as slaves, and wonder that they do not regard us as brethren. We drive them to mean occupations, and then reproach them for not embracing honorable professions. We long forbade them to possess land; and we complain that they chiefly occupy themselves in trade. We shut them out from all the paths of ambition; and then we despise them for taking refuge in avarice. During many ages we have, in all our dealings with them, abused our immense superiority of force; and then we are disgusted because they have recourse to that cunning which is the natural and universal defence of the weak against the violence of the strong. But were they always a mere money-changing, moneygetting, moneyhoarding race? Nobody knows better than my honorable friend the Member for the University of Oxford that there is nothing in their national character which unfits them for the highest duties of citizens. He knows that, in the infancy of civilisation, when our island was as savage as

New Guinea, when letters and arts were still unknown to Athens, when scarcely a thatched hut stood on what was afterwards the site of Rome, this contemned people had their fenced cities and cedar palaces, their splendid Temple, their fleets of merchant ships, their schools of sacred learning, their great statesmen and soldiers, their natural philosophers, their historians and their poets. What nation ever contended more manfully against overwhelming odds for its independence and religion? What nation ever, in its last agonies, gave such signal proofs of what may be accomplished by a brave despair? And if, in the course of many centuries, the oppressed descendants of warriors and sages have degenerated from the qualities of their fathers, if, while excluded from the blessings of law, and bowed down under the yoke of slavery, they have contracted some of the vices of outlaws and of slaves, shall we consider this as matter of reproach to them? Shall we not rather consider it as matter of shame and remorse to ourselves? Let us do justice to them. Let us open to them the door of the House of Commons. Let us open to them every career in which ability and energy can be displayed. Till we have done this, let us not presume to say that there is no genius among the countrymen of Isaiah, no heroism among the descendants of the Maccabees.

Sir, in supporting the motion of my honorable friend, I am, I firmly believe, supporting the honor and the interests of the Christian religion. I should think that I insulted that religion if I said that it cannot stand unaided by intolerant laws. Without such laws it was established, and without such laws it may be maintained. It triumphed over the superstitions of the most refined and of the most savage nations, over the graceful mythology of Greece and the bloody idolatry of the northern forests. It prevailed over the power and policy of the Roman empire. It tamed the barbarians by whom that empire was overthrown. But all these victories were gained not by the help of intolerance, but in spite of the opposition of intolerance. The whole history of Christianity proves that she has little indeed to fear from persecution as a foe, but much to fear from persecution as an ally. May she long continue to bless our country with her benignant influence, strong in her sublime philosophy, strong in her spotless morality, strong in those internal and external evidences to which the most powerful and comprehensive of human intellects have yielded assent, the last solace of those who have outlived every earthly hope, the last restraint of those who are raised above every earthly fear! But let not us, mistaking her character and her interests, fight the battle of truth with the weapons of error, and endeavour to support by oppression that religion which first taught the human race the great lesson of universal charity.

The Ten Hours Bill

On 29 April 1846, John Fielden, member of Parliament for Oldham in Lancashire and a humanitarian factory owner, moved the second reading of a bill for limiting the labor of young persons in factories to ten hours a day. Macaulay made his speech in favor of the bill on May 22. What was at stake, as all concerned knew, was not just limiting the hours worked by young persons, but accepting the consequence that as a result of this legislation the hours worked by adults would also be restricted. For without "young persons," it would be hard, if not impossible, to keep factories going.

The history of the Ten Hours Movement goes back to the early 1830s when Tory Radicals such as Richard Oastler and Michael Sadler (subsequently joined by Ashley, later Lord Shaftesbury) put themselves in the vanguard of agitation for shorter hours of labor for young factory workers. At that time Macaulay, Sadler's victorious opponent in the Leeds election of 1832, declared his firm opposition to any attempt by the state to interfere with such matters to the point of limiting daily hours of labour to ten. "To tell a man that he may have ten hours' work and twelve hours' wages is the same thing as to tell him that by swallowing a certain pill, he would get rid of diseases of thirty years' continuance," he said at the time.

By 1846 Macaulay had changed his mind. He was now willing

Delivered May 22, 1846.

to sanction such interference. He was particularly proud of this speech; and it is indeed a remarkable example of clear and concise argument supported by an impressive variety of historical illustrations. G. M. Young's comment about this speech is worth recalling: "The decoration is not laid on: like the pinnacles and flying buttresses of a cathedral, it is an integral part of the fabric. The speaker is thinking in images drawn from an inexhaustible store of historic reminiscence and flashed on the mind of the listener with the force and dexterity of a born story-teller." The second reading of Fielden's Bill was, in fact, defeated on the day Macaulay spoke, but it became law in 1847.

It is impossible, Sir, that I can remain silent after the appeal which has been made to me in so pointed a manner by my honorable friend the Member for Sheffield.[1] And, even if that appeal had not been made to me, I should have been very desirous to have an opportunity of explaining the grounds on which I shall vote for the second reading of this bill.

It is, I hope, unnecessary for me to assure my honorable friend that I utterly disapprove of those aspersions which have, both in this House and out of it, been thrown on the owners of factories. For that valuable class of men I have no feeling but respect and good will. I am convinced that with their interests the interests of the whole community, and especially of the labouring classes, are inseparably bound up. I can also with perfect sincerity declare that the vote which I shall give to-night will not be a factious vote. In no circumstances indeed should I think that the laws of political hostility warranted me in treating this question as a party question. But at the present moment I would much rather strengthen than weaken the hands of Her Majesty's Ministers. It is by no means pleasant to me to be under the necessity of opposing them. I assure them, I assure my friends on this side of the House with whom I am so unfortunate as to differ, and especially my honorable friend the Member for Sheffield who spoke, I must say, in rather too plaintive a tone, that I have no desire to obtain credit for humanity at their expense. I fully believe that their feeling towards the labouring

1. Mr. Ward.

people is quite as kind as mine. There is no difference between us as to ends: there is an honest difference of opinion as to means: and we surely ought to be able to discuss the points on which we differ without one angry emotion or one acrimonious word.

The details of the bill, Sir, will be more conveniently and more regularly discussed when we consider it in Committee. Our business at present is with the principle: and the principle, we are told by many gentlemen of great authority, is unsound. In their opinion, neither this bill, nor any other bill regulating the hours of labour, can be defended. This, they say, is one of those matters about which we ought not to legislate at all; one of those matters which settle themselves far better than any government can settle them. Now it is most important that this point should be fully cleared up. We certainly ought not to usurp functions which do not properly belong to us: but, on the other hand, we ought not to abdicate functions which do properly belong to us. I hardly know which is the greater pest to society, a paternal government, that is to say a prying, meddlesome government, which intrudes itself into every part of human life, and which thinks that it can do everything for everybody better than anybody can do anything for himself; or a careless, lounging government, which suffers grievances, such as it could at once remove, to grow and multiply, and which to all complaint and remonstrance has only one answer: "We must let things alone: we must let things take their course: we must let things find their level." There is no more important problem in politics than to ascertain the just mean between these two most pernicious extremes, to draw correctly the line which divides those cases in which it is the duty of the State to interfere from those cases in which it is the duty of the State to abstain from interference. In old times the besetting sin of rulers was undoubtedly an inordinate disposition to meddle. The lawgiver was always telling people how to keep their shops, how to till their fields, how to educate their children, how many dishes to have on their tables, how much a yard to give for the cloth which made their coats. He was always trying to remedy some evil which did not properly fall within his province; and the consequence was that he increased the evils which he attempted to remedy. He was so much shocked by the distress in-

separable from scarcity that he made statutes against fore-
stalling and regrating, and so turned the scarcity into a famine.
He was so much shocked by the cunning and hardheartedness of
moneylenders that he made laws against usury; and the consequence was that the borrower, who, if he had been left unpro-
tected, would have got money at ten per cent, could hardly, when
protected, get it at fifteen per cent. Some eminent political philosophers of the last century exposed with great ability the folly
of such legislation, and, by doing so, rendered a great service to
mankind. There has been a reaction, a reaction which has doubtless produced much good, but which, like most reactions, has not
been without evils and dangers. Our statesmen cannot now be
accused of being busybodies. But I am afraid that there is, even
in some of the ablest and most upright among them, a tendency
to the opposite fault. I will give an instance of what I mean.
Fifteen years ago it became evident that railroads would soon,
in every part of the kingdom, supersede to a great extent the old
highways. The tracing of the new routes which were to join all
the chief cities, ports, and naval arsenals of the island was a matter of the highest national importance. But, unfortunately, those
who should have acted for the nation refused to interfere. Consequently, numerous questions which were really public, questions which concerned the public convenience, the public prosperity, the public security, were treated as private questions. That
the whole society was interested in having a good system of internal communication seemed to be forgotten. The speculator
who wanted a large dividend on his shares, the landowner who
wanted a large price for his acres, obtained a full hearing. But
nobody applied to be heard on behalf of the community. The
effects of that great error we feel, and we shall not soon cease to
feel. Unless I am greatly mistaken, we are in danger of committing to-night an error of the same kind. The honorable Member for Montrose[2] and my honorable friend the Member for
Sheffield think that the question before us is merely a question
between the old and the new theories of commerce. They cannot
understand how any friend of free trade can wish the Legislature
to interfere between the capitalist and the labourer. They say,

2. Mr. Hume.

"You do not make a law to settle the price of gloves, or the texture of gloves, or the length of credit which the glover shall give. You leave it to him to determine whether he will charge high or low prices, whether he will use strong or flimsy materials, whether he will trust or insist on ready money. You acknowledge that these are matters which he ought to be left to settle with his customers, and that we ought not to interfere. It is possible that he may manage his shop ill. But it is certain that we shall manage it ill. On the same grounds on which you leave the seller of gloves and the buyer of gloves to make their own contract, you ought to leave the seller of labour and the buyer of labour to make their own contract."

I have a great respect, Sir, for those who reason thus: but I cannot see this matter in the light in which it appears to them; and, though I may distrust my own judgment, I must be guided by it. I am, I believe, as strongly attached as any member of this House to the principle of free trade, rightly understood. Trade, considered merely as trade, considered merely with reference to the pecuniary interest of the contracting parties, can hardly be too free. But there is a great deal of trade which cannot be considered merely as trade, and which affects higher than pecuniary interests. And to say that Government never ought to regulate such trade is a monstrous proposition, a proposition at which Adam Smith would have stood aghast. We impose some restrictions on trade for the purposes of police. Thus, we do not suffer everybody who has a cab and a horse to ply for passengers in the streets of London. We do not leave the fare to be determined by the supply and the demand. We do not permit a driver to extort a guinea for going half a mile on a rainy day when there is no other vehicle on the stand. We impose some restrictions on trade for the sake of revenue. Thus, we forbid a farmer to cultivate tobacco on his own ground. We impose some restrictions on trade for the sake of national defence. Thus we compel a man who would rather be ploughing or weaving to go into the militia; and we fix the amount of pay which he shall receive without asking his consent. Nor is there in all this anything inconsistent with the soundest political economy. For the science of political economy teaches us only that we ought not on commercial grounds to interfere with the liberty of commerce; and we, in the cases which

I have put, interfere with the liberty of commerce on higher than commercial grounds.

And now, Sir, to come closer to the case with which we have to deal, I say, first, that where the health of the community is concerned, it may be the duty of the State to interfere with the contracts of individuals; and to this proposition I am quite sure that Her Majesty's Government will cordially assent. I have just read a very interesting report signed by two members of that Government, the Duke of Buccleuch, and the noble earl who was lately Chief Commissioner of the Woods and Forests, and who is now Secretary for Ireland;[3] and, since that report was laid before the House, the noble earl himself has, with the sanction of the Cabinet, brought in a bill for the protection of the public health. By this bill it is provided that no man shall be permitted to build a house on his own land in any great town without giving notice to certain Commissioners. No man is to sink a cellar without the consent of these Commissioners. The house must not be of less than a prescribed width. No new house must be built without a drain. If an old house has no drain, the Commissioners may order the owner to make a drain. If he refuses, they make a drain for him, and send him in the bill. They may order him to whitewash his house. If he refuses, they may send people with pails and brushes to whitewash it for him, at his charge. Now, suppose that some proprietor of houses at Leeds or Manchester were to expostulate with the Government in the language in which the Government has expostulated with the supporters of this bill for the regulation of factories. Suppose that he were to say to the noble earl, "Your lordship professes to be a friend to free trade. Your lordship's doctrine is that everybody ought to be at liberty to buy cheap and to sell dear. Why then may not I run up a house as cheap as I can, and let my rooms as dear as I can? Your lordship does not like houses without drains. Do not take one of mine then. You think my bedrooms filthy. Nobody forces you to sleep in them. Use your own liberty: but do not restrain that of your neighbours. I can find many a family willing to pay a shilling a week for leave to live in what you call a hovel. And why am not I to take the shilling which they are willing to give me? And why

3. The Earl of Lincoln.

are not they to have such shelter as, for that shilling, I can afford them? Why did you send a man without my consent to clean my house, and then force me to pay for what I never ordered? My tenants thought the house clean enough for them; or they would not have been my tenants: and, if they and I were satisfied, why did you, in direct defiance of all the principles of free trade, interfere between us?" This reasoning, Sir, is exactly of a piece with the reasoning of the honorable Member for Montrose, and of my honorable friend the Member for Sheffield. If the noble earl will allow me to make a defence for him, I believe that he would answer the objection thus: "I hold," he would say, "the sound doctrine of free trade. But your doctrine of free trade is an exaggeration, a caricature of the sound doctrine; and by exhibiting such a caricature you bring discredit on the sound doctrine. We should have nothing to do with the contracts between you and your tenants, if those contracts affected only pecuniary interests. But higher than pecuniary interests are at stake. It concerns the commonwealth that the great body of the people should not live in a way which makes life wretched and short, which enfeebles the body and pollutes the mind. If, by living in houses which resemble hogstyes, great numbers of our countrymen have contracted the tastes of hogs, if they have become so familiar with filth and stench and contagion, that they burrow without reluctance in holes which would turn the stomach of any man of cleanly habits, that is only an additional proof that we have too long neglected our duties, and an additional reason for our now performing them."

Secondly, I say that where the public morality is concerned it may be the duty of the State to interfere with the contracts of individuals. Take the traffic in licentious books and pictures. Will anybody deny that the State may, with propriety, interdict that traffic? Or take the case of lotteries. I have, we will suppose, an estate for which I wish to get twenty thousand pounds. I announce my intention to issue a thousand tickets at twenty pounds each. The holder of the number which is first drawn is to have the estate. But the magistrate interferes; the contract between me and the purchasers of my tickets is annulled; and I am forced to pay a heavy penalty for having made such a contract. I appeal to the principle of free trade, as expounded by the honorable gentleman the Members for Montrose and Sheffield. I say to you, the legislators who have restricted my liberty, "What business have you to interfere between a buyer and a seller? If you think the speculation a bad one, do not take tickets. But do not interdict other people from judging for themselves." Surely you would answer, "You would be right if this were a mere question of trade: but it is a question of morality. We prohibit you from disposing of your property in this particular mode, because it is a mode which tends to encourage a most pernicious habit of mind, a habit of mind incompatible with all the qualities on which the well being of individuals and of nations depends."

It must then, I think, be admitted that, where health is concerned, and where morality is concerned, the State is justified in interfering with the contracts of individuals. And, if this be admitted, it follows that the case with which we now have to do is a case for interference.

Will it be denied that the health of a large part of the rising generation may be seriously affected by the contracts which this bill is intended to regulate? Can any man who has read the evidence which is before us, can any man who has ever observed young people, can any man who remembers his own sensations when he was young, doubt that twelve hours a day of labour in a factory is too much for a lad of thirteen?

Or will it be denied that this is a question in which public morality is concerned? Can any one doubt,—none, I am sure, of my friends around me doubts,—that education is a matter of the highest importance to the virtue and happiness of a people? Now we know that there can be no education without leisure. It is evident that, after deducting from the day twelve hours for labour in a factory, and the additional hours necessary for exercise, refreshment, and repose, there will not remain time enough for education.

I have now, I think, shown that this bill is not in principle objectionable; and yet I have not touched the strongest part of our case. I hold that, where public health is concerned, and where public morality is concerned, the State may be justified in regulating even the contracts of adults. But we propose to regulate only the contracts of infants. Now was there ever a civilised society in which the contracts of infants were not under some regu-

lation? Is there a single member of this House who will say that a
wealthy minor of thirteen ought to be at perfect liberty to execute
a conveyance of his estate, or to give a bond for fifty thousand
pounds? If anybody were so absurd as to say, "What has the
Legislature to do with the matter? Why cannot you leave trade
free? Why do you pretend to understand the boy's interest better
than he understands it?"—you would answer; "When he grows
up, he may squander his fortune away if he likes: but at present
the State is his guardian; and he shall not ruin himself till he is
old enough to know what he is about." The minors whom we
wish to protect have not indeed large property to throw away:
but they are not the less our wards. Their only inheritance, the
only fund to which they must look for their subsistence through
life, is the sound mind in the sound body. And is it not our duty
to prevent them from wasting that most precious wealth before
they know its value?

But, it is said, this bill, though it directly limits only the labour
of infants, will, by an indirect operation, limit also the labour of
adults. Now, Sir, though I am not prepared to vote for a bill
directly limiting the labour of adults, I will plainly say that I do
not think that the limitation of the labour of adults would necessarily produce all those frightful consequences which we have
heard predicted. You cheer me in very triumphant tones, as if I
had uttered some monstrous paradox. Pray, does it not occur to
any of you that the labour of adults is now limited in this country? Are you not aware that you are living in a society in which
the labour of adults is limited to six days in seven? It is you, not I,
who maintain a paradox opposed to the opinions and the practices of all nations and ages. Did you ever hear of a single civilised State since the beginning of the world in which a certain
portion of time was not set apart for the rest and recreation of
adults by public authority? In general, this arrangement has been
sanctioned by religion. The Egyptians, the Jews, the Greeks, the
Romans, had their holidays: the Hindoo has his holidays: the
Mussulman has his holidays: there are holidays in the Greek
Church, holidays in the Church of Rome, holidays in the Church
of England. Is it not amusing to hear a gentleman pronounce with
confidence that any legislation which limits the labour of adults
must produce consequences fatal to society, without once reflect-

ing that in the society in which he lives, and in every other society that exists, or ever has existed, there has been such legislation without any evil consequence? It is true that a Puritan Government in England, and an Atheistical Government in France,
abolished the old holidays as superstitious. But those governments felt it to be absolutely necessary to institute new holidays.
Civil festivals were substituted for religious festivals. You will
find among the ordinances of the Long Parliament a law providing that, in exchange for the days of rest and amusement which
the people had been used to enjoy at Easter, Whitsuntide, and
Christmas, the second Tuesday of every month should be given
to the working man, and that any apprentice who was forced to
work on the second Tuesday of any month might have his master
up before a magistrate. The French Jacobins decreed that the
Sunday should no longer be a day of rest; but they instituted another day of rest, the Decade. They swept away the holidays of
the Roman Catholic Church; but they instituted another set of
holidays, the Sansculottides, one sacred to Genius, one to Industry, one to Opinion, and so on. I say, therefore, that the practice
of limiting by law the time of the labour of adults is so far from
being, as some gentlemen seem to think, an unheard of and monstrous practice, that it is a practice as universal as cookery, as the
wearing of clothes, as the use of domestic animals.

And has this practice been proved by experience to be pernicious? Let us take the instance with which we are most familiar.
Let us inquire what has been the effect of those laws which, in
our own country, limit the labour of adults to six days in every
seven. It is quite unnecessary to discuss the question whether
Christians be or be not bound by a divine command to observe
the Sunday. For it is evident that, whether our weekly holiday be
of divine or of human institution, the effect on the temporal interests of society will be exactly the same. Now, is there a single
argument in the whole Speech of my honorable friend the Member for Sheffield which does not tell just as strongly against the
laws which enjoin the observance of the Sunday as against the
bill on our table? Surely, if his reasoning is good for hours, it
must be equally good for days.

He says, "If this limitation be good for the working people,
rely on it that they will find it out, and that they will themselves

establish it without any law." Why not reason in the same way about the Sunday? Why not say, "If it be a good thing for the people of London to shut their shops one day in seven, they will find it out, and will shut their shops without a law"? Sir, the answer is obvious. I have no doubt that, if you were to poll the shopkeepers of London, you would find an immense majority, probably a hundred to one, in favour of closing shops on the Sunday; and yet it is absolutely necessary to give to the wish of the majority the sanction of a law; for, if there were no such law, the minority, by opening their shops, would soon force the majority to do the same.

But, says my honorable friend, you cannot limit the labour of adults unless you fix wages. This proposition he lays down repeatedly, assures us that it is incontrovertible, and indeed seems to think it self-evident; for he has not taken the trouble to prove it. Sir, my answer shall be very short. We have, during many centuries, limited the labour of adults to six days in seven; and yet we have not fixed the rate of wages.

But, it is said, you cannot legislate for all trades; and therefore you had better not legislate for any. Look at the poor sempstress. She works far longer and harder than the factory child. She sometimes plies her needle fifteen, sixteen hours in the twenty-four. See how the housemaid works, up at six every morning, and toiling up stairs and down stairs till near midnight. You own that you cannot do anything for the sempstress and the housemaid. Why then trouble yourself about the factory child? Take care that by protecting one class you do not aggravate the hardships endured by the classes which you cannot protect. Why, Sir, might not all this be said, word for word, against the laws which enjoin the observance of the Sunday? There are classes of people whom you cannot prevent from working on the Sunday. There are classes of people whom, if you could, you ought not to prevent from working on the Sunday. Take the sempstress, of whom so much has been said. You cannot keep her from sewing and hemming all Sunday in her garret. But you do not think that a reason for suffering Covent Garden Market, and Leadenhall Market, and Smithfield Market, and all the shops from Mile End to Hyde Park to be open all Sunday. Nay, these factories about which we are debating,—does anybody propose that they shall be allowed to work all Sunday? See then how inconsistent you are. You think it unjust to limit the labour of the factory child to ten hours a day, because you cannot limit the labour of the sempstress. And yet you see no injustice in limiting the labour of the factory child, aye, and the factory man, to six days in the week, though you cannot limit the labour of the sempstress.

But, you say, by protecting one class we shall aggravate the sufferings of all the classes which we cannot protect. You say this; but you do not prove it; and all experience proves the contrary. We interfere on the Sunday to close the shops. We do not interfere with the labour of the housemaid. But are the housemaids of London more severely worked on the Sunday than on other days? The fact notoriously is the reverse. For your legislation keeps the public feeling in a right state, and thus protects indirectly those whom it cannot protect directly.

Will my honorable friend the Member for Sheffield maintain that the law which limits the number of working days has been injurious to the working population? I am certain that he will not. How then can he expect me to believe that a law which limits the number of working hours must necessarily be injurious to the working population? Yet he and those who agree with him seem to wonder at our dulness because we do not at once admit the truth of the doctrine which they propound on this subject. They reason thus. We cannot reduce the number of hours of labour in factories without reducing the amount of production. We cannot reduce the amount of production without reducing the remuneration of the labourer. Meanwhile, foreigners, who are at liberty to work till they drop down dead at their looms, will soon beat us out of all the markets of the world. Wages will go down fast. The condition of our working people will be far worse than it is; and our unwise interference will, like the unwise interference of our ancestors with the dealings of the corn factor and the money lender, increase the distress of the very class which we wish to relieve.

Now, Sir, I fully admit that there might be such a limitation of the hours of labour as would produce the evil consequences with which we are threatened: and this, no doubt, is a very good reason for legislating with great caution, for feeling our way, for looking well to all the details of this bill. But it is certainly not true that every limitation of the hours of labour must produce these consequences. And I am, I must say, surprised when I hear men of eminent ability and knowledge lay down the proposition that a diminution of the time of labour must be followed by a diminution of the wages of labour, as a proposition universally true, as a proposition capable of being strictly demonstrated, as a proposition about which there can be no more doubt than about any theorem in Euclid. Sir, I deny the truth of the proposition; and for this plain reason. We have already, by law, greatly reduced the time of labour in factories. Thirty years ago, the late Sir Robert Peel told the House that it was a common practice to make children of eight years of age toil in mills fifteen hours a day. A law has since been made which prohibits persons under eighteen years of age from working in mills more than twelve hours a day. That law was opposed on exactly the same grounds on which the bill before us is opposed. Parliament was told then, as it is told now, that with the time of labour the quantity of production would decrease, that with the quantity of production the wages would decrease, that our manufacturers would be unable to contend with foreign manufacturers, and that the condition of the labouring population instead of being made better by the interference of the Legislature would be made worse. Read over those debates; and you may imagine that you are reading the debate of this evening. Parliament disregarded these prophecies. The time of labour was limited. Have wages fallen? Has the cotton trade left Manchester for France or Germany? Has the condition of the working people become more miserable? Is it not universally acknowledged that the evils which were so confidently predicted have not come to pass? Let me be understood. I am not arguing that, because a law which reduced the hours of daily labour from fifteen to twelve did not reduce wages, a law reducing those hours from twelve to ten or eleven cannot possibly reduce wages. That would be very inconclusive reasoning. What I say is this, that, since a law which reduced the hours of daily labour from fifteen to twelve has not reduced wages, the proposition that every reduction of the hours of labour must necessarily reduce wages is a false proposition. There is evidently some flaw in that demonstration which my honorable friend thinks so complete; and what the flaw is we may perhaps discover if we look at the analogous case to which I have so often referred.

Sir, exactly three hundred years ago, great religious changes were taking place in England. Much was said and written, in that inquiring and innovating age, about the question whether Christians were under a religious obligation to rest from labour on one day in the week; and it is well known that the chief Reformers, both here and on the continent, denied the existence of any such obligation. Suppose then that, in 1546, Parliament had made a law that there should thenceforth be no distinction between the Sunday and any other day. Now, Sir, our opponents, if they are consistent with themselves, must hold that such a law would have immensely increased the wealth of the country and the remuneration of the working man. What an effect, if their principles be sound, must have been produced by the addition of one sixth to the time of labour! What an increase of production! What a rise of wages! How utterly unable must the foreign artisan, who still had his days of festivity and of repose, have found himself to maintain a competition with a people whose shops were open, whose markets were crowded, whose spades, and axes, and planes, and hods, and anvils, and looms were at work from morning till night on three hundred and sixty-five days a year! The Sundays of three hundred years make up fifty years of our working days. We know what the industry of fifty years can do. We know what marvels the industry of the last fifty years has wrought. The arguments of my honorable friend irresistibly lead us to this conclusion, that if, during the last three centuries, the Sunday had not been observed as a day of rest, we should have been a far richer, a far more highly civilised people than we now are, and that the labouring class especially would have been far better off than at present. But does he, does any Member of the House, seriously believe that this would have been the case? For my own part, I have not the smallest doubt that, if we and our ancestors had, during the last three centuries, worked just as hard on the Sundays as on the week days, we should have been at this moment a poorer people and a less civilised people than we are; that there would have been less production than there has been, that the wages of the labourer would have been lower than they are, and that some other nation would have been now making cotton stuffs and woollen stuffs and cutlery for the whole world.

Of course, Sir, I do not mean to say that a man will not produce more in a week by working seven days than by working six days. But I very much doubt whether, at the end of the year, he will generally have produced more by working seven days a week than by working six days a week; and I firmly believe that, at the end of twenty years, he will have produced much less by working seven days a week than by working six days a week. In the same manner I do not deny that a factory child will produce more, in a single day, by working twelve hours than by working ten hours, and by working fifteen hours than by working twelve hours. But I do deny that a great society in which children work fifteen, or even twelve hours a day, will, in the lifetime of a generation, produce as much as if those children had worked less. If we consider man merely in a commercial point of view, if we consider him merely as a machine for the production of worsted and calico, let us not forget what a piece of mechanism he is, how fearfully and wonderfully made. We do not treat a fine horse or a sagacious dog exactly as we treat a spinning jenny. Nor will any slave-holder, who has sense enough to know his own interest, treat his human chattels exactly as he treats his horses and his dogs. And would you treat the free labourer of England like a mere wheel or pulley? Rely on it that intense labour, beginning too early in life, continued too long every day, stunting the growth of the body, stunting the growth of the mind, leaving no time for healthful exercise, leaving no time for intellectual culture, must impair all those high qualities which have made our country great. Your overworked boys will become a feeble and ignoble race of men, the parents of a more feeble and more ignoble progeny; nor will it be long before the deterioration of the labourer will injuriously affect those very interests to which his physical and moral energies have been sacrificed. On the other hand, a day of rest recurring in every week, two or three hours of leisure, exercise, innocent amusement or useful study, recurring every day, must improve the whole man, physically, morally, intellectually; and the improvement of the man will improve all that the man produces. Why is it, Sir, that the Hindoo cotton manufacturer, close to whose door the cotton grows, cannot, in the bazaar of his own town, maintain a competition with the English cotton manufacturer, who has to send thousands of miles for the raw material, and who has then to send the wrought material thousands of miles to market? You will say that it is owing to the excellence of our machinery. And to what is the excellence of our machinery owing? How many of the improvements which have been made in our machinery do we owe to the ingenuity and patient thought of working men? Adam Smith tells us in the first chapter of his great work, that you can hardly go to a factory without seeing some very pretty machine,—that is his expression, —devised by some labouring man. Hargraves, the inventor of the spinning jenny, was a common artisan. Crompton, the inventor of the mule jenny, was a working man. How many hours of the labour of children would do so much for our manufactures as one of these improvements has done? And in what sort of society are such improvements most likely to be made? Surely in a society in which the faculties of the working people are developed by education. How long will you wait before any negro, working under the lash in Louisiana, will contrive a better machinery for squeezing the sugar canes? My honorable friend seems to me, in all his reasonings about the commercial prosperity of nations, to overlook entirely the chief cause on which that prosperity depends. What is it, Sir, that makes the great difference between country and country? Not the exuberance of soil; not the mildness of climate; not mines, nor havens, nor rivers. These things are indeed valuable when put to their proper use by human intelligence: but human intelligence can do much without them; and they without human intelligence can do nothing. They exist in the highest degree in regions of which the inhabitants are few, and squalid, and barbarous, and naked, and starving; while on sterile rocks, amidst unwholesome marshes, and under inclement skies, may be found immense populations, well fed, well lodged, well clad, well governed. Nature meant Egypt and Sicily to be the gardens of the world. They once were so. Is it anything in the earth or in the air that makes Scotland more prosperous than Egypt, that makes Holland more prosperous than Sicily? No; it was the Scotchman that made Scotland: it was the Dutchman that made Holland. Look at North America. Two centuries ago the sites on which now arise mills, and hotels, and banks, and colleges, and churches, and the Senate Houses of flourishing commonwealths, were deserts abandoned to the panther and the bear. What has made the change? Was it the rich mould, or the redundant rivers? No: the prairies were as fertile, the Ohio and the Hudson were as broad and as full then as now. Was the improvement the effect of some great transfer of capital from the old world to the new? No: the emigrants generally carried out with them no more than a pittance; but they carried out the English heart, and head, and arm; and the English heart and head and arm turned the wilderness into cornfield and orchard, and the huge trees of the primeval forest into cities and fleets. Man, man is the great instrument that produces wealth. The natural difference between Campania and Spitzbergen is trifling when compared with the difference between a country inhabited by men full of bodily and mental vigour, and a country inhabited by men sunk in bodily and mental decrepitude. Therefore it is that we are not poorer but richer, because we have, through many ages, rested from our labour one day in seven. That day is not lost. While industry is suspended, while the plough lies in the furrow, while the Exchange is silent, while no smoke ascends from the factory, a process is going on quite as important to the wealth of nations as any process which is performed on more busy days. Man, the machine of machines, the machine compared with which all the contrivances of the Watts and the Arkwrights are worthless, is repairing and winding up, so that he returns to his labours on the Monday with clearer intellect, with livelier spirits, with renewed corporal vigour. Never will I believe that what makes a population stronger, and healthier, and wiser, and better, can ultimately make it poorer. You try to frighten us by telling us that, in some German factories, the young work seventeen hours in the twenty-four, that they work so hard that among thousands there is not one who grows to such a stature that he can be admitted into the army; and you ask whether, if we pass this bill, we can possibly hold our own against such competition as this? Sir, I laugh at the thought of such competition. If ever we are forced to yield the foremost place among commercial nations, we shall yield it, not to a race of degenerate dwarfs, but to some people preeminently vigorous in body and in mind.

For these reasons, Sir, I approve of the principle of this bill, and shall, without hesitation, vote for the second reading. To what extent we ought to reduce the hours of labour is a question of more difficulty. I think that we are in the situation of a physician who has satisfied himself that there is a disease, and that there is a specific medicine for the disease, but who is not certain what quantity of that medicine the patient's constitution will bear. Such a physician would probably administer his remedy by small doses, and carefully watch its operation. I cannot help thinking that, by at once reducing the hours of labour from twelve to ten, we should hazard too much. The change is great, and ought to be cautiously and gradually made. Suppose that there should be an immediate fall of wages, which is not impossible. Might there not be a violent reaction? Might not the public take up a notion that our legislation had been erroneous in principle, though, in truth, our error would have been an error, not of principle, but merely of degree? Might not Parliament be induced to retrace its steps? Might we not find it difficult to maintain even the present limitation? The wisest course would, in my opinion, be to reduce the hours of labour from twelve to eleven, to observe the effect of that experiment, and if, as I hope and believe, the result should be satisfactory, then to make a further reduction from eleven to ten. This is a question, however, which will be with more advantage considered when we are in Committee.

One word, Sir, before I sit down, in answer to my noble friend near me.[4] He seems to think that this bill is ill timed. I own that I cannot agree with him. We carried up on Monday last to the bar of the Lords a bill which will remove the most hateful and pernicious restriction that ever was laid on trade. Nothing can be more proper than to apply, in the same week, a remedy to a great evil of a directly opposite kind. As lawgivers, we have two great faults to confess and to repair. We have done that which we ought not to have done. We have left undone that which we ought to have done. We have regulated that which we should have left to regulate itself. We have left unregulated that which we were bound to regulate. We have given to some branches of industry a protection which has proved their bane. We have with-

4. Lord Morpeth.

held from public health and public morals the protection which was their due. We have prevented the labourer from buying his loaf where he could get it cheapest; but we have not prevented him from ruining his body and mind by premature and immoderate toil. I hope that we have seen the last both of a vicious system of interference and of a vicious system of non-interference, and that our poorer countrymen will no longer have reason to attribute their sufferings either to our meddling or to our neglect.

Education

In 1847 elementary education in England was, as it had always been, in the hands of religious societies and was conducted on the voluntary system. The rapid growth of an industrial population in the nineteenth century made a new system imperative, but the efforts to establish it roused strong prejudices and raised many questions. Ought the state to intervene in education? Should education be secular? And compulsory? And would not the state favor Church of England schools over those run by nonconformists? The government had already established a committee of the Privy Council to administer a parliamentary grant in aid of elementary education; Macaulay's speech was made in support of a measure to increase that grant to £100,000. The speech shows, like that on the Ten Hours Bill, Macaulay's growing willingness, based on good sense and good feeling, to allow the state to intervene in matters previously thought to be outside its scope. In this he was a little ahead of the general opinion. The proposal for an increased grant was passed, but a bill for a genuinely national plan of elementary education did not become law until 1870.

You will not wonder, Sir, that I am desirous to catch your eye this evening. The first duty which I performed, as a Member of the Committee of Council which is charged with the superintendence

Delivered April 19, 1847.

of public instruction, was to give my hearty assent to the plan which the honorable Member for Finsbury calls on the House to condemn. I am one of those who have been accused in every part of the kingdom, and who are now accused in Parliament, of aiming, under specious pretences, a blow at the civil and religious liberties of the people. It is natural therefore that I should seize the earliest opportunity of vindicating myself from so grave a charge.

The honorable Member for Finsbury must excuse me if, in the remarks which I have to offer to the House, I should not follow very closely the order of his speech. The truth is that a mere answer to his speech would be no defence of myself or of my colleagues. I am surprised, I own, that a man of his acuteness and ability should, on such an occasion, have made such a speech. The country is excited from one end to the other by a great question of principle. On that question the Government has taken one side. The honorable Member stands forth as the chosen and trusted champion of a great party which takes the other side. We expected to hear from him a full exposition of the views of those in whose name he speaks. But, to our astonishment, he has scarcely even alluded to the controversy which has divided the whole nation. He has entertained us with sarcasms and personal anecdotes: he has talked much about matters of mere detail: but I must say that, after listening with close attention to all that he has said, I am quite unable to discover whether, on the only important point which is in issue, he agrees with us or with that large and active body of Nonconformists which is diametrically opposed to us. He has sate down without dropping one word from which it is possible to discover whether he thinks that education is or that it is not a matter with which the State ought to interfere. Yet that is the question about which the whole nation has, during several weeks, been writing, reading, speaking, hearing, thinking, petitioning, and on which it is now the duty of Parliament to pronounce a decision. That question once settled, there will be, I believe, very little room for dispute. If it be not competent to the State to interfere with the education of the people, the mode of interference recommended by the Committee of Council must of course be condemned. If it be the right and the duty of the State to make provision for the education of the people, the objections made to our plan will, in a very few words, be shown to be frivolous.

I shall take a course very different from that which has been taken by the honorable gentleman. I shall in the clearest manner profess my opinion on that great question of principle which he has studiously evaded; and for my opinion I shall give what seem to me to be unanswerable reasons.

I believe, Sir, that it is the right and the duty of the State to provide means of education for the common people. This proposition seems to me to be implied in every definition that has ever yet been given of the functions of a government. About the extent of those functions there has been much difference of opinion among ingenious men. There are some who hold that it is the business of a government to meddle with every part of the system of human life, to regulate trade by bounties and prohibitions, to regulate expenditure by sumptuary laws, to regulate literature by a censorship, to regulate religion by an inquisition. Others go to the opposite extreme, and assign to Government a very narrow sphere of action. But the very narrowest sphere that ever was assigned to governments by any school of political philosophy is quite wide enough for my purpose. On one point all the disputants are agreed. They unanimously acknowledge that it is the duty of every government to take order for giving security to the persons and property of the members of the community.

This being admitted, can it be denied that the education of the common people is a most effectual means of securing our persons and our property? Let Adam Smith answer that question for me. His authority, always high, is, on this subject, entitled to peculiar respect, because he extremely disliked busy, prying, interfering governments. He was for leaving literature, arts, sciences, to take care of themselves. He was not friendly to ecclesiastical establishments. He was of opinion, that the State ought not to meddle with the education of the rich. But he has expressly told us that a distinction is to be made, particularly in a commercial and highly civilised society, between the education of the rich and the education of the poor. The education of the poor, he says, is a matter which deeply concerns the commonwealth. Just as the magistrate ought to interfere for the purpose of preventing the leprosy from spreading among the people, he ought to interfere for the purpose of stopping the progress of the moral distempers which are inseparable from ignorance. Nor can this duty be neglected without danger to the public peace. If you leave the multitude uninstructed, there is serious risk that religious animosities may produce the most dreadful disorders. The most dreadful disorders! Those are Adam Smith's own words; and prophetic words they were. Scarcely had he given this warning to our rulers when his prediction was fulfilled in a manner never to be forgotten. I speak of the No Popery riots of 1780. I do not know that I could find in all history a stronger proof of the proposition, that the ignorance of the common people makes the property, the limbs, the lives of all classes insecure. Without the shadow of a grievance, at the summons of a madman, a hundred thousand people rise in insurrection. During a whole week, there is anarchy in the greatest and wealthiest of European cities. The parliament is besieged. Your predecessor sits trembling in his chair, and expects every moment to see the door beaten in by the ruffians whose roar he hears all round the house. The peers are pulled out of their coaches. The bishops in their lawn are forced to fly over the tiles. The chapels of foreign ambassadors, buildings made sacred by the law of nations are destroyed. The house of the Chief Justice is demolished. The little children of the Prime Minister are taken out of their beds and laid in their night clothes on the table of the Horse Guards, the only safe asylum from the fury of the rabble. The prisons are opened. Highwaymen, housebreakers, murderers, come forth to swell the mob by which they have been set free. Thirty-six fires are blazing at once in London. Then comes the retribution. Count up all the wretches who were shot, who were hanged, who were crushed, who drank themselves to death at the rivers of gin which ran down Holborn Hill; and you will find that battles have been lost and won with a smaller sacrifice of life. And what was the cause of this calamity, a calamity which, in the history of London, ranks with the great plague and the great fire? The cause was the ignorance of a population which had been suffered, in the neighbourhood of palaces, theatres, temples, to grow up as rude and stupid as any tribe of tattooed cannibals in New Zealand, I might say as any drove of beasts in Smithfield Market.

The instance is striking: but it is not solitary. To the same cause are to be ascribed the riots of Nottingham, the sack of Bristol, all the outrages of Ludd, and Swing, and Rebecca, beautiful and costly machinery broken to pieces in Yorkshire, barns and haystacks blazing in Kent, fences and buildings pulled down in Wales. Could such things have been done in a country in which the mind of the labourer had been opened by education, in which he had been taught to find pleasure in the exercise of his intellect, taught to revere his Maker, taught to respect legitimate authority, and taught at the same time to seek the redress of real wrongs by peaceful and constitutional means?

This then is my argument. It is the duty of Government to protect our persons and property from danger. The gross ignorance of the common people is a principal cause of danger to our persons and property. Therefore, it is the duty of the Government to take care that the common people shall not be grossly ignorant.

And what is the alternative? It is universally allowed that, by some means, Government must protect our persons and property. If you take away education, what means do you leave? You leave means such as only necessity can justify, means which inflict a fearful amount of pain, not only on the guilty, but on the innocent who are connected with the guilty. You leave guns and bayonets, stocks and whipping-posts, treadmills, solitary cells, penal colonies, gibbets. See then how the case stands. Here is an end which, as we all agree, governments are bound to attain. There are only two ways of attaining it. One of those ways is by making men better, and wiser, and happier. The other way is by making them infamous and miserable. Can it be doubted which way we ought to prefer? Is it not strange, is it not almost incredible, that pious and benevolent men should gravely propound the doctrine that the magistrate is bound to punish and at the same time bound not to teach? To me it seems quite clear that whoever has a right to hang has a right to educate. Can we think without shame and remorse that more than half of those wretches who have been tied up at Newgate in our time might have been living happily, that more than half of those who are now in our gaols might have been enjoying liberty and using that liberty well, that such a hell on earth as Norfolk Island need never have existed, if we had expended in training honest men but a small part of what we have expended in hunting and torturing rogues.

I would earnestly entreat every gentleman to look at a report which is contained in the Appendix to the First Volume of the Minutes of the Committee of Council. I speak of the report made by Mr. Seymour Tremenheare on the state of that part of Monmouthshire which is inhabited by a population chiefly employed in mining. He found that, in this district, towards the close of 1839, out of eleven thousand children who were of an age to attend school, eight thousand never went to any school at all, and that most of the remaining three thousand might almost as well have gone to no school as to the squalid hovels in which men who ought themselves to have been learners pretended to teach. In general these men had only one qualification for their employment; and that was their utter unfitness for every other employment. They were disabled miners, or broken hucksters. In their schools all was stench, and noise, and confusion. Now and then the clamour of the boys was silenced for two minutes by the furious menaces of the master; but it soon broke out again. The instruction given was of the lowest kind. Not one school in ten was provided with a single map. This is the way in which you suffered the minds of a great population to be formed. And now for the effects of your negligence. The barbarian inhabitants of this region rise in an insane rebellion against the Government. They come pouring down their valleys to Newport. They fire on the Queen's troops. They wound a magistrate. The soldiers fire in return; and too many of these wretched men pay with their lives the penalty of their crime. But is the crime theirs alone? Is it strange that they should listen to the only teaching that they had? How can you, who took no pains to instruct them, blame them for giving ear to the demagogue who took pains to delude them? We put them down, of course. We punished them. We had no choice. Order must be maintained; property must be protected; and, since we had omitted to take the best way of keeping these people quiet, we were under the necessity of keeping them quiet by the dread of the sword and the halter. But could any necessity be more cruel? And which of us would run the risk of being placed under such necessity a second time?

I say, therefore, that the education of the people is not only a means, but the best means, of attaining that which all allow to be a chief end of government; and, if this be so, it passes my faculties to understand how any man can gravely contend that Government has nothing to do with the education of the people.

My confidence in my opinion is strengthened when I recollect that I hold that opinion in common with all the greatest lawgivers, statesmen, and political philosophers of all nations and ages, with all the most illustrious champions of civil and spiritual freedom, and especially with those men whose names were once held in the highest veneration by the Protestant Dissenters of England. I might cite many of the most venerable names of the old world; but I would rather cite the example of that country which the supporters of the Voluntary system here are always recommending to us as a pattern. Go back to the days when the little society which has expanded into the opulent and enlightened commonwealth of Massachusetts began to exist. Our modern Dissenters will scarcely, I think, venture to speak contumeliously of those Puritans whose spirit Laud and his High Commission Court could not subdue, of those Puritans who were willing to leave home and kindred, and all the comforts and refinements of civilised life, to cross the ocean, to fix their abode in forests among wild beasts and wild men, rather than commit the sin of performing, in the House of God, one gesture which they believed to be displeasing to Him. Did those brave exiles think it inconsistent with civil or religious freedom that the State should take charge of the education of the people? No, Sir; one of the earliest laws enacted by the Puritan colonists was that every township, as soon as the Lord had increased it to the number of fifty houses, should appoint one to teach all children to write and read, and that every township of a hundred houses should set up a grammar school. Nor have the descendants of those who made this law ever ceased to hold that the public authorities were bound to provide the means of public instruction. Nor is this doctrine confined to New England. "Educate the people" was the first admonition addressed by Penn to the colony which he founded. "Educate the people" was the legacy of Washington to the nation which he had saved. "Educate the people" was the unceasing exhortation of Jefferson; and I quote Jefferson with peculiar pleasure, because, of all the eminent men that have ever lived, Adam Smith himself not excepted, Jefferson was the one who most abhorred everything like meddling on the part of governments. Yet the chief business of his later years was to establish a good system of State education in Virginia.

And, against such authority as this, what have you who take the other side to show? Can you mention a single great philosopher, a single man distinguished by his zeal for liberty, humanity, and truth, who, from the beginning of the world down to the time of this present Parliament, ever held your doctrines? You can oppose to the unanimous voice of all the wise and good, of all ages, and of both hemispheres, nothing but a clamour which was first heard a few months ago, a clamour in which you cannot join without condemning, not only all whose memory you profess to hold in reverence, but even your former selves.

This new theory of politics has at least the merit of originality. It may be fairly stated thus. All men have hitherto been utterly in the wrong as to the nature and objects of civil government. The great truth, hidden from every preceding generation, and at length revealed, in the year 1846, to some highly respectable ministers and elders of dissenting congregations, is this. Government is simply a great hangman. Government ought to do nothing except by harsh and degrading means. The one business of Government is to handcuff, and lock up, and scourge, and shoot, and stab, and strangle. It is odious tyranny in a government to attempt to prevent crime by informing the understanding and elevating the moral feeling of a people. A statesman may see hamlets turned, in the course of one generation, into great seaport towns and manufacturing towns. He may know that on the character of the vast population which is collected in those wonderful towns, depends the prosperity, the peace, the very existence of society. But he must not think of forming that character. He is an enemy of public liberty if he attempts to prevent those hundreds of thousands of his countrymen from becoming mere Yahoos. He may, indeed, build barrack after barrack to overawe them. If they break out into insurrection, he may send cavalry to sabre them: he may mow them down with grape shot: he may hang them, draw them, quarter them, anything but teach them. He may see, and may shudder as he sees, throughout large rural districts, millions of infants growing up from infancy to manhood as ignorant, as mere slaves of sensual appetite, as the beasts that perish. No matter. He is a traitor to the cause of civil and religious freedom if he does not look on with folded arms, while absurd hopes and evil passions ripen in that rank soil. He must wait for the day of his harvest. He must wait till the Jaquerie comes, till farm houses are burning, till threshing machines are broken in pieces; and then begins his business, which is simply to send one poor ignorant savage to the county gaol, and another to the antipodes, and a third to the gallows.

Such, Sir, is the new theory of government which was first propounded, in the year 1846, by some men of high note among the Nonconformists of England. It is difficult to understand how men of excellent abilities and excellent intentions,—and there are, I readily admit, such men among those who hold this theory, —can have fallen into so absurd and pernicious an error. One explanation only occurs to me. This is, I am inclined to believe, an instance of the operation of the great law of reaction. We have just come victorious out of a long and fierce contest for the liberty of trade. While that contest was undecided, much was said and written about the advantages of free competition, and about the danger of suffering the State to regulate matters which should be left to individuals. There has consequently arisen in the minds of persons who are led by words, and who are little in the habit of making distinctions, a disposition to apply to political questions and moral questions principles which are sound only when applied to commercial questions. These people, not content with having forced the Government to surrender a province wrongfuly usurped, now wish to wrest from the Government a domain held by a right which was never before questioned, and which cannot be questioned with the smallest show of reason. "If," they say, "free competition is a good thing in trade, it must surely be a good thing in education. The supply of other commodities, of sugar, for example, is left to adjust itself to the demand; and the consequence is, that we are better supplied with sugar than if the Government undertook to supply us. Why then should we doubt that the supply of instruction will, without the intervention of the Government, be found equal to the demand?"

Never was there a more false analogy. Whether a man is well supplied with sugar is a matter which concerns himself alone.

But whether he is well supplied with instruction is a matter which concerns his neighbours and the State. If he cannot afford to pay for sugar, he must go without sugar. But it is by no means fit that, because he cannot afford to pay for education, he should go without education. Between the rich and their instructors there may, as Adam Smith says, be free trade. The supply of music masters and Italian masters may be left to adjust itself to the demand. But what is to become of the millions who are too poor to procure without assistance the services of a decent school-master? We have indeed heard it said that even these millions will be supplied with teachers by the free competition of benevolent individuals who will vie with each other in rendering this service to mankind. No doubt there are many benevolent individuals who spend their time and money most laudably in setting up and supporting schools; and you may say, if you please, that there is, among these respectable persons, a competition to do good. But do not be imposed upon by words. Do not belive that this competition resembles the competition which is produced by the desire of wealth and by the fear of ruin. There is a great difference, be assured, between the rivalry of philan-thropists and the rivalry of grocers. The grocer knows that, if his wares are worse than those of other grocers, he shall soon go before the Bankrupt Court, and his wife and children will have no refuge but the workhouse: he knows that, if his shop obtains an honorable celebrity, he shall be able to set up a carriage and buy a villa: and this knowledge impels him to exertions com-pared with which the exertions of even every charitable people to serve the poor are but languid. It would be strange infatuation indeed to legislate on the supposition that a man cares for his fellow creatures as much as he cares for himself.

Unless, Sir, I greatly deceive myself, those arguments, which show that the Government ought not to leave to private people the task of providing for the national defence, will equally show that the Government ought not to leave to private people the task of providing for national education. On this subject, Mr. Hume has laid down the general law with admirable good sense and perspicuity. I mean David Hume, not the Member for Montrose, though that honorable gentleman will, I am confident, assent to the doctrine propounded by his illustrious namesake. David

Hume, Sir, justly says that most of the arts and trades which exist in the world produce so much advantage and pleasure to individuals, that the magistrate may safely leave it to individuals to encourage those arts and trades. But he adds that there are callings which, though they are highly useful, nay, absolutely necessary to society, yet do not administer to the peculiar pleasure or profit of any individual. The military calling is an instance. Here, says Hume, the government must interfere. It must take on itself to regulate these callings, and to stimulate the industry of the persons who follow these callings by pecuniary and honorary rewards.

Now, Sir, it seems to me that, on the same principle on which Government ought to superintend and to reward the soldier, Government ought to superintend and to reward the schoolmaster. I mean, of course, the schoolmaster of the common people. That his calling is useful, that his calling is necessary, will hardly be denied. Yet it is clear that his services will not be adequately remunerated if he is left to be remunerated by those whom he teaches, or by the voluntary contributions of the charitable. Is this disputed? Look at the facts. You tell us that schools will multiply and flourish exceedingly, if the Government will only abstain from interfering with them. Has not the Government long abstained from interfering with them? Has not everything been left, through many years, to individual exertion? If it were true that education, like trade, thrives most where the magistrate meddles least, the common people of England would now be the best educated in the world. Our schools would be model schools. Every one would have a well chosen little library, excellent maps, a small but neat apparatus for experiments in natural philosophy. A grown person unable to read and write would be pointed at like Giant O'Brien or the Polish Count. Our schoolmasters would be as eminently expert in all that relates to teaching as our cutlers, our cottonspinners, our engineers are allowed to be in their respective callings. They would, as a class, be held in high consideration; and their gains would be such that it would be easy to find men of respectable character and attainments to fill up vacancies.

Now, is this the case? Look at the charges of the judges, at the resolutions of the grand juries, at the reports of public officers, at the reports of voluntary associations. All tell the same sad and ignominious story. Take the reports of the Inspectors of Prisons. In the House of Correction at Hertford, of seven hundred prisoners one half could not read at all; only eight could read and write well. Of eight thousand prisoners who had passed through Maidstone gaol only fifty could read and write well. In Coldbath Fields Prison, the proportion that could read and write well seems to have been still smaller. Turn from the registers of prisoners to the registers of marriages. You will find that about a hundred and thirty thousand couples were married in the year 1844. More than forty thousand of the bridegrooms and more than sixty thousand of the brides did not sign their names, but made their marks. Nearly one third of the men and nearly one half of the women, who are in the prime of life, who are to be the parents of the Englishmen of the next generation, who are to bear a chief part in forming the minds of the Englishmen of the next generation, cannot write their own names. Remember, too, that, though people who cannot write their own names must be grossly ignorant, people may write their own names and yet have very little knowledge. Tens of thousands who were able to write their names had in all probability received only the wretched education of a common day school. We know what such a school too often is; a room crusted with filth, without light, without air, with a heap of fuel in one corner and a brood of chickens in another; the only machinery of instruction a dog-eared spellingbook and a broken slate; the masters the refuse of all other callings, discarded footmen, ruined pedlars, men who cannot work a sum in the rule of three, men who cannot write a common letter without blunders, men who do not know whether the earth is a sphere or a cube, men who do not know whether Jerusalem is in Asia or America. And to such men, men to whom none of us would entrust the key of his cellar, we have entrusted the mind of the rising generation, and, with the mind of the rising generation, the freedom, the happiness, the glory of our country.

Do you question the accuracy of this description? I will produce evidence to which I am sure that you will not venture to take an exception. Every gentleman here knows, I suppose, how important a place the Congregational Union holds among the

Nonconformists, and how prominent a part Mr. Edward Baines has taken in opposition to State education. A Committee of the Congregational Union drew up last year a report on the subject of education. That report was received by the Union; and the person who moved that it should be received was Mr. Edward Baines. That report contains the following passage: "If it were necessary to disclose facts to such an assembly as this, as to the ignorance and debasement of the neglected portions of our population in towns and rural districts, both adult and juvenile, it could easily be done. Private information communicated to the Board, personal observation and investigation of the various localities, with the published documents of the Registrar General, and the reports of the state of prisons in England and Wales, published by order of the House of Commons, would furnish enough to make us modest in speaking of what has been done for the humbler classes, and make us ashamed that the sons of the soil of England should have been so long neglected, and should present to the enlightened traveller from other shores such a sad spectacle of neglected cultivation, lost mental power, and spiritual degradation." Nothing can be more just. All the information which I have been able to obtain bears out the statements of the Congregational Union. I do believe that the ignorance and degradation of a large part of the community to which we belong ought to make us ashamed of ourselves. I do believe that an enlightened traveller from New York, from Geneva, or from Berlin, would be shocked to see so much barbarism in the close neighbourhood of so much wealth and civilisation. But is it not strange that the very gentlemen who tell us in such emphatic language that the people are shamefully ill educated, should yet persist in telling us that under a system of free competition the people are certain to be excellently educated? Only this morning the opponents of our plan circulated a paper in which they confidently predict that free competition will do all that is necessary, if we will only wait with patience. Wait with patience! Why, we have been waiting ever since the Heptarchy. How much longer are we to wait? Till the year 2847? Or till the year 3847? That the experiment has as yet failed you do not deny. And why should it have failed? Has it been tried in unfavourable circumstances. Not so; it has been tried in the richest, and in the freest, and in the most charitable country in all Europe. Has it been tried on too small a scale? Not so: millions have been subjected to it. Has it been tried during too short a time? Not so: it has been going on during ages. The cause of the failure then is plain. Our whole system has been unsound. We have applied the principle of free competition to a case to which that principle is not applicable.

But, Sir, if the state of the southern part of our island has furnished me with one strong argument, the state of the northern part furnishes me with another argument, which is, if possible, still more decisive. A hundred and fifty years ago England was one of the best governed and most prosperous countries in the world: Scotland was perhaps the rudest and poorest country that could lay any claim to civilisation. The name of Scotchman was then uttered in this part of the island with contempt. The ablest Scotch statesmen contemplated the degraded state of their poorer countrymen with a feeling approaching to despair. It is well known that Fletcher of Saltoun, a brave and accomplished man, a man who had drawn his sword for liberty, who had suffered proscription and exile for liberty, was so much disgusted and dismayed by the misery, the ignorance, the idleness, the lawlessness of the common people, that he proposed to make many thousands of them slaves. Nothing, he thought, but the discipline which kept order and inforced exertion among the negroes of a sugar colony, nothing but the lash and the stocks, could reclaim the vagabonds who infested every part of Scotland from their indolent and predatory habits, and compel them to support themselves by steady labour. He therefore, soon after the Revolution, published a pamphlet, in which he earnestly, and, as I believe, from the mere impulse of humanity and patriotism, recommended to the Estates of the Realm this sharp remedy, which alone, as he conceived, could remove the evil. Within a few months after the publication of that pamphlet a very different remedy was applied. The Parliament which sate at Edinburgh passed an act for the establishment of parochial schools. What followed? An improvement such as the world had never seen took place in the moral and intellectual character of the people. Soon, in spite of the rigour of the climate, in spite of the sterility of the earth, Scotland became a country which had no reason to envy the fairest portions of the globe. Wherever the Scotchman went,—and there were few parts of the world to which he did not go,—he carried his superiority with him. If he was admitted into a public office, he worked his way up to the highest post. If he got employment in a brewery or a factory, he was soon the foreman. If he took a shop, his trade was the best in the street. If he enlisted in the army, he became a colour-serjeant. If he went to a colony, he was the most thriving planter there. The Scotchman of the seventeenth century had been spoken of in London as we speak of the Esquimaux. The Scotchman of the eighteenth century was an object, not of scorn, but of envy. The cry was that, wherever he came, he got more than his share; that, mixed with Englishmen or mixed with Irishmen, he rose to the top as surely as oil rises to the top of water. And what had produced this great revolution? The Scotch air was still as cold, the Scotch rocks were still as bare as ever. All the natural qualities of the Scotchman were still what they had been when learned and benevolent men advised that he should be flogged, like a beast of burden, to his daily task. But the State had given him an education. That education was not, it is true, in all respects what it should have been. But, such as it was, it had done more for the bleak and dreary shores of the Forth and the Clyde than the richest of soils and the most genial of climates had done for Capua and Tarentum. Is there one member of this House, however strongly he may hold the doctrine that the Government ought not to interfere with the education of the people, who will stand up and say that, in his opinion, the Scotch would now have been a happier and a more enlightened people if they had been left, during the last five generations, to find instruction for themselves?

I say then, Sir, that, if the science of Government be an experimental science, this question is decided. We are in a condition to perform the inductive process according to the rules laid down in the Novum Organum. We have two nations closely connected, inhabiting the same island, sprung from the same blood, speaking the same language, governed by the same Sovereign and the same Legislature, holding essentially the same religious faith, having the same allies and the same enemies. Of these two nations one was, a hundred and fifty years ago, as respects opulence and civilisation, in the highest rank among European communities, the other in the lowest rank. The opulent and highly civilised nation leaves the education of the people to free competition. In the poor and half barbarous nation the education of the people is undertaken by the State. The result is that the first are last and the last first. The common people of Scotland,—it is vain to disguise the truth,—have passed the common people of England. Free competition, tried with every advantage, has produced effects of which, as the Congregational Union tells us, we ought to be ashamed, and which must lower us in the opinion of every intelligent foreigner. State education, tried under every disadvantage, has produced an improvement to which it would be difficult to find a parallel in any age or country. Such an experiment as this would be regarded as conclusive in surgery or chemistry, and ought, I think, to be regarded as equally conclusive in politics.

These, Sir, are the reasons which have satisfied me that it is the duty of the State to educate the people. Being firmly convinced of that truth, I shall not shrink from proclaiming it here and elsewhere, in defiance of the loudest clamour that agitators can raise. The remainder of my task is easy. For, if the great principle for which I have been contending is admitted, the objections which have been made to the details of our plan will vanish fast. I will deal with those objections in the order in which they stand in the amendment moved by the honorable member for Finsbury.

First among his objections he places the cost. Surely, Sir, no person who admits that it is our duty to train the minds of the rising generation can think a hundred thousand pounds too large a sum for that purpose. If we look at the matter in the lowest point of view, if we consider human beings merely as producers of wealth, the difference between an intelligent and a stupid population, estimated in pounds, shillings, and pence, exceeds a hundredfold the proposed outlay. Nor is this all. For every pound that you save in education, you will spend five in prosecutions, in prisons, in penal settlements. I cannot believe that the House, having never grudged anything that was asked for the purpose of maintaining order and protecting property by means of pain and fear, will begin to be niggardly as soon as it is proposed to effect the same objects by making the people wiser and better.

The next objection made by the honorable member to our plan is that it will increase the influence of the Crown. This sum of a hundred thousand pounds may, he apprehends, be employed in corruption and jobbing. Those schoolmasters who vote for ministerial candidates will obtain a share of the grant: those schoolmasters who vote for opponents of the ministry will apply for assistance in vain. Sir, the honorable member never would have made this objection if he had taken the trouble to understand the minutes which he has condemned. We propose to place this part of the public expenditure under checks which must make such abuses as the honorable Member anticipates morally impossible. Not only will there be those ordinary checks which are thought sufficient to prevent the misapplication of the many millions annually granted for the army, the navy, the ordnance, the civil government: not only must the Ministers of the Crown come every year to this House for a vote, and be prepared to render an account of the manner in which they have laid out what had been voted in the preceding year; but, when they have satisfied the House, when they have got their vote, they will still be unable to distribute the money at their discretion. Whatever they may do for any schoolmaster must be done in concert with those persons who, in the district where the schoolmaster lives, take an interest in education, and contribute out of their private means to the expense of education. When the honorable gentleman is afraid that we shall corrupt the schoolmasters, he forgets, first, that we do not appoint the schoolmasters; secondly, that we cannot dismiss the schoolmasters; thirdly, that managers who are altogether independent of us can, without our consent, dismiss the schoolmasters; and, fourthly that without the recommendation of those managers we can give nothing to the schoolmasters. Observe, too, that such a recommendation will not be one of those recommendations which goodnatured easy people are too apt to give to everybody who asks; nor will it at all resemble those recommendations which the Secretary of the Treasury is in the habit of receiving. For every pound which we pay on the recommendation of the managers, the managers themselves must pay two pounds. They must also provide the schoolmaster with a house out of their own funds before they can obtain for him a grant from the public funds. What chance of jobbing is there here? It is common enough, no doubt, for a Member of Parliament who votes with Government to ask that one of those who zealously supported him at the last election may have a place in the Excise or the Customs. But such a member would soon cease to solicit if the answer were, "Your friend shall have a place of fifty pounds a year, if you will give him a house and settle on him an income of a hundred a year." What chance then, I again ask, is there of jobbing? What, say some of the dissenters of Leeds, is to prevent a Tory Government, a High Church Government, from using this parliamentary grant to corrupt the schoolmasters of our borough, and to induce them to use all their influence in favour of a Tory and High Church candidate? Why, Sir, the dissenters of Leeds themselves have the power to prevent it. Let them subscribe to the schools: let them take a share in the management of the schools: let them refuse to recommend to the Committee of Council any schoolmaster whom they suspect of having voted at any election from corrupt motives: and the thing is done. Our plan, in truth, is made up of checks. My only doubt is whether the checks may not be found too numerous and too stringent. On our general conduct there is the ordinary check, the parliamentary check. And, as respects those minute details which it is impossible that this House can investigate, we shall be checked, in every town and in every rural district, by boards consisting of independent men zealous in the cause of education.

The truth is, Sir, that those who clamour most loudly against our plan, have never thought of ascertaining what it is. I see that a gentleman, who ought to have known better, has not been ashamed publicly to tell the world that our plan will cost the nation two millions a year, and will paralyse all the exertions of individuals to educate the people. These two assertions are uttered in one breath. And yet, if he who made them had read our minutes before he railed at them, he would have seen that his predictions are contradictory; that they cannot both be fulfilled; that, if individuals do not exert themselves, the country will have to pay nothing; and that, if the country has to pay two millions, it will be because individuals have exerted themselves with such wonderful, such incredible, vigour, as to raise four millions by voluntary contributions.

The next objection made by the honorable Member for Finsbury is that we have acted unconstitutionally, and have incroached on the functions of Parliament. The Committee of Council he seems to consider as an unlawful assembly. He calls it sometimes a self elected body and sometimes a self appointed body. Sir, these are words without meaning. The Committee is no more a self elected body than the Board of Trade. It is a body appointed by the Queen; and in appointing it Her Majesty has exercised, under the advice of her responsible Ministers, a prerogative as old as the monarchy. But, says the honorable member, the constitutional course would have been to apply for an Act of Parliament. On what ground? Nothing but an Act of Parliament can legalise that which is illegal. But whoever heard of an Act of Parliament to legalise what was already beyond all dispute legal? Of course, if we wished to send aliens out of the country, or to detain disaffected persons in custody without bringing them to trial, we must obtain an Act of Parliament empowering us to do so. But why should we ask for an Act of Parliament to empower us to do what anybody may do, what the honorable Member for Finsbury may do? Is there any doubt that he or anybody else may subscribe to a school, give a stipend to a monitor, or settle a retiring pension on a preceptor who has done good service? What any of the Queen's subjects may do the Queen may do. Suppose that her privy purse were so large that she could afford to employ a hundred thousand pounds in this beneficent manner; would an Act of Parliament be necessary to enable her to do so? Every part of our plan may lawfully be carried into execution by any person, Sovereign or subject, who has the inclination and the money. We have not the money; and for the money we come, in a strictly constitutional manner, to the House of Commons. The course which we have taken is in conformity with all precedent, as well as with all principle. There are military schools. No Act of Parliament was necessary to authorise the establishing of such schools. All that was necessary was a grant of money to defray the charge. When I was Secretary at War it was my duty to bring under Her Majesty's notice the situation of the female children of her soldiers. Many such children accompanied every regiment, and their education was grievously neglected. Her Majesty was graciously pleased to sign a warrant by which a girls' school was attached to each corps. No Act of Parliament was necessary. For to set up a school where girls might be taught to read, and write, and sew, and cook, was perfectly legal already. I might have set it up myself, if I had been rich enough. All that I had to ask from Parliament was the money. But I ought to beg pardon for arguing a point so clear.

The next objection to our plans is that they interfere with the religious convictions of Her Majesty's subjects. It has been sometimes insinuated, but it has never been proved, that the Committee of Council has shown undue favour to the Established Church. Sir, I have carefully read and considered the minutes; and I wish that every man who has exerted his eloquence against them had done the same. I say that I have carefully read and considered them, and that they seem to me to have been drawn up with exemplary impartiality. The benefits which we offer we offer to people of all religious persuasions alike. The dissenting managers of schools will have equal authority with the managers who belong to the Church. A boy who goes to meeting will be just as eligible to be a monitor, and will receive just as large a stipend, as if he went to the cathedral. The schoolmaster who is a nonconformist and the schoolmaster who is a conformist will enjoy the same emoluments, and will, after the same term of service, obtain, on the same conditions, the same retiring pension. I wish that some gentleman would, instead of using vague phrases about religious liberty and the rights of conscience, answer this plain question. Suppose that in one of our large towns there are four schools, a school connected with the Church, a school connected with the Independents, a Baptist school, and a Wesleyan school; what encouragement, pecuniary or honorary, will, by our plan, be given to the school connected with the Church, and withheld from any of the other three schools? Is it not indeed plain that, if by neglect or maladministration the Church school should get into a bad state, while the dissenting schools flourish, the dissenting schools will receive public money and the Church school will receive none?

It is true, I admit, that, in rural districts which are too poor to support more than one school, the religious community to which the majority belongs will have an advantage over other religious communities. But this is not our fault. If we are as impartial as it is possible to be, you surely do not expect more. If there should be a parish containing nine hundred churchmen and a hundred dissenters, if there should, in that parish, be a school connected with the Church, if the dissenters in that parish should be too poor to set up another school, undoubtedly the school connected with the Church will, in that parish, get all that we give; and the dissenters will get nothing. But observe that there is no partiality to the Church, as the Church, in this arrangement. The churchmen get public money, not because they are churchmen, but because they are the majority. The dissenters get nothing, not because they are dissenters, but because they are a small minority. There are districts where the case will be reversed, where there will be dissenting schools, and no Church schools. In such cases the dissenters will get what we have to give, and the churchmen will get nothing.

But, Sir, I ought not to say that a churchman gets nothing by a system which gives a good education to dissenters, or that a dissenter gets nothing by a system which gives a good education to churchmen. We are not, I hope, so much conformists, or so much nonconformists, as to forget that we are Englishmen and Christians. We all, Churchmen, Presbyterians, Independents, Baptists, Methodists, have an interest in this, that the great body of the people should be rescued from ignorance and barbarism. I mentioned Lord George Gordon's mob. That mob began, it is true, with the Roman Catholics: but, long before the tumults were over, there was not a respectable Protestant in London who was not in fear for his house, for his limbs, for his life, for the lives of those who were dearest to him. The honorable Member for Finsbury says that we call on men to pay for an education from which they derive no benefit. I deny that there is one honest and industrious man in the country who derives no benefit from living among honest and industrious neighbours rather than among rioters and vagabonds. This matter is as much a matter of common concern as the defence of our coast. Suppose that I were to say, "Why do you tax me to fortify Portsmouth? If the people of Portsmouth think that they cannot be safe without bastions and ravelins, let the people of Portsmouth pay the engineers and masons. Why am I to bear the charge of works from which I derive no advantage?" You would answer, and most justly, that there is no man in the island who does not derive advantage from these works, whether he resides within them or not. And, as every man, in whatever part of the island he may live, is bound to contribute to the support of those arsenals which are necessary for our common security, so is every man, to whatever sect he may belong, bound to contribute to the support of those schools on which, not less than on our arsenals, our common security depends.

I now come to the last words of the amendment. The honorable Member for Finsbury is apprehensive that our plan may interfere with the civil rights of Her Majesty's subjects. How a man's civil rights can be prejudiced by his learning to read and write, to multiply and divide, or even by his obtaining some knowledge of history and geography, I do not very well apprehend. One thing is clear, that persons sunk in that ignorance in which, as we are assured by the Congregational Union, great numbers of our countrymen are sunk, can be free only in name. It is hardly necessary for us to appoint a Select Committee for the purpose of inquiring whether knowledge be the ally or the enemy of liberty. He is, I must say, but a short-sighted friend of the common people who is eager to bestow on them a franchise which would make them all-powerful, and yet would withhold from them that instruction without which their power must be a curse to themselves and to the State.

This, Sir, is my defence. From the clamour of our accusers I appeal with confidence to the country to which we must, in no long time, render an account of our stewardship. I appeal with still more confidence to future generations, which, while enjoying all the blessings of an impartial and efficient system of public instruction, will find it difficult to believe that the authors of that system should have had to struggle with a vehement and pertinacious opposition, and still more difficult to believe that such an opposition was offered in the name of civil and religious freedom.

III. Minute on
Indian Education

Minute on Indian Education

Shortly after he reached India in 1834, Macaulay found himself embroiled in the struggle over the future of Indian education which had been raging within the General Committee on Public Instruction for some time. The committee was divided into two factions—the "Orientalists" who felt that the British government should continue to foster instruction in Sanskrit and Arabic as well as in English for students in institutions of higher learning sponsored by the committee; and the "Anglicists" who were convinced that the available funds should be employed more or less exclusively for the teaching of English. Both sides believed in varying degrees in the necessity for "Westernization" and in the importance of the Indian vernaculars for carrying out this purpose. But the Anglicist party, unlike the Orientalist, believed strongly that the principal effort on the part of the government had to be put into the teaching of English. Macaulay's minute, written in his capacity of Legal Member of Council, strongly favored the Anglicist side. In the event, the governor-general, Lord William Bentinck, adopted in principle (though not in every detail) the policies recommended by Macaulay. The correctness of these policies is still being argued about today, but there is no doubt that their consequences for India were immense.

As it seems to be the opinion of some of the gentlemen who

Dated February 2, 1835.

compose the Committee of Public Instruction, that the course which they have hitherto pursued was strictly prescribed by the British Parliament in 1813, and as, if that opinion be correct, a legislative Act will be necessary to warrant a change, I have thought it right to refrain from taking any part in the preparation of the adverse statements which are now before us, and to reserve what I had to say on the subject till it should come before me as a member of the Council of India.

It does not appear to me that the Act of Parliament can, by any art of construction, be made to bear the meaning which has been assigned to it. It contains nothing about the particular languages or sciences which are to be studied. A sum is set apart "for the revival and promotion of literature and the encouragement of the learned natives of India, and for the introduction and promotion of a knowledge of the sciences among the inhabitants of the British territories." It is argued, or rather taken for granted, that by literature the Parliament can have only meant Arabic and Sanscrit literature, that they never would have given the honourable appellation of a "learned native" to a native who was familiar with the poetry of Milton, the metaphysics of Locke, and the physics of Newton; but that they meant to designate by that name only such persons as might have studied in the sacred books of the Hindoos all the usages of cusa-grass, and all the mysteries of absorption into the Deity. This does not appear to be a very satisfactory interpretation. To take a parallel case; suppose that the Pacha of Egypt, a country once superior in knowledge to the nations of Europe, but now sunk far below them, were to appropriate a sum for the purpose of "reviving and promoting literature, and encouraging learned natives of Egypt," would anybody infer that he meant the youth of his pachalic to give years to the study of hieroglyphics, to search into all the doctrines disguised under the fable of Osiris, and to ascertain with all possible accuracy the ritual with which cats and onions were anciently adored? Would he be justly charged with inconsistency, if, instead of employing his young subjects in deciphering obelisks, he were to order them to be instructed in the English and French languages, and in all the sciences to which those languages are the chief keys?

The words on which the supporters of the old system rely do not bear them out, and other words follow which seem to be quite decisive on the other side. This lac of rupees is set apart, not only for "reviving literature in India," the phrase on which their whole interpretation is founded, but also for "the introduction and promotion of a knowledge of the sciences among the inhabitants of the British territories,"—words which are alone sufficient to authorize all the changes for which I contend.

If the Council agree in my construction, no legislative Act will be necessary. If they differ from me, I will prepare a short Act rescinding that clause of the Charter of 1813, from which the difficulty arises.

The argument which I have been considering affects only the form of proceeding. But the admirers of the Oriental system of education have used another argument, which, if we admit it to be valid, is decisive against all change. They conceive that the public faith is pledged to the present system, and that to alter the appropriation of any of the funds which have hitherto been spent in encouraging the study of Arabic and Sanscrit would be downright spoliation. It is not easy to understand by what process of reasoning they can have arrived at this conclusion. The grants which are made from the public purse for the encouragement of literature differed in no respect from the grants which are made from the same purse for other objects of real or supposed utility. We found a sanatarium on a spot which we suppose to be healthy. Do we thereby pledge ourselves to keep a sanatarium there, if the result should not answer our expectation? We commence the erection of a pier. Is it a violation of the public faith to stop the works, if we afterwards see reason to believe that the building will be useless? The rights of property are undoubtedly sacred. But nothing endangers those rights so much as the practice, now unhappily too common, of attributing them to things to which they do not belong. Those who would impart to abuses the sanctity of property are in truth imparting to the institution of property the unpopularity and fragility of abuses. If the Government has given to any person a formal assurance; nay, if the Government has excited in any person's mind a reasonable expectation that he shall receive a certain income as a teacher or a learner of Sanscrit or Arabic, I would respect that person's pecuniary interests—I would rather err on the side of liberality to individuals than suffer the public faith to be called in question. But to talk of a Government pledging itself to teach certain languages and certain sciences, though those languages may become useless, though those sciences may be exploded, seems to me quite unmeaning. There is not a single word in any public instructions from which it can be inferred that the Indian Government ever intended to give any pledge on this subject, or ever considered the destination of these funds as unalterably fixed. But, had it been otherwise, I should have denied the competence of our predecessors to bind us by any pledge on such a subject. Suppose that a Government had in the last century enacted in the most solemn manner that all its subjects should, to the end of time, be inoculated for the small-pox: would that Government be bound to persist in the practice after Jenner's discovery? These promises, of which nobody claims the performance, and from which nobody can grant a release; these vested rights, which vest in nobody; this property without proprietors; this robbery, which makes nobody poorer, may be comprehended by persons of higher faculties than mine—I consider this plea merely as a set form of words, regularly used both in England and India, in defence of every abuse for which no other plea can be set up.

I hold this lac of rupees to be quite at the disposal of the Governor-General in Council, for the purpose of promoting learning in India, in any way which may be thought most advisable. I hold his Lordship to be quite as free to direct that it shall no longer be employed in encouraging Arabic and Sanscrit, as he is to direct that the reward for killing tigers in Mysore shall be diminished, or that no more public money shall be expended on the chanting at the cathedral.

We now come to the gist of the matter. We have a fund to be employed as Government shall direct for the intellectual improvement of the people of this country. The simple question is, what is the most useful way of employing it?

All parties seem to be agreed on one point, that the dialects commonly spoken among the natives of this part of India contain neither Literary nor scientific information, and are, moreover so poor and rude that, until they are enriched from some other quarter, it will not be easy to translate any valuable work into them. It seems to be admitted on all sides that the intellectual improvement of those classes of the people who have the means of pursuing higher studies can at present be effected only by means of some language not vernacular amongst them.

What, then, shall that language be? One half of the Committee maintain that it should be the English. The other half strongly recommend the Arabic and Sanscrit. The whole question seems to me to be, which language is the best worth knowing?

I have no knowledge of either Sanscrit or Arabic.—But I have done what I could to form a correct estimate of their value. I have read translations of the most celebrated Arabic and Sanscrit works. I have conversed both here and at home with men distinguished by their proficiency in the Eastern tongues. I am quite ready to take the Oriental learning at the valuation of the Orientalists themselves. I have never found one among them who could deny that a single shelf of a good European library was worth the whole native literature of India and Arabia. The intrinsic superiority of the Western literature is, indeed, fully admitted by those members of the Committee who support the Oriental plan of education.

It will hardly be disputed, I suppose, that the department of literature in which the Eastern writers stand highest is poetry. And I certainly never met with any Orientalist who ventured to maintain that the Arabic and Sanscrit poetry could be compared to that of the great European nations. But, when we pass from works of imagination to works in which facts are recorded and general principles investigated, the superiority of the Europeans becomes absolutely immeasurable. It is, I believe, no exaggeration to say, that all the historical information which has been collected from all the books written in the Sanscrit language is less valuable than what may be found in the most paltry abridgments used at preparatory schools in England. In every branch of physical or moral philosophy the relative position of the two nations is nearly the same.

How, then, stands the case? We have to educate a people who cannot at present be educated by means of their mother-tongue. We must teach them some foreign language. The claims of our own language it is hardly necessary to recapitulate. It stands preeminent even among the languages of the West. It abounds with works of imagination not inferior to the noblest which Greece has bequeathed to us; with models of every species of eloquence; with historical compositions, which, considered merely as narratives, have seldom been surpassed, and which, considered as vehicles of ethical and political instruction, have never been equalled; with just and lively representations of human life and human nature; with the most profound speculations on metaphysics, morals, government, jurisprudence, and trade; with full and correct information respecting every experimental science which tends to preserve the health, to increase the comfort, or to expand the intellect of man. Whoever knows that language, has ready access to all the vast intellectual wealth, which all the wisest nations of the earth have created and hoarded in the course of ninety generations. It may safely be said that the literature now extant in that language is of far greater value than all the literature which three hundred years ago was extant in all the languages of the world together. Nor is this all. In India, English is the language spoken by the ruling class. It is spoken by the higher class of natives at the seats of Government. It is likely to become the language of commerce throughout the seas of the East. It is the language of two great European communities which are rising, the one in the south of Africa, the other in Australasia; communities which are every year becoming more important, and more closely connected with our Indian empire. Whether we look at the intrinsic value of our literature, or at the particular situation of this country, we shall see the strongest reason to think that, of all foreign tongues, the English tongue is that which would be the most useful to our native subjects.

The question now before us is simply whether, when it is in our power to teach this language, we shall teach languages in which, by universal confession, there are no books on any subject which deserve to be compared to our own; whether, when we can teach European science, we shall teach systems which, by universal confession, whenever they differ from those of Europe, differ for the worse; and whether, when we can patronise sound Philosophy and true History, we shall countenance, at the public expense, medical doctrines which would disgrace an English Farrier— Astronomy, which would move laughter in girls at an English boarding school—History, abounding with kings thirty feet high, and reigns thirty thousand years long—and Geography, made up of seas of treacle and seas of butter.

We are not without experience to guide us. History furnishes several analogous cases, and they all teach the same lesson. There are in modern times, to go no further, two memorable instances of a great impulse given to the mind of a whole society—of prejudices overthrown—of knowledge diffused—of taste purified—of arts and sciences planted in countries which had recently been ignorant and barbarous.

The first instance to which I refer is the great revival of letters among the Western nations at the close of the fifteenth and the beginning of the sixteenth century. At that time almost everything that was worth reading was contained in the writings of the ancient Greeks and Romans. Had our ancestors acted as the Committee of Public Instruction has hitherto acted; had they neglected the language of Cicero and Tacitus; had they confined their attention to the old dialects of our own island; had they printed nothing and taught nothing at the universities but Chronicles in Anglo-Saxon and Romances in Norman-French, would England have been what she now is? What the Greek and Latin were to the contemporaries of More and Ascham, our tongue is to the people of India. The literature of England is now more valuable than that of classical antiquity. I doubt whether the Sanscrit literature be as valuable as that of our Saxon and Norman progenitors. In some departments—in History, for example—I am certain that it is much less so.

Another instance may be said to be still before our eyes. Within the last hundred and twenty years, a nation which had previously been in a state as barbarous as that in which our ancestors were before the Crusades, has gradually emerged from the ignorance in which it was sunk, and has taken its place among civilised communities—I speak of Russia. There is now in that country a large educated class, abounding with persons fit to serve the state in the highest functions, and in nowise inferior to the most accomplished men who adorn the best circles of Paris and London. There is reason to hope that this vast empire, which in the time of our grandfathers was probably behind the Punjab, may, in the time of our grandchildren, be pressing close on France and

Britain in the career of improvement. And how was this change effected? Not by flattering national prejudices; not by feeding the mind of the young Muscovite with the old woman's stories which his rude fathers had believed: not by filling his head with lying legends about St. Nicholas: not by encouraging him to study the great question, whether the world was or was not created on the 13th of September: not by calling him "a learned native," when he has mastered all these points of knowledge: but by teaching him those foreign languages in which the greatest mass of information had been laid up, and thus putting all that information within his reach. The languages of Western Europe civilized Russia. I cannot doubt that they will do for the Hindoo what they have done for the Tartar.

And what are the arguments against that course which seems to be alike recommended by theory and by experience? It is said that we ought to secure the co-operation of the native public, and that we can do this only by teaching Sanscrit and Arabic.

I can by no means admit that, when a nation of high intellectual attainments undertakes to superintend the education of a nation comparatively ignorant, the learners are absolutely to prescribe the course which is to be taken by the teachers. It is not necessary, however, to say anything on this subject. For it is proved by unanswerable evidence that we are not at present securing the co-operation of the natives. It would be bad enough to consult their intellectual taste at the expense of their intellectual health. But we are consulting neither—we are withholding from them the learning for which they are craving; we are forcing on them the mock-learning which they nauseate.

This is proved by the fact that we are forced to pay our Arabic and Sanscrit students, while those who learn English are willing to pay us. All the declamations in the world about the love and reverence of the natives for their sacred dialects will never, in the mind of any impartial person, outweigh the undisputed fact, that we cannot find, in all our vast empire, a single student who will let us teach him those dialects unless we will pay him.

I have now before me the accounts of the Madrassa for one month—the month of December, 1833. The Arabic students appear to have been seventy-seven in number. All receive stipends from the public. The whole amount paid to them is above 500 rupees a month. On the other side of the account stands the following item: Deduct amount realised from the out-students of English for the months of May, June, and July last, 103 rupees.

I have been told that it is merely from want of local experience that I am surprised at these phenomena, and that it is not the fashion for students in India to study at their own charges. This only confirms me in my opinion. Nothing is more certain than that it never can in any part of the world be necessary to pay men for doing what they think pleasant and profitable. India is no exception to this rule. The people of India do not require to be paid for eating rice when they are hungry, or for wearing woollen cloth in the cold season. To come nearer to the case before us, the children who learn their letters and a little elementary Arithmetic from the village schoolmaster are not paid by him. He is paid for teaching them. Why, then, is it necessary to pay people to learn Sanscrit and Arabic? Evidently because it is universally felt that the Sanscrit and Arabic are languages the knowledge of which does not compensate for the trouble of acquiring them. On all such subjects the state of the market is the decisive test.

Other evidence is not wanting, if other evidence were required. A petition was presented last year to the Committee by several ex-students of the Sanscrit College. The petitioners stated they had studied in the college ten or twelve years; that they had made themselves acquainted with Hindoo literature and science; that they had received certificates of proficiency: and what is the fruit of all this? "Notwithstanding such testimonials," they say, "we have but little prospect of bettering our condition without the kind assistance of your Honourable Committee, the indifference with which we are generally looked upon by our countrymen leaving no hope of encouragement and assistance from them." They therefore beg that they may be recommended to the Governor-General for places under the Government, not places of high dignity or emolument, but such as may just enable them to exist. "We want means," they say, for a decent living, and for our progressive improvement, which, however, we cannot obtain without the assistance of Government, by whom we have been educated and maintained from childhood." They conclude by representing, very pathetically, that they are sure that it was never the intention of Government, after behaving so liberally to them during their education, to abandon them to destitution and neglect.

I have been used to see petitions to Government for compensation. All these petitions, even the most unreasonable of them, proceeded on the supposition that some loss had been sustained —that some wrong had been inflicted. These are surely the first petitioners who ever demanded compensation for having been educated gratis—for having been supported by the public during twelve years, and then sent forth into the world well-furnished with literature and science. They represent their education as an injury which gives them a claim on the Government for redress, as an injury for which the stipends paid to them during the infliction were a very inadequate compensation. And I doubt not that they are in the right. They have wasted the best years of life in learning what procures for them neither bread nor respect. Surely we might, with advantage, have saved the cost of making these persons useless and miserable; surely, men may be brought up to be burdens to the public and objects of contempt to their neighbours at a somewhat smaller charge to the state. But such is our policy. We do not even stand neuter in the contest between truth and falsehood. We are not content to leave the natives to the influence of their own hereditary prejudices. To the natural difficulties which obstruct the progress of sound science in the East we add fresh difficulties of our own making. Bounties and premiums, such as ought not to be given even for the propagation of truth, we lavish on false taste and false philosophy.

By acting thus we create the very evil which we fear. We are making that opposition which we do not find. What we spend on the Arabic and Sanscrit colleges is not merely a dead loss to the cause of truth: it is the bounty-money paid to raise up champions of error. It goes to form a nest, not merely of helpless place-hunters, but of bigots prompted alike by passion and by interest to raise a cry against every useful scheme of education. If there should be any opposition among the natives to the change which I recommend, that opposition will be the effect of our own system. It will be headed by persons supported by our stipends and trained in our colleges. The longer we persevere in our present course, the more formidable will that opposition be. It will be every year re-inforced by recruits whom we are paying. From the native society left to itself we have no difficulties to apprehend; all the murmuring will come from that oriental interest which we have, by artificial means, called into being and nursed into strength.

There is yet another fact, which is alone sufficient to prove that the feeling of the native public, when left to itself, is not such as the supporters of the old system represent it to be. The Committee have thought fit to lay out above a lac of rupees in printing Arabic and Sanscrit books. Those books find no purchasers. It is very rarely that a single copy is disposed of. Twenty-three thousand volumes, most of them folios and quartos, fill the libraries, or rather the lumber-rooms, of this body. The Committee contrive to get rid of some portion of their vast stock of Oriental literature by giving books away. But they cannot give so fast as they print. About twenty thousand rupees a year are spent in adding fresh masses of waste paper to a hoard which, I should think, is already sufficiently ample. During the last three years, about sixty thousand rupees have been expended in this manner. The sale of Arabic and Sanscrit books, during those three years, has not yielded quite one thousand rupees. In the mean time the School-book Society is selling seven or eight thousand English volumes every year, and not only pays the expenses of printing, but realizes a profit of 20 per cent on its outlay.

The fact that the Hindoo law is to be learned chiefly from Sanscrit books, and the Mahomedan law from Arabic books, has been much insisted on, but seems not to bear at all on the question. We are commanded by Parliament to ascertain and digest the laws of India. The assistance of a law commission has been given to us for that purpose. As soon as the code is promulgated, the Shasters and the Hedeya will be useless to a Moonsiff or Sudder Ameen. I hope and trust that, before the boys who are now entering at the Madrassa and the Sanscrit college have completed their studies, this great work will be finished. It would be manifestly absurd to educate the rising generation with a view to a state of things which we mean to alter before they reach manhood.

But there is yet another argument which seems even more untenable. It is said that the Sanscrit and Arabic are the languages in which the sacred books of a hundred millions of people are written, and that they are, on that account, entitled to peculiar encouragement. Assuredly it is the duty of the British Government in India to be not only tolerant, but neutral on all religious questions. But to encourage the study of a literature admitted to be of small intrinsic value only because that literature inculcates the most serious errors on the most important subjects, is a course hardly reconcilable with reason, with morality, or even with that very neutrality which ought, as we all agree, to be sacredly preserved. It is confessed that a language is barren of useful knowledge. We are told to teach it because it is fruitful of monstrous superstitions. We are to teach false history, false astronomy, false medicine, because we find them in company with a false religion. We abstain, and I trust shall always abstain, from giving any public encouragement to those who are engaged in the work of converting natives to Christianity. And, while we act thus, can we reasonably and decently bribe men out of the revenues of the state to waste their youth in learning how they are to purify themselves after touching an ass, or what text of the Vedas they are to repeat to expiate the crime of killing a goat?

It is taken for granted by the advocates of Oriental learning that no native of this country can possibly attain more than a mere smattering of English. They do not attempt to prove this; but they perpetually insinuate it. They designate the education which their opponents recommend as a mere spelling-book education. They assume it as undeniable, that the question is between a profound knowledge of Hindoo and Arabian literature and science on the one side, and a superficial knowledge of the rudiments of English on the other. This is not merely an assumption, but an assumption contrary to all reason and experience. We know that foreigners of all nations do learn our language sufficiently to have access to all the most abstruse knowledge which it contains, sufficiently to relish even the more delicate graces of our most idiomatic writers. There are in this very town natives who are quite competent to discuss political or scientific questions with fluency and precision in the English language. I have heard the very question on which I am now writing discussed by native gentlemen with a liberality and an intelligence which would do credit to any member of the Committee of Public Instruction. Indeed, it is unusual to find, even in the literary circles of the continent, any foreigner who can express himself in English with so much facility and correctness as we find in many Hindoos. Nobody, I suppose, will contend that English is so difficult to a Hindoo as Greek to an Englishman. Yet an intelligent English youth, in a much smaller number of years than our unfortunate pupils pass at the Sanscrit college, becomes able to read, to enjoy, and even to imitate, not unhappily, the composition of the best Greek authors. Less than half the time which enables an English youth to read Herodotus and Sophocles ought to enable a Hindoo to read Hume and Milton.

To sum up what I have said: I think it clear that we are not fettered by the Act of Parliament of 1813; that we are not fettered by any pledge expressed or implied; that we are free to employ our funds as we choose; that we ought to employ them in teaching what is best worth knowing; that English is better worth knowing than Sanscrit or Arabic; that the natives are desirous to be taught English, and are not desirous to be taught Sanscrit or Arabic; that neither as the languages of law, nor as the languages of religion, have the Sanscrit and Arabic any peculiar claim to our encouragement; that it is possible to make natives of this country thoroughly good English scholars, and that to this end our efforts ought to be directed.

In one point I fully agree with the gentlemen to whose general views I am opposed. I feel, with them, that it is impossible for us, with our limited means, to attempt to educate the body of the people. We must at present do our best to form a class who may be interpreters between us and the millions whom we govern; a class of persons, Indian in blood and colour, but English in taste, in opinions, in morals, and in intellect. To that class we may leave it to refine the vernacular dialects of the country, to enrich those dialects with terms of science borrowed from the Western nomenclature, and to render them by degrees fit vehicles for conveying knowledge to the great mass of the population.

I would strictly respect all existing interests. I would deal even generously with all individuals who have had fair reason to expect a pecuniary provision. But I would strike at the root of the bad system which has hitherto been fostered by us. I would at once stop the printing of Arabic and Sanscrit books; I would abolish the Madrassa and the Sanscrit college at Calcutta. Benares is the great seat of Brahmanical learning; Delhi, of Arabic learning. If we retain the Sanscrit college at Benares and the Mahomedan college at Delhi, we do enough, and much more than enough in my opinion, for the Eastern languages. If the Benares and Delhi colleges should be retained, I would at least recommend that no stipend shall be given to any students who may hereafter repair thither, but that the people shall be left to make their own choice between the rival systems of education without being bribed by us to learn what they have no desire to know. The funds which would thus be placed at our disposal would enable us to give larger encouragement to the Hindoo college at Calcutta, and to establish in the principal cities throughout the Presidencies of Fort William and Agra schools in which the English language might be well and thoroughly taught.

If the decision of his Lordship in Council should be such as I anticipate, I shall enter on the performance of my duties with the greatest zeal and alacrity. If, on the other hand, it be the opinion of the Government that the present system ought to remain unchanged, I beg that I may be permitted to retire from the chair of the Committee. I feel that I could not be of the smallest use there—I feel, also, that I should be lending my countenance to what I firmly believe to be a mere delusion. I believe that the present system tends, not to accelerate the progress of truth, but to delay the natural death of expiring errors. I conceive that we have at present no right to the respectable name of a Board of Public Instruction. We are a Board for wasting public money, for printing books which are of less value than the paper on which they are printed was while it was blank; for giving artificial encouragement to absurd history, absurd metaphysics, absurd physics, absurd theology; for raising up a breed of scholars who find their scholarship an encumbrance and a blemish, who live on the public while they are receiving their education, and whose education is so utterly useless to them that, when they have received it, they must either starve or live on the public all the rest of their lives. Entertaining these opinions, I am naturally desirous to decline all share in the responsibility of a body which, unless it alters its whole mode of proceeding, I must consider not merely as useless, but as positively noxious.

IV. History of England

History of England

Macaulay began to plan his History of England *while still in India. In July 1838 he wrote from Calcutta to the editor of the* Edinburgh Review *that he intended the first part to extend from 1688 to 1721; the second to run from the latter date, the beginning of Walpole's administration, to the American Revolution; and the third to go from there to the death of George IV in 1830. "The History," he continued, "would be an entire view of all the transactions which took place, between the Revolution which brought the Crown into harmony with the Parliament, and the Revolution which brought the Parliament into harmony with the nation." In the event, he did not come anywhere near to completing this ambitious project. The work as it now stands ends with the death of William III in 1702.*

Macaulay started to concentrate on writing the History *after the Whigs went out of office in the summer of 1841 and when he thus came to the end of his period of service as secretary at war. The first two volumes, bringing the story to the end of the reign of James II, appeared in December 1848 and were an immediate success. Thirteen thousand copies were sold in four months. The third and fourth volumes, ending with the peace of Ryswick in 1697, were published in December 1855. The reading public responded with even greater enthusiasm. Longmans sold twenty-six and a half thousand copies in ten weeks, and eleven weeks after publication, Macaulay received a check for twenty thousand pounds from the publishers. The fifth and last volume of the* History *was published posthumously, in March 1861.*

The two extracts from the History *included in this volume are taken from chapter 3, Macaulay's pioneering venture in social history, and from chapter 9, a striking example of the art of sustained and gripping narrative at its best. The first of these chapters attempts to depict the state of England in 1685 and is notable for the use made in it of literary sources as well as for the breadth of its approach. The second chapter describes William's landing in England and the events which led to the flight of James II.*

From

Chapter 3

I intend, in this chapter, to give a description of the state in which England was at the time when the crown passed from Charles the Second to his brother. Such a description, composed from scanty and dispersed materials, must necessarily be very imperfect. Yet it may perhaps correct some false notions which would make the subsequent narrative unintelligible or uninstructive.

If we would study with profit the history of our ancestors, we must be constantly on our guard against that delusion which the well known names of families, places, and offices naturally produce, and must never forget that the country of which we read was a very different country from that in which we live. In every experimental science there is a tendency towards perfection. In every human being there is a wish to ameliorate his own condition. These two principles have often sufficed, even when counteracted by great public calamities and by bad institutions, to carry civilisation rapidly forward. No ordinary misfortune, no ordinary misgovernment, will do so much to make a nation wretched, as the constant progress of physical knowledge and the constant effort of every man to better himself will do to make a nation prosperous. It has often been found that profuse expenditure, heavy taxation, absurd commercial restrictions, corrupt tribunals, disastrous wars, seditions, persecutions, conflagrations, inundations, have not been able to destroy capital so fast as the exertions of private citizens have been able to create it. It can easily be proved that, in our own land, the national wealth has, during at least six centuries, been almost uninterruptedly increasing; that it was greater under the Tudors than under the Plantagenets; that it was greater under the Stuarts than under the Tudors; that, in spite of battles, sieges, and confiscations, it was greater on the day of the Restoration than on the day when the Long Parliament met; that, in spite of maladministration, of extravagance, of public bankruptcy, of two costly and unsuccessful wars, of the pestilence and of the fire, it was greater on the day of the death of Charles the Second than on the day of his Restoration. This progress, having continued during many ages, became at length, about the middle of the eighteenth century, portentously rapid, and has proceeded, during the nineteenth, with accelerated velocity. In consequence partly of our geographical and partly of our moral position, we have, during several generations, been exempt from evils which have elsewhere impeded the efforts and destroyed the fruits of industry. While every part of the Continent, from Moscow to Lisbon, has been the theatre of bloody and devastating wars, no hostile standard has been seen here but as a trophy. While revolutions have taken place all around us, our government has never once been subverted by violence. During more than a hundred years there has been in our island no tumult of sufficient importance to be called an insurrection; nor has the law been once borne down either by popular fury or by regal tyranny: public credit has been held sacred: the administration of justice has been pure: even in times which might by Englishmen be justly called evil times, we have enjoyed what almost every other nation in the world would have considered as an ample measure of civil and religious freedom. Every man has felt entire confidence that the state would protect him in the possession of what had been earned by his diligence and hoarded by his selfdenial. Under the benignant influence of peace and liberty, science has flourished, and has been applied to practical purposes on a scale never before known. The consequence is that a change to which the history of the old world furnishes no parallel has taken place in our country. Could the England of 1685 be, by some magical process, set before our eyes, we should not know one landscape in a hundred or one building in ten thousand. The country gentleman would not recognise his own fields. The inhabitant of the town would not recognise his own street. Everything has been changed, but the great features of nature, and a few massive and durable works of human art. We might find out Snowdon and Windermere, the Cheddar Cliffs and Beachy Head. We might find out here and there a Norman minster, or a castle which witnessed the wars of the Roses. But, with such rare exceptions, everything would be strange to us. Many thousands of square miles which are now rich corn land and meadow, intersected by green hedgerows, and dotted with villages and pleasant country seats, would appear as moors overgrown with furze, or fens abandoned to wild ducks. We should see straggling huts built of wood and covered with thatch, where we now see manufacturing towns and seaports renowned to the farthest ends of the world. The capital itself would shrink to dimensions not much exceeding those of its present suburb on the south of the Thames. Not less strange to us would be the garb and manners of the people, the furniture and the equipages, the interior of the shops and dwellings. Such a change in the state of a nation seems to be at least as well entitled to the notice of a historian as any change of the dynasty or of the ministry.[1]

One of the first objects of an inquirer, who wishes to form a correct notion of the state of a community at a given time, must be to ascertain of how many persons that community then consisted. Unfortunately the population of England in 1685 cannot be ascertained with perfect accuracy. For no great state had then adopted the wise course of periodically numbering the people. All men were left to conjecture for themselves; and, as they generally conjectured without examining facts, and under the influence of strong passions and prejudices, their guesses were often ludicrously absurd. Even intelligent Londoners ordinarily talked of London as containing several millions of souls. It was confi-

1. During the interval which has elapsed since this chapter was written, England has continued to advance rapidly in material prosperity. I have left my text nearly as it originally stood; but I have added a few notes which may enable the reader to form some notion of the progress which has been made during the last nine years; and, in general, I would desire him to remember that there is scarcely a district which is not more populous, or a source of wealth which is not more productive, at present than in 1848. (1857.)

dently asserted by many that, during the thirty-five years which had elapsed between the accession of Charles the First and the Restoration, the population of the City had increased by two millions.[2] Even while the ravages of the plague and fire were recent, it was the fashion to say that the capital still had a million and a half of inhabitants.[3] Some persons, disgusted by these exaggerations, ran violently into the opposite extreme. Thus Isaac Vossius, a man of undoubted parts and learning, strenuously maintained that there were only two millions of human beings in England, Scotland, and Ireland taken together.[4]

We are not, however, left without the means of correcting the wild blunders into which some minds were hurried by national vanity and others by a morbid love of paradox. There are extant three computations which seem to be entitled to peculiar attention. They are entirely independent of each other: they proceed on different principles; and yet there is little difference in the results.

One of these computations was made in the year 1696 by Gregory King, Lancaster herald, a political arithmetician of great acuteness and judgment. The basis of his calculations was the number of houses returned in 1690 by the officers who made the last collection of the hearth money. The conclusion at which he arrived was that the population of England was nearly five millions and a half.[5]

About the same time King William the Third was desirous to ascertain the comparative strength of the religious sects into which the community was divided. An inquiry was instituted; and reports were laid before him from all the dioceses of the realm. According to these reports the number of his English

2. Observations on the Bills of Mortality, by Captain John Graunt (Sir William Petty), chap. xi.

4. Isaac Vossius, De Magnitudine Urbium Sinarum, 1685. Vossius, as we learn from Saint Evremond, talked on this subject oftener and longer than fashionable circles cared to listen.

3. "She doth comprehend
Full fifteen hundred thousand which do spend
Their days within."

Great Britain's Beauty, 1671.

5. King's Natural and Political Observations, 1696. This valuable treatise, which ought to be read as the author wrote it, and not as garbled by Davenant, will be found in some editions of Chalmer's Estimate.

subjects must have been about five million two hundred thousand.[6]

Lastly, in our own days, Mr. Finlaison, an actuary of eminent skill, subjected the ancient parochial registers of baptisms, marriages, and burials, to all the tests which the modern improvements in statistical science enabled him to apply. His opinion was, that, at the close of the seventeenth century, the population of England was a little under five million two hundred thousand souls.[7]

Of these three estimates, framed without concert by different persons from different sets of materials, the highest, which is that of King, does not exceed the lowest, which is that of Finlaison, by one twelfth. We may, therefore, with confidence pronounce that, when James the Second reigned, England contained between five million and five million five hundred thousand inhabitants. On the very highest supposition she then had less than one third of her present population, and less than three times the population which is now collected in her gigantic capital.

The increase of the people has been great in every part of the kingdom, but generally much greater in the northern than in the southern shires. In truth a large part of the country beyond Trent was, down to the eighteenth century, in a state of barbarism. Physical and moral causes had concurred to prevent civilisation from spreading to that region. The air was inclement; the soil was generally such as required skilful and industrious cultivation; and there could be little skill or industry in a tract which was often the theatre of war, and which, even when there was nominal peace, was constantly desolated by bands of Scottish marauders. Before the union of the two British crowns, and long after that union, there was as great a difference between Middlesex and Northumberland as there now is between Massachusetts and the settlements of those squatters who, far to the west of the Mississippi, administer a rude justice with the rifle and the

6. Dalrymple's Appendix to Part II, Book I. The practice of reckoning the population by sects was long fashionable. Gulliver says of the King of Brobdingnag; "He laughed at my odd arithmetic, as he was pleased to call it, in reckoning the numbers of our people by a computation drawn from the several sects among us in religion and politics."

7. Preface to the Population Returns of 1831.

dagger. In the reign of Charles the Second, the traces left by ages of slaughter and pillage were distinctly perceptible, many miles south of the Tweed, in the face of the country and in the lawless manners of the people. There was still a large class of moss-troopers, whose calling was to plunder dwellings and to drive away whole herds of cattle. It was found necessary, soon after the Restoration, to enact laws of great severity for the prevention of these outrages. The magistrates of Northumberland and Cumberland were authorised to raise bands of armed men for the defence of property and order; and provision was made for meeting the expense of these levies by local taxation.[8] The parishes were required to keep bloodhounds for the purpose of hunting the freebooters. Many old men who were living in the middle of the eighteenth century could well remember the time when those ferocious dogs were common.[9] Yet, even with such auxiliaries, it was often found impossible to track the robbers to their retreats among the hills and morasses. For the geography of that wild country was very imperfectly known. Even after the accession of George the Third, the path over the fells from Borrowdale to Ravenglas was still a secret carefully kept by the dalesmen, some of whom had probably in their youth escaped from the pursuit of justice by that road.[10] The seats of the gentry and the larger farmhouses were fortified. Oxen were penned at night beneath the overhanging battlements of the residence, which was known by the name of the Peel. The inmates slept with arms at their sides. Huge stones and boiling water were in readiness to crush and scald the plunderer who might venture to assail the little garrison. No traveller ventured into that country without making his will. The Judges on circuit, with the whole body of barristers, attorneys, clerks, and serving men, rode on horseback from Newcastle to Carlisle, armed and escorted by a strong guard under the command of the Sheriffs. It was necessary to carry provisions; for the country was a wilderness which afforded no supplies. The spot where the cavalcade halted to dine, under an immense oak, is not yet forgotten. The irregular vigour with

8. Statutes 14 Car. II. c. 22.; 18 & 19 Car. II. c. 3.; 29 & 30 Car. II. c. 2.

9. Nicholson and Bourne, Discourse on the Ancient State of the Border, 1777.

10. Gray's Journal of a Tour in the Lakes, Oct. 3, 1769.

which criminal justice was administered shocked observers whose lives had been passed in more tranquil districts. Juries, animated by hatred and by a sense of common danger, convicted house-breakers and cattle stealers with the promptitude of a court martial in a mutiny; and the convicts were hurried by scores to the gallows.[11] Within the memory of some whom this generation has seen, the sportsman who wandered in pursuit of game to the sources of the Tyne found the heaths round Keeldar Castle peopled by a race scarcely less savage than the Indians of California, and heard with surprise the half naked women chaunting a wild measure, while the men with brandished dirks danced a war dance.[12]

Slowly and with difficulty peace was established on the border. In the train of peace came industry and all the arts of life. Meanwhile it was discovered that the regions north of the Trent possessed in their coal beds a source of wealth far more precious than the gold mines of Peru. It was found that, in the neighbourhood of these beds, almost every manufacture might be most profitably carried on. A constant stream of emigrants began to roll northward. It appeared by the returns of 1841 that the ancient archiepiscopal province of York contained two sevenths of the population of England. At the time of the Revolution that province was believed to contain only one seventh of the population.[13] In Lancashire the number of inhabitants appears to have increased ninefold, while in Norfolk, Suffolk, and Northamptonshire it has hardly doubled.[14]

Of the taxation we can speak with more confidence and precision than of the population. The revenue of England, when Charles the Second died, was small, when compared with the resources which she even then possessed, or with the sums which were raised by the governments of the neighbouring countries.

11. North's Life of Guildford; Hutchinson's History of Cumberland, Parish of Brampton.

12. See Sir Walter Scott's Journal, Oct. 7, 1827, in his Life by Mr. Lockhart.

13. Dalrymple, Appendix to Part II, Book I. The returns of the hearth money lead to nearly the same conclusion. The hearths in the province of York were not a sixth of the hearths of England.

14. I do not, of course, pretend to strict accuracy here; but I believe that whoever will take the trouble to compare the last returns of hearth money in the reign of William the Third with the census of 1841, will come to a conclusion not very different from mine.

It had, from the time of the Restoration, been almost constantly increasing: yet it was little more than three fourths of the revenue of the United Provinces, and was hardly one fifth of the revenue of France.

The most important head of receipt was the excise, which, in the last year of the reign of Charles, produced five hundred and eighty-five thousand pounds, clear of all deductions. The net proceeds of the customs amounted in the same year to five hundred and thirty thousand pounds. These burdens did not lie very heavy on the nation. The tax on chimneys, though less productive, called forth far louder murmurs. The discontent excited by direct imposts is, indeed, almost always out of proportion to the quantity of money which they bring into the Exchequer; and the tax on chimneys was, even among direct imposts, peculiarly odious: for it could be levied only by means of domiciliary visits; and of such visits the English have always been impatient to a degree which the people of other countries can but faintly conceive. The poorer householders were frequently unable to pay their hearth money to the day. When this happened, their furniture was distrained without mercy: for the tax was farmed; and a farmer of taxes is, of all creditors, proverbially the most rapacious. The collectors were loudly accused of performing their unpopular duty with harshness and insolence. It was said that, as soon as they appeared at the threshold of a cottage, the children began to wail, and the old women ran to hide their earthenware. Nay, the single bed of a poor family had sometimes been carried away and sold. The net annual receipt from this tax was two hundred thousand pounds.[15]

15. There are in the Pepysian Library, some ballads of that age on the chimney money. I will give a specimen or two:
"The good old dames, whenever they the chimney man espied,
Unto their nooks they haste away, their pots and pipkins hide.
There is not one old dame in ten, and search the nation through,
But, if you talk of chimney men, will spare a curse or two."
    Again:
"Like plundering soldiers they'd enter the door,
And make a distress on the goods of the poor,
While frighted poor children distractedly cried:
This nothing abated their insolent pride."
    In the British Museum there are doggrel verses composed on the same subject and in the same spirit:
"Or, if through poverty it be not paid,

The fact that the sum raised in England by taxation, has, in a time not exceeding two long lives, been multiplied fortyfold, is strange, and may at first sight seem appalling. But those who are alarmed by the increase of the public burdens may perhaps be reassured when they have considered the increase of the public resources. In the year 1685, the value of the produce of the soil far exceeded the value of all the other fruits of human industry. Yet agriculture was in what would now be considered as a very rude and imperfect state. The arable land and pasture land were not supposed by the best political arithmeticians of that age to amount to much more than half the area of the kingdom.[16] The remainder was believed to consist of moor, forest, and fen. These computations are strongly confirmed by the road books and maps of the seventeenth century. From those books and maps it is clear that many routes which now pass through an endless succession of orchards, cornfields, hayfields, and beanfields, then ran through nothing but heath, swamp, and warren.[17] In the drawings of English landscapes made in that age for the Grand Duke Cosmo, scarce a hedgerow is to be seen, and numerous tracts, now rich with cultivation, appear as bare as Salisbury Plain.[18] At Enfield, hardly out of sight of the smoke of the capital, was a region of five and twenty miles in circumference, which contained only

---

For cruelty to tear away the single bed,
On which the poor man rests his weary head,
At once deprives him of his rest and bread."
  I take this opportunity, the first which occurs, of acknowledging most gratefully the kind and liberal manner in which the Master and Vicemaster of Magdalene College, Cambridge, gave me access to the valuable collections of Pepys.
  16. King's Natural and Political Conclusions. Davenant on the Balance of Trade.
  17. See the Itinerarium Angliæ, 1675, by John Ogilby, Cosmographer Royal. He describes great part of the land as wood, fen, heath on both sides, marsh on both sides. In some of his maps the roads through enclosed country are marked by lines, and the roads through unenclosed country by dots. The proportion of unenclosed country, which, if cultivated, must have been wretchedly cultivated, seems to have been very great. From Abingdon to Gloucester, for example, a distance of forty or fifty miles, there was not a single enclosure, and scarcely one enclosure between Biggleswade and Lincoln.
  18. Large copies of these highly interesting drawings are in the noble collection bequeathed by Mr. Grenville to the British Museum. See particularly the drawings of Exeter and Northampton.

three houses and scarcely any enclosed fields. Deer, as free as in an American forest, wandered there by thousands.[19] It is to be remarked, that wild animals of large size were then far more numerous than at present. The last wild boars, indeed, which had been preserved for the royal diversion, and had been allowed to ravage the cultivated land with their tusks, had been slaughtered by the exasperated rustics during the license of the civil war. The last wolf that has roamed our island had been slain in Scotland a short time before the close of the reign of Charles the Second. But many breeds, now extinct or rare, both of quadrupeds and birds, were still common. The fox, whose life is now, in many counties, held almost as sacred as that of a human being, was then considered as a mere nuisance. Oliver Saint John told the Long Parliament that Strafford was to be regarded, not as a stag or a hare, to whom some law was to be given, but as a fox, who was to be snared by any means, and knocked on the head without pity. This illustration would be by no means a happy one, if addressed to country gentlemen of our time: but in Saint John's days there were not seldom great massacres of foxes to which the peasantry thronged with all the dogs that could be mustered: traps were set: nets were spread: no quarter was given; and to shoot a female with cub was considered as a feat which merited the warmest gratitude of the neighbourhood. The red deer were then as common in Gloucestershire and Hampshire as they now are among the Grampian Hills. On one occasion Queen Anne, travelling to Portsmouth, saw a herd of no less than five hundred. The wild bull with his white mane was still to be found wandering in a few of the southern forests. The badger made his dark and tortuous hole on the side of every hill where the copsewood grew thick. The wild cats were frequently heard by night wailing round the lodges of the rangers of Whittlebury and Needwood. The yellow-breasted martin was still pursued in Cranbourne Chase for his fur, reputed inferior only to that of the sable. Fen eagles, measuring more than nine feet between the extremities of the wings, preyed on fish along the coast of Norfolk. On all the downs, from the British Channel to Yorkshire, huge bustards

19. Evelyn's Diary, June 2, 1675.

strayed in troops of fifty or sixty, and were often hunted with greyhounds. The marshes of Cambridgeshire and Lincolnshire were covered during some months of every year by immense clouds of cranes. Some of these races the progress of cultivation has extirpated. Of others the numbers are so much diminished that men crowd to gaze at a specimen as at a Bengal tiger, or a Polar bear.[20]

The progress of this great change can nowhere be more clearly traced than in the Statute Book. The number of enclosure acts passed since King George the Second came to the throne exceeds four thousand. The area enclosed under the authority of those acts exceeds, on a moderate calculation, ten thousand square miles. How many square miles, which were formerly uncultivated or ill cultivated, have, during the same period, been fenced and carefully tilled by the proprietors, without any application to the legislature, can only be conjectured. But it seems highly probable that a fourth part of England has been, in the course of little more than a century, turned from a wild into a garden.

Even in those parts of the kingdom which at the close of the reign of Charles the Second were the best cultivated, the farming, though greatly improved since the civil war, was not such as would now be thought skilful. To this day no effectual steps have been taken by public authority for the purpose of obtaining accurate accounts of the produce of the English soil. The historian must therefore follow, with some misgivings, the guidance of those writers on statistics whose reputation for diligence and fidelity stands highest. At present an average crop of wheat, rye, barley, oats, and beans, is supposed considerably to exceed thirty millions of quarters. The crop of wheat would be thought wretched if it did not exceed twelve millions of quarters. According to the computation made in the year 1696 by Gregory King, the whole quantity of wheat, rye, barley, oats, and beans, then annually grown in the kingdom, was somewhat less than ten

---

20. See White's Selborne; Bell's History of British Quadrupeds; Gentleman's Recreation, 1686; Aubrey's Natural History of Wiltshire, 1685; Morton's History of Northamptonshire, 1712; Willoughby's Ornithology, by Ray, 1678; Latham's General Synopsis of Birds; and Sir Thomas Browne's Account of Birds found in Norfolk.

millions of quarters. The wheat, which was then cultivated only on the strongest clay, and consumed only by those who were in easy circumstances, he estimated at less than two millions of quarters. Charles Davenant, an acute and well informed though most unprincipled and rancorous politician, differed from King as to some of the items of the account, but came to nearly the same general conclusions.[21]

The rotation of crops was very imperfectly understood. It was known, indeed, that some vegetables lately introduced into our island, particularly the turnip, afforded excellent nutriment in winter to sheep and oxen: but it was not yet the practice to feed cattle in this manner. It was therefore by no means easy to keep them alive during the season when the grass is scanty. They were killed and salted in great numbers at the beginning of the cold weather; and, during several months, even the gentry tasted scarcely any fresh animal food, except game and river fish, which were consequently much more important articles in housekeeping than at present. It appears from the Northumberland Household Book that, in the reign of Henry the Seventh, fresh meat was never eaten even by the gentlemen attendant on a great Earl, except during the short interval between Midsummer and Michaelmas. But in the course of two centuries an improvement had taken place; and under Charles the Second it was not till the beginning of November that families laid in their stock of salt provisions, then called Martinmas beef.[22]

The sheep and the ox of that time were diminutive when compared with the sheep and oxen which are now driven to our markets.[23] Our native horses, though serviceable, were held in small esteem, and fetched low prices. They were valued, one with another, by the ablest of those who computed the national wealth, at not more than fifty shillings each. Foreign breeds were greatly preferred. Spanish jennets were regarded as the finest chargers, and were imported for purposes of pageantry and war. The

21. King's Natural and Political Conclusions; Davenant on the Balance of Trade.

22. See the Almanacks of 1684 and 1685.

23. See Mr. M'Culloch's Statistical Account of the British Empire, Part III, chap. i, sec. 6.

coaches of the aristocracy were drawn by grey Flemish mares, which trotted, as it was thought, with a peculiar grace, and endured better than any cattle reared in our island the work of dragging a ponderous equipage over the rugged pavement of London. Neither the modern dray horse nor the modern race horse was then known. At a much later period the ancestors of the gigantic quadrupeds, which all foreigners now class among the chief wonders of London, were brought from the marshes of Walcheren; the ancestors of Childers and Eclipse from the sands of Arabia. Already, however, there was among our nobility and gentry a passion for the amusements of the turf. The importance of improving our studs by an infusion of new blood was strongly felt; and with this view a considerable number of barbs had lately been brought into the country. Two men whose authority on such subjects was held in great esteem, the Duke of Newcastle and Sir John Fenwick, pronounced that the meanest hack ever imported from Tangier would produce a finer progeny than could be expected from the best sire of our native breed. They would not readily have believed that a time would come when the princes and nobles of neighbouring lands would be as eager to obtain horses from England as ever the English had been to obtain horses from Barbary.[24]

The increase of vegetable and animal produce, though great, seems small when compared with the increase of our mineral wealth. In 1685 the tin of Cornwall, which had, more than two thousand years before, attracted the Tyrian sails beyond the pillars of Hercules, was still one of the most valuable subterranean productions of the island. The quantity annually extracted from the earth was found to be, some years later, sixteen hundred tons, probably about a third of what it now is.[25] But the veins of copper which lie in the same region were, in the time of Charles the Sec-

24. King and Davenant as before; the Duke of Newcastle on Horsemanship; Gentleman's Recreation, 1686. The "dappled Flanders mares" were marks of greatness in the time of Pope, and even later.

The vulgar proverb, that the grey mare is the better horse, originated, I suspect, in the preference generally given to the grey mares of Flanders over the finest coach horses of England.

25. See a curious note by Tonkin, in Lord De Dunstanville's edition of Carew's Survey of Cornwall.

ond, altogether neglected, nor did any landowner take them into the account in estimating the value of his property. Cornwall and Wales at present yield annually near fifteen thousand tons of copper, worth near a million and a half sterling; that is to say, worth about twice as much as the annual produce of all English mines of all descriptions in the seventeenth century.[26] The first bed of rock salt had been discovered in Cheshire not long after the Restoration, but does not appear to have been worked till much later. The salt which was obtained by a rude process from brine pits was held in no high estimation. The pans in which the manufacture was carried on exhaled a sulphurous stench; and, when the evaporation was complete, the substance which was left was scarcely fit to be used with food. Physicians attributed the scorbutic and pulmonary complaints which were common among the English to this unwholesome condiment. It was therefore seldom used by the upper and middle classes; and there was a regular and considerable importation from France. At present our springs and mines not only supply our own immense demand, but send annually more than seven hundred millions of pounds of excellent salt to foreign countries.[27]

Far more important has been the improvement of our iron works. Such works had long existed in our island, but had not prospered, and had been regarded with no favourable eye by the government and by the public. It was not then the practice to employ coal for smelting the ore; and the rapid consumption of wood excited the alarm of politicians. As early as the reign of Elizabeth there had been loud complaints that whole forests were cut down for the purpose of feeding the furnaces; and the Parliament had interfered to prohibit the manufacturers from burning timber. The manufacture consequently languished. At the close of the reign of Charles the Second, great part of the iron which was used in this country was imported from abroad; and the whole quantity cast here annually seems not to have exceeded ten

26. Borlase's Natural History of Cornwall, 1758. The quantity of copper now produced, I have taken from parliamentary returns. Davenant, in 1700, estimated the annual produce of all the mines of England at between seven and eight hundred thousand pounds.

27. Philosophical Transactions, No. 53, Nov. 1669; No. 66, Dec. 1670; No. 103, May 1674; No. 156, Feb. 1683¾.

thousand tons. At present the trade is thought to be in a depressed state if less than a million of tons are produced in a year.[28]

One mineral, perhaps more important than iron itself, remains to be mentioned. Coal, though very little used in any species of manufacture, was already the ordinary fuel in some districts which were fortunate enough to possess large beds, and in the capital, which could easily be supplied by water carriage. It seems reasonable to believe that at least one half of the quantity then extracted from the pits was consumed in London. The consumption of London seemed to the writers of that age enormous, and was often mentioned by them as a proof of the greatness of the imperial city. They scarcely hoped to be believed when they affirmed that two hundred and eighty thousand chaldrons, that is to say, about three hundred and fifty thousand tons, were, in the last year of the reign of Charles the Second, brought to the Thames. At present three millions and a half of tons are required yearly by the metropolis; and the whole annual produce cannot, on the most moderate computation, be estimated at less than thirty millions of tons.[29]

While these great changes have been in progress, the rent of land, has, as might be expected, been almost constantly rising. In some districts it has multiplied more than tenfold. In some it has not more than doubled. It has probably, on the average, quadrupled.

Of the rent, a large proportion was divided among the country gentlemen, a class of persons whose position and character it is most important that we should clearly understand; for by their influence and by their passions the fate of the nation was, at several important conjunctures, determined.

We should be much mistaken if we pictured to ourselves the squires of the seventeenth century as men bearing a close resem-

28. Yarranton, England's Improvement by Sea and Land, 1677; Porter's Progress of the Nation. See also a remarkably perspicuous history, in small compass, of the English iron works, in Mr. M'Culloch's Statistical Account of the British Empire.

29. See Chamberlayne's State of England, 1684, 1687; Angliæ Metropolis, 1691; M'Culloch's Statistical Account of the British Empire, Part III, chap. ii (edition of 1847). In 1845 the quantity of coal brought into London appeared, by the parliamentary returns, to be 3,460,000 tons. (1848.) In 1854 the quantity of coal brought into London amounted to 4,378,000 tons. (1857.)

blance to their descendants, the county members and chairmen of quarter sessions with whom we are familiar. The modern country gentleman generally receives a liberal education, passes from a distinguished school to a distinguished college, and has ample opportunity to become an excellent scholar. He has generally seen something of foreign countries. A considerable part of his life has generally been passed in the capital; and the refinements of the capital follow him into the country. There is perhaps no class of dwellings so pleasing as the rural seats of the English gentry. In the parks and pleasure grounds, nature, dressed yet not disguised by art, wears her most alluring form. In the buildings, good sense and good taste combine to produce a happy union of the comfortable and the graceful. The pictures, the musical instruments, the library, would in any other country be considered as proving the owner to be an eminently polished and accomplished man. A country gentleman who witnessed the Revolution was probably in receipt of about a fourth part of the rent which his acres now yield to his posterity. He was, therefore, as compared with his posterity, a poor man, and was generally under the necessity of residing, with little interruption, on his estate. To travel on the Continent, to maintain an establishment in London, or even to visit London frequently, were pleasures in which only the great proprietors could indulge. It may be confidently affirmed that of the squires whose names were then in the Commissions of Peace and Lieutenancy not one in twenty went to town once in five years, or had ever in his life wandered so far as Paris. Many lords of manors had received an education differing little from that of their menial servants. The heir of an estate often passed his boyhood and youth at the seat of his family with no better tutors than grooms and gamekeepers, and scarce attained learning enough to sign his name to a Mittimus. If he went to school and to college, he generally returned before he was twenty to the seclusion of the old hall, and there, unless his mind were very happily constituted by nature, soon forgot his academical pursuits in rural business and pleasures. His chief serious employment was the care of his property. He examined samples of grain, handled pigs, and, on market days, made bargains over a tankard with drovers and hop merchants. His chief pleasures were commonly derived from field sports and from an unrefined sensuality. His language and pronunciation were such as we should now expect to hear only from the most ignorant clowns. His oaths, coarse jests, and scurrilous terms of abuse, were uttered with the broadest accent of his province. It was easy to discern, from the first words which he spoke, whether he came from Somersetshire or Yorkshire. He troubled himself little about decorating his abode, and, if he attempted decoration, seldom produced anything but deformity. The litter of a farmyard gathered under the windows of his bedchamber, and the cabbages and gooseberry bushes grew close to his hall door. His table was loaded with coarse plenty; and guests were cordially welcomed to it. But, as the habit of drinking to excess was general in the class to which he belonged, and as his fortune did not enable him to intoxicate large assemblies daily with claret or canary, strong beer was the ordinary beverage. The quantity of beer consumed in those days was indeed enormous. For beer then was to the middle and lower classes, not only all that beer now is, but all that wine, tea, and ardent spirits now are. It was only at great houses, or on great occasions, that foreign drink was placed on the board. The ladies of the house, whose business it had commonly been to cook the repast, retired as soon as the dishes had been devoured, and left the gentlemen to their ale and tobacco. The coarse jollity of the afternoon was often prolonged till the revellers were laid under the table.

It was very seldom that the country gentleman caught glimpses of the great world; and what he saw of it tended rather to confuse than to enlighten his understanding. His opinions respecting religion, government, foreign countries and former times, having been derived, not from study, from observation, or from conversation with enlightened companions, but from such traditions as were current in his own small circle, were the opinions of a child. He adhered to them, however, with the obstinacy which is generally found in ignorant men accustomed to be fed with flattery. His animosities were numerous and bitter. He hated Frenchmen and Italians, Scotchmen and Irishmen, Papists and Presbyterians, Independents and Baptists, Quakers and Jews. Towards London and Londoners he felt an aversion which more than once produced important political effects. His wife and daughter were in tastes and acquirements below a housekeeper or a stillroom maid of the present day. They stitched and spun, brewed gooseberry wine, cured marigolds, and made the crust for the venison pasty.

From this description it might be supposed that the English esquire of the seventeenth century did not materially differ from a rustic miller or alehouse keeper of our time. There are, however, some important parts of his character still to be noted, which will greatly modify this estimate. Unlettered as he was and unpolished, he was still in some most important points a gentleman. He was a member of a proud and powerful aristocracy, and was distinguished by many both of the good and of the bad qualities which belong to aristocrats. His family pride was beyond that of a Talbot or a Howard. He knew the genealogies and coats of arms of all his neighbours, and could tell which of them had assumed supporters without any right, and which of them were so unfortunate as to be greatgrandsons of aldermen. He was a magistrate, and, as such, administered gratuitously to those who dwelt around him a rude patriarchal justice, which, in spite of innumerable blunders and of occasional acts of tyranny, was yet better than no justice at all. He was an officer of the trainbands; and his military dignity, though it might move the mirth of gallants who had served a campaign in Flanders, raised his character in his own eyes and in the eyes of his neighbours. Nor indeed was his soldiership justly a subject of derision. In every county there were elderly gentlemen who had seen service which was no child's play. One had been knighted by Charles the First, after the battle of Edgehill. Another still wore a patch over the scar which he had received at Naseby. A third had defended his old house till Fairfax had blown in the door with a petard. The presence of these old Cavaliers, with their old swords and holsters, and with their old stories about Goring and Lunsford, gave to the musters of militia an earnest and warlike aspect which would otherwise have been wanting. Even those country gentlemen who were too young to have themselves exchanged blows with the cuirassiers of the Parliament had, from childhood, been surrounded by the traces of recent war, and fed with stories of the martial exploits of their fathers and uncles. Thus the character of the English esquire of the seventeenth century was compounded of two elements which we seldom or never find united. His ignorance and uncouthness, his low tastes and gross phrases, would, in our time, be considered as indicating a nature and a breeding thoroughly plebeian. Yet he was essentially a patrician, and had, in large measure, both the virtues and the vices which flourish among men set from their birth in high place, and used to respect themselves and to be respected by others. It is not easy for a generation accustomed to find chivalrous sentiments only in company with liberal studies and polished manners to image to itself a man with the deportment, the vocabulary, and the accent of a carter, yet punctilious on matters of genealogy and precedence, and ready to risk his life rather than see a stain cast on the honour of his house. It is however only by thus joining together things seldom or never found together in our own experience, that we can form a just idea of that rustic aristocracy which constituted the main strength of the armies of Charles the First, and which long supported, with strange fidelity, the interest of his descendants.

The gross, uneducated, untravelled country gentleman was commonly a Tory: but, though devotedly attached to hereditary monarchy, he had no partiality for courtiers and ministers. He thought, not without reason, that Whitehall was filled with the most corrupt of mankind, and that of the great sums which the House of Commons had voted to the crown since the Restoration part had been embezzled by cunning politicians, and part squandered on buffoons and foreign courtesans. His stout English heart swelled with indignation at the thought that the government of his country should be subject to French dictation. Being himself generally an old Cavalier, or the son of an old Cavalier, he reflected with bitter resentment on the ingratitude with which the Stuarts had requited their best friends. Those who heard him grumble at the neglect with which he was treated, and at the profusion with which wealth was lavished on the bastards of Nell Gwynn and Madam Carwell, would have supposed him ripe for rebellion. But all this ill humour lasted only till the throne was really in danger. It was precisely when those whom the sovereign had loaded with wealth and honours shrank from his side that the country gentlemen, so surly and mutinous in the season of his prosperity, rallied round him in a body. Thus, after murmuring twenty years at the misgovernment of Charles the Second, they came to his rescue in his extremity, when his own Secretaries of State and the Lords of his own Treasury had deserted him, and enabled him to gain a complete victory over the opposition; nor can there be any doubt that they would have shown equal loyalty to his brother James, if James would, even at the last moment, have refrained from outraging their strongest feeling. For there was one institution, and one only, which they prized even more than hereditary monarchy; and that institution was the Church of England. Their love of the Church was not, indeed, the effect of study or meditation. Few among them could have given any reason, drawn from Scripture or ecclesiastical history, for adhering to her doctrines, her ritual, and her polity; nor were they, as a class, by any means strict observers of that code of morality which is common to all Christian sects. But the experience of many ages proves that men may be ready to fight to the death, and to persecute without pity, for a religion whose creed they do not understand, and whose precepts they habitually disobey.[30]

The rural clergy were even more vehement in Toryism than the rural gentry, and were a class scarcely less important. It is to be observed, however, that the individual clergyman, as compared with the individual gentleman, then ranked much lower than in our days. The main support of the Church was derived from the tithe; and the tithe bore to the rent a much smaller ratio than at present. King estimated the whole income of the parochial and collegiate clergy at only four hundred and eighty thousand pounds a year; Davenant at only five hundred and forty-four thousand a year. It is certainly now more than seven times as great as the larger of these two sums. The average rent of the land has not, according to any estimate, increased proportionally. It follows that the rectors and vicars must have been, as compared with the neighbouring knights and squires, much poorer in the seventeenth than in the nineteenth century.

The place of the clergyman in society had been completely changed by the Reformation. Before that event, ecclesiastics had formed the majority of the House of Lords, had, in wealth and splendour, equalled, and sometimes outshone, the greatest of the temporal barons, and had generally held the highest civil offices.

30. My notion of the country gentleman of the seventeenth century has been derived from sources too numerous to be recapitulated. I must leave my description to the judgment of those who have studied the history and the lighter literature of that age.

Many of the Treasurers, and almost all the Chancellors of the Plantagenets were Bishops. The Lord Keeper of the Privy Seal and the Master of the Rolls were ordinarily churchmen. Churchmen transacted the most important diplomatic business. Indeed, all that large portion of the administration which rude and warlike nobles were incompetent to conduct was considered as especially belonging to divines. Men, therefore, who were averse to the life of camps, and who were, at the same time, desirous to rise in the state, commonly received the tonsure. Among them were sons of all the most illustrious families, and near kinsmen of the throne, Scroops and Nevilles, Bourchiers, Staffords, and Poles. To the religious houses belonged the rents of immense domains, and all that large portion of the tithe which is now in the hands of laymen. Down to the middle of the reign of Henry the Eighth, therefore, no line of life was so attractive to ambitious and covetous natures as the priesthood. Then came a violent revolution. The abolition of the monasteries deprived the Church at once of the greater part of her wealth, and of her predominance in the Upper House of Parliament. There was no longer an Abbot of Glastonbury or an Abbot of Reading seated among the peers, and possessed of revenues equal to those of a powerful Earl. The princely splendour of William of Wykeham and of William of Waynflete had disappeared. The scarlet hat of the Cardinal, the silver cross of the Legate, were no more. The clergy had also lost the ascendency which is the natural reward of superior mental cultivation. Once the circumstance that a man could read had raised a presumption that he was in orders. But, in an age which produced such laymen as William Cecil and Nicholas Bacon, Roger Ascham and Thomas Smith, Walter Mildmay and Francis Walsingham, there was no reason for calling away prelates from their dioceses to negotiate treaties, to superintend the finances, or to administer justice. The spiritual character not only ceased to be a qualification for high civil office, but began to be regarded as a disqualification. Those worldly motives, therefore, which had formerly induced so many able, aspiring, and high born youths to assume the ecclesiastical habit, ceased to operate. Not one parish in two hundred then afforded what a man of family considered as a maintenance. There were still indeed prizes in the Church: but they were few; and even the highest were mean, when compared with the glory which had once surrounded the princes of the hierarchy. The state kept by Parker and Grindal seemed beggarly to those who remembered the imperial pomp of Wolsey, his palaces, which had become the favourite abodes of royalty, Whitehall and Hampton Court, the three sumptuous tables daily spread in his refectory, the forty-four gorgeous copes in his chapel, his running footmen in rich liveries, and his body guards with gilded poleaxes. Thus the sacerdotal office lost its attraction for the higher classes. During the century which followed the accession of Elizabeth, scarce a single person of noble descent took orders. At the close of the reign of Charles the Second, two sons of peers were Bishops; four or five sons of peers were priests, and held valuable preferment: but these rare exceptions did not take away the reproach which lay on the body. The clergy were regarded as, on the whole, a plebeian class.[31] And, indeed, for one who made the figure of a gentleman, ten were mere menial servants. A large proportion of those divines who had no benefices, or whose benefices were too small to afford a comfortable revenue, lived in the houses of laymen. It had long been evident that this practice tended to degrade the priestly character. Laud had exerted himself to effect a change; and Charles the First had repeatedly issued positive orders that none but men of high rank should presume to keep domestic chaplains.[32] But these injunctions had become obsolete. Indeed, during the domination of the Puritans, many of the ejected ministers of the Church of England could obtain bread and shelter only by attaching themselves to the households of royalist gentlemen; and the habits which had been formed in those times of trouble continued long after the reestablishment of monarchy and episcopacy. In the mansions of men of liberal sentiments and cultivated understandings, the chaplain was doubtless treated with urbanity and kindness. His conversa-

31. In the eighteenth century the great increase in the value of benefices produced a change. The younger sons of the nobility were allured back to the clerical profession. Warburton in a letter to Hurd, dated the 5th of July 1752, mentions this change, which was then recent. "Our grandees have at last found their way back into the Church. I only wonder they have been so long about it. But be assured that nothing but a new religious revolution, to sweep away the fragments that Henry the Eighth left after banqueting his courtiers, will drive them out again."

32. See Heylin's Cyprianus Anglicus.

tion, his literary assistance, his spiritual advice, were considered as an ample return for his food, his lodging, and his stipend. But this was not the general feeling of the country gentlemen. The coarse and ignorant squire, who thought that it belonged to his dignity to have grace said every day at his table by an ecclesiastic in full canonicals, found means to reconcile dignity with economy. A young Levite—such was the phrase then in use—might be had for his board, a small garret, and ten pounds a year, and might not only perform his own professional functions, might not only be the most patient of butts and of listeners, might not only be always ready in fine weather for bowls, and in rainy weather for shovelboard, but might also save the expense of a gardener, or of a groom. Sometimes the reverend man nailed up the apricots; and sometimes he curried the coach horses. He cast up the farrier's bills. He walked ten miles with a message or a parcel. He was permitted to dine with the family; but he was expected to content himself with the plainest fare. He might fill himself with the corned beef and the carrots: but, as soon as the tarts and cheesecakes made their appearance, he quitted his seat, and stood aloof till he was summoned to return thanks for the repast, from a great part of which he had been excluded.[33]

Perhaps, after some years of service, he was presented to a living sufficient to support him: but he often found it necessary to purchase his preferment by a species of Simony, which furnished an inexhaustible subject of pleasantry to three or four generations of scoffers. With his cure he was expected to take a wife. The wife had ordinarily been in the patron's service; and it was well if she was not suspected of standing too high in the patron's favour. Indeed, the nature of the matrimonial connections which the clergymen of that age were in the habit of forming is the most certain indication of the place which the order held in the social system. An Oxonian, writing a few months after the death of Charles the Second, complained bitterly, not only that the country attorney and the country apothecary looked down with disdain on the country clergyman, but that one of the lessons most

---

33. Eachard, Causes of the Contempt of the Clergy; Oldham, Satire addressed to a Friend about to leave the University; Tatler, 255, 258. That the English clergy were a lowborn class, is remarked in the Travels of the Grand Duke Cosmo, Appendix A.

earnestly inculcated on every girl of honourable family was to give no encouragement to a lover in orders, and that, if any young lady forgot this precept, she was almost as much disgraced as by an illicit amour.[34] Clarendon, who assuredly bore no ill will to the priesthood, mentions it as a sign of the confusion of ranks which the great rebellion had produced, that some damsels of noble families had bestowed themselves on divines.[35] A waiting woman was generally considered as the most suitable helpmate for a parson. Queen Elizabeth, as head of the Church, had given what seemed to be a formal sanction to this prejudice, by issuing special orders that no clergyman should presume to espouse a servant girl, without the consent of the master or mistress.[36] During several generations accordingly the relation between divines and hand-maidens was a theme for endless jest; nor would it be easy to find, in the comedy of the seventeenth century, a single instance of a clergyman who wins a spouse above the rank of a cook.[37] Even so late as the time of George the Second, the keenest of all observers of life and manners, himself a priest, remarked that, in a great household, the chaplain was the resource of a lady's maid whose character had been blown upon, and who was therefore forced to give up hopes of catching the steward.[38]

In general the divine who quitted his chaplainship for a benefice and a wife found that he had only exchanged one class of vexations for another. Hardly one living in fifty enabled the

34. "A causidico, medicastro, ipasque artificum farragine, ecclesiæ rector aut vicarius contemnitur et fit ludibrio. Gentis et familiæ nitor sacris ordinibus pollutus censetur: fœminisque natalitio insignibus unicum inculcatur sæpius præceptum, ne modestiæ naufragium faciant, aut, (quod idem auribus tam delicatulis sonat,) ne clerico se nuptas dari patiantur."—Angliæ Notitia, by T. Wood, of New College, Oxford, 1686.

35. Clarendon's Life, ii, 21.

36. See the Injunctions of 1559, in Bishop Sparrow's Collection. Jeremy Collier, in his Essay on Pride, speaks of this injunction with a bitterness which proves that his own pride had not been effectually tamed.

37. Roger and Abigail in Fletcher's Scornful Lady, Bull and the Nurse in Vanbrugh's Relapse, Smirk and Susan in Shadwell's Lancashire Witches, are instances.

38. Swift's Directions to Servants. I may add that Swift, in his Essay on the Fates of Clergymen, has elaborately traced the career of two divines, Eugenius and Corusodes, the man of parts and the dunce. Differing in everything else, they both marry low women. Eugenius has to take up with a farmer's widow, and Corusodes with a cast off mistress.

incumbent to bring up a family comfortably. As children multiplied and grew, the household of the priest became more and more beggarly. Holes appeared more and more plainly in the thatch of his parsonage and in his single cassock. Often it was only by toiling on his glebe, by feeding swine, and by loading dungcarts, that he could obtain daily bread; nor did his utmost exertions always prevent the bailiffs from taking his concordance and his inkstand in execution. It was a white day on which he was admitted into the kitchen of a great house, and regaled by the servants with cold meat and ale. His children were brought up like the children of the neighbouring peasantry. His boys followed the plough; and his girls went out to service.[39] Study he found impossible: for the advowson of his living would hardly have sold for a sum sufficient to purchase a good theological library; and he might be considered as unusually lucky if he had ten or twelve dogeared volumes among the pots and pans on his shelves. Even a keen and strong intellect might be expected to rust in so unfavourable a situation.

Assuredly there was at that time no lack in the English Church of ministers distinguished by abilities and learning. But it is to be observed that these ministers were not scattered among the rural population. They were brought together at a few places where the means of acquiring knowledge were abundant, and where the opportunities of vigorous intellectual exercise were frequent.[40] At such places were to be found divines qualified by parts, by eloquence, by wide knowledge of literature, of science, and of life, to defend their Church victoriously against heretics and sceptics, to command the attention of frivolous and worldly congregations, to guide the deliberations of senates, and to make religion respectable, even in the most dissolute of courts. Some laboured to fathom the abysses of metaphysical theology: some were deeply versed in biblical criticism; and some threw light

39. Even in Tom Jones, published two generations later, Mrs. Seagrim, the wife of a gamekeeper, and Mrs. Honour, a waitingwoman, boast of their descent from clergymen. "It is to be hoped," says Fielding, "such instances will in future ages, when some provision is made for the families of the inferior clergy, appear stranger than they can be thought at present."

40. This distinction between country clergy and town clergy is strongly marked by Eachard, and cannot but be observed by every person who has studied the ecclesiastical history of that age.

on the darkest parts of ecclesiastical history. Some proved themselves consummate masters of logic. Some cultivated rhetoric with such assiduity and success that their discourses are still justly valued as models of style. These eminent men were to be found, with scarcely a single exception, at the Universities, at the great Cathedrals, or in the capital. Barrow had lately died at Cambridge; and Pearson had gone thence to the episcopal bench. Cudworth and Henry More were still living there. South and Pococke, Jane and Aldrich, were at Oxford. Prideaux was in the close of Norwich, and Whitby in the close of Salisbury. But it was chiefly by the London clergy, who were always spoken of as a class apart, that the fame of their profession for learning and eloquence was upheld. The principal pulpits of the metropolis were occupied about this time by a crowd of distinguished men, from among whom was selected a large proportion of the rulers of the Church. Sherlock preached at the Temple, Tillotson at Lincoln's Inn, Wake and Jeremy Collier at Gray's Inn, Burnet at the Rolls, Stillingfleet at Saint Paul's Cathedral, Patrick at Saint Paul's in Covent Garden, Fowler at Saint Giles's, Cripplegate, Sharp at Saint Giles's in the Fields, Tenison at Saint Martin's, Sprat at Saint Margaret's, Beveridge at Saint Peter's in Cornhill. Of these twelve men, all of high note in ecclesiastical history, ten became Bishops, and four Archbishops. Meanwhile almost the only important theological works which came forth from a rural parsonage were those of George Bull, afterwards Bishop of Saint David's; and Bull never would have produced those works, had he not inherited an estate, by the sale of which he was enabled to collect a library, such as probably no other country clergyman in England possessed.[41]

Thus the Anglican priesthood was divided into two sections, which, in acquirements, in manners, and in social position, differed widely from each other. One section, trained for cities and courts, comprised men familiar with all ancient and modern learning; men able to encounter Hobbes or Bossuet at all the weapons of controversy; men who could, in their sermons, set forth the majesty and beauty of Christianity with such justness of

41. Nelson's Life of Bull. As to the extreme difficulty which the country clergy found in procuring books, see the Life of Thomas Bray, the founder of the Society for the Propagation of the Gospel.

thought, and such energy of language, that the indolent Charles roused himself to listen, and the fastidious Buckingham forgot to sneer; men whose address, politeness, and knowledge of the world qualified them to manage the consciences of the wealthy and noble; men with whom Halifax loved to discuss the interests of empires, and from whom Dryden was not ashamed to own that he had learned to write.[42] The other section was destined to ruder and humbler service. It was dispersed over the country, and consisted chiefly of persons not at all wealthier, and not much more refined, than small farmers or upper servants. Yet it was in these rustic priests, who derived but a scanty subsistence from their tithe sheaves and tithe pigs, and who had not the smallest chance of ever attaining high professional honours, that the professional spirit was strongest. Among those divines who were the boast of the Universities and the delight of the capital, and who had attained, or might reasonably expect to attain, opulence and lordly rank, a party, respectable in numbers, and more respectable in character, leaned towards constitutional principles of government, lived on friendly terms with Presbyterians, Independents, and Baptists, would gladly have seen a full toleration granted to all Protestant sects, and would even have consented to make alterations in the Liturgy, for the purpose of conciliating honest and candid Nonconformists. But such latitudinarianism was held in horror by the country parson. He took, indeed, more pride in his ragged gown than his superiors in their lawn and their scarlet hoods. The very consciousness that there was little in his worldly circumstances to distinguish him from the villagers to whom he preached led him to hold immoderately high the dignity of that sacerdotal office which was his single title to reverence. Having lived in seclusion, and having had little opportunity of correcting his opinions by reading or conversation, he held and taught the doctrines of indefeasible hereditary right, of passive obedience, and of nonresistance, in all their crude absurdity. Having been long engaged in a petty war against the neighbouring dissenters, he too often hated them for the wrong

42. "I have frequently heard him (Dryden) own with pleasure, that if he had any talent for English prose it was owing to his having often read the writings of the great Archbishop Tillotson."—Congreve's Dedication of Dryden's Plays.

which he had done them, and found no fault with the Five Mile Act and the Conventicle Act, except that those odious laws had not a sharper edge. Whatever influence his office gave him was exerted with passionate zeal on the Tory side; and that influence was immense. It would be a great error to imagine, because the country rector was in general not regarded as a gentleman, because he could not dare to aspire to the hand of one of the young ladies at the manor house, because he was not asked into the parlours of the great, but was left to drink and smoke with grooms and butlers, that the power of the clerical body was smaller than at present. The influence of a class is by no means proportioned to the consideration which the members of that class enjoy in their individual capacity. A Cardinal is a much more exalted personage than a begging friar: but it would be a grievous mistake to suppose that the College of Cardinals has exercised a greater dominion over the public mind of Europe than the Order of Saint Francis. In Ireland, at present, a peer holds a far higher station in society than a Roman Catholic priest: yet there are in Munster and Connaught few counties where a combination of priests would not carry an election against a combination of peers. In the seventeenth century the pulpit was to a large portion of the population what the periodical press now is. Scarce any of the clowns who came to the parish church ever saw a Gazette or a political pamphlet. Ill informed as their spiritual pastor might be, he was yet better informed than themselves: he had every week an opportunity of haranguing them; and his harangues were never answered. At every important conjuncture, invectives against the Whigs and exhortations to obey the Lord's anointed resounded at once from many thousands of pulpits; and the effect was formidable indeed. Of all the causes which, after the dissolution of the Oxford Parliament, produced the violent reaction against the Exclusionists, the most potent seems to have been the oratory of the country clergy.

The power which the country gentlemen and the country clergymen exercised in the rural districts was in some measure counterbalanced by the power of the yeomanry, an eminently manly and truehearted race. The petty proprietors who cultivated their own fields with their own hands, and enjoyed a modest competence, without affecting to have scutcheons and crests, or aspiring to sit on the bench of justice, then formed a much more important part of the nation than at present. If we may trust the best statistical writers of that age, not less than a hundred and sixty thousand proprietors, who with their families must have made up more than a seventh of the whole population, derived their subsistence from little freehold estates. The average income of these small landholders, an income made up of rent, profit, and wages, was estimated at between sixty and seventy pounds a year. It was computed that the number of persons who tilled their own land was greater than the number of those who farmed the land of others.[43] A large portion of the yeomanry had, from the time of the Reformation, leaned towards Puritanism, had, in the civil war, taken the side of the Parliament, had, after the Restoration, persisted in hearing Presbyterian and Independent preachers, had, at elections, strenuously supported the Exclusionists, and had continued, even after the discovery of the Rye House plot and the proscription of the Whig leaders, to regard Popery and arbitrary power with unmitigated hostility.

. . . .

The position of London, relatively to the other towns of the empire, was, in the time of Charles the Second, far higher than at present. For at present the population of London is little more than six times the population of Manchester or of Liverpool. In the days of Charles the Second the population of London was more than seventeen times the population of Bristol or of Norwich. It may be doubted whether any other instance can be mentioned of a great kingdom in which the first city was more than seventeen times as large as the second. There is reason to believe that, in 1685, London had been, during about half a century, the most populous capital in Europe. The inhabitants, who are now at least nineteen hundred thousand, were then probably little more than half a million.[44] London had in the world only one commercial rival, now long ago outstripped, the mighty and opulent Amsterdam. English writers boasted of the forest of masts and yardarms which covered the river from the Bridge to

43. I have taken Davenant's estimate, which is a little lower than King's.
44. According to King, 530,000. (1848.) In 1851 the population of London exceeded 2,300,000. (1857.)

the Tower, and of the stupendous sums which were collected at the Custom House in Thames Street. There is, indeed, no doubt that the trade of the metropolis then bore a far greater proportion than at present to the whole trade of the country; yet to our generation the honest vaunting of our ancestors must appear almost ludicrous. The shipping which they thought incredibly great appears not to have exceeded seventy thousand tons. This was, indeed, then more than a third of the whole tonnage of the kingdom, but is now less than a fourth of the tonnage of Newcastle, and is nearly equalled by the tonnage of the steam vessels of the Thames. The customs of London amounted, in 1685, to about three hundred and thirty thousand pounds a year. In our time the net duty paid annually, at the same place, exceeds ten millions.[45]

Whoever examines the maps of London which were published towards the close of the reign of Charles the Second will see that only the nucleus of the present capital then existed. The town did not, as now, fade by imperceptible degrees into the country. No long avenues of villas, embowered in lilacs and laburnums, extended from the great centre of wealth and civilisation almost to the boundaries of Middlesex and far into the heart of Kent and Surrey. In the east, no part of the immense line of warehouses and artificial lakes which now stretches from the Tower to Blackwall had even been projected. On the west, scarcely one of those stately piles of building which are inhabited by the noble and wealthy was in existence; and Chelsea, which is now peopled by more than forty thousand human beings, was a quiet country village with about a thousand inhabitants.[46] On the north, cattle fed, and sportsmen wandered with dogs and guns, over the site of the borough of Marylebone, and over far the greater part of the space now covered by the boroughs of Finsbury and of the Tower Hamlets. Islington was almost a

45. Macpherson's History of Commerce; Chalmers's Estimate; Chamberlayne's State of England, 1684. The tonnage of the steamers belonging to the port of London was, at the end of 1847, about 60,000 tons. The customs of the port, from 1842 to 1845, very nearly averaged £11,000,000. (1848.) In 1854 the tonnage of the steamers of the port of London amounted to 138,000 tons, without reckoning vessels of less than fifty tons. (1857.)

46. Lyson's Environs of London. The baptisms at Chelsea, between 1680 and 1690, were only 42 a year.

solitude; and poets loved to contrast its silence and repose with the din and turmoil of the monster London.[47] On the south the capital is now connected with its suburb by several bridges, not inferior in magnificence and solidity to the noblest works of the Cæsars. In 1685, a single line of irregular arches, overhung by piles of mean and crazy houses, and garnished, after a fashion worthy of the naked barbarians of Dahomy, with scores of mouldering heads, impeded the navigation of the river.

Of the metropolis, the City, properly so called, was the most important division. At the time of the Restoration it had been built, for the most part, of wood and plaster; the few bricks that were used were ill baked; the booths where goods were exposed to sale projected far into the streets, and were overhung by the upper stories. A few specimens of this architecture may still be seen in those districts which were not reached by the great fire. That fire had, in a few days, covered a space of little less than a square mile with the ruins of eighty-nine churches and of thirteen thousand houses. But the City had risen again with a celerity which had excited the admiration of neighbouring countries. Unfortunately, the old lines of the streets had been to a great extent preserved; and those lines, originally traced in an age when even princesses performed their journeys on horseback, were often too narrow to allow wheeled carriages to pass each other with ease, and were therefore ill adapted for the residence of wealthy persons in an age when a coach and six was a fashionable luxury. The style of building was, however, far superior to that of the City which had perished. The ordinary material was brick, of much better quality than had formerly been used. On the sites of the ancient parish churches had arisen a multitude of new domes, towers, and spires which bore the mark of the fertile genius of Wren. In every place save one the traces of the great devastation had been completely effaced. But the crowds of workmen, the scaffolds, and the masses of hewn stone were still to be seen where the noblest of Protestant temples was slowly rising on the ruins of the old Cathedral of Saint Paul.[48]

47. Cowley, Discourse of Solitude.
48. The fullest and most trustworthy information about the state of the buildings of London at this time is to be derived from the maps and drawings in the British Museum and in the Pepysian Library. The badness of the bricks

The whole character of the City has, since that time, under-gone a complete change. At present the bankers, the merchants, and the chief shopkeepers repair thither on six mornings of every week for the transaction of business: but they reside in other quarters of the metropolis, or at suburban country seats sur-rounded by shrubberies and flower gardens. This revolution in private habits has produced a political revolution of no small importance. The City is no longer regarded by the wealthiest traders with that attachment which every man naturally feels for his home. It is no longer associated in their minds with domestic affections and endearments. The fireside, the nursery, the social table, the quiet bed are not there. Lombard Street and Threadneedle Street are merely places where men toil and ac-cumulate. They go elsewhere to enjoy and to expend. On a Sun-day, or in an evening after the hours of business, some courts and alleys, which a few hours before had been alive with hurry-ing feet and anxious faces, are as silent as the glades of a forest. The chiefs of the mercantile interest are no longer citizens. They avoid, they almost contemn, municipal honours and duties. Those honours and duties are abandoned to men who, though useful and highly respectable, seldom belong to the princely commer-cial houses of which the names are renowned throughout the world.

In the seventeenth century the City was the merchant's resi-dence. Those mansions of the great old burghers which still exist have been turned into counting houses and warehouses: but it is evident that they were originally not inferior in magnif-icence to the dwellings which were then inhabited by the nobility. They sometimes stand in retired and gloomy courts, and are accessible only by inconvenient passages: but their dimensions are ample, and their aspect stately. The entrances are decorated with richly carved pillars and canopies. The staircases and land-ing places are not wanting in grandeur. The floors are some-times of wood, tessellated after the fashion of France. The palace

---

in the old buildings of London is particularly mentioned in the Travels of the Grand Duke Cosmo. There is an account of the works at Saint Paul's in Ward's London Spy. I am almost ashamed to quote such nauseous balderdash; but I have been forced to descend even lower, if possible, in search af materials.

of Sir Robert Clayton, in the Old Jewry, contained a superb banqueting room wainscoted with cedar, and adorned with battles of gods and giants in fresco.[49] Sir Dudley North expended four thousand pounds, a sum which would then have been important to a Duke, on the rich furniture of his reception rooms in Basinghall Street.[50] In such abodes, under the last Stuarts, the heads of the great firms lived splendidly and hospitably. To their dwelling place they were bound by the strongest ties of interest and affection. There they had passed their youth, had made their friendships, had courted their wives, had seen their children grow up, had laid the remains of their parents in the earth, and expected that their own remains would be laid. That intense patriotism which is peculiar to the members of societies congregated within a narrow space was, in such circumstances, strongly developed. London was, to the Londoner, what Athens was to the Athenian of the age of Pericles, what Florence was to the Florentine of the fifteenth century. The citizen was proud of the grandeur of his city, punctilious about her claims to respect, ambitious of her offices, and zealous for her franchises.

At the close of the reign of Charles the Second the pride of the Londoners was smarting from a cruel mortification. The old charter had been taken away; and the magistracy had been remodelled. All the civic functionaries were Tories: and the Whigs, though in numbers and in wealth superior to their opponents, found themselves excluded from every local dignity. Nevertheless, the external splendour of the municipal government was not diminished, nay, was rather increased by this change. For, under the administration of some Puritans who had lately borne rule, the ancient fame of the City for good cheer had declined: but under the new magistrates, who belonged to a more festive party, and at whose boards guests of rank and fashion from beyond Temple Bar were often seen, the Guildhall and the halls of the great companies were enlivened by many sumptuous banquets. During these repasts, odes, composed by the poet laureate of the corporation, in praise of the King, the Duke, and the Mayor, were sung to music. The drinking was

49. Evelyn's Diary, Sept. 20, 1672.
50. Roger North's Life of Sir Dudley North.

deep, the shouting loud. An observant Tory, who had often shared in these revels, has remarked that the practice of huzzaing after drinking healths dates from this joyous period.[51]

The magnificence displayed by the first civic magistrate was almost regal. The gilded coach, indeed, which is now annually admired by the crowd, was not yet a part of his state. On great occasions he appeared on horseback, attended by a long cavalcade inferior in magnificence only to that which, before a coronation, escorted the sovereign from the Tower to Westminster. The Lord Mayor was never seen in public without his rich robe, his hood of black velvet, his gold chain, his jewel, and a great attendance of harbingers and guards.[52] Nor did the world find anything ludicrous in the pomp which constantly surrounded him. For it was not more than became the place which, as wielding the strength and representing the dignity of the City of London, he was entitled to occupy in the state. That City, being then not only without equal in the country, but without second, had, during five and forty years, exercised almost as great an influence on the politics of England as Paris has, in our own time, exercised on the politics of France. In intelligence London was greatly in advance of every other part of the kingdom. A government, supported and trusted by London, could in a day obtain such pecuniary means as it would have taken months to collect from the rest of the island. Nor were the military resources of the capital to be despised. The power which the Lord Lieutenants exercised in other parts of the kingdom was in London entrusted to a Commission of eminent citizens. Under the orders of this Commission were twelve regiments of foot and two regiments of horse. An army of drapers' apprentices and journeymen tailors, with common councilmen for captains and aldermen for colonels, might not indeed have been able to stand its ground against regular troops; but there were then very few regular troops in the kingdom. A town, therefore, which could send forth, at

51. North's Examen. This amusing writer has preserved a specimen of the sublime raptures in which the Pindar of the City indulged:
"The worshipful Sir John Moor!
After age that name adore!"
52. Chamberlayne's State of England, 1684; Angliæ Metropolis, 1690; Seymour's London, 1734.

an hour's notice, thousands of men, abounding in natural courage, provided with tolerable weapons, and not altogether untinctured with martial discipline, could not but be a valuable ally and a formidable enemy. It was not forgotten that Hampden and Pym had been protected from lawless tyranny by the London trainbands; that, in the great crisis of the civil war, the London trainbands had marched to raise the siege of Gloucester; or that, in the movement against the military tyrants which followed the downfall of Richard Cromwell, the London trainbands had borne a signal part. In truth, it is no exaggeration to say that, but for the hostility of the City, Charles the First would never have been vanquished, and that, without the help of the City, Charles the Second could scarcely have been restored.

These considerations may serve to explain why, in spite of that attraction which had, during a long course of years, gradually drawn the aristocracy westward, a few men of high rank had continued, till a very recent period, to dwell in the vicinity of the Exchange and of the Guildhall. Shaftesbury and Buckingham, while engaged in bitter and unscrupulous opposition to the government, had thought that they could nowhere carry on their intrigues so conveniently or so securely as under the protection of the City magistrates and the City militia. Shaftesbury had therefore lived in Aldersgate Street, at a house which may still be easily known by pilasters and wreaths, the graceful work of Inigo. Buckingham had ordered his mansion near Charing Cross, once the abode of the Archbishops of York, to be pulled down; and, while streets and alleys which are still named after him were rising on that site, chose to reside in Dowgate.[53]

These, however, were rare exceptions. Almost all the noble families of England had long migrated beyond the walls. The district where most of their town houses stood lies between the City and the regions which are now considered as fashionable. A few great men still retained their hereditary hotels in the Strand. The stately dwellings on the south and west of Lincoln's Inn Fields, the Piazza of Covent Garden, Southampton Square, which is now called Bloomsbury Square, and King's Square in Soho

53. North's Examen, 116; Wood, Ath. Ox. Shaftesbury; The Duke of B.'s Litany.

Fields, which is now called Soho Square, were among the favourite spots. Foreign princes were carried to see Bloomsbury Square, as one of the wonders of England.[54] Soho Square, which had just been built, was to our ancestors a subject of pride with which their posterity will hardly sympathise. Monmouth Square had been the name while the fortunes of the Duke of Monmouth flourished; and on the southern side towered his mansion. The front, though ungraceful, was lofty and richly adorned. The walls of the principal apartments were finely sculptured with fruit, foliage, and armorial bearings, and were hung with embroidered satin.[55] Every trace of this magnificence has long disappeared; and no aristocratical mansion is to be found in that once aristocratical quarter. A little way north from Holborn, and on the verge of the pastures and cornfields, rose two celebrated palaces, each with an ample garden. One of them, then called Southampton House, and subsequently Bedford House, was removed about fifty years ago to make room for a new city, which now covers, with its squares, streets, and churches, a vast area, renowned in the seventeenth century for peaches and snipes. The other, Montague House, celebrated for its frescoes and furniture, was, a few months after the death of Charles the Second, burned to the ground, and was speedily succeeded by a more magnificent Montague House, which, having been long the repository of such various and precious treasures of art, science, and learning as were scarcely ever before assembled under a single roof, has now given place to an edifice more magnificent still.[56]

Nearer to the Court, on a space called Saint James's Fields, had just been built Saint James's Square and Jermyn Street. Saint James's Church had recently been opened for the accommodation of the inhabitants of this new quarter.[57] Golden Square, which was in the next generation inhabited by lords and ministers of state, had not yet been begun. Indeed the only dwellings to be

54. Travels of the Grand Duke Cosmo.
55. Chamberlayne's State of England, 1684; Pennant's London; Smith's Life of Nollekens.
56. Evelyn's Diary, Oct. 10, 1683, Jan. 19, 1685⁄6.
57. Stat. 1 Jac. II, c. 22.; Evelyn's Diary, Dec. 7, 1684.

seen on the north of Piccadilly were three or four isolated and almost rural mansions, of which the most celebrated was the costly pile erected by Clarendon, and nicknamed Dunkirk House. It had been purchased after its founder's downfall by the Duke of Albemarle. The Clarendon Hotel and Albemarle Street still preserve the memory of the site.

He who then rambled to what is now the gayest and most crowded part of Regent Street found himself in a solitude, and was sometimes so fortunate as to have a shot at a woodcock.[58] On the north the Oxford road ran between hedges. Three or four hundred yards to the south were the garden walls of a few great houses which were considered as quite out of town. On the west was a meadow renowned for a spring from which, long afterwards, Conduit Street was named. On the east was a field not to be passed without a shudder by any Londoner of that age. There, as in a place far from the haunts of men, had been dug, twenty years before, when the great plague was raging, a pit into which the dead carts had nightly shot corpses by scores. It was popularly believed that the earth was deeply tainted with infection, and could not be disturbed without imminent risk to human life. No foundations were laid there till two generations had passed without any return of the pestilence, and till the ghastly spot had long been surrounded by buildings.[59]

We should greatly err if we were to suppose that any of the streets and squares then bore the same aspect as at present. The great majority of the houses, indeed, have, since that time, been wholly, or in great part, rebuilt. If the most fashionable parts of the capital could be placed before us, such as they then were, we should be disgusted by their squalid appearance, and poisoned by their noisome atmosphere.

In Covent Garden a filthy and noisy market was held close to the dwellings of the great. Fruit women screamed, carters fought, cabbage stalks and rotten apples accumulated in heaps at the

58. Old General Oglethorpe, who died in 1785, used to boast that he had shot birds here in Anne's reign. See Pennant's London, and the Gentleman's Magazine for July 1785.

59. The pest field will be seen in maps of London as late as the end of George the First's reign.

thresholds of the Countess of Berkshire and of the Bishop of Durham.[60]

The centre of Lincoln's Inn Fields was an open space where the rabble congregated every evening, within a few yards of Cardigan House and Winchester House, to hear mountebanks harangue, to see bears dance, and to set dogs at oxen. Rubbish was shot in every part of the area. Horses were exercised there. The beggars were as noisy and importunate as in the worst governed cities of the Continent. A Lincoln's Inn mumper was a proverb. The whole fraternity knew the arms and liveries of every charitably disposed grandee in the neighbourhood, and, as soon as his lordship's coach and six appeared, came hopping and crawling in crowds to persecute him. These disorders lasted, in spite of many accidents, and of some legal proceedings, till, in the reign of George the Second, Sir Joseph Jekyll, Master of the Rolls, was knocked down and nearly killed in the middle of the square. Then at length palisades were set up, and a pleasant garden laid out.[61]

Saint James's Square was a receptable for all the offal and cinders, for all the dead cats and dead dogs of Westminster. At one time a cudgel player kept the ring there. At another time an impudent squatter settled himself there, and built a shed for rubbish under the windows of the gilded saloons in which the first magnates of the realm, Norfolk, Ormond, Kent, and Pembroke, gave banquets and balls. It was not till these nuisances had lasted through a whole generation, and till much had been written about them, that the inhabitants applied to Parliament for permission to put up rails, and to plant trees.[62]

60. See a very curious plan of Covent Garden made about 1690, and engraved for Smith's History of Westminster. See also Hogarth's Morning, painted while some of the houses in the Piazza were still occupied by people of fashion.

61. London Spy; Tom Brown's Comical View of London and Westminster; Turner's Propositions for the employing of the Poor, 1678; Daily Courant and Daily Journal of June 7, 1733; Case of Michael v. Allestree, in 1676, 2 Levinz, p. 172. Michael had been run over by two horses which Allestree was breaking in Lincoln's Inn Fields. The declaration set forth that the defendant "porta deux chivals ungovernable en un coach, et improvide, incaute, et absque debita consideratione ineptitudinis loci la eux drive pur eux faire tractable et apt pur un coach, quels chivals, pur ceo que, per leur ferocite, ne poient estre rule, curre sur le plaintiff et le noie."

62. Stat. 12 Geo. I, c. 25; Commons' Journals, Feb. 25. March 2, 172⅝;

When such was the state of the region inhabited by the most luxurious portion of society, we may easily believe that the great body of the population suffered what would now be considered as insupportable grievances. The pavement was detestable: all foreigners cried shame upon it. The drainage was so bad that in rainy weather the gutters soon became torrents. Several facetious poets have commemorated the fury with which these black rivulets roared down Snow Hill and Ludgate Hill, bearing to Fleet Ditch a vast tribute of animal and vegetable filth from the stalls of butchers and greengrocers. This flood was profusely thrown to right and left by coaches and carts. To keep as far from the carriage road as possible was therefore the wish of every pedestrian. The mild and timid gave the wall. The bold and athletic took it. If two roisterers met, they cocked their hats in each other's faces, and pushed each other about till the weaker was shoved towards the kennel. If he was a mere bully he sneaked off, muttering that he should find a time. If he was pugnacious, the encounter probably ended in a duel behind Montague House.[63]

The houses were not numbered. There would indeed have been little advantage in numbering them; for of the coachmen, chairmen, porters, and errand boys of London, a very small proportion could read. It was necessary to use marks which the most ignorant could understand. The shops were therefore distinguished by painted or sculptured signs, which gave a gay and grotesque aspect to the streets. The walk from Charing Cross to Whitechapel lay through an endless succession of Saracens' Heads, Royal Oaks, Blue Bears, and Golden Lambs, which disappeared when they were no longer required for the direction of the common people.

When the evening closed in, the difficulty and danger of walking about London became serious indeed. The garret windows were opened, and pails were emptied, with little regard to

---

London Gardener, 1712; Evening Post, March 23, 1731. I have not been able to find this number of the Evening Post; I therefore quote it on the faith of Mr. Malcolm, who mentions it in his History of London.

63. Lettres sur les Anglois, written early in the reign of William the Third; Swift's City Shower; Gay's Trivia. Johnson used to relate a curious conversation which he had with his mother about giving and taking the wall.

those who were passing below. Falls, bruises, and broken bones were of constant occurrence. For, till the last year of the reign of Charles the Second, most of the streets were left in profound darkness. Thieves and robbers plied their trade with impunity: yet they were hardly so terrible to peaceable citizens as another class of ruffians. It was a favourite amusement of dissolute young gentlemen to swagger by night about the town, breaking windows, upsetting sedans, beating quiet men, and offering rude caresses to pretty women. Several dynasties of these tyrants had, since the Restoration, domineered over the streets. The Muns and Tityre Tus had given place to the Hectors, and the Hectors had been recently succeeded by the Scourers. At a later period arose the Nicker, the Hawcubite, and the yet more dreaded name of Mohawk.[64] The machinery for keeping the peace was utterly contemptible. There was an Act of Common Council which provided that more than a thousand watchmen should be constantly on the alert in the city, from sunset to sunrise, and that every inhabitant should take his turn of duty. But this Act was negligently executed. Few of those who were summoned left their homes; and those few generally found it more agreeable to tipple in alehouses than to pace the streets.[65]

It ought to be noticed that, in the last year of the reign of Charles the Second, began a great change in the police of London, a change which has perhaps added as much to the happiness of the body of the people as revolutions of much greater fame. An ingenious projector, named Edward Heming, obtained letters patent conveying to him, for a term of years, the exclusive right of lighting up London. He undertook, for a moderate con-

---

64. Oldham's Imitation of the 3d Satire of Juvenal, 1682; Shadwell's Scourers, 1690. Many other authorities will readily occur to all who are acquainted with the popular literature of that and the succeeding generation. It may be suspected that some of the Tityre Tus, like good Cavaliers, broke Milton's windows shortly after the Restoration. I am confident that he was thinking of those pests of London when he dictated the noble lines:
"And in luxurious cities, when the noise
Of riot ascends above their loftiest towers,
And injury and outrage, and when night
Darkens the streets, then wander forth the sons
Of Belial, flown with insolence and wine."
65. Seymour's London.

sideration, to place a light before every tenth door, on moonless nights, from Michaelmas to Lady Day, and from six to twelve of the clock. Those who now see the capital all the year round, from dusk to dawn, blazing with a splendour beside which the illuminations for La Hogue and Blenheim would have looked pale, may perhaps smile to think of Heming's lanterns, which glimmered feebly before one house in ten during a small part of one night in three. But such was not the feeling of his contemporaries. His scheme was enthusiastically applauded, and furiously attacked. The friends of improvement extolled him as the greatest of all the benefactors of his city. What, they asked, were the boasted inventions of Archimedes, when compared with the achievement of the man who had turned the nocturnal shades into noon day? In spite of these eloquent eulogies the cause of darkness was not left undefended. There were fools in that age who opposed the introduction of what was called the new light as strenuously as fools in our age have opposed the introduction of vaccination and railroads, as strenuously as the fools of an age anterior to the dawn of history doubtless opposed the introduction of the plough and of alphabetical writing. Many years after the date of Heming's patent there were extensive districts in which no lamp was seen.[66]

We may easily imagine what, in such times, must have been the state of the quarters of London which were peopled by the outcasts of society. Among those quarters one had attained a scandalous preeminence. On the confines of the City and the Temple had been founded, in the thirteenth century, a House of Carmelite Friars, distinguished by their white hoods. The precinct of this house had, before the Reformation, been a sanctuary for criminals, and still retained the privilege of protecting debtors from arrest. Insolvents consequently were to be found in every dwelling, from cellar to garret. Of these a large proportion were knaves and libertines, and were followed to their asylum by women more abandoned than themselves. The civil power was unable to keep order in a district swarming with such inhabitants; and thus Whitefriars became the favourite

66. Angliæ Metropolis, 1690, Sect. 17, entitled, "Of the new lights"; Seymour's London.

resort of all who wished to be emancipated from the restraints of the law. Though the immunities legally belonging to the place extended only to cases of debt, cheats, false witnesses, forgers, and highwaymen found refuge there. For amidst a rabble so desperate no peace officer's life was in safety. At the cry of "Rescue," bullies with swords and cudgels, and termagant hags with spits and broomsticks, poured forth by hundreds; and the intruder was fortunate if he escaped back into Fleet Street, hustled, stripped, and pumped upon. Even the warrant of the Chief Justice of England could not be executed without the help of a company of musketeers. Such relics of the barbarism of the darkest ages were to be found within a short walk of the chambers where Somers was studying history and law, of the chapel where Tillotson was preaching, of the coffee house where Dryden was passing judgment on poems and plays, and of the hall where the Royal Society was examining the astronomical system of Isaac Newton.[67]

Each of the two cities which made up the capital of England had its own centre of attraction. In the metropolis of commerce the point of convergence was the Exchange; in the metropolis of fashion the Palace. But the Palace did not retain its influence so long as the Exchange. The Revolution completely altered the relations between the Court and the higher classes of society. It was by degrees discovered that the King, in his individual capacity, had very little to give; that coronets and garters, bishoprics and embassies, lordships of the Treasury and tellerships of the Exchequer, nay, even charges in the royal stud and bedchamber, were really bestowed, not by him, but by his advisers. Every ambitious and covetous man perceived that he would consult his own interest far better by acquiring the dominion of a Cornish borough, and by rendering good service to the ministry during a critical session, than by becoming the companion, or even the minion, of his prince. It was therefore in the antechambers, not of George the First and of George the Second, but of Walpole and of Pelham, that the daily crowd of courtiers was to be found. It is also to be remarked that the same Revolution, which made

67. Stowe's Survey of London; Shadwell's Squire of Alsatia; Ward's London Spy; Stat. 8 & 9, Gul. III, cap. 27.

it impossible that our Kings should use the patronage of the state merely for the purpose of gratifying their personal predilections, gave us several Kings unfitted by their education and habits to be gracious and affable hosts. They had been born and bred on the Continent. They never felt themselves at home in our island. If they spoke our language, they spoke it inelegantly and with effort. Our national character they never fully understood. Our national manners they hardly attempted to acquire. The most important part of their duty they performed better than any ruler who had preceded them: for they governed strictly according to law: but they could not be the first gentlemen of the realm, the heads of polite society. If ever they unbent, it was in a very small circle where hardly an English face was to be seen; and they were never so happy as when they could escape for a summer to their native land. They had indeed their days of reception for our nobility and gentry; but the reception was mere matter of form, and became at last as solemn a ceremony as a funeral.

Not such was the court of Charles the Second. Whitehall, when he dwelt there, was the focus of political intrigue and of fashionable gaiety. Half the jobbing and half the flirting of the metropolis went on under his roof. Whoever could make himself agreeable to the prince, or could secure the good offices of the mistress, might hope to rise in the world without rendering any service to the government, without being even known by sight to any minister of state. This courtier got a frigate, and that a company; a third, the pardon of a rich offender; a fourth, a lease of crown land on easy terms. If the King notified his pleasure that a briefless lawyer should be made a judge, or that a libertine baronet should be made a peer, the gravest counsellors, after a little murmuring, submitted.[68] Interest, therefore, drew a constant press of suitors to the gates of the palace; and those gates always stood wide. The King kept open house every day, and all day long, for the good society of London, the extreme Whigs only excepted. Hardly any gentleman had any difficulty in making his way to the royal presence. The levee was exactly what the word

68. See Sir Roger North's account of the way in which Wright was made a judge, and Clarendon's account of the way in which Sir George Savile was made a peer.

imports. Some men of quality came every morning to stand round their master, to chat with him while his wig was combed and his cravat tied, and to accompany him in his early walk through the Park. All persons who had been properly introduced might, without any special invitation, go to see him dine, sup, dance, and play at hazard, and might have the pleasure of hearing him tell stories, which indeed he told remarkably well, about his flight from Worcester, and about the misery which he had endured when he was a state prisoner in the hands of the canting meddling preachers of Scotland. Bystanders whom His Majesty recognised often came in for a courteous word. This proved a far more successful kingcraft than any that his father or grandfather had practised. It was not easy for the most austere republican of the school of Marvel to resist the fascination of so much goodhumour and affability: and many a veteran Cavalier, in whose heart the remembrance of unrequited sacrifices and services had been festering during twenty years, was compensated in one moment for wounds and sequestrations by his sovereign's kind nod, and "God bless you, my old friend!"

Whitehall naturally became the chief staple of news. Whenever there was a rumour that anything important had happened or was about to happen, people hastened thither to obtain intelligence from the fountain head. The galleries presented the appearance of a modern club room at an anxious time. They were full of people enquiring whether the Dutch mail was in, what tidings the express from France had brought, whether John Sobiesky had beaten the Turks, whether the Doge of Genoa was really at Paris. These were matters about which it was safe to talk aloud. But there were subjects concerning which information was asked and given in whispers. Had Halifax got the better of Rochester? Was there to be a Parliament? Was the Duke of York really going to Scotland? Had Monmouth really been summoned from the Hague? Men tried to read the countenance of every minister as he went through the throng to and from the royal closet. All sorts of auguries were drawn from the tone in which His Majesty spoke to the Lord President, or from the laugh with which His Majesty honoured a jest of the Lord Privy Seal; and in a few hours the hopes and fears inspired by such slight indications had spread to all the coffee houses from Saint James's to the Tower.[69]

The coffee house must not be dismissed with a cursory mention. It might indeed at that time have been not improperly called a most important political institution. No Parliament had sat for years. The municipal council of the City had ceased to speak the sense of the citizens. Public meetings, harangues, resolutions, and the rest of the modern machinery of agitation had not yet come into fashion. Nothing resembling the modern newspaper existed. In such circumstances the coffee houses were the chief organs through which the public opinion of the metropolis vented itself.

The first of these establishments had been set up, in the time of the Commonwealth, by a Turkey merchant, who had acquired among the Mahometans a taste for their favourite beverage. The convenience of being able to make appointments in any part of the town, and of being able to pass evenings socially at a very small charge, was so great that the fashion spread fast. Every man of the upper or middle class went daily to his coffee house to learn the news and to discuss it. Every coffee house had one or more orators to whose eloquence the crowd listened with admiration, and who soon became, what the journalists of our time have been called, a fourth Estate of the realm. The Court had long seen with uneasiness the growth of this new power in the state. An attempt had been made, during Danby's administration, to close the coffee houses. But men of all parties missed their usual places of resort so much that there was an universal outcry. The government did not venture, in opposition to a feeling so strong and general, to enforce a regulation of which the legality might well be questioned. Since that time ten years had elapsed, and during those years the number and influence of the coffee houses had been constantly increasing. Foreigners remarked that the coffee house was that which especially distin-

69. The sources from which I have drawn my information about the state of the Court are too numerous to recapitulate. Among them are the Despatches of Barillon, Van Citters, Ronquillo, and Adda, the Travels of the Grand Duke Cosmo, the works of Roger North, the Diaries of Pepys, Evelyn, and Teonge, and the Memoirs of Grammont and Reresby.

guished London from all other cities; that the coffee house was the Londoner's home, and that those who wished to find a gentleman commonly asked, not whether he lived in Fleet Street or Chancery Lane, but whether he frequented the Grecian or the Rainbow. Nobody was excluded from these places who laid down his penny at the bar. Yet every rank and profession, and every shade of religious and political opinion, had its own head quarters. There were houses near Saint James's Park where fops congregated, their heads and shoulders covered with black or flaxen wigs, not less ample than those which are now worn by the Chancellor and by the Speaker of the House of Commons. The wig came from Paris; and so did the rest of the fine gentleman's ornaments, his embroidered coat, his fringed gloves, and the tassel which upheld his pantaloons. The conversation was in that dialect which, long after it had ceased to be spoken in fashionable circles, continued, in the mouth of Lord Foppington, to excite the mirth of theatres.[70] The atmosphere was like that of a perfumer's shop. Tobacco in any other form than that of richly scented snuff was held in abomination. If any clown, ignorant of the usages of the house, called for a pipe, the sneers of the whole assembly and the short answers of the waiters soon convinced him that he had better go somewhere else. Nor, indeed, would he have had far to go. For, in general, the coffee rooms reeked with tobacco like a guardroom; and strangers sometimes expressed their surprise that so many people should leave their own firesides to sit in the midst of eternal fog and stench. Nowhere was the smoking more constant than at Will's. That celebrated house, situated between Covent Garden and Bow Street, was sacred to polite letters. There the talk was about poetical justice and the unities of place and time. There was a faction for Perrault and the moderns, a faction for Boileau and the ancients. One group debated whether Paradise Lost ought not to have been in rhyme. To another an envious poetaster demonstrated that Venice Preserved ought to have been hooted from the stage. Under no roof

---

70. The chief peculiarity of this dialect was that, in a large class of words, the O was pronounced like A. Thus Lord was pronounced Lard. See Vanbrugh's Relapse. Lord Sunderland was a great master of this court tune, as Roger North calls it; and Titus Oates affected it in the hope of passing for a fine gentleman. Examen, 77, 254.

was a greater variety of figures to be seen. There were Earls in stars and garters, clergymen in cassocks and bands, pert Templars, sheepish lads from the Universities, translators and index-makers in ragged coats of frieze. The great press was to get near the chair where John Dryden sate. In winter that chair was always in the warmest nook by the fire; in summer it stood in the balcony. To bow to the Laureate, and to hear his opinion of Racine's last tragedy or of Bossu's treatise on epic poetry, was thought a privilege. A pinch from his snuff box was an honour sufficient to turn the head of a young enthusiast. There were coffee houses where the first medical men might be consulted. Doctor John Radcliffe, who, in the year 1685, rose to the largest practice in London, came daily, at the hour when the Exchange was full, from his house in Bow Street, then a fashionable part of the capital, to Garraway's, and was to be found, surrounded by surgeons and apothecaries, at a particular table. There were Puritan coffee houses where no oath was heard, and where lank-haired men discussed election and reprobation through their noses; Jew coffee houses where dark-eyed money changers from Venice and from Amsterdam greeted each other; and Popish coffee houses where, as good Protestants believed, Jesuits planned, over their cups, another great fire, and cast silver bullets to shoot the King.[71]

These gregarious habits had no small share in forming the character of the Londoner of that age. He was, indeed, a different being from the rustic Englishman. There was not then the inter-course which now exists between the two classes. Only very great men were in the habit of dividing the year between town and country. Few esquires came to the capital thrice in their lives. Nor was it yet the practice of all citizens in easy circum-stances to breathe the fresh air of the fields and woods during some weeks of every summer. A cockney, in a rural village, was stared at as much as if he had intruded into a Kraal of Hotten-

71. Lettres sur les Anglois; Tom Brown's Tour; Ward's London Spy; The Character of a Coffee House, 1673; Rules and Orders of the Coffee House, 1764; Coffee Houses vindicated, 1675; A Satyr against Coffee; North's Examen, 138; Life of Guildford, 152; Life of Sir Dudley North, 149; Life of Dr. Radcliffe, published by Curll in 1715. The liveliest description of Will's is in the City and Country Mouse. There is a remarkable passage about the influence of the coffee house orators in Halstead's Succinct Genealogies, printed in 1685.

tots. On the other hand, when the lord of a Lincolnshire or Shropshire manor appeared in Fleet Street, he was as easily distinguished from the resident population as a Turk or a Lascar. His dress, his gait, his accent, the manner in which he gazed at the shops, stumbled into the gutters, ran against the porters, and stood under the waterspouts, marked him out as an excellent subject for the operations of swindlers and banterers. Bullies jostled him into the kennel. Hackney coachmen splashed him from head to foot. Thieves explored with perfect security the huge pockets of his horseman's coat, while he stood entranced by the splendour of the Lord Mayor's show. Moneydroppers, sore from the cart's tail, introduced themselves to him, and appeared to him the most honest friendly gentlemen that he had ever seen. Painted women, the refuse of Lewkner Lane and Whetstone Park, passed themselves on him for countesses and maids of honour. If he asked his way to Saint James's, his informants sent him to Mile End. If he went into a shop, he was instantly discerned to be a fit purchaser of everything that nobody else would buy, of secondhand embroidery, copper rings, and watches that would not go. If he rambled into any fashionable coffee house, he became a mark for the insolent derision of fops and the grave waggery of Templars. Enraged and mortified, he soon returned to his mansion, and there, in the homage of his tenants and the conversation of his boon companions, found consolation for the vexations and humiliations which he had undergone. There he was once more a great man, and saw nothing above himself except when at the assizes he took his seat on the bench near the Judge, or when at the muster of the militia he saluted the Lord Lieutenant.

The chief cause which made the fusion of the different elements of society so imperfect was the extreme difficulty which our ancestors found in passing from place to place. Of all inventions, the alphabet and the printing press alone excepted, those inventions which abridge distance have done most for the civilisation of our species. Every improvement of the means of locomotion benefits mankind morally and intellectually as well as materially, and not only facilitates the interchange of the various productions of nature and art, but tends to remove national and provincial antipathies, and to bind together all the branches of the

great human family. In the seventeenth century the inhabitants
of London were, for almost every practical purpose, farther from
Reading than they now are from Edinburgh, and farther from
Edinburgh than they now are from Vienna.

The subjects of Charles the Second were not, it is true, quite
unacquainted with that principle which has, in our own time,
produced an unprecedented revolution in human affairs, which
has enabled navies to advance in face of wind and tide, and
brigades of troops, attended by all their baggage and artillery,
to traverse kingdoms at a pace equal to that of the fleetest race
horse. The Marquess of Worcester had recently observed the
expansive power of moisture rarefied by heat. After many experiments he had succeeded in constructing a rude steam engine,
which he called a fire water work, and which he pronounced to
be an admirable and most forcible instrument of propulsion.[72]
But the Marquess was suspected to be a madman, and known to
be a Papist. His inventions, therefore, found no favourable reception. His fire water work might, perhaps, furnish matter for
conversation at a meeting of the Royal Society, but was not
applied to any practical purpose. There were no railways, except
a few made of timber, on which coals were carried from the
mouths of the Northumbrian pits to the banks of the Tyne.[73]
There was very little internal communication by water. A few
attempts had been made to deepen and embank the natural
streams, but with slender success. Hardly a single navigable
canal had been even projected. The English of that day were in
the habit of talking with mingled admiration and despair of the
immense trench by which Lewis the Fourteenth had made a junc-
tion between the Atlantic and the Mediterranean. They little
thought that their country would, in the course of a few generations, be intersected, at the cost of private adventurers, by artificial
rivers making up more than four times the length of the Thames,
the Severn, and the Trent together.

.   .   .   .

The mode in which correspondence was carried on between
distant places may excite the scorn of the present generation; yet
it was such as might have moved the admiration and envy of

72. Century of Inventions, 1663, No. 68.
73. North's Life of Guildford, 136.

the polished nations of antiquity, or of the contemporaries of Raleigh and Cecil. A rude and imperfect establishment of posts for the conveyance of letters had been set up by Charles the First, and had been swept away by the civil war. Under the Commonwealth the design was resumed. At the Restoration the proceeds of the Post Office, after all expenses had been paid, were settled on the Duke of York. On most lines of road the mails went out and came in only on the alternate days. In Cornwall, in the fens of Lincolnshire, and among the hills and lakes of Cumberland, letters were received only once a week. During a royal progress a daily post was despatched from the capital to the place where the court sojourned. There was also daily communication between London and the Downs; and the same privilege was sometimes extended to Tunbridge Wells and Bath at the seasons when those places were crowded by the great. The bags were carried on horseback day and night at the rate of about five miles an hour.[74]

The revenue of this establishment was not derived solely from the charge for the transmission of letters. The Post Office alone was entitled to furnish post horses; and, from the care with which this monopoly was guarded, we may infer that it was found profitable.[75] If, indeed, a traveller had waited half an hour without being supplied, he might hire a horse wherever he could.

To facilitate correspondence between one part of London and another was not originally one of the objects of the Post Office. But, in the reign of Charles the Second, an enterprising citizen of London, William Dockwray, set up, at great expense, a penny post, which delivered letters and parcels six or eight times a day in the busy and crowded streets near the Exchange, and four times a day in the outskirts of the capital. This improvement was, as usual, strenuously resisted. The porters complained that their interests were attacked, and tore down the placards in which the scheme was announced to the public. The excitement caused by Godfrey's death, and by the discovery of Coleman's papers, was then at the height. A cry was therefore raised that the penny post was a Popish contrivance. The great Doctor Oates, it was

74. Stat. 12 Car. II, c. 35; Chamberlayne's State of England, 1684; Angliæ Metropolis, 1690; London Gazette, June 22, 1685, August 15, 1687.
75. Lond. Gaz. Sept. 14, 1685.

affirmed, had hinted a suspicion that the Jesuits were at the bottom of the scheme, and that the bags, if examined, would be found full of treason.[76] The utility of the enterprise was, however, so great and obvious that all opposition proved fruitless. As soon as it became clear that the speculation would be lucrative, the Duke of York complained of it as an infraction of his monopoly; and the courts of law decided in his favour.[77]

The revenue of the Post Office was from the first constantly increasing. In the year of the Restoration a committee of the House of Commons, after strict enquiry, had estimated the net receipt at about twenty thousand pounds. At the close of the reign of Charles the Second, the net receipt was little short of fifty thousand pounds; and this was then thought a stupendous sum. The gross receipt was about seventy thousand pounds. The charge for conveying a single letter was twopence for eighty miles, and threepence for a longer distance. The postage increased in proportion to the weight of the packet.[78] At present a single letter is carried to the extremity of Scotland or of Ireland for a penny; and the monopoly of post horses has long ceased to exist. Yet the gross annual receipts of the department amount to more than eighteen hundred thousand pounds, and the net receipts to more than seven hundred thousand pounds. It is, therefore, scarcely possible to doubt that the number of letters now conveyed by mail is seventy times the number which was so conveyed at the time of the accession of James the Second.[79]

No part of the load which the old mails carried out was more important than the newsletters. In 1685 nothing like the London daily paper of our time existed, or could exist. Neither the necessary capital nor the necessary skill was to be found. Freedom too was wanting, a want as fatal as that of either capital or skill. The press was not indeed at that moment under a general censorship. The licensing act, which had been passed soon after the Restoration, had expired in 1679. Any person might therefore

76. Smith's Current Intelligence, March 30 and April 3, 1680.

77. Angliæ Metropolis, 1690.

78. Commons' Journals, Sept. 4, 1660, March 1, 168⅚; Chamberlayne, 1684; Davenant on the Public Revenue, Discourse IV.

79. I have left the text as it stood in 1848. In the year 1856 the gross receipt of the Post Office was more than £2,800,000; and the net receipt was about £1,200,000. The number of letters conveyed by post was 478,000,000. (1857.)

print, at his own risk, a history, a sermon, or a poem, without the previous approbation of any officer; but the Judges were unanimously of opinion that this liberty did not extend to Gazettes, and that, by the common law of England, no man, not authorised by the crown, had a right to publish political news.[80] While the Whig party was still formidable, the government thought it expedient occasionally to connive at the violation of this rule. During the great battle of the Exclusion Bill, many newspapers were suffered to appear, the Protestant Intelligence, the Current Intelligence, the Domestic Intelligence, the True News, the London Mercury.[81] None of these was published oftener than twice a week. None exceeded in size a single small leaf. The quantity of matter which one of them contained in a year was not more than is often found in two numbers of the Times. After the defeat of the Whigs it was no longer necessary for the King to be sparing in the use of that which all his Judges had pronounced to be his undoubted prerogative. At the close of his reign no newspaper was suffered to appear without his allowance: and his allowance was given exclusively to the London Gazette. The London Gazette came out only on Mondays and Thursdays. The contents generally were a royal proclamation, two or three Tory addresses, notices of two or three promotions, an account of a skirmish between the imperial troops and the Janissaries on the Danube, a description of a highwayman, an announcement of a grand cockfight between two persons of honour, and an advertisement offering a reward for a strayed dog. The whole made up two pages of moderate size. Whatever was communicated respecting matters of the highest moment was communicated in the most meagre and formal style. Sometimes, indeed, when the government was disposed to gratify the public curiosity respecting an important transaction, a broadside was put forth giving fuller details than could be found in the Gazette: but neither the Gazette nor any supplementary broadside printed by authority ever contained any intelligence which it did not suit the purposes of the Court to publish. The most important parliamentary debates, the most important state

80. London Gazette, May 5 and 17, 1680.
81. There is a very curious, and, I should think, unique collection of these papers in the British Museum.

trials, recorded in our history, were passed over in profound silence.[82] In the capital the coffee houses supplied in some measure the place of a journal. Thither the Londoners flocked, as the Athenians of old flocked to the market place, to hear whether there was any news. There men might learn how brutally a Whig had been treated the day before in Westminster Hall, what horrible accounts the letters from Edinburgh gave of the torturing of Covenanters, how grossly the Navy Board had cheated the crown in the victualling of the fleet, and what grave charges the Lord Privy Seal had brought against the Treasury in the matter of the hearth money. But people who lived at a distance from the great theatre of political contention could be kept regularly informed of what was passing there only by means of newsletters. To prepare such letters became a calling in London, as it now is among the natives of India. The newswriter rambled from coffee room to coffee room, collecting reports, squeezed himself into the Sessions House at the Old Bailey if there was an interesting trial, nay, perhaps obtained admission to the gallery of Whitehall, and noticed how the King and Duke looked. In this way he gathered materials for weekly epistles destined to enlighten some county town or some bench of rustic magistrates. Such were the sources from which the inhabitants of the largest provincial cities, and the great body of the gentry and clergy, learned almost all that they knew of the history of their own time. We must suppose that at Cambridge there were as many persons curious to know what was passing in the world as at almost any place in the kingdom, out of London. Yet at Cambridge, during a great part of the reign of Charles the Second, the Doctors of Laws and the Masters of Arts had no regular supply of news except through the London Gazette. At length the services of one of the collectors of intelligence in the capital were employed. That was a memorable day on which the first newsletter from London was laid on the table of the only coffee room in Cambridge.[83] At the seat of a man of fortune in the country the newsletter was

82. For example, there is not a word in the Gazette about the important parliamentary proceedings of November 1685, or about the trial and acquittal of the seven Bishops.

83. Roger North's Life of Dr. John North. On the subject of newsletters, see the Examen, 133.

309

impatiently expected. Within a week after it had arrived it had been thumbed by twenty families. It furnished the neighbouring squires with matter for talk over their October, and the neighbouring rectors with topics for sharp sermons against Whiggery or Popery. Many of these curious journals might doubtless still be detected by a diligent search in the archives of old families. Some are to be found in our public libraries; and one series, which is not the least valuable part of the literary treasures collected by Sir James Mackintosh, will be occasionally quoted in the course of this work.[84]

It is scarcely necessary to say there were then no provincial newspapers. Indeed, except in the capital and at the two Universities, there was scarcely a printer in the kingdom. The only press in England north of Trent appears to have been at York.[85]

It was not only by means of the London Gazette that the government undertook to furnish political instruction to the people. That journal contained a scanty supply of news without comment. Another journal, published under the patronage of the court, consisted of comment without news. This paper, called the Observator, was edited by an old Tory pamphleteer named Roger Lestrange. Lestrange was by no means deficient in readiness and shrewdness; and his diction, though coarse, and disfigured by a mean and flippant jargon which then passed for wit in the green room and the tavern, was not without keenness and vigour. But his nature, at once ferocious and ignoble, showed itself in every line that he penned. When the first Observators appeared there was some excuse for his acrimony. For the Whigs were then powerful; and he had to contend against numerous adversaries,

84. I take this opportunity of expressing my warm gratitude to the family of my dear and honoured friend Sir James Mackintosh for confiding to me the materials collected by him at a time when he meditated a work similar to that which I have undertaken. I have never seen, and I do not believe that there anywhere exists, within the same compass, so noble a collection of extracts from public and private archives. The judgment with which Sir James, in great masses of the rudest ore of history, selected what was valuable, and rejected what was worthless, can be fully appreciated only by one who has toiled after him in the same mine.

85. Life of Thomas Gent. A complete list of all printing houses in 1724 will be found in Nichols's Literary Anecdotes of the eighteenth century. There had then been a great increase within a few years in the number of presses; and yet there were thirty-four counties in which there was no printer, one of those counties being Lancashire.

whose unscrupulous violence might seem to justify unsparing retaliation. But in 1685 all opposition had been crushed. A generous spirit would have disdained to insult a party which could not reply, and to aggravate the misery of prisoners, of exiles, of bereaved families: but from the malice of Lestrange the grave was no hiding place, and the house of mourning no sanctuary. In the last month of the reign of Charles the Second, William Jenkyn, an aged dissenting pastor of great note, who had been cruelly persecuted for no crime but that of worshipping God according to the fashion generally followed throughout Protestant Europe, died of hardships and privations in Newgate. The outbreak of popular sympathy could not be repressed. The corpse was followed to the grave by a train of a hundred and fifty coaches. Even courtiers looked sad. Even the unthinking King showed some signs of concern. Lestrange alone set up a howl of savage exultation, laughed at the weak compassion of the Trimmers, proclaimed that the blasphemous old imposter had met with a most righteous punishment, and vowed to wage war, not only to the death, but after death, with all the mock saints and martyrs.[86] Such was the spirit of the paper which was at this time the oracle of the Tory party, and especially of the parochial clergy.

Literature which could be carried by the post bag then formed the greater part of the intellectual nutriment ruminated by the country divines and country justices. The difficulty and expense of conveying large packets from place to place was so great, that an extensive work was longer in making its way from Paternoster Row to Devonshire or Lancashire than it now is in reaching Kentucky. How scantily a rural parsonage was then furnished, even with books the most necessary to a theologian, has already been remarked. The houses of the gentry were not more plentifully supplied. Few knights of the shire had libraries so good as may now perpetually be found in a servants' hall, or in the back parlour of a small shopkeeper. An esquire passed among his neighbours for a great scholar, if Hudibras and Baker's Chronicle, Tarlton's Jests and the Seven Champions of Christendom, lay in his hall window among the fishing rods and fowling pieces. No circulating library, no book society, then existed even in the capi-

86. Observator, Jan. 29 and 31, 1685; Calamy's Life of Baxter; Nonconformist Memorial.

tal: but in the capital those students who could not afford to purchase largely had a resource. The shops of the great booksellers, near Saint Paul's Churchyard, were crowded every day and all day long with readers; and a known customer was often permitted to carry a volume home. In the country there was no such accommodation; and every man was under the necessity of buying whatever he wished to read.[87]

As to the lady of the manor and her daughters, their literary stores generally consisted of a prayer book and a receipt book. But in truth they lost little by living in rural seclusion. For, even in the highest ranks, and in those situations which afforded the greatest facilities for mental improvement, the English women of that generation were decidedly worse educated than they have been at any other time since the revival of learning. At an earlier period they had studied the masterpieces of ancient genius. In the present day they seldom bestow much attention on the dead languages; but they are familiar with the tongue of Pascal and Molière, with the tongue of Dante and Tasso, with the tongue of Goethe and Schiller; nor is there any purer or more graceful English than that which accomplished women now speak and write. But, during the latter part of the seventeenth century, the culture of the female mind seems to have been almost entirely neglected. If a damsel had the least smattering of literature she was regarded as a prodigy. Ladies highly born, highly bred, and naturally quick witted, were unable to write a line in their mother tongue without solecisms and faults of spelling such as a charity girl would now be ashamed to commit.[88]

The explanation may easily be found. Extravagant licentiousness, the natural effect of extravagant austerity, was now the

87. Cotton seems, from his Angler, to have found room for his whole library in his hall window; and Cotton was a man of letters. Even when Franklin first visited London in 1724, circulating libraries were unknown there. The crowd at the booksellers' shops in Little Britain is mentioned by Roger North in his life of his brother John.

88. One instance will suffice. Queen Mary, the daughter of James, had excellent natural abilities, had been educated by a Bishop, was fond of history and poetry, and was regarded by very eminent men as a superior woman. There is, in the library at the Hague, a superb English Bible which was delivered to her when she was crowned in Westminster Abbey. In the titlepage are these words in her own hand, "This book was given the King and I, at our crownation. Marie R."

splendour which was set off to full advantage by contrast. France, indeed, had at that time an empire over mankind, such as even the Roman Republic never attained. For, when Rome was politically dominant, she was in arts and letters the humble pupil of Greece. France had, over the surrounding countries, at once the ascendency which Rome had over Greece, and the ascendency which Greece had over Rome. French was fast becoming the universal language, the language of fashionable society, the language of diplomacy. At several courts princes and nobles spoke it more accurately and politely than their mother tongue. In our island there was less of this servility than on the Continent. Neither our good nor our bad qualities were those of imitators. Yet even here homage was paid, awkwardly indeed and sullenly, to the literary supremacy of our neighbours. The melodious Tuscan, so familiar to the gallants and ladies of the court of Elizabeth, sank into contempt. A gentleman who quoted Horace or Terence was considered in good company as a pompous pedant. But to garnish his conversation with scraps of French was the best proof which he could give of his parts and attainments.[90] New canons of criticism, new models of style came into fashion. The quaint ingenuity which had deformed the verses of Donne, and had been a blemish on those of Cowley, disappeared from our poetry. Our prose became less majestic, less artfully involved, less variously musical than that of an earlier age, but more lucid, more easy, and better fitted for controversy and narrative. In these changes it is impossible not to recognise the influence of French precept and of French example. Great masters of our language, in their most dignified compositions, affected to use French words, when English words, quite as expressive and sonorous, were at hand[91]: and from France was imported the

90. Butler, in a satire of great asperity, says,
>"For, though to smatter words of Greek
>And Latin be the rhetorique
>Of pedants counted, and vainglorious,
>To smatter French is meritorious."

91. The most offensive instance which I remember is in a poem on the coronation of Charles the Second by Dryden, who certainly could not plead poverty as an excuse for borrowing words from any foreign tongue:
>"Hither in summer evenings you repair
>To taste the fraicheur of the cooler air."

tragedy in rhyme, an exotic which, in our soil, drooped, and speedily died.

It would have been well if our writers had also copied the decorum which their great French contemporaries, with few exceptions, preserved; for the profligacy of the English plays, satires, songs, and novels of that age is a deep blot on our national fame. The evil may easily be traced to its source. The wits and the Puritans had never been on friendly terms. There was no sympathy between the two classes. They looked on the whole system of human life from different points and in different lights. The earnest of each was the jest of the other. The pleasures of each were the torments of the other. To the stern precisian even the innocent sport of the fancy seemed a crime. To light and festive natures the solemnity of the zealous brethren furnished copious matter of ridicule. From the Reformation to the civil war, almost every writer, gifted with a fine sense of the ludicrous, had taken some opportunity of assailing the straighthaired, snuffling, whining saints, who christened their children out of the Book of Nehemiah, who groaned in spirit at the sight of Jack in the Green, and who thought it impious to taste plum porridge on Christmas day. At length a time came when the laughers began to look grave in their turn. The rigid, ungainly zealots, after having furnished much good sport during two generations, rose up in arms, conquered, ruled, and grimly smiling, trod down under their feet the whole crowd of mockers. The wounds inflicted by gay and petulant malice were retaliated with the gloomy and implacable malice peculiar to bigots who mistake their own rancour for virtue. The theatres were closed. The players were flogged. The press was put under the guardianship of austere licensers. The Muses were banished from their own favourite haunts, Cambridge and Oxford. Cowley, Crashaw, and Cleveland were ejected from their fellowships. The young candidate for academical honours was no longer required to write Ovidian epistles or Virgilian pastorals, but was strictly interrogated by a synod of lowering Supralapsarians as to the day and hour when he experienced the new birth. Such a system was of course fruitful of hypocrites. Under sober clothing and under visages composed to the expression of austerity lay hid during several years the intense desire of license and of revenge. At length that desire was gratified. The Restoration emancipated thousands of minds from a yoke which had become insupportable. The old fight recommenced, but with an animosity altogether new. It was now not a sportive combat, but a war to the death. The Roundhead had no better quarter to expect from those whom he had persecuted than a cruel slavedriver can expect from insurgent slaves still bearing the marks of his collars and his scourges.

The war between wit and Puritanism soon became a war between wit and morality. The hostility excited by a grotesque caricature of virtue did not spare virtue herself. Whatever the canting Roundhead had regarded with reverence was insulted. Whatever he had proscribed was favoured. Because he had been scrupulous about trifles, all scruples were treated with derision. Because he had covered his failings with the mask of devotion, men were encouraged to obtrude with Cynic impudence all their most scandalous vices on the public eye. Because he had punished illicit love with barbarous severity, virgin purity and conjugal fidelity were made a jest. To that sanctimonious jargon which was his Shibboleth, was opposed another jargon not less absurd and much more odious. As he never opened his mouth except in scriptural phrase, the new breed of wits and fine gentlemen never opened their mouths without uttering ribaldry of which a porter would now be ashamed, and without calling on their Maker to curse them, sink them, confound them, blast them, and damn them.

It is not strange, therefore, that our polite literature, when it revived with the revival of the old civil and ecclesiastical polity, should have been profoundly immoral. A few eminent men, who belonged to an earlier and better age, were exempt from the general contagion. The verse of Waller still breathed the sentiments which had animated a more chivalrous generation. Cowley, distinguished as a loyalist and as a man of letters, raised his voice courageously against the immorality which disgraced both letters and loyalty. A mightier poet, tried at once by pain, danger, poverty, obloquy, and blindness, meditated, undisturbed by the obscene tumult which raged all around him, a song so sublime and so holy that it would not have misbecome the lips of those ethereal Virtues whom he saw, with that inner eye which no calamity could darken, flinging down on the jasper pavement their crowns of amaranth and gold. The vigorous and fertile genius of Butler, if it did not altogether escape the prevailing infection, took the disease in a mild form. But these were men whose minds had been trained in a world which had passed away. They gave place in no long time to a younger generation of wits; and of that generation, from Dryden down to Durfey, the common characteristic was hardhearted, shameless, swaggering licentiousness, at once inelegant and inhuman. The influence of these writers was doubtless noxious, yet less noxious than it would have been had they been less depraved. The poison which they administered was so strong that it was, in no long time, rejected with nausea. None of them understood the dangerous art of associating images of unlawful pleasure with all that is endearing and ennobling. None of them was aware that a certain decorum is essential even to voluptuousness, that drapery may be more alluring than exposure, and that the imagination may be far more powerfully moved by delicate hints which impel it to exert itself, than by gross descriptions which it takes in passively.

The spirit of the Antipuritan reaction pervades almost the whole polite literature of the reign of Charles the Second. But the very quintessence of that spirit will be found in the comic drama. The playhouses, shut by the meddling fanatic in the day of his power, were again crowded. To their old attractions new and more powerful attractions had been added. Scenery, dresses, and decorations, such as would now be thought mean or absurd, but such as would have been esteemed incredibly magnificent by those who, early in the seventeenth century, sate on the filthy benches of the Hope, or under the thatched roof of the Rose, dazzled the eyes of the multitude. The fascination of sex was called in to aid the fascination of art: and the young spectator saw, with emotions unknown to the contemporaries of Shakspeare and Jonson, tender and sprightly heroines personated by lovely women. From the day on which the theatres were reopened they became seminaries of vice; and the evil propagated itself. The profligacy of the representations soon drove away sober people. The frivolous and dissolute who remained required every year stronger and stronger stimulants. Thus the artists corrupted the spectators, and the spectators the artists, till the turpitude of the drama became such as must astonish all who are not aware that extreme relaxation is the natural effect of extreme restraint, and that an age of hypocrisy is, in the regular course of things, followed by an age of impudence.

Nothing is more characteristic of the times than the care with which the poets contrived to put all their loosest verses into the mouths of women. The compositions in which the greatest license was taken were the epilogues. They were almost always recited by favourite actresses; and nothing charmed the depraved audience so much as to hear lines grossly indecent repeated by a beautiful girl, who was supposed to have not yet lost her innocence.[92]

Our theatre was indebted in that age for many plots and characters to Spain, to France, and to the old English masters: but whatever our dramatists touched they tainted. In their imitations the houses of Calderon's stately and highspirited Castilian gentlemen became sties of vice, Shakspeare's Viola a procuress, Molière's Misanthrope a ravisher, Molière's Agnes an adultress. Nothing could be so pure or so heroic but that it became foul and ignoble by transfusion through those foul and ignoble minds.

Such was the state of the drama; and the drama was the department of polite literature in which a poet had the best chance of obtaining a subsistence by his pen. The sale of books was so small that a man of the greatest name could hardly expect more than a pittance for the copyright of the best performance. There cannot be a stronger instance than the fate of Dryden's last production, the Fables. That volume was published when he was universally admitted to be the chief of living English poets. It contains about twelve thousand lines. The versification is admirable, the narratives and descriptions full of life. To this day Palamon and Arcite, Cymon and Iphigenia, Theodore and Honoria, are the delight both of critics and of schoolboys. The collection includes Alexander's Feast, the noblest ode in our language. For the copyright Dryden received two hundred and fifty pounds, less than in our days has sometimes been paid for two articles in a review.[93] Nor does the bargain seem to have been a hard one. For the book went off slowly; and the second edition was not required till the author had been ten years in his grave. By writing for the theatre it was possible to earn a much larger sum with

92. Jeremy Collier has censured this odious practice with his usual force and keenness.

93. The contract will be found in Sir Walter Scott's edition of Dryden.

much less trouble. Southern made seven hundred pounds by one play.[94] Otway was raised from beggary to temporary affluence by the success of his Don Carlos.[95] Shadwell cleared a hundred and thirty pounds by a single representation of the Squire of Alsatia.[96] The consequence was that every man who had to live by his wit wrote plays, whether he had any internal vocation to write plays or not. It was thus with Dryden. As a satirist he has rivalled Juvenal. As a didactic poet he perhaps might, with care and meditation, have rivalled Lucretius. Of lyric poets he is, if not the most sublime, the most brilliant and spiritstirring. But nature, profuse to him of many rare gifts, had withheld from him the dramatic faculty. Nevertheless all the energies of his best years were wasted on dramatic composition. He had too much judgment not to be aware that in the power of exhibiting character by means of dialogue he was deficient. That deficiency he did his best to conceal, sometimes by surprising and amusing incidents, sometimes by stately declamation, sometimes by harmonious numbers, sometimes by ribaldry but too well suited to the taste of a profane and licentious pit. Yet he never obtained any theatrical success equal to that which rewarded the exertions of some men far inferior to him in general powers. He thought himself fortunate if he cleared a hundred guineas by a play; a scanty remuneration, yet apparently larger than he could have earned in any other way by the same quantity of labour.[97]

The recompense which the wits of that age could obtain from the public was so small, that they were under the necessity of eking out their incomes by levying contributions on the great. Every rich and goodnatured lord was pestered by authors with a mendicancy so importunate, and a flattery so abject, as may in our time seem incredible. The patron to whom a work was inscribed was expected to reward the writer with a purse of gold. The fee paid for the dedication of a book was often much larger than the sum which any publisher would give for the copyright. Books were therefore frequently printed merely that they might be dedicated. This traffic in praise produced the effect which might have

94. See the Life of Southern, by Shiels.
95. See Rochester's Trial of the Poets.
96. Some Account of the English stage.
97. Life of Southern, by Shiels.

been expected. Adulation pushed to the verge, sometimes of nonsense, and sometimes of impiety, was not thought to disgrace a poet. Independence, veracity, selfrespect, were things not required by the world from him. In truth, he was in morals something between a pandar and a beggar.

To the other vices which degraded the literary character was added, towards the close of the reign of Charles the Second, the most savage intemperance of party spirit. The wits, as a class, had been impelled by their old hatred of Puritanism to take the side of the court, and had been found useful allies. Dryden, in particular, had done good service to the government. His Absalom and Achitophel, the greatest satire of modern times, had amazed the town, had made its way with unprecedented rapidity even into rural districts, and had, wherever it appeared, bitterly annoyed the Exclusionists, and raised the courage of the Tories. But we must not, in the admiration which we naturally feel for noble diction and versification, forget the great distinctions of good and evil. The spirit by which Dryden and several of his compeers were at this time animated against the Whigs deserves to be called fiendish. The servile Judges and Sheriffs of those evil days could not shed blood so fast as the poets cried out for it. Calls for more victims, hideous jests on hanging, bitter taunts on those who, having stood by the King in the hour of danger, now advised him to deal mercifully and generously by his vanquished enemies, were publicly recited on the stage, and, that nothing might be wanting to the guilt and the shame, were recited by women, who, having long been taught to discard all modesty, were now taught to discard all compassion.[98]

It is a remarkable fact that, while the lighter literature of England was thus becoming a nuisance and a national disgrace, the English genius was effecting in science a revolution which will, to the end of time, be reckoned among the highest achievements of the human intellect. Bacon had sown the good seed in a sluggish soil and an ungenial season. He had not expected an early crop, and in his last testament had solemnly bequeathed his fame to the next age. During a whole generation his philosophy

98. If any reader thinks my expressions too severe, I would advise him to read Dryden's Epilogue to the Duke of Guise, and to observe that it was spoken by a woman.

had, amidst tumults, wars, and proscriptions, been slowly ripening in a few well constituted minds. While factions were struggling for dominion over each other, a small body of sages had turned away with benevolent disdain from the conflict, and had devoted themselves to the nobler work of extending the dominion of man over matter. As soon as tranquillity was restored, these teachers easily found attentive audience. For the discipline through which the nation had passed had brought the public mind to a temper well fitted for the reception of the Verulamian doctrine. The civil troubles had stimulated the faculties of the educated classes, and had called forth a restless activity and an insatiable curiosity, such as had not before been known among us. Yet the effect of those troubles was that schemes of political and religious reform were generally regarded with suspicion and contempt. During twenty years the chief employment of busy and ingenious men had been to frame constitutions with first magistrates, without first magistrates, with hereditary senates, with senates appointed by lot, with annual senates, with perpetual senates. In these plans nothing was omitted. All the detail, all the nomenclature, all the ceremonial of the imaginary government was fully set forth, Polemarchs and Phylarchs, Tribes and Galaxies, the Lord Archon and the Lord Strategus. Which ballot boxes were to be green and which red, which balls were to be of gold and which of silver, which magistrates were to wear hats and which black velvet caps with peaks, how the mace was to be carried and when the heralds were to uncover, these, and a hundred more such trifles, were gravely considered and arranged by men of no common capacity and learning.[99] But the time for these visions had gone by; and, if any steadfast republican still continued to amuse himself with them, fear of public derision and of a criminal information generally induced him to keep his fancies to himself. It was now unpopular and unsafe to mutter a word against the fundamental laws of the monarchy: but daring and ingenious men might indemnify themselves by treating with disdain what had lately been considered as the fundamental laws of nature. The torrent which had been dammed up in one channel rushed violently into another. The revolutionary spirit, ceasing to

99. See particulary Harrington's Oceana.

operate in politics, began to exert itself with unprecedented vigour and hardihood in every department of physics. The year 1660, the era of the restoration of the old constitution, is also the era from which dates the ascendency of the new philosophy. In that year the Royal Society, destined to be a chief agent in a long series of glorious and saluatory reforms, began to exist.[100] In a few months the experimental science became all the mode. The transfusion of blood, the ponderation of air, the fixation of mercury, succeeded to that place in the public mind which had been lately occupied by the controversies of the Rota. Dreams of perfect forms of government made way for dreams of wings with which men were to fly from the Tower to the Abbey, and of doublekeeled ships which were never to founder in the fiercest storm. All classes were hurried along by the prevailing sentiment. Cavalier and Roundhead, Churchman and Puritan, were for once allied. Divines, jurists, statesmen, nobles, princes, swelled the triumph of the Baconian philosophy. Poets sang with emulous fervour the approach of the golden age. Cowley, in lines weighty with thought and resplendent with wit, urged the chosen seed to take possession of the promised land flowing with milk and honey, that land which their great deliverer and lawgiver had seen, as from the summit of Pisgah, but had not been permitted to enter.[101] Dryden, with more zeal than knowledge, joined his voice to the general acclamation, and foretold things which neither he nor anybody else understood. The Royal Society, he predicted, would soon lead us to the extreme verge of the globe, and there delight us with a better view of the moon.[102] Two able and aspiring prelates, Ward, Bishop of Salisbury, and Wilkins, Bishop of Chester, were conspicuous among the leaders of the movement. Its history was eloquently written by a younger divine, who was rising to high distinction in his profession, Thomas Sprat, afterwards Bishop of Rochester. Both Chief Justice Hale and Lord Keeper Guildford stole some hours from the business of

100. See Sprat's History of the Royal Society.
101. Cowley's Ode to the Royal Society.
102. "Then we upon the globe's last verge shall go,
    And view the ocean leaning on the sky;
    From thence our rolling neighbours we shall know,
    And on the lunar world securely pry."
                           Annus Mirabilis, 164.

their courts to write on hydrostatics. Indeed it was under the immediate direction of Guildford that the first barometers ever exposed to sale in London were constructed.[103] Chemistry divided, for a time, with wine and love, with the stage and the gaming table, with the intrigues of a courtier and the intrigues of a demagogue, the attention of the fickle Buckingham. Rupert has the credit of having invented mezzotinto; and from him is named that curious bubble of glass which has long amused children and puzzled philosophers. Charles himself had a laboratory at Whitehall, and was far more active and attentive there than at the council board. It was almost necessary to the character of a fine gentleman to have something to say about airpumps and telescopes; and even fine ladies, now and then, thought it becoming to affect a taste for science, went in coaches and six to visit the Gresham curiosities, and broke forth into cries of delight at finding that a magnet really attracted a needle, and that a microscope really made a fly look as large as a sparrow.[104]

In this, as in every great stir of the human mind, there was doubtless something which might well move a smile. It is the universal law that whatever pursuit, whatever doctrine, becomes fashionable, shall lose a portion of that dignity which it had possessed while it was confined to a small but earnest minority, and was loved for its own sake alone. It is true that the follies of some persons who, without any real aptitude for science, professed a passion for it, furnished matter of contemptuous mirth to a few malignant satirists who belonged to the preceding generation, and were not disposed to unlearn the lore of their youth.[105] But it is not less true that the great work of interpreting nature was performed by the English of that age as it had never before been performed in any age by any nation. The spirit of Francis Bacon was abroad, a spirit admirably compounded of audacity and sobriety. There was a strong persuasion that the whole world was full of secrets of high moment to the happiness of man, and that man had, by his Maker, been entrusted with the key which,

103. North's Life of Guildford.
104. Pepys's Diary, May 30, 1667.
105. Butler was, I think, the only man of real genius who, between the Restoration and the Revolution, showed a bitter enmity to the new philosophy, as it was then called. See the Satire on the Royal Society, and the Elephant in the Moon.

rightly used, would give access to them. There was at the same time a conviction that in physics it was impossible to arrive at the knowledge of general laws except by the careful observation of particular facts. Deeply impressed with these great truths, the professors of the new philosophy applied themselves to their task, and, before a quarter of a century had expired, they had given ample earnest of what has since been achieved. Already a reform of agriculture had been commenced. New vegetables were cultivated. New implements of husbandry were employed. New manures were applied to the soil.[106] Evelyn had, under the formal sanction of the Royal Society, given instruction to his countrymen in planting. Temple, in his intervals of leisure, had tried many experiments in horticulture, and had proved that many delicate fruits, the natives of more favoured climates, might, with the help of art, be grown on English ground. Medicine, which in France was still in abject bondage, and afforded an inexhaustible subject of just ridicule to Molière, had in England become an experimental and progressive science, and every day made some new advance, in defiance of Hippocrates and Galen. The attention of speculative men had been, for the first time, directed to the important subject of sanitary police. The great plague of 1665 induced them to consider with care the defective architecture, draining, and ventilation of the capital. The great fire of 1666 afforded an opportunity for effecting extensive improvements. The whole matter was diligently examined by the Royal Society; and to the suggestions of that body must be partly attributed the changes which, though far short of what the public welfare required, yet made a wide difference between the new and the old London, and probably put a final close to the ravages of pestilence in our country.[107] At the same time one of the founders of the Society, Sir William Petty, created the science of political arithmetic, the humble but indispensable haidmaid of political philosophy. No kingdom of nature was left unexplored. To that period belong the chemical discoveries of Boyle, and the earliest botanical researches of Sloane. It was then that Ray made

---

106. The eagerness with which the agriculturists of that age tried experiments and introduced improvements is well described by Aubrey. See the Natural History of Wiltshire, 1685.

107. Sprat's History of the Royal Society.

a new classification of birds and fishes, and that the attention of Woodward was first drawn towards fossils and shells. One after another phantoms which had haunted the world through ages of darkness fled before the light. Astrology and alchymy became jests. Soon there was scarcely a county in which some of the Quorum did not smile contemptuously when an old woman was brought before them for riding on broomsticks or giving cattle the murrain. But it was in those noblest and most arduous departments of knowledge in which induction and mathematical demonstration cooperate for the discovery of truth, that the English genius won in that age the most memorable triumphs. John Wallis placed the whole system of statics on a new foundation. Edmund Halley investigated the properties of the atmosphere, the ebb and flow of the sea, the laws of magnetism, and the course of the comets; nor did he shrink from toil, peril, and exile in the cause of science. While he, on the rock of Saint Helena, mapped the constellations of the southern hemisphere, our national observatory was rising at Greenwich; and John Flamsteed, the first Astronomer Royal, was commencing that long series of observations which is never mentioned without respect and gratitude in any part of the globe. But the glory of these men, eminent as they were, is cast into the shade by the transcendent lustre of one immortal name. In Isaac Newton two kinds of intellectual power, which have little in common, and which are not often found together in a very high degree of vigour, but which nevertheless are equally necessary in the most sublime departments of physics, were united as they have never been united before or since. There may have been minds as happily constituted as his for the cultivation of pure mathematical science: there may have been minds as happily constituted for the cultivation of science purely experimental: but in no other mind have the demonstrative faculty and the inductive faculty coexisted in such supreme excellence and perfect harmony. Perhaps in the days of Scotists and Thomists even his intellect might have run to waste, as many intellects ran to waste which were inferior only to his. Happily the spirit of the age on which his lot was cast, gave the right direction to his mind; and his mind reacted with tenfold force on the spirit of the age. In the year 1685 his fame, though splendid, was only dawning; but his genius was in the meridian. His great work, that work which effected a revolution in the most important provinces of natural philosophy, had been completed, but was not yet published, and was just about to be submitted to the consideration of the Royal Society.

It is not very easy to explain why the nation which was so far before its neighbours in science should in art have been far behind them. Yet such was the fact. It is true that in architecture, an art which is half a science, an art in which none but a geometrician can excel, an art which has no standard of grace but what is directly or indirectly dependent on utility, an art of which the creations derive a part, at least, of their majesty from mere bulk, our country could boast of one truly great man, Christopher Wren; and the fire which laid London in ruins had given him an opportunity, unprecedented in modern history, of displaying his powers. The austere beauty of the Athenian portico, the gloomy sublimity of the Gothic arcade, he was, like almost all his contemporaries, incapable of emulating, and perhaps incapable of appreciating: but no man, born on our side of the Alps, has imitated with so much success the magnificence of the palacelike churches of Italy. Even the superb Lewis has left to posterity no work which can bear a comparison with Saint Paul's. But at the close of the reign of Charles the Second there was not a single English painter or statuary whose name is now remembered. This sterility is somewhat mysterious; for painters and statuaries were by no means a despised or an ill paid class. Their social position was at least as high as at present. Their gains, when compared with the wealth of the nation and with the remuneration of other descriptions of intellectual labour, were even larger than at present. Indeed the munificent patronage which was extended to artists drew them to our shores in multitudes. Lely, who has preserved to us the rich curls, the full lips, and the languishing eyes of the frail beauties celebrated by Hamilton, was a Westphalian. He had died in 1680, having long lived splendidly, having received the honour of knighthood, and having accumulated a good estate out of the fruits of his skill. His noble collection of drawings and pictures was, after his decease, exhibited by the royal permission in the Banqueting House at Whitehall, and was sold by auction for the almost incredible sum of twenty-six thousand pounds, a sum which bore a greater proportion to the fortunes of the rich men of that day than a hundred thousand pounds would bear to the fortunes of the rich men of our time.[108] Lely was succeeded by his countryman Godfrey Kneller, who was made first a knight and then a baronet, and who, after keeping up a sumptuous establishment, and after losing much money by unlucky speculations, was still able to bequeath a large fortune to his family. The two Vandeveldes, natives of Holland, had been tempted by English liberality to settle here, and had produced for the King and his nobles some of the finest sea pieces in the world. Another Dutchman, Simon Varelst, painted glorious sunflowers and tulips for prices such as had never before been known. Verrio, a Neapolitan, covered ceilings and staircases with Gorgons and Muses, Nymphs and Satyrs, Virtues and Vices, Gods quaffing nectar, and laurelled princes riding in triumph. The income which he derived from his performances enabled him to keep one of the most expensive tables in England. For his pieces at Windsor alone he received seven thousand pounds, a sum then sufficient to make a gentleman of moderate wishes perfectly easy for life, a sum greatly exceeding all that Dryden, during a literary life of forty years, obtained from the booksellers.[109] Verrio's assistant and successor, Lewis Laguerre, came from France. The two most celebrated sculptors of that day were also foreigners. Cibber, whose pathetic emblems of Fury and Melancholy still adorn Bedlam, was a Dane. Gibbons, to whose graceful fancy and delicate touch many of our palaces, colleges, and churches owe their finest decorations, was a Dutchman. Even the designs for the coin were made by French artists. Indeed, it was not till the reign of George the Second that our country could glory in a great painter; and George the Third was on the throne before she had reason to be proud of any of her sculptors.

It is time that this description of the England which Charles the Second governed should draw to a close. Yet one subject of the highest moment still remains untouched. Nothing has yet been said of the great body of the people, of those who held the ploughs, who tended the oxen, who toiled at the looms of Nor-

108. Walpole's Anecdotes of Painting; London Gazette, May 31, 1683; North's Life of Guildford.
109. The great prices paid to Varelst and Verrio are mentioned in Walpole's Anecdotes of Painting.

wich, and squared the Portland stone for Saint Paul's. Nor can very much be said. The most numerous class is precisely the class respecting which we have the most meagre information. In those times philanthropists did not yet regard it as a sacred duty, nor had demagogues yet found it a lucrative trade, to talk and write about the distress of the labourer. History was too much occupied with courts and camps to spare a line for the hut of the peasant or the garret of the mechanic. The press now often sends forth in a day a greater quantity of discussion and declamation about the condition of the working man than was published during the twenty-eight years which elapsed between the Restoration and the Revolution. But it would be a great error to infer from the increase of complaint that there has been any increase of misery.

The great criterion of the state of the common people is the amount of their wages; and as four-fifths of the common people were, in the seventeenth century, employed in agriculture, it is especially important to ascertain what were then the wages of agricultural industry. On this subject we have the means of arriving at conclusions sufficiently exact for our purpose.

Sir William Petty, whose mere assertion carries great weight, informs us that a labourer was by no means in the lowest state who received for a day's work fourpence with food, or eightpence without food. Four shillings a week therefore were, according to Petty's calculation, fair agricultural wages.[110]

That this calculation was not remote from the truth we have abundant proof. About the beginning of the year 1685 the justices of Warwickshire, in the exercise of a power entrusted to them by an act of Elizabeth, fixed, at their quarter sessions, a scale of wages for the county, and notified that every employer who gave more than the authorised sum, and every working man who received more, would be liable to punishment. The wages of the common agricultural labourer, from March to September, were fixed at the precise amount mentioned by Petty, namely four shillings a week without food. From September to March the wages were to be only three and sixpence a week.[111]

But in that age, as in ours, the earnings of the peasant were

110. Petty's Political Arithmetic.
111. Stat. 5 Eliz. c. 4; Archæologia, vol. xi.

very different in different parts of the kingdom. The wages of Warwickshire were probably about the average, and those of the counties near the Scottish border below it: but there were more favoured districts. In the same year, 1685, a gentleman of Devonshire, named Richard Dunning, published a small tract, in which he described the condition of the poor of that county. That he understood his subject well it is impossible to doubt; for a few months later his work was reprinted, and was, by the magistrates assembled in quarter sessions at Exeter, strongly recommended to the attention of all parochial officers. According to him, the wages of the Devonshire peasant were, without food, about five shillings a week.[112]

Still better was the condition of the labourer in the neighbourhood of Bury Saint Edmund's. The magistrates of Suffolk met there in the spring of 1682 to fix a rate of wages, and resolved that, where the labourer was not boarded, he should have five shillings a week in winter, and six in summer.[113]

In 1661 the justices at Chelmsford had fixed the wages of the Essex labourer, who was not boarded, at six shillings in winter and seven in summer. This seems to have been the highest remuneration given in the kingdom for agricultural labour between the Restoration and the Revolution; and it is to be observed that, in the year in which this order was made, the necessaries of life were immoderately dear. Wheat was at seventy shillings the quarter, which would even now be considered as almost a famine price.[114]

These facts are in perfect accordance with another fact which seems to deserve consideration. It is evident that, in a country where no man can be compelled to become a soldier, the ranks of an army cannot be filled if the government offers much less than the wages of common rustic labour. At present the pay and beer money of a private in a regiment of the line amount to seven shillings and sevenpence a week. This stipend, coupled with the hope of a pension, does not attract the English youth in sufficient numbers; and it is found necessary to supply the defi-

112. Plain and easy Method showing how the office of Overseer of the Poor may be managed, by Richard Dunning; 1st edition, 1685; 2d edition, 1686.
113. Cullum's History of Hawsted.
114. Ruggles on the Poor.

ciency by enlisting largely from among the poorer population of Munster and Connaught. The pay of the private foot soldier in 1685 was only four shillings and eightpence a week; yet it is certain that the government in that year found no difficulty in obtaining many thousands of English recruits at very short notice. The pay of the private foot soldier in the army of the Commonwealth had been seven shillings a week, that is to say, as much as a corporal received under Charles the Second;[115] and seven shillings a week had been found sufficient to fill the ranks with men decidedly superior to the generality of the people. On the whole, therefore, it seems reasonable to conclude that, in the reign of Charles the Second, the ordinary wages of the peasant did not exceed four shillings a week; but that, in some parts of the kingdom, five shillings, six shillings, and, during the summer months, even seven shillings were paid. At present a district where a labouring man earns only seven shillings a week is thought to be in a state shocking to humanity. The average is very much higher; and, in prosperous counties, the weekly wages of husbandmen amount to twelve, fourteen, and even sixteen shillings.

The remuneration of workmen employed in manufactures has always been higher than that of the tillers of the soil. In the year 1680, a member of the House of Commons remarked that the high wages paid in this country made it impossible for our textures to maintain a competition with the produce of the Indian looms. An English mechanic, he said, instead of slaving like a native of Bengal for a piece of copper, exacted a shilling a day.[116] Other evidence is extant, which proves that a shilling a day was the pay to which the English manufacturer then thought himself entitled, but that he was often forced to work for less. The common people of that age were not in the habit of meeting for public discussion, of haranguing, or of petitioning Parliament. No newspaper pleaded their cause. It was in rude rhyme that their love and hatred, their exultation and their distress found utterance. A great part of their history is to be learned only from

115. See, in Thurloe's State Papers, the memorandum of the Dutch Deputies, dated August 2/12. 1653.

116. The orator was Mr. John Basset, member for Barnstaple. See Smith's Memoirs of Wool, chapter lxviii.

their ballads. One of the most remarkable of the popular lays chaunted about the streets of Norwich and Leeds in the time of Charles the Second may still be read on the original broadside. It is the vehement and bitter cry of labour against capital. It describes the good old times when every artisan employed in the woollen manufacture lived as well as a farmer. But those times were past. Sixpence a day was now all that could be earned by hard labour at the loom. If the poor complained that they could not live on such a pittance, they were told that they were free to take it or leave it. For so miserable a recompense were the producers of wealth compelled to toil, rising early and lying down late, while the master clothier, eating, sleeping, and idling, became rich by their exertions. A shilling a day, the poet declares, is what the weaver would have, if justice were done.[117] We may therefore conclude that, in the generation which preceded the Revolution, a workman employed in the great staple manufacture of England thought himself fairly paid if he gained six shillings a week.

It may here be noticed that the practice of setting children prematurely to work, a practice which the state, the legitimate protector of those who cannot protect themselves, has, in our time, wisely and humanely interdicted, prevailed in the seventeenth century to an extent which, when compared with the extent of the manufacturing system, seems almost incredible. At Norwich, the chief seat of the clothing trade, a little creature

117. This ballad is in the British Museum. The precise year is not given; but the Imprimatur of Roger Lestrange fixes the date sufficiently for my purpose. I will quote some of the lines. The master clothier is introduced speaking as follows:

"In former ages we used to give,
So that our workfolks like farmers did live;
But the times are changed, we will make them know.
* * * * * *
"We will make them to work hard for sixpence a day,
Though a shilling they deserve if they had their just pay;
If at all they murmur and say 'tis too small,
We bid them choose whether they'll work at all.
And thus we do gain all our wealth and estate,
By many poor men that work early and late.
Then hey for the clothing trade! It goes on brave;
We scorn for to toyl and moyl, nor yet to slave.
Our workmen do work hard, but we live at ease,
We go when we will, and we come when we please."

of six years old was thought fit for labour. Several writers of that time, and among them some who were considered as eminently benevolent, mention, with exultation, the fact that, in that single city, boys and girls of very tender age created wealth exceeding what was necessary for their own subsistence by twelve thousand pounds a year.[118] The more carefully we examine the history of the past, the more reason shall we find to dissent from those who imagine that our age has been fruitful of new social evils. The truth is that the evils are, with scarcely an exception, old. That which is new is the intelligence which discerns and the humanity which remedies them.

When we pass from the weavers of cloth to a different class of artisans, our enquiries will still lead us to nearly the same conclusions. During several generations, the Commissioners of Greenwich Hospital have kept a register of the wages paid to different classes of workmen who have been employed in the repairs of the building. From this valuable record it appears that, in the course of a hundred and twenty years, the daily earnings of the bricklayer have risen from half a crown to four and tenpence, those of the mason from half a crown to five and threepence, those of the carpenter from half a crown to five and fivepence, and those of the plumber from three shillings to five and sixpence.

It seems clear, therefore, that the wages of labour, estimated in money, were, in 1685, not more than half of what they now are; and there were few articles important to the working man of which the price was not, in 1685, more than half of what it now is. Beer was undoubtedly much cheaper in that age than at present. Meat was also cheaper, but was still so dear that hundreds of thousands of families scarcely knew the taste of it.[119] In the cost of wheat there has been very little change. The average price of the quarter, during the last twelve years of Charles

118. Chamberlayne's State of England; Petty's Political Arithmetic, chapter viii; Dunning's Plain and Easy Method; Firmin's Proposition for the Employing of the Poor. It ought to be observed that Firmin was an eminent philanthropist.

119. King in his Natural and Political Conclusions roughly estimated the common people of England at 880,000 families. Of these families, 440,000, according to him, ate animal food twice a week. The remaining 440,000 ate it not at all, or at most not oftener than once a week.

the Second, was fifty shillings. Bread, therefore, such as is now given to the immates of a workhouse, was then seldom seen, even on the trencher of a yeoman or of a shopkeeper. The great majority of the nation lived almost entirely on rye, barley, and oats.

The produce of tropical countries, the produce of the mines, the produce of machinery, was positively dearer than at present. Among the commodities for which the labourer would have had to pay higher in 1685 than his posterity now pay were sugar, salt, coals, candles, soap, shoes, stockings, and generally all articles of clothing and all articles of bedding. It may be added, that the old coats and blankets would have been, not only more costly, but less serviceable than the modern fabrics.

It must be remembered that those labourers who were able to maintain themselves and their families by means of wages were not the most necessitous members of the community. Beneath them lay a large class which could not subsist without some aid from the parish. There can hardly be a more important test of the condition of the common people than the ratio which this class bears to the whole society. At present the men, women, and children who receive relief appear from the official returns to be, in bad years, one-tenth of the inhabitants of England, and, in good years, one-thirteenth. Gregory King estimated them in his time at about a fourth; and this estimate, which all our respect for his authority will scarcely prevent us from calling extravagant, was pronounced by Davenant eminently judicious.

We are not quite without the means of forming an estimate for ourselves. The poor rate was undoubtedly the heaviest tax borne by our ancestors in those days. It was computed, in the reign of Charles the Second, at near seven hundred thousand pounds a year, much more than the produce either of the excise or of the customs, and little less than half the entire revenue of the crown. The poor rate went on increasing rapidly, and appears to have risen in a short time to between eight and nine hundred thousand a year, that is to say, to one-sixth of what it now is. The population was then less than a third of what it now is. The minimum of wages, estimated in money, was half of what it now is; and we can therefore hardly suppose that the average allowance made to a pauper can have been more than half of what it now is. It seems to follow that the proportion of the English people which received parochial relief then must have been larger than the proportion which receives relief now. It is good to speak on such questions with diffidence: but it has certainly never yet been proved that pauperism was a less heavy burden or a less serious social evil during the last quarter of the seventeenth century than it is in our own time.[120]

In one respect it must be admitted that the progress of civilisation has diminished the physical comforts of a portion of the poorest class. It has already been mentioned that, before the Revolution, many thousands of square miles, now enclosed and cultivated, were marsh, forest, and heath. Of this wild land much was, by law, common, and much of what was not common by law was worth so little that the proprietors suffered it to be common in fact. In such a tract, squatters and trespassers were tolerated to an extent now unknown. The peasant who dwelt there could, at little or no charge, procure occasionally some palatable addition to his hard fare, and provide himself with fuel for the winter. He kept a flock of geese on what is now an orchard rich with apple blossoms. He snared wild fowl on the fen which has long since been drained and divided into corn fields and turnip fields. He cut turf among the furze bushes on the moat which is now a meadow bright with clover and renowned for butter and cheese. The progress of agriculture and the increase of population necessarily deprived him of these privileges. But against this disadvantage a long list of advantages is to be set off. Of the blessings which civilisation and philosophy bring with them a large proportion is common to all ranks,

120. Fourteenth Report of the Poor Law Commissioners, Appendix B, No. 2, Appendix C, No. 1, 1848. Of the two estimates of the poor rate mentioned in the text one was formed by Arthur Moore, the other, some years later, by Richard Dunning. Moore's estimate will be found in Davenant's Essay on Ways and Means; Dunning's in Sir Frederic Eden's valuable work on the poor. King and Davenant estimate the paupers and beggars in 1696, at the incredible number of 1,330,000 out of a population of 5,500,000. In 1846 the number of persons who received relief appears from the official returns to have been only 1,332,089 out of a population of about 17,000,000. It ought also to be observed that, in those returns, a pauper must very often be reckoned more than once.

I would advise the reader to consult De Foe's pamphlet entitled "Giving Alms no Charity," and with the Greenwich tables which will be found in Mr. M'Culloch's Commercial Dictionary under the head Prices.

and would, if withdrawn, be missed as painfully by the labourer as by the peer. The marketplace which the rustic can now reach with his cart in an hour was, a hundred and sixty years ago, a day's journey from him. The street which now affords to the artisan, during the whole night, a secure, a convenient, and a brilliantly lighted walk was, a hundred and sixty years ago, so dark after sunset that he would not have been able to see his hand, so ill paved that he would have run constant risk of breaking his neck, and so ill watched that he would have been in imminent danger of being knocked down and plundered of his small earnings. Every bricklayer who falls from a scaffold, every sweeper of a crossing who is run over by a carriage, may now have his wounds dressed and his limbs set with a skill such as, a hundred and sixty years ago, all the wealth of a great lord like Ormond, or of a merchant prince like Clayton, could not have purchased. Some frightful diseases have been extirpated by science; and some have been banished by police. The term of human life has been lengthened over the whole kingdom, and especially in the towns. The year 1685 was not accounted sickly; yet in the year 1685 more than one in twenty-three of the inhabitants of the capital died.[121] At present only one inhabitant of the capital in forty dies annually. The difference in salubrity between the London of the nineteenth century and the London of the seventeenth century is very far greater than the difference between London in an ordinary year and London in a year of cholera.

Still more important is the benefit which all orders of society, and especially the lower orders, have derived from the mollifying influence of civilisation on the national character. The groundwork of that character has indeed been the same through many generations, in the sense in which the groundwork of the character of an individual may be said to be the same when he is a rude and thoughtless schoolboy and when he is a refined and accomplished man. It is pleasing to reflect that the public mind of England has softened while it has ripened, and that we have, in the course of ages, become, not only a wiser, but also a kinder people. There is scarcely a page of the history or lighter literature of the seventeenth century which does not contain some

---

121. The deaths were 23,222. Petty's Political Arithmetic.

proof that our ancestors were less humane than their posterity. The discipline of workshops, of schools, of private families, though not more efficient than at present, was infinitely harsher. Masters, well born and bred, were in the habit of beating their servants. Pedagogues knew no way of imparting knowledge but by beating their pupils. Husbands, of decent station, were not ashamed to beat their wives. The implacability of hostile factions was such as we can scarcely conceive. Whigs were disposed to murmur because Stafford was suffered to die without seeing his bowels burned before his face. Tories reviled and insulted Russell as his coach passed from the Tower to the scaffold in Lincoln's Inn Fields.[122] As little mercy was shown by the populace to sufferers of a humbler rank. If an offender was put into the pillory, it was well if he escaped with life from the shower of brickbats and paving stones.[123] If he was tied to the cart's tail, the crowd pressed round him, imploring the hangman to give it the fellow well, and make him howl.[124] Gentlemen arranged parties of pleasure to Bridewell on court days, for the purpose of seeing the wretched women who beat hemp there whipped.[125] A man pressed to death for refusing to plead, a woman burned for coining, excited less sympathy than is now felt for a galled horse or an overdriven ox. Fights compared with which a boxing match is a refined and humane spectacle were among the favourite diversions of a large part of the town. Multitudes assembled to see gladiators hack each other to pieces with deadly weapons, and shouted with delight when one of the combatants lost a finger or an eye. The prisons were hells on earth, seminaries of every crime and of every disease. At the assizes the lean and yellow culprits brought with them from their cells to the dock an atmosphere of stench and pestilence which sometimes avenged them signally on bench, bar, and jury. But on all this misery society looked with profound indifference. Nowhere could be found that sensitive and restless compassion which has, in our time, extended a powerful protection to the factory child, to the

122. Burnet, i, 560.
123. Muggleton's Acts of the Witnesses of the Spirit.
124. Tom Brown describes such a scene in lines which I do not venture to quote.
125. Ward's London Spy.

337

Hindoo widow, to the negro slave, which pries into the stores and watercasks of every emigrant ship, which winces at every lash laid on the back of a drunken soldier, which will not suffer the thief in the hulks to be ill fed or overworked, and which has repeatedly endeavoured to save the life even of the murderer. It is true that compassion ought, like all other feelings, to be under the government of reason, and has, for want of such government, produced some ridiculous and some deplorable effects. But the more we study the annals of the past the more shall we rejoice that we live in a merciful age, in an age in which cruelty is abhorred, and in which pain, even when deserved, is inflicted reluctantly and from a sense of duty. Every class doubtless has gained largely by this great moral change: but the class which has gained most is the poorest, the most dependent, and the most defenceless.

The general effect of the evidence which has been submitted to the reader seems hardly to admit of doubt. Yet, in spite of evidence, many will still image to themselves the England of the Stuarts as a more pleasant country than the England in which we live. It may at first sight seem strange that society, while constantly moving forward with eager speed, should be constantly looking backward with tender regret. But these two propensities, inconsistent as they may appear, can easily be resolved into the same principle. Both spring from our impatience of the state in which we actually are. That impatience, while it stimulates us to surpass preceding generations, disposes us to overrate their happiness. It is, in some sense, unreasonable and ungrateful in us to be constantly discontented with a condition which is constantly improving. But, in truth, there is constant improvement precisely because there is constant discontent. If we were perfectly satisfied with the present, we should cease to contrive, to labour, and to save with a view to the future. And it is natural that, being dissatisfied with the present, we should form a too favourable estimate of the past.

In truth we are under a deception similar to that which misleads the traveller in the Arabian desert. Beneath the caravan all is dry and bare: but far in advance, and far in the rear, is the semblance of refreshing waters. The pilgrims hasten forward and find nothing but sand where, an hour before, they had seen a lake. They turn their eyes and see a lake where, an hour before, they were toiling through sand. A similar illusion seems to haunt nations through every stage of the long progress from poverty and barbarism to the highest degrees of opulence and civilisation. But, if we resolutely chase the mirage backward, we shall find it recede before us into the regions of fabulous antiquity. It is now the fashion to place the golden age of England in times when noblemen were destitute of comforts the want of which would be intolerable to a modern footman, when farmers and shopkeepers breakfasted on loaves the very sight of which would raise a riot in a modern workhouse, when to have a clean shirt once a week was a privilege reserved for the higher class of gentry, when men died faster in the purest country air than they now die in the most pestilential lanes of our towns, and when men died faster in the lanes of our towns than they now die on the coast of Guiana. We too shall, in our turn, be outstripped, and in our turn be envied. It may well be, in the twentieth century, that the peasant of Dorsetshire may think himself miserably paid with twenty shillings a week; that the carpenter at Greenwich may receive ten shillings a day; that labouring men may be as little used to dine without meat as they now are to eat rye bread; that sanitary police and medical discoveries may have added several more years to the average length of human life; that numerous comforts and luxuries which are now unknown, or confined to a few, may be within the reach of every diligent and thrifty working man. And yet it may then be the mode to assert that the increase of wealth and the progress of science have benefited the few at the expense of the many, and to talk of the reign of Queen Victoria as the time when England was truly merry England, when all classes were bound together by brotherly sympathy, when the rich did not grind the faces of the poor, and when the poor did not envy the splendour of the rich.

From
Chapter 9

On the sixteenth of October, according to the English reckoning, was held a solemn sitting of the States of Holland. The Prince came to bid them farewell. He thanked them for the kindness with which they had watched over him when he was left an orphan child, for the confidence which they had reposed in him during his administration, and for the assistance which they had granted him at this momentous crisis. He entreated them to believe that he had always meant and endeavoured to promote the interest of his country. He was now quitting them, perhaps never to return. If he should fall in defence of the reformed religion and of the independence of Europe, he commended his beloved wife to their care. The Grand Pensionary answered in a faltering voice; and in all that grave senate there was none who could refrain from shedding tears. But the iron stoicism of William never gave way; and he stood among his weeping friends calm and austere as if he had been about to leave them only for a short visit to his hunting grounds at Loo.[1]

The deputies of the principal towns accompanied him to his yacht. Even the representatives of Amsterdam, so long the chief seat of opposition to his administration, joined in paying him

The opening portion of this chapter has been omitted.

1. Register of the Proceedings of the States of Holland and West Friesland; Burnet, i, 782.

this compliment. Public prayers were offered for him on that day in all the churches of the Hague.

In the evening he arrived at Helvoetsluys and went on board of a frigate called the Brill. His flag was immediately hoisted. It displayed the arms of Nassau quartered with those of England. The motto, embroidered in letters three feet long, was happily chosen. The House of Orange had long used the elliptical device, "I will maintain." The ellipsis was now filled up with words of high import, "The liberties of England and the Protestant religion."

The Prince had not been many hours on board when the wind became fair. On the nineteenth the armament put out to sea, and traversed, before a strong breeze, about half the distance between the Dutch and English coasts. Then the wind changed, blew hard from the west, and swelled into a violent tempest. The ships, scattered and in great distress, regained the shore of Holland as they best might. The Brill reached Helvoetsluys on the twenty-first. The Prince's fellow passengers had observed with admiration that neither peril nor mortification had for one moment disturbed his composure. He now, though suffering from sea sickness, refused to go on shore: for he conceived that, by remaining on board, he should in the most effectual manner notify to Europe that the late misfortune had only delayed for a very short time the execution of his purpose. In two or three days the fleet reassembled. One vessel only had been cast away. Not a single soldier or sailor was missing. Some horses had perished: but this loss the Prince with great expedition repaired; and, before the London Gazette had spread the news of his mishap, he was again ready to sail.[2]

His Declaration preceded him only by a few hours. On the first of November it began to be mentioned in mysterious whispers by the politicians of London, was passed secretly from man to man, and was slipped into the boxes of the post office. One of the agents was arrested, and the packets of which he was in charge were carried to Whitehall. The King read, and was greatly troubled. His first impulse was to hide the paper from all human eyes.

2. London Gazette, October 29, 1688; Burnet, i, 782; Bentinck to his wife, October 21/31, Oct. 22/Nov. 1, Oct. 24/Nov. 3, Oct. 27/Nov. 6, 1688.

He threw into the fire every copy which had been brought to him, except one; and that one he would scarcely trust out of his own hands.[3]

The paragraph in the manifesto which disturbed him most was that in which it was said that some of the Peers, Spiritual and Temporal, had invited the Prince of Orange to invade England. Halifax, Clarendon, and Nottingham were then in London. They were immediately summoned to the palace and interrogated. Halifax, though conscious of innocence, refused at first to make any answer. "Your Majesty asks me," said he, "whether I have committed high treason. If I am suspected, let me be brought before my peers. And how can Your Majesty place any dependence on the answer of a culprit whose life is at stake? Even if I had invited His Highness over, I should without scruple plead Not Guilty." The King declared that he did not at all consider Halifax as a culprit, and that he had asked the question as one gentleman asks another who has been calumniated whether there be the least foundation for the calumny. "In that case," said Halifax, "I have no objection to aver, as a gentleman speaking to a gentleman, on my honour, which is as sacred as my oath, that I have not invited the Prince of Orange over."[4] Clarendon and Nottingham said the same. The King was still more anxious to ascertain the temper of the Prelates. If they were hostile to him, his throne was indeed in danger. But it could not be. There was something monstrous in the supposition that any Bishop of the Church of England could rebel against his Sovereign. Compton was called into the royal closet, and was asked whether he believed that there was the slightest ground for the Prince's assertion. The Bishop was in a strait; for he was himself one of the seven who had signed the invitation; and his conscience, not a very enlightened conscience, would not suffer him, it seems, to utter a direct falsehood. "Sir," he said, "I am quite confident that there is not one of my brethren who is not as guiltless as myself in this matter." The equivocation was ingenious: but whether the difference between the sin of such an equivocation and the sin of a lie be worth any expense of ingenuity may per-

3. Van Citters, Nov. 2/11, 1688; Adda, Nov. 2/12.
4. Ronquillo, Nov. 12/22, 1688. "Estas respuestas," says Ronquillo, "son ciertas, aunque mas las encubrian en la corte."

haps be doubted. The King was satisfied. "I fully acquit you all," he said. "But I think it necessary that you should publicly contradict the slanderous charge brought against you in the Prince's Declaration." The Bishop very naturally begged that he might be allowed to read the paper which he was required to contradict: but the King would not suffer him to look at it.

On the following day appeared a proclamation threatening with the severest punishment all who should circulate, or who should even dare to read, William's manifesto.[5] The Primate and the few Spiritual Peers who happened to be then in London had orders to wait upon the King. Preston was in attendance with the Prince's Declaration in his hand. "My Lords," said James, "listen to this passage. It concerns you." Preston then read the sentence in which the Spiritual Peers were mentioned. The King proceeded: "I do not believe one word of this: I am satisfied of your innocence: but I think it fit to let you know of what you are accused."

The Primate, with many dutiful expressions, protested that the King did him no more than justice. "I was born in Your Majesty's allegiance. I have repeatedly confirmed that allegiance by my oath. I can have but one King at one time. I have not invited the Prince over; and I do not believe that a single one of my brethren has done so." "I am sure I have not," said Crewe of Durham. "Nor I," said Cartwright of Chester. Crewe and Cartwright might well be believed; for both had sate in the Ecclesiastical Commission. When Compton's turn came, he parried the question with an adroitness which a Jesuit might have envied. "I gave Your Majesty my answer yesterday."

James repeated again and again that he fully acquitted them all. Nevertheless it would, in his judgment, be for his service and for their own honour that they should publicly vindicate themselves. He therefore required them to draw up a paper setting forth their abhorrence of the Prince's design. They remained silent: their silence was supposed to imply consent; and they were suffered to withdraw.[6]

Meanwhile the fleet of William was on the German Ocean. It was on the evening of Thursday the first of November that

5. London Gazette, Nov. 5, 1668. The Proclamation is dated November 2.
6. Tanner MSS.

he put to sea the second time. The wind blew fresh from the east. The armament, during twelve hours, held a course towards the northwest. The light vessels sent out by the English Admiral for the purpose of obtaining intelligence brought back news which confirmed the prevailing opinion that the enemy would try to land in Yorkshire. All at once, on a signal from the Prince's ship, the whole fleet tacked, and made sail for the British Channel. The same breeze which favoured the voyage of the invaders prevented Dartmouth from coming out of the Thames. His ships were forced to strike yards and topmasts; and two of his frigates, which had gained the open sea, were shattered by the violence of the weather and driven back into the river.[7]

The Dutch fleet ran fast before the gale, and reached the Straits at about ten in the morning of Saturday, the third of November. William himself, in the Brill, led the way. More than six hundred vessels, with canvass spread to a favourable wind, followed in his train. The transports were in the centre. The men of war, more than fifty in number, formed an outer rampart. Herbert, with the title of Lieutenant Admiral General, commanded the whole fleet. His post was in the rear, and many English sailors, inflamed against Popery, and attracted by high pay, served under him. It was not without great difficulty that the Prince had prevailed on some Dutch officers of high reputation to submit to the authority of a stranger. But the arrangement was eminently judicious. There was, in the King's fleet, much discontent and an ardent zeal for the Protestant faith. But within the memory of old mariners the Dutch and English navies had thrice, with heroic spirit and various fortune, contended for the empire of the sea. Our sailors had not forgotten the broom with which Tromp had threatened to sweep the Channel, or the fire which De Ruyter had lighted in the dockyards of the Medway. Had the rival nations been once more brought face to face on the element of which both claimed the sovereignty, all other thoughts might have given place to mutual animosity. A bloody and obstinate battle might have been fought. Defeat would have been fatal to William's enterprise. Even victory would have

7. Burnet, i, 787; Rapin; Whittle's Exact Diary; Expedition of the Prince of Orange to England, 1688; History of the Desertion, 1688; Dartmouth to James, Nov. 5, 1688, in Dalrymple.

deranged all his deeply mediated schemes of policy. He therefore wisely determined that the pursuers, if they overtook him, should be hailed in their own mother tongue, and adjured, by an admiral under whom they had served, and whom they esteemed, not to fight against old messmates for Popish tyranny. Such an appeal might possibly avert a conflict. If a conflict took place, one English commander would be opposed to another; nor would the pride of the islanders be wounded by learning that Dartmouth had been compelled to strike to Herbert.[8]

Happily William's precautions were not necessary. Soon after midday he passed the Straits. His fleet spread to within a league of Dover on the north and of Calais on the south. The men of war on the extreme right and left saluted both fortresses at once. The troops appeared under arms on the decks. The flourish of trumpets, the clash of cymbals, and the rolling of drums were distinctly heard at once on the English and French shores. An innumerable company of gazers blackened the white beach of Kent. Another mighty multitude covered the coast of Picardy. Rapin de Thoyras, who, driven by persecution from his country, had taken service in the Dutch army, and now went with the Prince to England, described the spectacle, many years later, as the most magnificent and affecting that was ever seen by human eyes. At sunset the armament was off Beachy Head. Then the lights were kindled. The sea was in a blaze for many miles. But the eyes of all the steersmen were directed throughout the night to three huge lanterns which flamed on the stern of the Brill.[9]

Meanwhile a courier had been riding post from Dover Castle to Whitehall with news that the Dutch had passed the Straits and were steering westward. It was necessary to make an immediate change in all the military arrangements. Messengers were despatched in every direction. Officers were roused from their

8. Avaux, July 12/22, Aug. 14/24, 1688. On this subject, Mr. De Jonge, who is connected by affinity with the descendants of the Dutch Admiral Evertsen, has kindly communicated to me some interesting information derived from family papers. In a letter to Bentinck, dated Sept. 6/16, 1688, William insists strongly on the importance of avoiding an action, and begs Bentinck to represent this to Herbert. "Ce n'est pas le tems de faire voir sa bravoure, ni de se battre si l'on le peut éviter. Je luy l'ai déjà dit: mais il sera nécessaire que vous le répétiez, et que vous le luy fassiez bien comprendre."

9. Rapin's History; Whittle's Exact Diary. I have seen a contemporary Dutch chart of the order in which the fleet sailed.

beds at dead of night. At three on the Sunday morning there was a great muster by torchlight in Hyde Park. The King had sent several regiments northward in the expectation that William would land in Yorkshire. Expresses were despatched to recall them. All the forces except those which were necessary to keep the peace of the capital were ordered to move to the West. Salisbury was appointed as the place of rendezvous; but, as it was thought possible that Portsmouth might be the first point of attack, three battalions of guards and a strong body of cavalry set out for that fortress. In a few hours it was known that Portsmouth was safe; and these troops then received orders to change their route and to hasten to Salisbury.[10]

When Sunday the fourth of November dawned, the cliffs of the Isle of Wight were full in view of the Dutch armament. That day was the anniversary both of William's birth and of his marriage. Sail was slackened during part of the morning; and divine service was performed on board of the ships. In the afternoon and through the night the fleet held on its course. Torbay was the place where the Prince intended to land. But the morning of Monday the fifth of November was hazy. The pilot of the Brill could not discern the sea marks, and carried the fleet too far to the west. The danger was great. To return in the face of the wind was impossible. Plymouth was the next port. But at Plymouth a garrison had been posted under the command of the Earl of Bath. The landing might be opposed; and a check might produce serious consequences. There could be little doubt, moreover, that by this time the royal fleet had got out of the Thames and was hastening full sail down the Channel. Russell saw the whole extent of the peril, and exclaimed to Burnet, "You may go to prayers, Doctor. All is over." At that moment the wind changed: a soft breeze sprang up from the south: the mist dispersed: the sun shone forth; and, under the mild light of an autumnal noon, the fleet turned back, passed round the lofty cape of Berry Head, and rode safe in the harbour of Torbay.[11]

10. Adda, Nov. 5/15, 1688; Newsletter in the Mackintosh Collection; Van Citters, Nov. 6/16.

11. Burnet, i, 788; Extracts from the Legge Papers in the Mackintosh Collection.

Since William looked on that harbour its aspect has greatly changed. The amphitheatre which surrounds the spacious basin now exhibits everywhere the signs of prosperity and civilisation. At the northeastern extremity has sprung up a great watering place, to which strangers are attracted from the most remote parts of our island by the Italian softness of the air: for in that climate the myrtle flourishes unsheltered; and even the winter is milder than the Northumbrian April. The inhabitants are about ten thousand in number. The newly built churches and chapels, the baths and libraries, the hotels and public gardens, the infirmary and the museum, the white streets, rising terrace above terrace, the gay villas peeping from the midst of shrubberies and flower beds, present a spectacle widely different from any that in the seventeenth century England could show. At the opposite end of the bay lies, sheltered by Berry Head, the stirring market town of Brixham, the wealthiest seat of our fishing trade. A pier and a haven were formed there at the beginning of the present century, but have been found insufficient for the increasing traffic. The population is about six thousand souls. The shipping amounts to more than two hundred sail. The tonnage exceeds many times the tonnage of the port of Liverpool under the kings of the House of Stuart. But Torbay, when the Dutch fleet cast anchor there, was known only as a haven where ships sometimes took refuge from the tempests of the Atlantic. Its quiet shores were undisturbed by the bustle either of commerce or of pleasure; and the huts of ploughmen and fishermen were thinly scattered over what is now the site of crowded marts and of luxurious pavilions.

The peasantry of the coast of Devonshire remembered the name of Monmouth with affection, and held Popery in detestation. They therefore crowded down to the seaside with provisions and offers of service. The disembarkation instantly commenced. Sixty boats conveyed the troops to the coast. Mackay was sent on shore first with the British regiments. The Prince soon followed. He landed where the quay of Brixham now stands. The whole aspect of the place has been altered. Where we now see a port crowded with shipping, and a marketplace swarming with buyers and sellers, the waves then broke on a desolate beach; but a fragment of the rock on which the deliverer stepped from his boat has been carefully preserved, and is set up as an object of public veneration in the centre of that busy wharf.

As soon as the Prince had planted his foot on dry ground he called for horses. Two beasts, such as the small yeomen of that time were in the habit of riding, were procured from the neighbouring village. Willam and Schomberg mounted and proceeded to examine the country.

As soon as Burnet was on shore he hastened to the Prince. An amusing dialogue took place between them. Burnet poured forth his congratulations with genuine delight, and then eagerly asked what were His Highness's plans. Military men are seldom disposed to take counsel with gownsmen on military matters; and William regarded the interference of unprofessional advisers, in questions relating to war, with even more than the disgust ordinarily felt by soldiers on such occasions. But he was at that moment in an excellent humour, and, instead of signifying his displeasure by a short and cutting reprimand, graciously extended his hand, and answered his chaplain's question by another question: "Well, Doctor, what do you think of predestination now?" The reproof was so delicate that Burnet, whose perceptions were not very fine, did not perceive it. He answered with great fervour that he should never forget the signal manner in which Providence had favoured their undertaking.[12]

During the first day the troops who had gone on shore had many discomforts to endure. The earth was soaked with rain. The baggage was still on board of the ships. Officers of high rank were compelled to sleep in wet clothes on the wet ground: the Prince himself had no better quarters than a hut afforded. His banner was displayed on the thatched roof; and some bedding brought from the Brill was spread for him on the floor.[13] There was some difficulty about landing the horses; and it seemed probable that this operation would occupy several days. But on the following morning the prospect cleared. The wind was gentle. The water in the bay was as even as glass. Some fishermen

12. I think that nobody who compares Burnet's account of this conversation with Dartmouth's can doubt that I have correctly represented what passed.

13. I have seen a contemporary Dutch print of the disembarkation. Some men are bringing the Prince's bedding into the hut on which his flag is flying.

pointed out a place where the ships could be brought within sixty feet of the beach. This was done; and in three hours many hundreds of horses swam safely to shore.

The disembarkation had hardly been effected when the wind rose again, and swelled into a fierce gale from the west. The enemy coming in pursuit down the Channel had been stopped by the same change of weather which enabled William to land. During two days the King's fleet lay on an unruffled sea in sight of Beachy Head. At length Dartmouth was able to proceed. He passed the Isle of Wight, and one of his ships came in sight of the Dutch topmasts in Torbay. Just at this moment he was encountered by the tempest, and compelled to take shelter in the harbour of Portsmouth.[14] At that time James, who was not incompetent to form a judgment on a question of seamanship, declared himself perfectly satisfied that his Admiral had done all that man could do, and had yielded only to the irresistible hostility of the winds and waves. At a later period the unfortunate prince began, with little reason, to suspect Dartmouth of treachery, or at least of slackness.[15]

The weather had indeed served the Protestant cause so well that some men of more piety than judgment fully believed the ordinary laws of nature to have been suspended for the preservation of the liberty and religion of England. Exactly a hundred years before, they said, the Armada, invincible by man, had been scattered by the wrath of God. Civil freedom and divine truth were again in jeopardy; and again the obedient elements had fought for the good cause. The wind had blown strong from the east while the Prince wished to sail down the Channel, had turned to the south when he wished to enter Torbay, had sunk to a calm during the disembarkation, and, as soon as the disembarkation was completed, had risen to a storm, and had met the pursuers in the face. Nor did men omit to remark that, by an extraordinary coincidence, the Prince had reached our shores on a day on which the Church of England commemorated, by prayer and thanksgiving, the wonderful escape of the royal House and of the

14. Burnet, i, 789; Legge Papers.
15. On Nov. 9, 1688, James wrote to Dartmouth thus: "Nobody could work otherwise than you did. I am sure all knowing seamen must be of the same mind." But see the Life of James, ii, 207, Orig. Mem.

three Estates from the blackest plot ever devised by Papists. Carstairs, whose suggestions were sure to meet with attention from the Prince, recommended that, as soon as the landing had been effected, public thanks should be offered to God for the protection so conspicuously accorded to the great enterprise. This advice was taken, and with excellent effect. The troops, taught to regard themselves as favourites of heaven, were inspired with new courage; and the English people formed the most favourable opinion of a general and an army so attentive to the duties of religion.

On Tuesday, the sixth of November, William's army began to march up the country. Some regiments advanced as far as Newton Abbot. A stone, set up in the midst of that little town, still marks the spot where the Prince's Declaration was solemnly read to the people. The movements of the troops were slow: for the rain fell in torrents; and the roads of England were then in a state which seemed frightful to persons accustomed to the excellent communications of Holland. William took up his quarters, during two days, at Ford, a seat of the ancient and illustrious family of Courtenay, in the neighbourhood of Newton Abbot. He was magnificently lodged and feasted there: but it is remarkable that the owner of the house, though a strong Whig, did not choose to be the first to put life and fortune in peril, and cautiously abstained from doing anything which, if the King should prevail, could be treated as a crime.

Exeter, in the meantime, was greatly agitated. Lamplugh, the bishop, as soon as he heard that the Dutch were at Torbay, set off in terror for London. The Dean fled from the deanery. The magistrates were for the King, the body of the inhabitants for the Prince. Everything was in confusion when, on the morning of Thursday, the eighth of November, a body of troops, under the command of Mordaunt, appeared before the city. With Mordaunt came Burnet, to whom William had entrusted the duty of protecting the clergy of the Cathedral from injury and insult.[16] The Mayor and Aldermen had ordered the gates to be closed, but yielded on the first summons. The deanery was prepared for the reception of the Prince. On the following day, Fri-

16. Burnet, i, 790.

day the ninth, he arrived. The magistrates had been pressed to receive him in state at the entrance of the city, but had steadfastly refused. The pomp of that day, however, could well spare them. Such a sight had never been seen in Devonshire. Many of the citizens went forth half a day's journey to meet the champion of their religion. All the neighbouring villages poured forth their inhabitants. A great crowd, consisting chiefly of young peasants, brandishing their cudgels, had assembled on the top of Haldon Hill, whence the army, marching from Chudleigh, first descried the rich valley of the Exe, and the two massive towers rising from the cloud of smoke which overhung the capital of the West. The road, all down the long descent, and through the plain to the banks of the river, was lined, mile after mile, with spectators. From the West Gate to the Cathedral Close, the pressing and shouting on each side was such as reminded Londoners of the crowds on the Lord Mayor's day. The houses were gaily decorated. Doors, windows, balconies, and roofs were thronged with gazers. An eye accustomed to the pomp of war would have found much to criticise in the spectacle. For several toilsome marches in the rain, through roads where one who travelled on foot sank at every step up to the ankles in clay, had not improved the appearance either of the men or of their accoutrements. But the people of Devonshire, altogether unused to the splendour of well ordered camps, were overwhelmed with delight and awe. Descriptions of the martial pageant were circulated all over the kingdom. They contained much that was well fitted to gratify the vulgar appetite for the marvellous. For the Dutch army, composed of men who had been born in various climates, and had served under various standards, presented an aspect at once grotesque, gorgeous, and terrible to islanders who had, in general, a very indistinct notion of foreign countries. First rode Macclesfield at the head of two hundred gentlemen, mostly of English blood, glittering in helmets and cuirasses, and mounted on Flemish war horses. Each was attended by a negro, brought from the sugar plantations on the coast of Guiana. The citizens of Exeter, who had never seen so many specimens of the African race, gazed with wonder on those black faces set off by embroidered turbans and white feathers. Then, with drawn broadswords, came a squadron of

Swedish horsemen in black armour and fur cloaks. They were regarded with a strange interest; for it was rumoured that they were natives of a land where the ocean was frozen and where the night lasted through half the year, and that they had themselves slain the huge bears whose skins they wore. Next, surrounded by a goodly company of gentlemen and pages, was borne aloft the Prince's banner. On its broad folds the crowd which covered the roofs and filled the windows read with delight that memorable inscription, "The Protestant religion and the liberties of England." But the acclamations redoubled when, attended by forty running footmen, the Prince himself appeared, armed on back and breast, wearing a white plume and mounted on a white charger. With how martial an air he curbed his horse, how thoughtful and commanding was the expression of his ample forehead and falcon eye, may still be seen on the canvass of Kneller. Once those grave features relaxed into a smile. It was when an ancient woman, perhaps one of the zealous Puritans who, through twenty-eight years of persecution, had waited with firm faith for the consolation of Israel, perhaps the mother of some rebel who had perished in the carnage of Sedgemoor, or in the more fearful carnage of the Bloody Circuit, broke from the crowd, rushed through the drawn swords and curvetting horses, touched the hand of the deliverer, and cried out that now she was happy. Near to the Prince was one who divided with him the gaze of the multitude. That, men said, was the great Count Schomberg, the first soldier in Europe, since Turenne and Condé were gone, the man whose genius and valour had saved the Portuguese monarchy on the field of Montes Claros, the man who had earned a still higher glory by resigning the truncheon of a Marshal of France for the sake of the true religion. It was not forgotten that the two heroes who, indissolubly united by their common Protestantism, were entering Exeter together, had twelve years before been opposed to each other under the walls of Maestricht, and that the energy of the young Prince had not then been found a match for the cool science of the veteran who now rode in friendship by his side. Then came a long column of the whiskered infantry of Switzerland, distinguished in all the Continental wars of two centuries by pre-eminent valour and discipline, but never till that week seen on

English ground. And then marched a succession of bands designated, as was the fashion of that age, after their leaders, Bentinck, Solmes, and Ginkell, Talmash and Mackay. With peculiar pleasure Englishmen might look on one gallant regiment which still bore the name of the honoured and lamented Ossory. The effect of the spectacle was heightened by the recollection of more than one renowned event in which the warriors now pouring through the West Gate had borne a share. For they had seen service very different from that of the Devonshire militia or of the camp at Hounslow. Some of them had repelled the fiery onset of the French on the field of Seneff; and others had crossed swords with the infidels in the cause of Christendom on that great day when the siege of Vienna was raised. The very senses of the multitude were fooled by imagination. Newsletters conveyed to every part of the kingdom fabulous accounts of the size and strength of the invaders. It was affirmed that they were, with scarcely an exception, above six feet high, and that they wielded such huge pikes, swords, and muskets, as had never before been seen in England. Nor did the wonder of the population diminish when the artillery arrived, twenty-one huge pieces of brass cannon, which were with difficulty tugged along by sixteen cart horses to each. Much curiosity was excited by a strange structure mounted on wheels. It proved to be a movable smithy, furnished with all tools and materials necessary for repairing arms and carriages. But nothing caused so much astonishment as the bridge of boats, which was laid with great speed on the Exe for the conveyance of waggons, and afterwards as speedily taken to pieces and carried away. It was made, if report said true, after a pattern contrived by the Christians who were warring against the Great Turk on the Danube. The foreigners inspired as much good will as admiration. Their politic leader took care to distribute the quarters in such a manner as to cause the smallest possible inconvenience to the inhabitants of Exeter and of the neighbouring villages. The most rigid discipline was maintained. Not only were pillage and outrage effectually prevented, but the troops were required to demean themselves with civility towards all classes. Those who had formed their notions of an army from the conduct of Kirke and his Lambs were amazed to see soldiers who never swore at a landlady or took an egg without paying for it. In return for this moderation the people furnished the troops with provisions in great abundance and at reasonable prices.[17]

Much depended on the course which, at this great crisis, the clergy of the Church of England might take; and the members of the Chapter of Exeter were the first who were called upon to declare their sentiments. Burnet informed the Canons, now left without a head by the flight of the Dean, that they could not be permitted to use the prayer for the Prince of Wales, and that a solemn service must be performed in honour of the safe arrival of the Prince. The Canons did not choose to appear in their stalls; but some of the choristers and prebendaries attended. William repaired in military state to the Cathedral. As he passed under the gorgeous screen, that renowned organ, scarcely surpassed by any of those which are the boast of his native Holland, gave out a peal of triumph. He mounted the Bishop's seat, a stately throne rich with the carving of the fifteenth century. Burnet stood below; and a crowd of warriors and nobles appeared on the right hand and on the left. The singers, robed in white, sang the Te Deum. When the chaunt was over, Burnet read the Prince's Declaration: but, as soon as the first words were uttered, prebendaries and singers crowded in all haste out of the choir. At the close

---

17. See Whittle's Diary, the Expedition of His Highness, and the Letter from Exon published at the time. I have myself seen two manuscript newsletters describing the pomp of the Prince's entrance into Exeter. A few months later a bad poet wrote a play, entitled "The late Revolution." One scene is laid at Exeter. "Enter battalions of the Prince's army, on their march into the city, with colours flying, drums beating, and the citizens shouting." A nobleman named Misopapas says,

"Can you guess, my lord,
How dreadful guilt and fear has represented
Your army to the court? Your number and your stature
Are both advanced; all six foot high at least,
In bearskins clad, Swiss, Swedes, and Brandenburghers."

In a song which appeared just after the entrance into Exeter, the Irish are described as mere dwarfs in comparison of the giants whom William commanded:

"Poor Berwick, how will thy dear joys
Oppose this famed viaggio?
Thy tallest sparks will be mere toys
To Brandenburgh and Swedish boys,
Coraggio! Coraggio!"

Addison alludes, in the Freeholder, to the extraordinary effect which these romantic stories produced.

354

Burnet cried in a loud voice, "God save the Prince of Orange!" and many fervent voices answered, "Amen."[18]

On Sunday, the eleventh of November, Burnet preached before the Prince in the Cathedral, and dilated on the signal mercy vouchsafed by God to the English Church and nation. At the same time a singular event happened in a humbler place of worship. Ferguson resolved to preach at the Presbyterian meeting house. The minister and elders would not consent: but the turbulent and halfwitted knave, fancying that the times of Fleetwood and Harrison were come again, forced the door, went through the congregation sword in hand, mounted the pulpit, and there poured forth a fiery invective against the King. The time for such follies had gone by; and this exhibition excited nothing but derision and disgust.[19]

While these things were passing in Devonshire the ferment was great in London. The Prince's Declaration, in spite of all precautions, was now in every man's hands. On the sixth of November James, still uncertain on what part of the coast the invaders had landed, summoned the Primate and three other Bishops, Compton of London, White of Peterborough, and Sprat of Rochester, to a conference in the closet. The King listened graciously while the prelates made warm professions of loyalty, and assured them that he did not suspect them. "But where," said he, "is the paper that you were to bring me?" "Sir," answered Sancroft, "we have brought no paper. We are not solicitous to clear our fame to the world. It is no new thing to us to be reviled and falsely accused. Our consciences acquit us: Your Majesty acquits us; and we are satisfied." "Yes," said the King, "but a declaration from you is necessary to my service." He then produced a copy of the Prince's manifesto. "See," he said, "how you are mentioned here." "Sir," answered one of the Bishops, "not one person in five hundred believes this manifesto to be genuine." "No!" cried the King fiercely: "then those five hundred would bring the Prince of Orange to cut my throat." "God forbid," exclaimed the prelates in concert. But the King's understanding, never very clear, was now quite bewildered. One of his peculiari-

18. Expedition of the Prince of Orange; Oldmixon, 755; Whittle's Diary; Eachard, iii, 911; London Gazette, Nov. 15, 1688.

19. London Gazette, Nov. 15, 1688; Expedition of the Prince of Orange.

ties was that, whenever his opinion was not adopted, he fancied that his veracity was questioned. "This paper not genuine!" he exclaimed, turning over the leaves with his hands. "Am I not worthy to be believed? Is my word not to be taken?" "At all events, sir," said one of the Bishops, "this is not an ecclesiastical matter. It lies within the sphere of the civil power. God has entrusted Your Majesty with the sword: and it is not for us to invade your functions." Then the Archbishop, with that gentle and temperate malice which inflicts the deepest wounds, declared that he must be excused from setting his hand to any political document. "I and my brethren, sir," he said, "have already smarted severely for meddling with affairs of state; and we shall be very cautious how we do so again. We once subscribed a petition of the most harmless kind: we presented it in the most respectful manner; and we found that we had committed a high offence. We were saved from ruin only by the merciful protection of God. And, sir, the ground then taken by Your Majesty's Attorney and Solicitor was that, out of Parliament, we were private men, and that it was criminal presumption in private men to meddle with politics. They attacked us so fiercely that for my part I gave myself over for lost." "I thank you for that, my Lord of Canterbury," said the King: "I should have hoped that you would not have thought yourself lost by falling into my hands." Such a speech might have become the mouth of a merciful sovereign, but it came with a bad grace from a prince who had burned a woman alive for harbouring one of his flying enemies, from a prince round whose knees his own nephew had clung in vain agonies of supplication. The Archbishop was not to be so silenced. He resumed his story, and recounted the insults which the creatures of the Court had offered to the Church of England, among which some ridicule thrown on his own style occupied a conspicuous place. The King had nothing to say but that there was no use in repeating old grievances, and that he had hoped that these things had been quite forgotten. He, who never forgot the smallest injury that he had suffered, could not understand how others should remember for a few weeks the most deadly injuries that he had inflicted.

At length the conversation came back to the point from which it had wandered. The King insisted on having from the Bishops a paper declaring their abhorrence of the Prince's enterprise. They, with many professions of the most submissive loyalty, pertinaciously refused. The Prince, they said, asserted that he had been invited by temporal as well as by spiritual peers. The imputation was common. Why should not the purgation be common also? "I see how it is," said the King. "Some of the temporal peers have been with you, and have persuaded you to cross me in this matter." The Bishops solemnly averred that it was not so. But it would, they said, seem strange that, on a question involving grave political and military considerations, the temporal peers should be entirely passed over, and the prelates alone should be required to take a prominent part. "But this," said James, "is my method. I am your King. It is for me to judge what is best. I will go my own way; and I call on you to assist me." The Bishops assured him that they would assist him in their proper department, as Christian ministers with their prayers, and as peers of the realm with their advice in his Parliament. James, who wanted neither the prayers of heretics nor the advice of Parliaments, was bitterly disappointed. After a long altercation, "I have done," he said, "I will urge you no further. Since you will not help me, I must trust to myself and to my own arms."[20]

The Bishops had hardly left the royal presence, when a courier arrived with the news that on the preceding day the Prince of Orange had landed in Devonshire. During the following week London was violently agitated. On Sunday, the eleventh of November, a rumour was circulated that knives, gridirons, and caldrons, intended for the torturing of heretics, were concealed in the monastery which had been established under the King's protection at Clerkenwell. Great multitudes assembled round the building, and were about to demolish it, when a military force arrived. The crowd was dispersed, and several of the rioters were slain. An inquest sate on the bodies, and came to a decision which strongly indicated the temper of the public mind. The jury found that certain loyal and well disposed persons, who had gone to put down the meetings of traitors and public enemies at a mass house, had been wilfully murdered by the soldiers; and this strange verdict was signed by all the jurors. The ecclesiastics at Clerkenwell,

20. Life of James, ii, 210, Orig. Mem.; Sprat's Narrative; Van Citters, Nov. 6/16, 1688.

naturally alarmed by these symptoms of popular feeling, were desirous to place their property in safety. They succeeded in removing most of their furniture before any report of their intentions got abroad. But at length the suspicions of the rabble were excited. The last two carts were stopped in Holborn, and all that they contained was publicly burned in the middle of the street. So great was the alarm among the Catholics that all their places of worship were closed, except those which belonged to the royal family and to foreign Ambassadors.[21]

On the whole, however, things as yet looked not unfavourably for James. The invaders had been more than a week on English ground. Yet no man of note had joined them. No rebellion had broken out in the north or the east. No servant of the crown appeared to have betrayed his trust. The royal army was assembling fast at Salisbury, and, though inferior in discipline to that of William, was superior in numbers.

The Prince was undoubtedly surprised and mortified by the slackness of those who had invited him to England. By the common people of Devonshire, indeed, he had been received with every sign of good will: but no nobleman, no gentleman of high consideration, had yet repaired to his quarters. The explanation of this singular fact is probably to be found in the circumstance that he had landed in a part of the island where he had not been expected. His friends in the north had made their arrangements for a rising, on the supposition that he would be among them with an army. His friends in the west had made no arrangements at all, and were naturally disconcerted at finding themselves suddenly called upon to take the lead in a movement so important and perilous. They had also fresh in their recollection, and indeed full in their sight, the disastrous consequences of rebellion, gibbets, heads, mangled quarters, families still in deep mourning for brave sufferers who had loved their country well but not wisely. After a warning so terrible and so recent, some hesitation was natural. It was equally natural, however, that William, who, trusting to promises from England, had put to hazard, not only his own fame and fortunes, but also the prosperity and independence of his native land, should feel deeply mortified. He was,

21. Luttrell's Diary; Newsletter in the Mackintosh Collection; Adda, Nov. 16/26, 1688.

indeed, so indignant, that he talked of falling back to Torbay, reembarking his troops, returning to Holland, and leaving those who had betrayed him to the fate which they deserved. At length, on Monday, the twelfth of November, a gentleman named Burrington, who resided in the neighbourhood of Crediton, joined the Prince's standard, and his example was followed by several of his neighbours.

Men of higher consequence had already set out from different parts of the country for Exeter. The first of these was John Lord Lovelace, distinguished by his taste, by his magnificence, and by the audacious and intemperate vehemence of his Whiggism. He had been five or six times arrested for political offences. The last crime laid to his charge was, that he had contemptuously denied the validity of a warrant, signed by a Roman Catholic Justice of the Peace. He had been brought before the Privy Council and strictly examined, but to little purpose. He resolutely refused to criminate himself; and the evidence against him was insufficient. He was dismissed; but, before he retired, James exclaimed in great heat, "My Lord, this is not the first trick that you have played me." "Sir," answered Lovelace, with undaunted spirit, "I never played any trick to Your Majesty, or to any other person. Whoever has accused me to Your Majesty of playing tricks is a liar."[22] Lovelace had subsequently been admitted into the confidence of those who planned the Revolution. His mansion, built by his ancestors out of the spoils of Spanish galleons from the Indies, rose on the ruins of a house of Our Lady in that beautiful valley through which the Thames, not yet defiled by the precincts of a great capital, nor rising and falling with the flow and ebb of the sea, rolls under woods of beech round the gentle hills of Berkshire. Beneath the stately saloon, adorned by Italian pencils, was a subterraneous vault, in which the bones of ancient monks had sometimes been found. In this dark chamber some zealous and daring opponents of the government had held many midnight conferences during that anxious time when England was impatiently expecting the Protestant wind.[23] The season for action had now arrived. Lovelace, with seventy followers, well armed and mounted, quitted his dwelling, and directed his course

22. Johnstone, Feb. 27, 1688; Van Citters of the same date.
23. Lysons, Magna Britannia Berkshire.

westward. He reached Gloucestershire without difficulty. But Beaufort, who governed that country, was exerting all his great authority and influence in support of the crown. The militia had been called out. A strong party had been posted at Cirencester. When Lovelace arrived there he was informed that he could not be suffered to pass. It was necessary for him either to relinquish his undertaking or to fight his way through. He resolved to force a passage; and his friends and tenants stood gallantly by him. A sharp conflict took place. The militia lost an officer and six or seven men; but at length the followers of Lovelace were over-powered: he was made a prisoner, and sent to Gloucester Castle.[24]

Others were more fortunate. On the day on which the skirmish took place at Cirencester, Richard Savage, Lord Colchester, son and heir of the Earl Rivers, and father, by a lawless amour, of that unhappy poet whose misdeeds and misfortunes form one of the darkest portions of literary history, came with between sixty and seventy horse to Exeter. With him arrived the bold and tur-bulent Thomas Wharton. A few hours later came Edward Rus-sell, son of the Earl of Bedford, and brother of the virtuous no-bleman whose blood had been shed on the scaffold. Another arrival still more important was speedily announced. Colchester, Wharton, and Russell belonged to that party which had been constantly opposed to the Court. James Bertie, Earl of Abingdon, had, on the contrary, been regarded as a supporter of arbitrary government. He had been true to James in the days of the Ex-clusion Bill. He had, as Lord Lieutenant of Oxfordshire, acted with vigour and severity against the adherents of Monmouth, and had lighted bonfires to celebrate the defeat of Argyle. But dread of Popery had driven him into opposition and rebellion. He was the first peer of the realm who made his appearance at the quarters of the Prince of Orange.[25]

But the King had less to fear from those who openly arrayed themselves against his authority, than from the dark conspiracy which had spread its ramifications through his army and his fam-ily. Of that conspiracy Churchill, unrivalled in sagacity and ad-dress, endowed by nature with a certain cool intrepidity which never failed him either in fighting or lying, high in military rank,

24. London Gazette, Nov. 15, 1688; Luttrell's Diary.
25. Burnet, i, 790; Life of William, 1703.

and high in the favour of the Princess Anne, must be regarded as the soul. It was not yet time for him to strike the decisive blow. But even thus early he inflicted, by the instrumentality of a subordinate agent, a wound, serious if not deadly, on the royal cause.

Edward Viscount Cornbury, eldest son of the Earl of Clarendon, was a young man of slender abilities, loose principles, and violent temper. He had been early taught to consider his relationship to the Princess Anne as the groundwork of his fortunes, and had been exhorted to pay her assiduous court. It had never occurred to his father that the hereditary loyalty of the Hydes could run any risk of contamination in the household of the King's favourite daughter: but in that household the Churchills held absolute sway; and Cornbury became their tool. He commanded one of the regiments of dragoons which had been sent westward. Such dispositions had been made that, on the fourteenth of November, he was, during a few hours, the senior officer at Salisbury, and all the troops assembled there were subject to his authority. It seems extraordinary that, at such a crisis, the army on which everything depended should have been left, even for a moment, under the command of a young Colonel, who had neither abilities nor experience. There can be little doubt that so strange an arrangement was the result of deep design, and as little doubt to what head and to what heart the design is to be imputed.

Suddenly three of the regiments of cavalry which had assembled at Salisbury were ordered to march westward. Cornbury put himself at their head, and conducted them first to Blandford and thence to Dorchester. From Dorchester, after a halt of an hour or two, they set out for Axminster. Some of the officers began to be uneasy, and demanded an explanation of these strange movements. Cornbury replied that he had instructions to make a night attack on some troops which the Prince of Orange had posted at Honiton. But suspicon was awake. Searching questions were put, and were evasively answered. At last Cornbury was pressed to produce his orders. He perceived, not only that it would be impossible for him to carry over all the three regiments, as he had hoped, but that he was himself in a situation of considerable peril. He accordingly stole away with a few followers to the Dutch quarters. Most of his troops returned to Salisbury: but some who had been detached from the main body, and who had no suspicion of the designs of their commander, proceeded to Honiton. There they found themselves in the midst of a large force which was fully prepared to receive them. Resistance was impossible. Their leader pressed them to take service under William. A gratuity of a month's pay was offered to them, and was by most of them accepted.[26]

The news of these events reached London on the fifteenth. James had been on the morning of that day in high good humour. Bishop Lamplugh had just presented himself at court on his arrival from Exeter, and had been most graciously received. "My Lord," said the King, "you are a genuine old Cavalier." The archbishopric of York, which had now been vacant more than two years and a half, was immediately bestowed on Lamplugh as the reward of loyalty. That afternoon, just as the King was sitting down to dinner, arrived an express with the tidings of Cornbury's defection. James turned away from his untasted meal, swallowed a crust of bread and a glass of wine, and retired to his closet. He afterwards learned that, as he was rising from table, several of the Lords in whom he reposed the greatest confidence were shaking hands and congratulating each other in the adjoining gallery. When the news was carried to the Queen's apartments she and her ladies broke out into tears and loud cries of sorrow.[27]

The blow was indeed a heavy one. It was true that the direct loss to the crown and the direct gain to the invaders hardly amounted to two hundred men and as many horses. But where could the King henceforth expect to find those sentiments in which consists the strength of states and of armies? Cornbury was the heir of a house conspicuous for its attachment to monarchy. His father Clarendon, his uncle Rochester, were men whose loyalty was supposed to be proof to all temptation. What must be the strength of that feeling against which the most deeply rooted hereditary prejudices were of no avail, of that feeling which could reconcile a young officer of high birth to desertion, aggravated by breach of trust and by gross falsehood? That Cornbury

26. Life of James, ii, 215, Orig. Mem.; Burnet, i, 790; Clarendon's Diary, Nov. 15, 1688; London Gazette, Nov. 17.

27. Life of James, ii, 218; Clarendon's Diary, Nov. 15, 1688; Van Citters, Nov. 16/26.

was not a man of brilliant parts or enterprising temper made the event more alarming. It was impossible to doubt that he had in some quarter a powerful and artful prompter. Who that prompter was soon became evident. In the meantime no man in the royal camp could feel assured that he was not surrounded by traitors. Political rank, military rank, the honour of a nobleman, the honour of a soldier, the strongest professions, the purest Cavalier blood, could no longer afford security. Every man might reasonably doubt whether every order which he received from his superior was not meant to serve the purposes of the enemy. That prompt obedience without which an army is merely a rabble was necessarily at an end. What discipline could there be among soldiers who had just been saved from a snare by refusing to follow their commanding officer on a secret expedition, and by insisting on a sight of his orders?

Cornbury was soon kept in countenance by a crowd of deserters superior to him in rank and capacity: but during a few days he stood alone in his shame, and was bitterly reviled by many who afterwards imitated his example and envied his dishonourable precedence. Among these was his own father. The first outbreak of Clarendon's rage and sorrow was highly pathetic. "Oh God!" he ejaculated, "that a son of mine should be a rebel!" A fortnight later he made up his mind to be a rebel himself. Yet it would be unjust to pronounce him a mere hypocrite. In revolutions men live fast: the experience of years is crowded into hours: old habits of thought and action are violently broken; and novelties, which at first sight inspire dread and disgust, become in a few days familiar, endurable, attractive. Many men of far purer virtue and higher spirit than Clarendon were prepared, before that memorable year ended, to do what they would have pronounced wicked and infamous when it began.

The unhappy father composed himself as well as he could, and sent to ask a private audience of the King. It was granted. James said, with more than his usual graciousness, that he from his heart pitied Cornbury's relations, and should not hold them at all accountable for the crime of their unworthy kinsman. Clarendon went home, scarcely daring to look his friends in the face. Soon, however, he learned with surprise that the act, which had, as he at first thought, for ever dishonoured his family, was applauded by some persons of high station. His niece, the Princess of Denmark, asked him why he shut himself up. He answered that he had been overwhelmed with confusion by his son's villany. Anne seemed not at all to understand this feeling. "People," she said, "are very uneasy about Popery. I believe that many of the army will do the same."[28]

And now the King, greatly disturbed, called together the principal officers who were still in London. Churchill, who was about this time promoted to the rank of Lieutenant General, made his appearance with that bland serenity which neither peril nor infamy could ever disturb. The meeting was attended by Henry Fitzroy, Duke of Grafton, whose audacity and activity made him conspicuous among the natural children of Charles the Second. Grafton was colonel of the first regiment of Foot Guards. He seems to have been at this time completely under Churchill's influence, and was prepared to desert the royal standard as soon as the favourable moment should arrive. Two other traitors were in the circle, Kirke and Trelawney, who commanded those two fierce and lawless bands then known as the Tangier regiments. Both of them had, like the other Protestant officers of the army, long seen with extreme displeasure the partiality which the King had shown to members of his own Church; and Trelawney remembered with bitter resentment the persecution of his brother the Bishop of Bristol. James addressed the assembly in language worthy of a better man and of a better cause. It might be, he said, that some of the officers had conscientious scruples about fighting for him. If so, he was willing to receive back their commissions. But he adjured them as gentlemen and soldiers not to imitate the shameful example of Cornbury. All seemed moved; and none more than Churchill. He was the first to vow with well feigned enthusiasm that he would shed the last drop of his blood in the service of his gracious master: Grafton was loud and forward in similar protestations; and the example was followed by Kirke and Trelawney.[29]

Deceived by these professions, the King prepared to set out for Salisbury. Before his departure he was informed that a considerable number of peers, temporal and spiritual, desired to be

28. Clarendon's Diary, Nov. 15, 16, 17, 20, 1688.
29. Life of James, ii, 219, Orig. Mem.

admitted to an audience. They came, with Sancroft at their head, to present a petition, praying that a free and legal Parliament might be called, and that a negotiation might be opened with the Prince of Orange.

The history of this petition is curious. The thought seems to have occurred at once to two great chiefs of parties who had long been rivals and enemies, Rochester and Halifax. They both, independently of one another, consulted the Bishops. The Bishops warmly approved the suggestion. It was then proposed that a general meeting of peers should be called to deliberate on the form of an address to the King. It was term time; and in term time men of rank and fashion then lounged every day in Westminster Hall as they now lounge in the clubs of Pall Mall and Saint James's Street. Nothing could be easier than for the Lords who assembled there to step aside into some adjoining room and to hold a consultation. But unexpected difficulties arose. Halifax became first cold and then adverse. It was his nature to discover objections to everything; and on this occasion his sagacity was quickened by rivalry. The scheme, which he had approved while he regarded it as his own, began to displease him as soon as he found that it was also the scheme of Rochester, by whom he had been long thwarted and at length supplanted, and whom he disliked as much as it was in his easy nature to dislike anybody. Nottingham was at that time much under the influence of Halifax. They both declared that they would not join in the address if Rochester signed it. Clarendon expostulated in vain. "I mean no disrespect," said Halifax, "to my Lord Rochester: but he has been a member of the Ecclesiastical Commission: the proceedings of that court must soon be the subject of a very serious enquiry; and it is not fit that one who has sate there should take any part in our petition." Nottingham, with strong expressions of personal esteem for Rochester, avowed the same opinion. The authority of the two dissentient Lords prevented several other noblemen from subscribing the address; but the Hydes and the Bishops persisted. Nineteen signatures were procured; and the petitioners waited in a body on the King.[30]

He received their address ungraciously. He assured them, in-

30. Clarendon's Diary, from Nov. 8 to Nov. 17, 1688.

deed, that he passionately desired the meeting of a free Parliament; and he promised them, on the faith of a King, that he would call one as soon as the Prince of Orange should have left the island. "But how," said he, "can a Parliament be free when an enemy is in the kingdom, and can return near a hundred votes?" To the prelates he spoke with peculiar acrimony. "I could not," he said, "prevail on you the other day to declare against this invasion: but you are ready enough to declare against me. Then you would not meddle with politics. You have no scruple about meddling now. You have excited this rebellious temper among your flocks; and now you foment it. You would be better employed in teaching them how to obey than in teaching me how to govern." He was much incensed against his nephew Grafton, whose signature stood next to that of Sancroft, and said to the young man, with great asperity, "You know nothing about religion: you care nothing about it; and yet, forsooth, you must pretend to have a conscience." "It is true, sir," answered Grafton, with impudent frankness, "that I have very little conscience: but I belong to a party which has a great deal."[31]

Bitter as was the King's language to the petitioners, it was far less bitter than that which he held after they had withdrawn. He had done, he said, far too much already in the hope of satisfying an undutiful and ungrateful people. He had always hated the thought of concession: but he had suffered himself to be talked over; and now he, like his father before him, had found that concession only made subjects more encroaching. He would yield nothing more, not an atom; and, after his fashion, he vehemently repeated many times, "Not an atom." Not only would he make no overtures to the invaders, but he would receive none. If the Dutch sent flags of truce, the first messenger should be dismissed without an answer; the second should be hanged.[32] In such a mood James set out for Salisbury. His last act before his departure was to appoint a Council of five Lords to represent him in

31. Life of James, ii, 212. Orig. Mem.; Clarendon's Diary, Nov. 17, 1688; Van Citters, Nov. 20/30; Burnet, i, 791; Some Reflections upon the most Humble Petition to the King's most Excellent Majesty, 1688; Modest Vindication of the Petition; First Collection of Papers relating to English Affairs, 1688.
32. Adda, Nov. 19/29, 1688.

London during his absence. Of the five, two were Papists, and by law incapable of office. Joined with them was Jeffreys, a Protestant indeed, but more detested by the nation than any Papist. To the other two members of this board, Preston and Goldolphin, no serious objection could be made. On the day on which the King left London the Prince of Wales was sent to Portsmouth. That fortress was strongly garrisoned, and was under the government of Berwick. The fleet commanded by Dartmouth lay close at hand: and it was supposed that, if things went ill, the royal infant would, without difficulty, be conveyed from Portsmouth to France.[33]

On the nineteenth James reached Salisbury, and took up his quarters in the episcopal palace. Evil news was now fast pouring in upon him from all sides. The western counties had at length risen. As soon as the news of Cornbury's desertion was known, many wealthy landowners took heart and hastened to Exeter. Among them was Sir William Portman of Bryanstone, one of the greatest men in Dorsetshire, and Sir Francis Warre of Hestercombe, whose interest was great in Somersetshire.[34] But the most important of the new comers was Seymour, who had recently inherited a baronetcy which added nothing to his dignity, and who, in birth, in political influence, and in parliamentary abilities, was beyond comparison the foremost among the Tory gentlemen of England. At his first audience he is said to have exhibited his characteristic pride in a way which surprised and amused the Prince. "I think, Sir Edward," said William, meaning to be very civil, "that you are of the family of the Duke of Somerset." "Pardon me, sir," said Sir Edward, who never forgot that he was the head of the elder branch of the Seymours: "the Duke of Somerset is of my family."[35]

The quarters of William now began to present the appearance of a court. More than sixty men of rank and fortune were lodged at Exeter; and the daily display of rich liveries, and of coaches

33. Life of James, 220, 221.
34. Eachard's History of the Revolution.
35. Seymour's reply to William is related by many writers. It much resembles a story which is told of the Manriquez family. They, it is said, took for their device the words, "Nos no descendemos de los Reyes; sino los Reyes descienden de nos."—Carpentariana.

drawn by six horses, in the Cathedral Close, gave to that quiet precinct something of the splendour and gaiety of Whitehall. The common people were eager to take arms; and it would have been easy to form many battalions of infantry. But Schomberg, who thought little of soldiers fresh from the plough, maintained that, if the expedition could not succeed without such help, it would not succeed at all; and William, who had as much professional feeling as Schomberg, concurred in this opinion. Commissions therefore for raising new regiments were very sparingly given; and none but picked recruits were enlisted.

It was now thought desirable that the Prince should give a public reception to the whole body of noblemen and gentlemen who had assembled at Exeter. He addressed them in a short but dignified and well considered speech. He was not, he said, acquainted with the faces of all whom he saw. But he had a list of their names, and knew how high they stood in the estimation of their country. He gently chid their tardiness, but expressed a confident hope that it was not yet too late to save the kingdom. "Therefore," he said, "gentlemen, friends, and fellow Protestants, we bid you and all your followers most heartily welcome to our court and camp."[36]

Seymour, a keen politician, long accustomed to the tactics of faction, saw in a moment that the party which had begun to rally round the Prince stood in need of organisation. It was as yet, he said, a mere rope of sand: no common object had been publicly and formally avowed: nobody was pledged to anything. As soon as the assembly at the deanery broke up, he sent for Burnet, and suggested that an association should be formed, and that all the English adherents of the Prince should put their hands to an instrument binding them to be true to their leader and to each other. Burnet carried the suggestion to the Prince and to Shrewsbury, by both of whom it was approved. A meeting was held in the Cathedral. A short paper drawn up by Burnet was produced, approved, and eagerly signed. The subscribers engaged to pursue in concert the objects set forth in the Prince's Declaration; to stand by him and by each other; to take signal vengeance on all who should

36. Fourth Collection of Papers, 1688; Letter from Exon; Burnet, i, 792.

make any attempt on his person; and, even if such an attempt should unhappily succeed, to persist in their undertaking till the liberties and the religion of the nation should be effectually secured.[37]

About the same time a messenger arrived at Exeter from the Earl of Bath, who commanded at Plymouth. Bath declared that he placed himself, his troops, and the fortress which he governed at the Prince's disposal. The invaders therefore had now not a single enemy in their rear.[38]

While the West was thus rising to confront the King, the North was all in a flame behind him. On the sixteenth Delamere took arms in Cheshire. He convoked his tenants, called upon them to stand by him, promised that, if they fell in the cause, their leases should be renewed to their children, and exhorted every one who had a good horse either to take the field or to provide a substitute.[39] He appeared at Manchester with fifty men armed and mounted, and his force had trebled before he reached Boaden Downs.

The neighbouring counties were violently agitated. It had been arranged that Danby should seize York, and that Devonshire should appear at Nottingham. At Nottingham no resistance was anticipated. But at York there was a small garrison under the command of Sir John Reresby. Danby acted with rare dexterity. A meeting of the gentry and freeholders of Yorkshire had been summoned for the twenty-second of November to address the King on the state of affairs. All the Deputy Lieutenants of the three Ridings, several noblemen, and a multitude of opulent esquires and substantial yeomen had been attracted to the provincial capital. Four troops of militia had been drawn out under arms to preserve the public peace. The Common Hall was crowded with freeholders, and the discussion had begun, when a cry was suddenly raised that the Papists were up, and were slaying the Protestants. The Papists of York were much more likely to be employed in seeking for hiding places than in attacking enemies

37. Burnet, i, 792; History of the Desertion; Second Collection of Papers, 1688.
38. Letter of Bath to the Prince of Orange, Nov. 18, 1688; Dalrymple.
39. First Collection of Papers, 1688; London Gazette, November 22.

who outnumbered them in the proportion of a hundred to one. But at that time no story of Popish atrocity could be so wild and marvellous as not to find ready belief. The meeting separated in dismay. The whole city was in confusion. At this moment Danby at the head of about a hundred horsemen rode up to the militia, and raised the cry "No Popery! A free Parliament! The Protestant religion!" The militia echoed the shout. The garrison was instantly surprised and disarmed. The governor was placed under arrest. The gates were closed. Sentinels were posted everywhere. The populace was suffered to pull down a Roman Catholic chapel; but no other harm appears to have been done. On the following morning the Guildhall was crowded with the first gentlemen of the shire, and with the principal magistrates of the city. The Lord Mayor was placed in the chair. Danby proposed a Declaration setting forth the reasons which had induced the friends of the constitution and of the Protestant religion to rise in arms. This Declaration was eagerly adopted, and received in a few hours the signatures of six peers, of five baronets, of six knights, and of many gentlemen of high consideration.[40]

Devonshire meantime, at the head of a great body of friends and dependents, quitted the palace which he was rearing at Chatsworth, and appeared in arms at Derby. There he formally delivered to the municipal authorities a paper setting forth the reasons which had moved him to this enterprise. He then proceeded to Nottingham, which soon became the head quarters of the Northern insurrection. Here a proclamation was put forth couched in bold and severe terms. The name of rebellion, it was said, was a bugbear which could frighten no reasonable man. Was it rebellion to defend those laws and that religion which every king of England bound himself by oath to maintain? How that oath had lately been observed was a question on which, it was to be hoped, a free Parliament would soon pronounce. In the meantime, the insurgents declared that they held it to be not rebellion, but legitimate self defence, to resist a tyrant who knew no law but his own will. The Northern rising became every day more formidable. Four powerful and wealthy Earls, Manchester, Stamford, Rutland, and Chesterfield, repaired to Nottingham,

40. Reresby's Memoirs; Life of James, ii, 231. Orig. Mem.

and were joined there by Lord Cholmondeley and by Lord Grey de Ruthyn.[41]

All this time the hostile armies in the south were approaching each other. The Prince of Orange, when he learned that the King had arrived at Salisbury, thought it time to leave Exeter. He placed that city and the surrounding country under the government of Sir Edward Seymour, and set out on Wednesday the twenty-first of November, escorted by many of the most considerable gentlemen of the western counties, for Axminster, where he remained several days.

The King was eager to fight; and it was obviously his interest to do so. Every hour took away something from his own strength, and added something to the strength of his enemies. It was most important, too, that his troops should be blooded. A great battle, however it might terminate, could not but injure the Prince's popularity. All this William perfectly understood, and determined to avoid an action as long as possible. It is said that, when Schomberg was told that the enemy were advancing and were determined to fight, he answered, with the composure of a tactician confident in his skill, "That will be just as we may choose." It was, however, impossible to prevent all skirmishing between the advanced guards of the armies. William was desirous that in such skirmishing nothing might happen which could wound the pride or rouse the vindictive feelings of the nation which he meant to deliver. He therefore, with admirable prudence, placed his British regiments in the situations where there was most risk of collision. The outposts of the royal army were Irish. The consequence was that, in the little combats of this short campaign, the invaders had on their side the hearty sympathy of all Englishmen.

The first of these encounters took place at Wincanton. Mackay's regiment, composed of British soldiers, lay near a body of the King's Irish troops, commanded by their countryman, the gallant Sarsfield. Mackay sent out a small party under a lieutenant named Campbell, to procure horses for the baggage. Campbell found what he wanted at Wincanton, and was just leaving that town on his return, when a strong detachment of Sarsfield's

41. Cibber's Apology; History of the Desertion; Luttrell's Diary; Second Collection of Papers, 1688.

troops approached. The Irish were four to one: but Campbell resolved to fight it out to the last. With a handful of resolute men he took his stand in the road. The rest of his soldiers lined the hedges which overhung the highway on the right and on the left. The enemy came up. "Stand," cried Campbell; "for whom are you?" "I am for King James," answered the leader of the other party. "And I for the Prince of Orange," cried Campbell. "We will prince you," answered the Irishman with a curse. "Fire!" exclaimed Campbell; and a sharp fire was instantly poured in from both the hedges. The King's troops received three well aimed volleys before they could make any return. At length they succeeded in carrying one of the hedges; and would have overpowered the little band which was opposed to them, had not the country people, who mortally hated the Irish, given a false alarm that more of the Prince's troops were coming up. Sarsfield recalled his men and fell back; and Campbell proceeded on his march unmolested with the baggage horses. This affair, creditable undoubtedly to the valour and discipline of the Prince's army, was magnified by report into a victory won against great odds by British Protestants over Popish barbarians who had been brought from Connaught to oppress our island.[42]

A few hours after this skirmish an event took place which put an end to all risk of a more serious struggle between the armies. Churchill and some of his principal accomplices were assembled at Salisbury. Two of the conspirators, Kirke and Trelawney, had proceeded to Warminster, where their regiments were posted. All was ripe for the execution of the long meditated treason.

Churchill advised the King to visit Warminster, and to inspect the troops stationed there. James assented; and his coach was at the door of the episcopal palace when his nose began to bleed violently. He was forced to postpone his expedition and to put himself under medical treatment. Three days elapsed before the hemorrhage was entirely subdued; and during those three days alarming rumours reached his ears.

It was impossible that a conspiracy so widely spread as that of which Churchill was the head could be kept altogether secret. There was no evidence which could be laid before a jury or a

42. Whittle's Diary; History of the Desertion; Luttrell's Diary.

court martial; but strange whispers wandered about the camp. Feversham, who held the chief command, reported that there was a bad spirit in the army. It was hinted to the King that some who were near his person were not his friends, and that it would be a wise precaution to send Churchill and Grafton under a guard to Portsmouth. James rejected this counsel. A propensity to suspicion was not among his vices. Indeed the confidence which he reposed in professions of fidelity and attachment was such as might rather have been expected from a goodhearted and inexperienced stripling than from a politician who was far advanced in life, who had seen much of the world, who had suffered much from the villanous arts, and whose own character was by no means a favourable specimen of human nature. It would be difficult to mention any other man who, having himself so little scruple about breaking faith with his neighbours, was so slow to believe that his neighbours could break faith with him. Nevertheless the reports which he had received of the state of his army disturbed him greatly. He was now no longer impatient for a battle. He even began to think of retreating. On the evening of Saturday, the twenty-fourth of November, he called a council of war. The meeting was attended by those officers against whom he had been most earnestly cautioned. Feversham expressed an opinion that it was desirable to fall back. Churchill argued on the other side. The consultation lasted till midnight. At length the King declared that he had decided for a retreat. Churchill saw or imagined that he was distrusted, and, though gifted with a rare self command, could not conceal his uneasiness. Before the day broke he fled to the Prince's quarters, accompanied by Grafton.[43]

Churchill left behind him a letter of explanation. It was written with that decorum which he never failed to preserve in the midst of guilt and dishonour. He acknowledged that he owed everything to the royal favour. Interest, he said, and gratitude impelled him in the same direction. Under no other government could he hope to be so great and prosperous as he had been: but all such considerations must yield to a paramount duty. He was a Protestant; and he could not conscientiously draw his sword

43. Life of James, ii, 222, Orig. Mem.; Barillon, Nov. 21/Dec. 1, 1688; Sheridan MS.

against the Protestant cause. As to the rest he would ever be ready to hazard life and fortune in defence of the sacred person and of the lawful rights of his gracious master.[44]

Next morning all was confusion in the royal camp. The King's friends were in dismay. His enemies could not conceal their exultation. The consternation of James was increased by news which arrived on the same day from Warminster. Kirke, who commanded at that post, had refused to obey orders which he had received from Salisbury. There could no longer be any doubt that he too was in league with the Prince of Orange. It was rumoured that he had actually gone over with all his troops to the enemy: and the rumour, though false, was, during some hours, fully believed.[45] A new light flashed on the mind of the unhappy King. He thought that he understood why he had been pressed, a few days before, to visit Warminster. There he would have found himself helpless, at the mercy of the conspirators, and in the vicinity of the hostile outposts. Those who might have attempted to defend him would have been easily overpowered. He would have been carried a prisoner to the head quarters of the invading army. Perhaps some still blacker treason might have been committed; for men who have once engaged in a wicked and perilous enterprise are no longer their own masters, and are often impelled, by a fatality which is part of their just punishment, to crimes such as they would at first have shuddered to contemplate. Surely it was not without the special intervention of some guardian Saint that a King devoted to the Catholic Church had, at the very moment when he was blindly hastening to captivity, perhaps to death, been suddenly arrested by what he had then thought a disastrous malady.

All these things confirmed James in the resolution which he had taken on the preceding evening. Orders were given for an immediate retreat. Salisbury was in an uproar. The camp broke up with the confusion of a flight. No man knew whom to trust or whom to obey. The material strength of the army was little diminished: but its moral strength had been destroyed. Many

44. First Collection of Papers, 1688.
45. Letter from Middleton to Preston, dated Salisbury, Nov. 25. "Villany upon villany," says Middleton, "the last still greater than the former." Life of James, ii, 224, 225, Orig. Mem.

whom shame would have restrained from leading the way to the Prince's quarters were eager to imitate an example which they never would have set; and many, who would have stood by their King while he appeared to be resolutely advancing against the invaders, felt no inclination to follow a receding standard.[46]

James went that day as far as Andover. He was attended by his son in law Prince George, and by the Duke of Ormond. Both were among the conspirators, and would probably have accompanied Churchill, had he not, in consequence of what had passed at the council of war, thought it expedient to take his departure suddenly. The impenetrable stupidity of Prince George served his turn on this occasion better than cunning would have done. It was his habit, when any news was told him, to exclaim in French, "Est-il-possible?" "Is it possible?" This catchword was now of great use to him. "Est-il-possible?" he cried, when he had been made to understand that Churchill and Grafton were missing. And when the ill tidings came from Warminster, he again ejaculated, "Est-il-possible?"

Prince George and Ormond were invited to sup with the King at Andover. The meal must have been a sad one. The King was overwhelmed by his misfortunes. His son in law was the dullest of companions. "I have tried Prince George sober," said Charles the Second; "and I have tried him drunk; and, drunk or sober, there is nothing in him."[47] Ormond, who was through life taciturn and bashful, was not likely to be in high spirits at such a moment. At length the repast terminated. The King retired to rest. Horses were in waiting for the Prince and Ormond, who, as soon as they left the table, mounted and rode off. They were accompanied by the Earl of Drumlanrig, eldest son of the Duke of Queensberry. The defection of this young nobleman was no insignificant event. For Queensberry was the head of the Protestant Episcopalians of Scotland, a class compared with whom the bitterest English Tories might be called Whiggish; and Drumlanrig himself was Lieutenant Colonel of Dundee's regiment, a band more detested by the Whigs than even Kirke's lambs. This fresh calamity was announced to the King on the following morning. He was less disturbed by the news than might have been

46. History of the Desertion; Luttrell's Diary.
47. Dartmouth's note on Burnet, i, 643.

expected. The shock which he had undergone twenty-four hours before had prepared him for almost any disaster; and it was impossible to be seriously angry with Prince George, who was hardly an accountable being, for having yielded to the arts of such a tempter as Churchill. "What!" said James, "Is Est-il-possible gone too? After all, a good trooper would have been a greater loss."[48] In truth the King's whole anger seems, at this time, to have been concentrated, and not without cause, on one object. He set off for London, breathing vengeance against Churchill, and learned, on arriving, a new crime of the arch-deceiver. The Princess Anne had been some hours missing.

Anne, who had no will but that of the Churchills, had been induced by them to notify under her own hand to William, a week before, her approbation of his enterprise. She assured him that she was entirely in the hands of her friends, and that she would remain in the palace, or take refuge in the City, as they might determine.[49] On Sunday the twenty-fifth of November, she, and those who thought for her, were under the necessity of coming to a sudden resolution. That afternoon a courier from Salisbury brought tidings that Churchill had disappeared, that he had been accompanied by Grafton, that Kirke had proved false, and that the royal forces were in full retreat. There was, as usually happened when great news, good or bad, arrived in town, an immense crowd that evening in the galleries of Whitehall. Curiosity and anxiety sate on every face. The Queen broke forth into natural expressions of indignation against the chief traitor, and did not altogether spare his too partial mistress. The sentinels were doubled round that part of the palace which Anne occupied. The Princess was in dismay. In a few hours her father would be at Westminster. It was not likely that he would treat her personally with severity; but that he would permit her any longer to enjoy the society of her friend was not to be hoped. It could hardly be doubted that Sarah would be placed under arrest, and would be subjected to a strict examination by shrewd and rigorous inquisitors. Her papers would be seized. Perhaps evidence affecting her life might be discovered. If so, the worst might

48. Clarendon's Diary, Nov. 26; Life of James, ii, 224; Prince George's letter to the King has often been printed.
49. The letter, dated Nov. 18, will be found in Dalrymple.

well be dreaded. The vengeance of the implacable King knew no distinction of sex. For offences much smaller than those which might probably be brought home to Lady Churchill he had sent women to the scaffold and the stake. Strong affection braced the feeble mind of the Princess. There was no tie which she would not break, no risk which she would not run, for the object of her idolatrous affection. "I will jump out of the window," she cried, "rather than be found here by my father." The favourite undertook to manage an escape. She communicated in all haste with some of the chiefs of the conspiracy. In a few hours everything was arranged. That evening Anne retired to her chamber as usual. At dead of night she rose, and, accompanied by her friend Sarah and two other female attendants, stole down the back stairs in a dressing gown and slippers. The fugitives gained the open street unchallenged. A hackney coach was in waiting for them there. Two men guarded the humble vehicle. One of them was Compton, Bishop of London, the Princess's old tutor: the other was the magnificent and accomplished Dorset, whom the extremity of the public danger had roused from his luxurious repose. The coach drove instantly to Aldersgate Street, where the town residence of the Bishops of London then stood, within the shadow of their Cathedral. There the Princess passed the night. On the following morning she set out for Epping Forest. In that wild tract Dorset possessed a venerable mansion, which has long since been destroyed. In his hospitable dwelling, the favourite resort, during many years, of wits and poets, the fugitives made a short stay. They could not safely attempt to reach William's quarters; for the road thither lay through a country occupied by the royal forces. It was therefore determined that Anne should take refuge with the northern insurgents. Compton wholly laid aside, for the time, his sacerdotal character. Danger and conflict had rekindled in him all the military ardour which he had felt twenty-eight years before, when he rode in the Life Guards. He preceded the Princess's carriage in a buff coat and jackboots, with a sword at his side and pistols in his holsters. Long before she reached Nottingham, she was surrounded by a body guard of gentlemen who volunteered to escort her. They invited the Bishop to act as their colonel; and he consented with an alacrity which gave great scandal to rigid Churchmen, and did not much raise his character even in the opinion of Whigs.[50]

When, on the morning of the twenty-sixth, Anne's apartment was found empty, the consternation was great in Whitehall. While the Ladies of her Bed-chamber ran up and down the courts of the palace, screaming and wringing their hands, while Lord Craven, who commanded the Foot Guards, was questioning the sentinels in the gallery, while the Chancellor was sealing up the papers of the Churchills, the Princess's nurse broke into the royal apartments crying out that the dear lady had been murdered by the Papists. The news flew to Westminster Hall. There the story was that Her Highness had been hurried away by force to a place of confinement. When it could no longer be denied that her flight had been voluntary, numerous fictions were invented to account for it. She had been grossly insulted: she had been threatened: nay, though she was in that situation in which woman is entitled to peculiar tenderness, she had been beaten by her cruel stepmother. The populace, which years of misrule had made suspicious and irritable, was so much excited by these calumnies that the Queen was scarcely safe. Many Roman Catholics, and some Protestant Tories whose loyalty was proof to all trials, repaired to the palace that they might be in readiness to defend her in the event of an outbreak. In the midst of this distress and terror arrived the news of Prince George's flight. The courier who brought these evil tidings was fast followed by the King himself. The evening was closing in when James arrived, and was informed that his daughter had disappeared. After all that he had suffered, this affliction forced a cry of misery from his lips. "God help me!" he said; "my own children have forsaken me."[51]

That evening he sate in Council with his principal ministers till a late hour. It was determined that he should summon all the

50. Clarendon's Diary, Nov. 25, 26, 1688; Van Citters, Nov. 26/Dec. 6; Ellis Correspondence, Dec. 19; Duchess of Marlborough's Vindication; Burnet, i, 792; Compton to the Prince of Orange, Dec. 2, 1688, in Dalrymple. The Bishop's military costume is mentioned in innumerable pamphlets and lampoons.

51. Dartmouth's note on Burnet, i, 792; Van Citters, Nov. 26/Dec. 6, 1688; Life of James, ii, 226, Orig. Mem.; Clarendon's Diary, Nov. 26; Revolution Politics.

Lords Spiritual and Temporal who were then in London to attend him on the following day, and that he should solemnly ask their advice. Accordingly, on the afternoon of Tuesday the twenty-seventh, the Lords met in the diningroom of the palace. The assembly consisted of nine prelates and between thirty and forty noblemen, all Protestants. The two Secretaries of State, Middleton and Preston, though not peers of England, were in attendance. The King himself presided. The traces of severe bodily and mental suffering were discernible in his countenance and deportment. He opened the proceedings by referring to the petition which had been put into his hands just before he set out for Salisbury. The prayer of that petition was that he would convoke a free Parliament. Situated as he then was, he had not, he said, thought it right to comply. But, during his absence from London, great changes had taken place. He had also observed that his people everywhere seemed anxious that the Houses should meet. He had therefore commanded the attendance of his faithful Peers in order to ask their counsel.

For a time there was silence. Then Oxford, whose pedigree, unrivalled in antiquity and splendour, gave him a kind of primacy in the meeting, said that, in his opinion, those Lords who had signed the petition to which His Majesty had referred ought now to explain their views.

These words called up Rochester. He defended the petition, and declared that he still saw no hope for the throne or the country but in a Parliament. He would not, he said, venture to affirm that, in so disastrous an extremity, even that remedy would be efficacious: but he had no other remedy to propose. He added that it might be advisable to open a negotiation with the Prince of Orange. Jeffreys and Godolphin followed; and both declared that they agreed with Rochester.

Then Clarendon rose, and, to the astonishment of all, who remembered his loud professions of loyalty, and the agony of shame and sorrow into which he had been thrown, only a few days before, by the news of his son's defection, broke forth into a vehement invective against tyranny and Popery. "Even now," he said, "His Majesty is raising in London a regiment into which no Protestant is admitted." "That is not true," cried James, in great agitation from the head of the board. Clarendon persisted, and left this offensive topic only to pass to a topic still more offensive. He accused the unfortunate King of pusillanimity. Why retreat from Salisbury? Why not try the event of a battle? Could people be blamed for submitting to the invader when they saw their sovereign run away at the head of his army? James felt these insults keenly, and remembered them long. Indeed even Whigs thought the language of Clarendon indecent and ungenerous. Halifax spoke in a very different tone. During several years of peril he had defended with admirable ability the civil and ecclesiastical constitution of his country against the prerogative. But his serene intellect, singularly unsusceptible of enthusiasm, and singularly averse to extremes, began to lean towards the cause of royalty at the very moment at which those noisy Royalists who had lately execrated the Trimmers as little better than rebels were everywhere rising in rebellion. It was his ambition to be, at this conjuncture, the peacemaker between the throne and the nation. His talents and character fitted him for that office; and, if he failed, the failure is to be ascribed to causes against which no human skill could contend, and chiefly to the folly, faithlessness, and obstinacy of the Prince whom he tried to save.

Halifax now gave utterance to much unpalatable truth, but with a delicacy which brought on him the reproach of flattery from spirits too abject to understand that what would justly be called flattery when offered to the powerful is a debt of humanity to the fallen. With many expressions of sympathy and deference, he declared it to be his opinion that the King must make up his mind to great sacrifices. It was not enough to convoke a Parliament or to open a negotiation with the Prince of Orange. Some at least of the grievances of which the nation complained should be instantly redressed without waiting till redress was demanded by the Houses or by the captain of the hostile army. Nottingham, in language equally respectful, declared that he agreed with Halifax. The chief concessions which these Lords pressed the King to make were three. He ought, they said, forthwith to dismiss all Roman Catholics from office, to separate himself wholly from France, and to grant an unlimited amnesty to those who were in arms against him. The last of these propositions, it should seem, admitted of no dispute. For, though some of those who were banded together against the King had acted towards him in a manner which might not unreasonably excite his bitter resentment, it was more likely that he would soon be at their mercy than that they would ever be at his. It would have been childish to open a negotiation with William, and yet to denounce vengeance against men whom William could not without infamy abandon. But the clouded understanding and implacable temper of James held out long against the arguments of those who laboured to convince him that it would be wise to pardon offences which he could not punish. "I cannot do it," he exclaimed: "I must make examples; Churchill above all; Churchill whom I raised so high. He and he alone has done all this. He has corrupted my army. He has corrupted my child. He would have put me into the hands of the Prince of Orange, but for God's special providence. My Lords, you are strangely anxious for the safety of traitors. None of you troubles himself about my safety." In answer to this burst of impotent anger, those who had recommended the amnesty represented with profound respect, but with firmness, that a prince attacked by powerful enemies can be safe only by conquering or by conciliating. "If Your Majesty, after all that has happened, has still any hope of safety in arms, we have done: but if not, you can be safe only by regaining the affections of your people." After a long and animated debate the King broke up the meeting. "My Lords," he said, "you have used great freedom: but I do not take it ill of you. I have made up my mind on one point. I shall call a Parliament. The other suggestions which have been offered are of grave importance; and you will not be surprised that I take a night to reflect on them before I decide."[52]

52. Life of James, ii, 236, Orig. Mem.; Burnet, i ,794; Luttrell's Diary; Clarendon's Diary, November 27, 1688; Van Citters, Nov. 27/Dec. 7 and Nov. 30/Dec. 10.

Van Citters evidently had his intelligence from one of the Lords who were present. As the matter is important, I will give two short passages from his despatches. The King said, "Dat het by na voor hem unmogelyck was te pardoneren persoonen wie so hoog in syn reguarde schuldig stonden, vooral seer uytvarende jegens den Lord Churchill, wien hy hadde groot gemaakt, en nogtans meynde de eenigste oorsake van alle dese desertie en van de retraite van hare Coninglycke Hoogheden te wesen." One of the lords, probably Halifax or

At first James seemed disposed to make excellent use of the time which he had taken for consideration. The Chancellor was directed to issue writs convoking a Parliament for the thirteenth of January. Halifax was sent for to the closet, had a long audience, and spoke with much more freedom than he had thought it decorous to use in the presence of a large assembly. He was informed that he had been appointed a Commissioner to treat with the Prince of Orange. With him were joined Nottingham and Godolphin. The King declared that he was prepared to make great sacrifices for the sake of peace. Halifax answered that great sacrifices would doubtless be required. "Your Majesty," he said, "must not expect that those who have the power in their hands will consent to any terms which would leave the laws at the mercy of the prerogative." With this distinct explanation of his views, he accepted the Commission which the King wished him to undertake.[53] The concessions which a few hours before had been so obstinately refused were now made in the most liberal manner. A proclamation was put forth by which the King not only granted a free pardon to all who were in rebellion against him, but declared them eligible to be members of the approaching Parliament. It was not even required as a condition of eligibility that they should lay down their arms. The same Gazette which announced that the Houses were about to meet contained a notification that Sir Edward Hales, who, as a Papist, as a renegade, as the foremost champion of the dispensing power, and as the harsh gaoler of the Bishops, was one of the most unpopular men in the realm, had ceased to be Lieutenant of the Tower, and had been succeeded by his late prisoner, Bevil Skelton, who, though he

---

Nottingham, "seer hadde geurgeert op de securiteyt van de lords die nu met syn Hoogheyt geengageert staan. Soo hoorick," says Van Citters, "dat syn Majesteyt onder anderen soude gesegt hebben; 'Men spreekt al voor de securiteyt voor andere en niet voor de myne.' Waar op een der Pairs resolut dan met groot respect soude geantwoordt hebben dat, soo syne Majesteyt's wapenen in staat waren om hem te connen mainteneren, dat dan sulk syne securiteyte koude wesen; soo niet, en soo de difficulteyt dan nog te surmonteren was, dat het den moeste geschieden door de meeste condescendance, en hoe meer die was, en hy genegen om aan de natic contentement te geven, dat syne securiteyt ook des te grooter soude wesen."

53. Letter of the Bishop of Saint Asaph to the Prince of Orange, Dec. 17, 1688.

held no high place in the esteem of his countrymen, was at least not disqualified by law for public trust.[54]

But these concessions were meant only to blind the Lords and the nation to the King's real designs. He had secretly determined that, even in this extremity, he would yield nothing. On the very day on which he issued the proclamation of amnesty, he fully explained his intentions to Barillon. "This negotiation," said James, "is a mere feint. I must send Commissioners to my nephew, that I may gain time to ship off my wife and the Prince of Wales. You know the temper of my troops. None but the Irish will stand by me; and the Irish are not in sufficient force to resist the enemy. A Parliament would impose on me conditions which I could not endure. I should be forced to undo all that I have done for the Catholics, and to break with the King of France. As soon, therefore, as the Queen and my child are safe, I will leave England, and take refuge in Ireland, in Scotland, or with your master."[55]

Already James had made preparations for carrying this scheme into effect. Dover had been sent to Portsmouth with instructions to take charge of the Prince of Wales; and Dartmouth, who commanded the fleet there, had been ordered to obey Dover's directions in all things concerning the royal infant, and to have a yacht manned by trusty sailors in readiness to sail for France at a moment's notice.[56] The King now sent positive orders that the child should instantly be conveyed to the nearest Continental port.[57] Next to the Prince of Wales the chief object of anxiety was the Great Seal. To that symbol of kingly authority our jurists have always ascribed a peculiar and almost mysterious importance. It is held that, if the Keeper of the Seal should affix it, without taking the royal pleasure, to a patent of peerage or to a pardon, though he may be guilty of a high offence, the instrument cannot be questioned by any court of law, and can be annulled only by an Act of Parliament. James seems to have

54. London Gazette, Nov. 29, Dec. 3, 1688; Clarendon's Diary, Nov. 29, 30.
55. Barillon, December 1/11, 1688.
56. James to Dartmouth, Nov. 25, 1688. The letters are in Dalrymple.
57. James to Dartmouth, Dec. 1, 1688.

been afraid that his enemies might get this organ of his will into their hands, and might thus give a legal validity to acts which might affect him injuriously. Nor will his apprehensions be thought unreasonable when it is remembered that, exactly a hundred years later, the Great Seal of a King was used, with the assent of the Lords and the Commons, and with the approbation of many great statesmen and lawyers, for the purpose of transferring his prerogatives to his son. Lest the talisman which possessed such formidable powers should be abused, James determined that it should be kept within a few yards of his own closet. Jeffreys was therefore ordered to quit the costly mansion which he had lately built in Duke Street, and to take up his residence in a small apartment at Whitehall.[58]

The King had made all his preparations for flight, when an unexpected impediment compelled him to postpone the execution of his design. His agents at Portsmouth began to entertain scruples. Even Dover, though a member of the Jesuitical cabal, showed signs of hesitation. Dartmouth was still less disposed to comply with the royal wishes. He was zealous for the crown, and had done all that he could do, with a disaffected fleet, and in the face of an adverse wind, to prevent the Dutch from landing in England: but he was also zealous for the Established Church, and was by no means friendly to the policy of that government of which he was the defender. The mutinous temper of the officers and men under his command had caused him much anxiety; and he had been greatly relieved by the news that a free Parliament had been convoked, and that Commissioners had been named to treat with the Prince of Orange. The joy was clamorous throughout the fleet. An address, warmly thanking the King for these gracious concessions to public feeling, was drawn up on board of the flag ship. The Admiral signed first. Thirty-eight Captains wrote their names under his. This paper on its way to Whitehall crossed the messenger who brought to Portsmouth the order that the Prince of Wales should instantly be conveyed to France. Dartmouth learned, with bitter grief and resentment, that the free Parliament, the general amnesty, the negotiation, were all parts of a great fraud on the nation, and that in this fraud he was ex-

58. Luttrell's Diary.

pected to be an accomplice. His conduct on this occasion was the most honourable part of a not very honourable life. In a sensible and spirited letter he declared that he had already carried his obedience to the furthest point to which a Protestant and an Englishman could go. To put the heir apparent of the British crown into the hands of Lewis would be nothing less than treason against the monarchy. The nation, already too much alienated from the Sovereign, would be roused to madness. The Prince of Wales would either not return at all, or would return attended by a French army. If His Royal Highness remained in the island, the worst that could be apprehended was that he would be brought up a member of the national Church; and that he might be so brought up ought to be the prayer of every loyal subject. Dartmouth concluded by declaring that he would risk his life in defence of the throne, but that he would be no party to the transporting of the Prince into France.[59]

This letter deranged all the projects of James. He learned too that he could not on this occasion expect from his Admiral even passive obedience. For Dartmouth had gone so far as to station several sloops at the mouth of the harbour of Portsmouth with orders to suffer no vessel to pass out unexamined. A change of plan was necessary. The child must be brought back to London, and sent thence to France. An interval of some days must elapse before this could be done. During that interval the public mind must be amused by the hope of a Parliament and the semblance of a negotiation. Writs were sent out for the elections. Trumpeters went backward and forward between the capital and the Dutch head quarters. At length passes for the King's Commissioners arrived; and the three Lords set out on their embassy.

They left the capital in a state of fearful distraction. The passions which, during three troubled years, had been gradually gathering force, now, emancipated from the restraint of fear, and stimulated by victory and sympathy, showed themselves without disguise, even in the precincts of the royal dwelling. The

59. Second Collection of Papers, 1688; Dartmouth's Letter, dated December 3, 1688, will be found in Dalrymple; Life of James, ii, 233, Orig. Mem. James accuses Dartmouth of having got up an address from the fleet demanding a Parliament. This is a mere calumny. The address is one of thanks to the King for having called a Parliament, and was framed before Dartmouth had the least suspicion that His Majesty was deceiving the nation.

grand jury of Middlesex found a bill against the Earl of Salisbury for turning Papist.[60] The Lord Mayor ordered the houses of the Roman Catholics of the city to be searched for arms. The mob broke into the house of one respectable merchant who held the unpopular faith, in order to ascertain whether he had not run a mine from his cellars under the neighbouring parish church, for the purpose of blowing up parson and congregation.[61] The hawkers bawled about the streets a hue and cry after Father Petre, who had withdrawn himself, and not before it was time, from his apartments in Whitehall.[62] Wharton's celebrated song, with many additional verses, was chaunted more loudly than ever in all the streets of the capital. The very sentinels who guarded the palace hummed, as they paced their rounds,

> "The English confusion to Popery drink,
> Lillibullero bullen a la."

The secret presses of London worked without ceasing. Many papers daily came into circulation by means which the magistracy could not discover, or would not check. One of these has been preserved from oblivion by the skilful audacity with which it was written, and by the immense effect which it produced. It purported to be a supplemental declaration under the hand and seal of the Prince of Orange: but it was written in a style very different from that of his genuine manifesto. Vengeance alien from the usages of Christian and civilised nations was denounced against all Papists who should dare to espouse the royal cause. They should be treated, not as soldiers or gentlemen, but as freebooters. The ferocity and licentiousness of the invading army, which had hitherto been restrained with a strong hand, should be let loose on them. Good Protestants, and especially those who inhabited the capital, were adjured, as they valued all that was dear to them, and commanded, on peril of the Prince's highest displeasure, to seize, disarm, and imprison their Roman Catholic neighbours. This document, it is said, was found by a Whig bookseller one morning under his shop door. He

60. Luttrell's Diary.
61. Adda, Dec. 7/17, 1688.
62. The Nuncio says, "Se lo avesse fatto prima di ora, per il Rè ne sarebbe stato meglio."

made haste to print it. Many copies were dispersed by the post, and passed rapidly from hand to hand. Discerning readers had no difficulty in pronouncing it a forgery devised by some unquiet and unprincipled adventurer, such as, in troubled times, are always busied in the foulest and darkest offices of faction. But the multitude was completely duped. Indeed to such a height had national and religious feeling been excited against the Irish Papists that most of those who believed the spurious proclamation to be genuine were inclined to applaud it as a seasonable exhibition of vigour. When it was known that no such document had really proceeded from William, men asked anxiously what impostor had so daringly and so successfully personated His Highness. Some suspected Ferguson, others Johnson. At length, after the lapse of twenty-seven years, Hugh Speke avowed the forgery, and demanded from the House of Brunswick a reward for so eminent a service rendered to the Protestant religion. He asserted, in the tone of a man who conceives himself to have done something eminently virtuous and honourable, that, when the Dutch invasion had thrown Whitehall into consternation, he had offered his services to the Court, had pretended to be estranged from the Whigs, and had promised to act as a spy upon them; that he had thus obtained admittance to the royal closet, had vowed fidelity, had been promised large pecuniary rewards, and had procured blank passes which enabled him to travel backwards and forwards across the hostile lines. All these things he protested that he had done solely in order that he might, unsuspected, aim a deadly blow at the government, and produce a violent outbreak of popular feeling against the Roman Catholics. The forged proclamation he claimed as one of his contrivances: but whether his claim were well founded may be doubted. He delayed to make it so long that we may reasonably suspect him of having waited for the death of those who could confute him; and he produced no evidence but his own.[63]

While these things happened in London, every post from every part of the country brought tidings of some new insurrection. Lumley had seized Newcastle. The inhabitants had welcomed

63. See the Secret History of the Revolution, by Hugh Speke, 1715. In the London Library is a copy of this rare work with a manuscript note which seems to be in Speke's own hand.

him with transport. The statue of the King, which stood on a lofty pedestal of marble, had been pulled down and hurled into the Tyne. The third of December was long remembered at Hull as the Towntaking Day. That place had a garrison commanded by Lord Langdale, a Roman Catholic. The Protestant officers concerted with the magistracy a plan of revolt: Langdale and his adherents were arrested; and soldiers and citizens united in declaring for the Protestant religion and a free Parliament.[64]

The Eastern counties were up. The Duke of Norfolk, attended by three hundred gentlemen armed and mounted, appeared in the stately marketplace of Norwich. The Mayor and Aldermen met him there, and engaged to stand by him against Popery and arbitrary power.[65] Lord Herbert of Cherbury and Sir Edward Harley took up arms in Worcestershire.[66] Bristol, the second city of the realm, opened its gates to Shrewsbury. Trelawney, the Bishop, who had entirely unlearned in the Tower the doctrine of nonresistance, was the first to welcome the Prince's troops. Such was the temper of the inhabitants that it was thought unnecessary to leave any garrison among them.[67] The people of Gloucester rose and delivered Lovelace from confinement. An irregular army soon gathered round him. Some of his horsemen had only halters for bridles. Many of his infantry had only clubs for weapons. But this force, such as it was, marched unopposed through counties once devoted to the House of Stuart, and at length entered Oxford in triumph. The magistrates came in state to welcome the insurgents. The University itself, exasperated by recent injuries, was little disposed to pass censures on rebellion. Already some of the Heads of Houses had despatched one of their number to assure the Prince of Orange that they were cordially with him, and that they would gladly coin their plate for his service. The Whig chief, therefore, rode through the capital of Toryism amidst general acclamation. Be-

64. Brand's History of Newcastle; Tickell's History of Hull.

65. An account of what passed at Norwich may still be seen in several collections on the original broadside. See also the Fourth Collection of Papers, 1688.

66. Life of James, ii, 233; MS. Memoir of the Harley family in the Mackintosh Collection.

67. Van Citters, Dec. 9/19, 1688; Letter of the Bishop of Bristol to the Prince of Orange, Dec. 5, 1688, in Dalrymple.

fore him the drums beat Lillibullero. Behind him came a long stream of horse and foot. The whole High Street was gay with orange ribands. For already the orange riband had the double signification which, after the lapse of one hundred and sixty years, it still retains. Already it was the emblem to the Protestant Englishman of civil and religious freedom, to the Roman Catholic Celt of subjugation and persecution.[68]

While foes were thus rising up all round the King, friends were fast shrinking from his side. The idea of resistance had become familiar to every mind. Many, who had been struck with horror when they heard of the first defections, now blamed themselves for having been so slow to discern the signs of the times. There was no longer any difficulty or danger in repairing to William. The King, in calling on the nation to elect representatives, had, by implication, authorised all men to repair to the places where they had votes or interest; and many of those places were already occupied by invaders or insurgents. Clarendon eagerly caught at this opportunity of deserting the falling cause. He knew that his speech in the Council of Peers had given deadly offence; and he was mortified by finding that he was not to be one of the royal Commissioners. He had estates in Wiltshire; and he determined that his son, the son of whom he had lately spoken with grief and horror, should be a candidate for that county. Under pretence of looking after the election, Clarendon set out for the West. He was speedily followed by the Earl of Oxford, and by others who had hitherto disclaimed all connection with the Prince's enterprise.[69]

By this time the invaders, steadily though slowly advancing, were within seventy miles of London. Though midwinter was approaching, the weather was fine: the way was pleasant; and the turf of Salisbury Plain seemed luxuriously smooth to men who had been toiling through the miry ruts of the Devonshire and Somersetshire highways. The route of the army lay close by Stonehenge; and regiment after regiment halted to examine that mysterious ruin, celebrated all over the Continent as the greatest wonder of our island. William entered Salisbury with

68. Van Citters, Nov. 27/Dec. 7, 1688; Clarendon's Diary, Dec. 11; Song on Lord Lovelace's entry into Oxford, 1688; Burnet, i, 793.
69. Clarendon's Diary, Dec. 2, 3, 4, 5, 1688.

the same military pomp which he had displayed at Exeter, and was lodged there in the palace which the King had occupied a few days before.[70]

The Prince's train was now swelled by the Earls of Clarendon and Oxford, and by other men of high rank, who had, till within a few days, been considered as zealous Royalists. Van Citters also made his appearance at the Dutch head quarters. He had been during some weeks almost a prisoner in his house near Whitehall, under the constant observation of relays of spies. Yet, in spite of those spies, or perhaps by their help, he had succeeded in obtaining full and accurate intelligence of all that passed in the palace; and now, full fraught with valuable information about men and things, he came to assist the deliberations of William.[71]

Thus far the Prince's enterprise had prospered beyond the anticipations of the most sanguine. And now, according to the general law which governs human affairs, prosperity began to produce disunion. The Englishmen assembled at Salisbury were divided into two parties. One party consisted of Whigs who had always regarded the doctrines of passive obedience and of indefeasible hereditary right as slavish superstitions. Many of them had passed years in exile. All had been long shut out from participation in the favours of the crown. They now exulted in the near prospect of greatness and of vengeance. Burning with resentment, flushed with victory and hope, they would hear of no compromise. Nothing less than the deposition of their enemy would content them; nor can it be disputed that herein they were perfectly consistent. They had exerted themselves, nine years earlier, to exclude him from the throne, because they thought it likely that he would be a bad King. It could therefore scarcely be expected that they would willingly leave him on the throne, now that he had turned out a far worse King than any reasonable man could have anticipated.

On the other hand, not a few of William's followers were zealous Tories, who had, till very recently, held the doctrine of nonresistance in the most absolute form, but whose faith in that doctrine had, for a moment, given way to the strong passions excited by the ingratitude of the King and by the peril of the

70. Whittle's Exact Diary; Eachard's History of the Revolution.
71. Van Citters, Nov. 20/30, Dec. 9/19, 1688.

Church. No situation could be more painful or perplexing than that of the old Cavalier who found himself in arms against the throne. The scruples which had not prevented him from repairing to the Dutch camp began to torment him cruelly as soon as he was there. His mind misgave him that he had committed a crime. At all events he had exposed himself to reproach, by acting in diametrical opposition to the professions of his whole life. He felt insurmountable disgust for his new allies. They were people whom, ever since he could remember, he had been reviling and persecuting, Presbyterians, Independents, Anabaptists, old soldiers of Cromwell, brisk boys of Shaftesbury, accomplices in the Rye House plot, captains of the Western insurrection. He naturally wished to find out some salvo which might soothe his conscience, which might vindicate his consistency, and which might put a distinction between him and the crew of schismatical rebels whom he had always despised and abhorred, but with whom he was now in danger of being confounded. He therefore disclaimed with vehemence all thought of taking the crown from that anointed head which the ordinance of heaven and the fundamental laws of the realm had made sacred. His dearest wish was to see a reconciliation effected on terms which would not lower the royal dignity. He was no traitor. He was not, in truth, resisting the kingly authority. He was in arms only because he was convinced that the best service which could be rendered to the throne was to rescue His Majesty, by a little gentle coercion, from the hands of wicked counsellors.

The evils which the mutual animosity of these factions tended to produce were, to a great extent, averted by the ascendency and by the wisdom of the Prince. Surrounded by eager disputants, officious advisers, abject flatterers, vigilant spies, malicious talebearers, he remained serene and inscrutable. He preserved silence while silence was possible. When he was forced to speak, the earnest and peremptory tone in which he uttered his well weighed opinions soon silenced everybody else. Whatever some of his too zealous adherents might say, he uttered not a word indicating any design on the English crown. He was doubtless well aware that between him and that crown were still interposed obstacles which no prudence might be able to surmount, and which a single false step would make insurmountable. His only chance of obtaining the splendid prize was not to seize it rudely, but to wait till, without any appearance of exertion or stratagem on his part, his secret wish should be accomplished by the force of circumstances, by the blunders of his opponents, and by the free choice of the Estates of the Realm. Those who ventured to interrogate him learned nothing, and yet could not accuse him of shuffling. He quietly referred them to his Declaration, and assured them that his views had undergone no change since that instrument had been drawn up. So skilfully did he manage his followers that their discord seems rather to have strengthened than to have weakened his hands: but it broke forth with violence when his control was withdrawn, interrupted the harmony of convivial meetings, and did not respect even the sanctity of the house of God. Clarendon, who tried to hide from others and from himself, by an ostentatious display of loyal sentiments, the plain fact that he was a rebel, was shocked to hear some of his new associates laughing over their wine at the royal amnesty which had just been graciously offered to them. They wanted no pardon, they said. They would make the King ask pardon before they had done with him. Still more alarming and disgusting to every good Tory was an incident which happened at Salisbury Cathedral. As soon as the officiating minister began to read the collect for the King, Burnet, among whose many good qualities selfcommand and a fine sense of the becoming cannot be reckoned, rose from his knees, sate down in his stall, and uttered some contemptuous noises which disturbed the devotions of the congregation.[72]

In a short time the factions which divided the Prince's camp had an opportunity of measuring their strength. The royal Commissioners were on their way to him. Several days had elapsed since they had been appointed; and it was thought strange that, in a case of such urgency, there should be such delay. But in truth neither James nor William was desirous that negotiations should speedily commence; for James wished only to gain time sufficient for sending his wife and son into France; and the position of William became every day more commanding. At length the Prince caused it to be notified to the Commissioners that he

72. Clarendon's Diary, Dec. 6, 7, 1688.

would meet them at Hungerford. He probably selected this place because, lying at an equal distance from Salisbury and from Oxford, it was well situated for a rendezvous of his most important adherents. At Salisbury were those noblemen and gentlemen who had accompanied him from Holland or had joined him in the West; and at Oxford were many chiefs of the Northern insurrection.

Late on Thursday, the sixth of December, he reached Hungerford. The little town was soon crowded with men of rank and note who came thither from opposite quarters. The Prince was escorted by a strong body of troops. The northern Lords brought with them hundreds of irregular cavalry, whose accoutrements and horsemanship moved the mirth of men accustomed to the splendid aspect and exact movements of regular armies.[73]

While the Prince lay at Hungerford a sharp encounter took place between two hundred and fifty of his troops and six hundred Irish who were posted at Reading. The superior discipline of the invaders was signally proved on this occasion. Though greatly outnumbered, they, at one onset, drove the King's forces in confusion through the streets of the town into the marketplace. There the Irish attempted to rally; but, being vigorously attacked in front, and fired upon at the same time by the inhabitants from the windows of the neighbouring houses, they soon lost heart, and fled with the loss of their colours and of fifty men. Of the conquerers only five fell. The satisfaction which this news gave to the Lords and gentlemen who had joined William was unmixed. There was nothing in what had happened to gall their national feelings. The Dutch had not beaten the English, but had assisted an English town to free itself from the insupportable dominion of the Irish.[74]

On the morning of Saturday, the eighth of December, the King's Commissioners reached Hungerford. The Prince's body guard was drawn up to receive them with military respect. Bentinck welcomed them, and proposed to conduct them immediately to his master. They expressed a hope that the Prince would favour them with a private audience; but they were informed

73. Clarendon's Diary, Dec. 7, 1688.
74. History of the Desertion; Van Citters, Dec. 9/19, 1688; Exact Diary; Oldmixon, 760.

that he had resolved to hear them and answer them in public. They were ushered into his bedchamber, where they found him surrounded by a crowd of noblemen and gentlemen. Halifax, whose rank, age, and abilities entitled him to precedence, was spokesman. The proposition which the Commissioners had been instructed to make was that the points in dispute should be referred to the Parliament, for which the writs were already sealing, and that in the mean time the Prince's army would not come within thirty or forty miles of London. Halifax, having explained that this was the basis on which he and his colleagues were prepared to treat, put into William's hand a letter from the King, and retired. William opened the letter and seemed unusually moved. It was the first letter which he had received from his father in law since they had become avowed enemies. Once they had been on good terms and had written to each other familiarly; nor had they, even when they had begun to regard each other with suspicion and aversion, banished from their correspondence those forms of kindness which persons nearly related by blood and marriage commonly use. The letter which the Commissioners had brought was drawn up by a secretary in diplomatic form and in the French language. "I have had many letters from the King," said William, "but they were all in English and in his own hand." He spoke with a sensibility which he was little in the habit of displaying. Perhaps he thought at that moment how much reproach his enterprise, just, beneficent, and necessary as it was, must bring on him and on the wife who was devoted to him. Perhaps he repined at the hard fate which had placed him in such a situation that he could fulfil his public duties only by breaking through domestic ties, and envied the happier condition of those who are not responsible for the welfare of nations and Churches. But such thoughts, if they rose in his mind, were firmly suppressed. He requested the Lords and gentlemen whom he had convoked on this occasion to consult together, unrestrained by his presence, as to the answer which ought to be returned. To himself, however, he reserved the power of deciding in the last resort, after hearing their opinion. He then left them, and retired to Littlecote Hall, a manor house situated about two miles off, and renowned down to our own times, not more on account of its venerable architecture and furniture than on account of a horrible and mysterious crime which was perpetrated there in the days of the Tudors.[75]

Before he left Hungerford, he was told that Halifax had expressed a great desire to see Burnet. In this desire there was nothing strange; for Halifax and Burnet had long been on terms of friendship. No two men, indeed, could resemble each other less. Burnet was utterly destitute of delicacy and tact. Halifax's taste was fastidious, and his sense of the ludicrous morbidly quick. Burnet viewed every act and every character through a medium distorted and coloured by party spirit. The tendency of Halifax's mind was always to see the faults of his allies more strongly than the faults of his opponents. Burnet was, with all his infirmities, and through all the vicissitudes of a life passed in circumstances not very favourable to piety, a sincerely pious man. The sceptical and sarcastic Halifax lay under the imputation of infidelity. Halifax therefore often incurred Burnet's indignant censure; and Burnet was often the butt of Halifax's keen and polished pleasantry. Yet they were drawn to each other by a mutual attraction, liked each other's conversation, appreciated each other's abilities, interchanged opinions freely, and interchanged also good offices in perilous times. It was not, however, merely from personal regard that Halifax now wished to see his old acquaintance. The Commissioners must have been anxious to know what was the Prince's real aim. He had refused to see them in private; and little could be learned from what he might say in a formal and public interview. Almost all those who were admitted to his confidence were men taciturn and impenetrable as himself. Burnet was the only exception. He was notoriously garrulous and indiscreet. Yet circumstances had made it necessary to trust him; and he would doubtless, under the dexterous management of Halifax, have poured out secrets as fast as words. William knew this well, and, when he was informed that Halifax was asking for the Doctor, could not refrain from exclaiming, "If they get together there will be fine tattling." Burnet was forbidden to see the Commissioners in private: but he was assured

75. See a very interesting note on the fifth canto of Sir Walter Scott's Rokeby.

in very courteous terms that his fidelity was regarded by the Prince as above all suspicion, and, that there might be no ground for complaint, the prohibition was made general.

That afternoon the noblemen and gentlemen whose advice William had asked met in the great room of the principal inn at Hungerford. Oxford was placed in the chair; and the King's overtures were taken into consideration. It soon appeared that the assembly was divided into two parties, a party anxious to come to terms with the King, and a party bent on his destruction. The latter party had the numerical superiority: but it was observed that Shrewsbury, who of all the English nobles was supposed to enjoy the largest share of William's confidence, though a Whig, sided on this occasion with the Tories. After much altercation the question was put. The majority was for rejecting the proposition which the royal Commissioners had been instructed to make. The resolution of the assembly was reported to the Prince at Little-cote. On no occasion during the whole course of his eventful life did he show more prudence and selfcommand. He could not wish the negotiation to succeed. But he was far too wise a man not to know that, if unreasonable demands made by him should cause it to fail, public feeling would no longer be on his side. He therefore overruled the opinion of his two eager followers, and declared his determination to treat on the basis proposed by the King. Many of the Lords and gentlemen assembled at Hungerford remonstrated: a whole day was spent in bickering: but William's purpose was immovable. He declared himself willing to refer all the questions in dispute to the Parliament which had just been summoned, and not to advance within forty miles of London. On his side he made some demands which even those who were least disposed to commend him allowed to be moderate. He insisted that the existing statutes should be obeyed till they should be altered by competent authority, and that all persons who held offices without a legal qualification should be forthwith dismissed. The deliberations of the Parliament, he justly conceived, could not be free if it was to sit surrounded by Irish regiments while he and his army lay at a distance of several marches. He therefore thought it reasonable that, since his troops were not to advance within forty miles of London on the west, the King's troops should fall back as far to the east. There would thus be, round the spot where the Houses were to meet, a wide circle of neutral ground. Within that circle, indeed, there were two fastnesses of great importance to the people of the capital, the Tower, which commanded their dwellings, and Tilbury Fort, which commanded their maritime trade. It was impossible to leave these places ungarrisoned. William therefore proposed that they should be temporarily entrusted to the care of the City of London. It might possibly be convenient that, when the Parliament assembled, the King should repair to Westminster with a body guard. The Prince announced that, in that case, he should claim the right of repairing thither with a equal number of soldiers. It seemed to him just that, while military operations were suspended, both the armies should be considered as alike engaged in the service of the English nation, and should be alike maintained out of the English revenue. Lastly, he required some guarantee that the King would not take advantage of the armistice for the purpose of introducing a French force into England. The point where there was most danger was Portsmouth. The Prince did not insist that this important fortress should be delivered up to him, but proposed that it should, during the truce, be under the government of an officer in whom both himself and James could confide.

The propositions of William were framed with a punctilious fairness, such as might have been expected rather from a disinterested umpire pronouncing an award than from a victorious prince dictating to a helpless enemy. No fault could be found with them by the partisans of the King. But among the Whigs there was much murmuring. They wanted no reconciliation with their old master. They thought themselves absolved from all allegiance to him. They were not disposed to recognise the authority of a Parliament convoked by his writ. They were adverse to an armistice; and they could not conceive why, if there was to be an armistice, it should be an armistice on equal terms. By all the laws of war the stronger party had a right to take advantage of his strength; and what was there in the character of James to justify any extraordinary indulgence? Those who reasoned thus little knew from how elevated a point of view, and with how discerning an eye, the leader whom they censured contemplated the whole situation of England and Europe. They were eager

397

to ruin James, and would therefore either have refused to treat with him on any conditions, or have imposed on him conditions insupportably hard. To the success of William's vast and profound scheme of policy it was necessary that James should ruin himself by rejecting conditions ostentatiously liberal. The event proved the wisdom of the course which the majority of the Englishmen at Hungerford were inclined to condemn.

On Sunday, the ninth of December, the Prince's demands were put in writing, and delivered to Halifax. The Commissioners dined at Littlecote. A splendid assemblage had been invited to meet them. The old hall, hung with coats of mail which had seen the wars of the Roses, and with portraits of gallants who had adorned the court of Philip and Mary, was now crowded with Peers and Generals. In such a throng a short question and answer might be exchanged without attracting notice. Halifax seized this opportunity, the first which had presented itself, of extracting all that Burnet knew or thought. "What is it that you want?" said the dexterous diplomatist: "do you wish to get the King into your power?" "Not at all," said Burnet: "we would not do the least harm to his person." "And if he were to go away?" said Halifax. "There is nothing," said Burnet, "so much to be wished." There can be no doubt that Burnet expressed the general sentiment of the Whigs in the Prince's camp. They were all desirous that James should fly from the country: but only a few of the wisest among them understood how important it was that his flight should be ascribed by the nation to his own folly and perverseness, and not to harsh usage and well grounded apprehension. It seems probable that, even in the extremity to which he was now reduced, all his enemies united would have been unable to effect his complete overthrow had he not been his own worst enemy: but while his Commissioners were labouring to save him, he was labouring as earnestly to make all their efforts useless[76]

His plans were at length ripe for execution. The pretended

76. My account of what passed at Hungerford is taken from Clarendon's Diary, December 8, 9, 1688; Burnet, i, 794; the Paper delivered to the Prince by the Commissioners, and the Prince's Answer; Sir Patrick Hume's Diary; Van Citters, December 9/19.

negotiation had answered its purpose. On the same day on which the three Lords reached Hungerford the Prince of Wales arrived at Westminster. It had been intended that he should come over London Bridge; and some Irish troops were sent to Southwark to meet him. But they were received by a great multitude with such hooting and execration that they thought it advisable to re-tire with all speed. The poor child crossed the Thames at Kings-ton, and was brought into Whitehall so privately that many be-lieved him to be still at Portsmouth.[77]

To send him and the Queen out of the country without delay was now the first object of James. But who could be trusted to manage the escape? Dartmouth was accounted the most loyal of Protestant Tories; and Dartmouth had refused. Dover was a creature of the Jesuits; and even Dover had hesitated. It was not very easy to find an Englishman of rank and honour who would undertake to place the heir apparent of the English crown in the hands of the King of France. In these circumstances, James be-thought him of a French nobleman who then resided in London, Antonine Count of Lauzun. Of this man it has been said that his life was stranger than the dreams of other people. At an early age he had been the intimate associate of Lewis, and had been encouraged to expect the highest employments under the French crown. Then his fortunes had undergone an eclipse. Lewis had driven from him the friend of his youth with bitter reproaches, and had, it was said, scarcely refrained from adding blows. The fallen favourite had been sent prisoner to a fortress: but he had emerged from his confinement, had again enjoyed the smiles of his master, and had gained the heart of one of the greatest ladies in Europe, Anna Maria, daughter of Gaston Duke of Orleans, granddaughter of King Henry the Fourth, and heir-ess of the immense domains of the house of Montpensier. The lovers were bent on marriage. The royal consent was obtained. During a few hours Lauzun was regarded by the court as an adopted member of the house of Bourbon. The portion which the princess brought with her might well have been an object

---

77. Life of James, ii, 237. Burnet, strange to say, had not heard, or had forgotten, that the prince was brought back to London: i, 796.

of competition to sovereigns; three great dukedoms, an independent principality with its own mint and with its own tribunals, and an income greatly exceeding the whole revenue of the kingdom of Scotland. But this splendid prospect had been overcast. The match had been broken off. The aspiring suitor had been, during many years, shut up in a remote castle. At length Lewis relented. Lauzun was forbidden to appear in the royal presence, but was allowed to enjoy liberty at a distance from the court. He visited England, and was well received at the palace of James and in the fashionable circles of London; for in that age the gentlemen of France were regarded throughout Europe as models of grace; and many Chevaliers and Viscounts, who had never been admitted to the interior circle at Versailles, found themselves objects of general curiosity and admiration at Whitehall. Lauzun was in every respect the man for the present emergency. He had courage and a sense of honour, had been accustomed to eccentric adventures, and, with the keen observation and ironical pleasantry of a finished man of the world, had a strong propensity to knight errantry. All his national feelings and all his personal interests impelled him to undertake the adventure from which the most devoted subjects of the English crown seemed to shrink. As the guardian, at a perilous crisis, of the Queen of Great Britain and of the Prince of Wales, he might return with honour to his native land: he might once more be admitted to see Lewis dress and dine, and might, after so many vicissitudes, recommence, in the decline of life, the strangely fascinating chase of royal favour.

Animated by such feelings, Lauzun eagerly accepted the high trust which was offered to him. The arrangements for the flight were promptly made: a vessel was ordered to be in readiness at Gravesend: but to reach Gravesend was not easy. The City was in a state of extreme agitation. The slightest cause sufficed to bring a crowd together. No foreigner could appear in the streets without risk of being stopped, questioned, and carried before a magistrate as a Jesuit in disguise. It was, therefore, necessary to take the road on the south of the Thames. No precaution which could quiet suspicion was omitted. The King and Queen retired to rest as usual. When the palace had been some time profoundly quiet, James rose and called a servant who was in attendance. "You will find," said the King, "a man at the door of the ante-chamber: bring him hither." The servant obeyed, and Lauzun was ushered into the royal bedchamber. "I confide to you," said James, "my Queen and my son; everything must be risked to carry them into France." Lauzun, with a truly chivalrous spirit, re-turned thanks for the dangerous honour which had been con-ferred on him, and begged permission to avail himself of the assistance of his friend Saint Victor, a gentleman of Provence, whose courage and faith had been often tried. The services of so valuable an assistant were readily accepted. Lauzun gave his hand to Mary. Saint Victor wrapped up in his warm cloak the ill fated heir of so many Kings. The party stole down the back stairs, and embarked in an open skiff. It was a miserable voyage. The night was bleak: the rain fell: the wind roared: the water was rough: at length the boat reached Lambeth; and the fugitives landed near an inn, where a coach and horses were in waiting. Some time elapsed before the horses could be harnessed. Mary, afraid that her face might be known, would not enter the house. She re-mained with her child, cowering for shelter from the storm under the tower of Lambeth Church, and distracted by terror whenever the ostler approached her with his lantern. Two of her women attended her, one who gave suck to the Prince, and one whose office was to rock his cradle; but they could be of little use to their mistress; for both were foreigners who could hardly speak the English language, and who shuddered at the rigour of the En-glish climate. The only consolatory circumstance was that the little boy was well, and uttered not a single cry. At length the coach was ready. Saint Victor followed it on horseback. The fugitives reached Gravesend safely, and embarked in the yacht which waited for them. They found there Lord Powis and his wife. Three Irish officers were also on board. These men had been sent thither in order that they might assist Lauzun in any desperate emergency; for it was thought not impossible that the captain of the ship might prove false; and it was fully determined that, on the first suspicion of treachery, he should be stabbed to the heart. There was, however, no necessity for violence. The yacht proceeded down the river with a fair wind; and Saint Victor, having seen her under sail, spurred back with the good news to Whitehall.[78]

On the morning of Monday, the tenth of December, the King learned that his wife and son had begun their voyage with a fair prospect of reaching their destination. About the same time a courier arrived at the palace with despatches from Hungerford. Had James been a little more discerning, or a little less obstinate, those despatches would have induced him to reconsider all his plans. The Commissioners wrote hopefully. The conditions proposed by the conqueror were strangely liberal. The King himself could not refrain from exclaiming that they were more favourable than he could have expected. He might indeed not unreasonably suspect that they had been framed with no friendly design: but this mattered nothing; for, whether they were offered in the hope that, by closing with them, he would lay the ground for a happy reconciliation, or, as is more likely, in the hope that, by rejecting them, he would exhibit himself to the whole nation as utterly unreasonable and incorrigible, his course was equally clear. In either case his policy was to accept them promptly and to observe them faithfully.

But it soon appeared that William had perfectly understood the character with which he had to deal, and, in offering those terms which the Whigs at Hungerford had censured as too indulgent, had risked nothing. The solemn farce by which the public had been amused since the retreat of the royal army from Salisbury was prolonged during a few hours. All the Lords who were still in the capital were invited to the palace that they might be informed of the progress of the negotiation which had been opened by their advice. Another meeting of Peers was appointed for the following day. The Lord Mayor and the Sheriffs of London were summoned to attend the King. He exhorted them to perform their duties vigorously, and owned that he had thought it expedient to send his wife and child out of the country, but assured them that he would himself remain at his post. While

78. Life of James, ii, 246; Père d'Orléans, Révolutions d'Angleterre, xi; Madame de Sévigné, Dec. 14/24, 1688; Dangeau, Mémoires, Dec. 13/23. As to Lauzun, see the Memoirs of Mademoiselle and of the Duke of Saint Simon, and the Characters of Labruyère.

he uttered this unkingly and unmanly falsehood, his fixed purpose was to depart before daybreak. Already he had entrusted his most valuable movables to the care of several foreign Ambassadors. His most important papers had been deposited with the Tuscan minister. But before the flight there was still something to be done. The tyrant pleased himself with the thought that he might avenge himself on a people who had been impatient of his despotism by inflicting on them at parting all the evils of anarchy. He ordered the Great Seal and the writs for the new Parliament to be brought to his apartment. The writs he threw into the fire. Some which had been already sent out he annulled by an instrument drawn up in legal form. To Feversham he wrote a letter which could be understood only as a command to disband the army. Still, however, he concealed, even from his chief ministers, his intention of absconding. Just before he retired he directed Jeffreys to be in the closet early on the morrow, and, while stepping into bed, whispered to Mulgrave that the news from Hungerford was highly satisfactory. Everybody withdrew except the Duke of Northumberland. This young man, a natural son of Charles the Second by the Duchess of Cleveland, commanded a troop of Life Guards, and was a Lord of the Bedchamber. It seems to have been then the custom of the court that, in the Queen's absence, a Lord of the Bedchamber should sleep on a pallet in the King's room; and it was Northumberland's turn to perform this duty.

At three in the morning of Tuesday the eleventh of December, James rose, took the Great Seal in his hand, laid his commands on Northumberland not to open the door of the bedchamber till the usual hour, and disappeared through a secret passage, the same passage probably through which Huddleston had been brought to the bedside of the late King. Sir Edward Hales was in attendance with a hackney coach. James was conveyed to Millbank, where he crossed the Thames in a small wherry. As he passed Lambeth he flung the Great Seal into the midst of the stream, where, after many months, it was accidentally caught by a fishing net and dragged up.

At Vauxhall he landed. A carriage and horses had been stationed there for him; and he immediately took the road towards

Sheerness, where a hoy belonging to the Custom House had been ordered to await his arrival.[79]

79. History of the Desertion; Life of James, ii, 251, Orig. Mem.; Mulgrave's Account of the Revolution; Burnet, i, 795.

V. Verses

Verses

Macaulay was a facile versifier all his life, but he knew that his poetic gift was a slender one and published only a single volume of verse, the Lays of Ancient Rome in 1842. Like all that he wrote, however, his verse is always vigorous, and this small selection will suggest the varieties of its tone. "A Radical War Song" is a characteristic squib, written in 1820, partly no doubt to please his Tory father. The "Battle of Naseby" and "The Cavalier's March to London" appeared in 1824 in Knight's Quarterly Magazine, to which Macaulay contributed while he was still in residence at Cambridge. These show brilliantly Macaulay's knack for catching the colorful elements in a historical subject and his flair for mimicking the idiom of sects and parties. "The Epitaph on a Jacobite" (1847) is one of Macaulay's very finest pieces of writing, skillfully evocative and moving. The "Lines Written on the Night of the 30th of July, 1847" are interesting for their rather overcharged expression of Macaulay's idea of himself, provoked by his defeat in the parliamentary election at Edinburgh.

A Radical War Song

Awake, arise, the hour is come,
    For rows and revolutions;
There's no receipt like pike and drum
    For crazy constitutions.
Close, close the shop! Break, break the loom,
    Desert your hearths and furrows,
And throng in arms to seal the doom
    Of England's rotten boroughs.

We'll stretch that tort'ring Castlereagh
    On his own Dublin rack, sir;
We'll drown the King in Eau de vie,
    The Laureate in his sack, sir,
Old Eldon and his sordid hag
    In molten gold we'll smother,
And stifle in his own green bag
    The Doctor and his brother.

In chains we'll hang in fair Guildhall
    The City's famed Recorder,
And next on proud St. Stephen's fall,
    Though Wynne should squeak to order.
In vain our tyrants then shall try
    To 'scape our martial law, sir;

In vain the trembling Speaker cry
    That "Strangers must withdraw," sir.

Copley to hang offends no text;
    A rat is not a man, sir:
With schedules and with tax bills next
    We'll bury pious Van, sir.
The slaves who loved the Income Tax,
    We'll crush by scores, like mites, sir,
And him, the wretch who freed the blacks,
    And more enslaved the whites, sir.

The peer shall dangle from his gate,
    The bishop from his steeple,
Till all recanting, own, the State
    Means nothing but the People.
We'll fix the church's revenues
    On Apostolic basis,
One coat, one scrip, one pair of shoes
    Shall pay their strange grimaces.

We'll strap the bar's deluding train
    In their own darling halter,
And with his big church bible brain
    The parson at the altar.
Hail glorious hour, when fair Reform
    Shall bless our longing nation,
And Hunt receive commands to form
    A new administration.

Carlisle shall sit enthroned, where sat
    Our Cranmer and our Secker;
And Watson show his snow-white hat
    In England's rich Exchequer.
The breast of Thistlewood shall wear
    Our Wellesley's star and sash, man;
And many a mausoleum fair
    Shall rise to honest Cashman.

Then, then beneath the nine-tailed cat
　　Shall they who used it writhe, sir;
And curates lean, and rectors fat,
　　Shall dig the ground they tithe, sir.
Down with your Bayleys, and your Bests,
　　Your Giffords, and your Gurneys:
We'll clear the island of the pests,
　　Which mortals name attorneys.

Down with your sheriffs, and your mayors,
　　Your registrars, and proctors,
We'll live without the lawyer's cares,
　　And die without the doctor's.
No discontented fair shall pout
　　To see her spouse so stupid;
We'll tread the torch of Hymen out,
　　And live content with Cupid.

Then, when the high-born and the great
　　Are humbled to our level,
On all the wealth of Church and State,
　　Like aldermen, we'll revel.
We'll live when hushed the battle's din,
　　In smoking and in cards, sir,
In drinking unexcised gin,
　　And wooing fair Poissardes, sir.

Songs of the Civil War
The Battle of Naseby

*The Battle of Naseby,
by Obadiah Bind-Their-Kings-in-Chains-
and-Their-Nobles-with-Links-of-Iron,
Serjeant in Ireton's Regiment*

Oh! wherefore come ye forth, in triumph from the
  North,
  With your hands, and your feet, and your raiment all
  red?
And wherefore doth your rout send forth a joyous shout?
  And whence be the grapes of the wine-press which ye
  tread?

Oh evil was the root, and bitter was the fruit,
  And crimson was the juice of the vintage that we trod;
For we trampled on the throng of the haughty and the
  strong,
  Who sate in the high places, and slew the saints of
  God.

It was about the noon of a glorious day of June,
  That we saw their banners dance, and their cuirasses
  shine,
And the Man of Blood was there, with his long essenced
  hair,

And Astley, and Sir Marmaduke, and Rupert of the
Rhine.

Like a servant of the Lord, with his Bible and his sword,
The General rode along us to form us to the fight,
When a murmuring sound broke out, and swell'd into a
shout,
Among the godless horsemen upon the tyrant's right.

And hark! like the roar of the billows on the shore,
The cry of battle rises along their charging line!
For God! for the Cause! for the Church! for the Laws!
For Charles King of England, and Rupert of the Rhine!

The furious German comes, with his clarions and his
drums,
His bravoes of Alsatia, and pages of Whitehall;
They are bursting on our flanks. Grasp your pikes, close
your ranks;
For Rupert never comes but to conquer or to fall.

They are here! They rush on! We are broken! We are
gone!
Our left is borne before them like stubble on the blast.
O Lord, put forth thy might! O Lord, defend the right!
Stand back to back, in God's name, and fight it to the
last.

Stout Skippon hath a wound; the centre hath given
ground:
Hark! hark!—What means the trampling of horsemen on our rear?
Whose banner do I see, boys? 'Tis he, thank God, 'tis he,
boys.
Bear up another minute: brave Oliver is here.

Their heads all stooping low, their points all in a row,
Like a whirlwind on the trees, like a deluge on the
dykes,

Our cuirassiers have burst on the ranks of the Accurst,
   And at a shock have scattered the forest of his pikes.

Fast, fast, the gallants ride, in some safe nook to hide
   Their coward heads, predestined to rot on Temple
     Bar:
And he—he turns, he flies:—shame on those cruel eyes
   That bore to look on torture, and dare not look on
     war.

Ho! comrades, scour the plain; and, ere ye strip the
     slain,
   First give another stab to make your search secure,
Then shake from sleeves and pockets their broad-pieces
     and lockets,
   The tokens of the wanton, the plunder of the poor.

Fools! your doublets shone with gold, and your hearts
     were gay and bold,
   When you kissed your lily hands to your lemans to-
     day;
And to-morrow shall the fox, from her chambers in the
     rocks,
   Lead forth her tawny cubs to howl above the prey.

Where be your tongues that late mocked at heaven and
     hell and fate,
   And the fingers that once were so busy with your
     blades,
Your perfum'd satin clothes, your catches and your oaths,
   Your stage-plays and your sonnets, your diamonds and
     your spades?

Down, down, for ever down with the mitre and the
     crown,
   With the Belial of the Court, and the Mammon of the
     Pope;
There is woe in Oxford Halls: there is wail in Durham's
     Stalls:

The Jesuit smites his bosom: the Bishop rends his
cope.

And She of the seven hills shall mourn her children's ills,
   And tremble when she thinks on the edge of England's
   sword;
And the Kings of earth in fear shall shudder when they
hear
   What the hand of God hath wrought for the Houses
   and the Word.

Songs of the Civil War
The Cavalier's March to London

Here warlike coblers railed from tops of casks
At lords and love-locks, monarchy and masques.
There many a graceless page blaspheming reel'd,
From his dear cards and bumpers, to the field:
The famished rooks, impatient of delay,
Gnaw their cogg'd dice and curse the lingering prey:
His sad Andromache, with fruitless care,
Paints her wan lips and braids her borrowed hair:
For Church and King he quits his favourite arts,
Forsakes his Knaves, forsakes his Queen of Hearts:
For Church and King he burns to stain with gore
His doublet, stained with nought but sack before.

From a MS. Poem.

To horse! to horse! brave Cavaliers!
   To horse for Church and Crown!
Strike, strike your tents! snatch up your spears!
   And ho for London town!
The imperial harlot, doom'd a prey
   To our avenging fires,
Sends up the voice of her dismay
   From all her hundred spires.

The Strand resounds with maidens' shrieks,

415

The 'Change with merchants' sighs,
And blushes stand on brazen cheeks,
    And tears in iron eyes;
And, pale with fasting and with fright,
    Each Puritan Committee
Hath summon'd forth to prayer and fight
    The Roundheads of the City.

And soon shall London's sentries hear
    The thunder of our drum,
And London's dames, in wilder fear,
    Shall cry, Alack! They come!
Fling the fascines;—tear up the spikes
    And forward, one and all.
Down, down with all their train-band pikes,
    Down with their mud-built wall.

Quarter?—Foul fall your whining noise,
    Ye recreant spawn of fraud!
No quarter! Think on Strafford, boys.
    No quarter! Think on Laud.
What ho! The craven slaves retire.
    On! Trample them to mud,
No quarter!—Charge.—No quarter!—Fire.
    No quarter!—Blood!—Blood!—Blood!—

Where next? In sooth there lacks no witch,
    Brave lads, to tell us where,
Sure London's sons be passing rich,
    Her daughters wondrous fair:
And let that dastard be the theme
    Of many a board's derision,
Who quails for sermon, cuff, or scream
    Of any sweet Precisian.

Their lean divines, of solemn brow,
    Sworn foes to throne and steeple,
From an unwonted pulpit now
    Shall edify the people:
Till the tir'd hangman, in despair,

Shall curse his blunted shears,
And vainly pinch, and scrape, and tear,
　　Around their leathern ears.

We'll hang, above his own Guildhall,
　　The city's grave Recorder,
And on the den of thieves we'll fall,
　　Though Pym should speak to order.
In vain the lank-haired gang shall try
　　To cheat our martial law;
In vain shall Lenthall trembling cry
　　That strangers must withdraw.

Of bench and woolsack, tub and chair,
　　We'll build a glorious pyre,
And tons of rebel parchment there
　　Shall crackle in the fire.
With them shall perish, cheek by jowl,
　　Petition, psalm, and libel,
The Colonel's canting muster-roll,
　　The Chaplain's dog-ear'd bible.

We'll tread a measure round the blaze
　　Where England's pest expires,
And lead along the dance's maze
　　The beauties of the friars:
Then smiles in every face shall shine,
　　And joy in every soul.
Bring forth, bring forth the oldest wine,
　　And crown the largest bowl.

And as with nod and laugh ye sip
　　The goblet's rich carnation,
Whose bursting bubbles seem to tip
　　The wink of invitation;
Drink to those names,—those glorious names,—
　　Those names no time shall sever,—
Drink, in a draught as deep as Thames,
　　Our Church and King for ever!

Epitaph on a Jacobite

To my true king I offered free from stain
Courage and faith; vain faith, and courage vain.
For him, I threw lands, honours, wealth, away,
And one dear hope, that was more prized than they.
For him I languished in a foreign clime,
Grey-haired with sorrow in my manhood's prime;
Heard on Lavernia Scargill's whispering trees,
And pined by Arno for my lovelier Tees;
Beheld each night my home in fevered sleep,
Each morning started from the dream to weep;
Till God, who saw me tried too sorely, gave
The resting place I asked, an early grave.
Oh thou, whom chance leads to this nameless stone,
From that proud country which was once mine own,
By those white cliffs I never more must see,
By that dear language which I spake like thee,
Forget all feuds, and shed one English tear
O'er English dust. A broken heart lies here.

Lines Written on the Night
of the 30th of July, 1847

The day of tumult, strife, defeat, was o'er;
   Worn out with toil, and noise, and scorn, and spleen,
I slumbered, and in slumber saw once more
   A room in an old mansion, long unseen.

That room, methought, was curtained from the light;
   Yet through the curtains shone the moon's cold ray
Full on a cradle, where, in linen white,
   Sleeping life's first soft sleep, an infant lay.

Pale flickered on the hearth the dying flame,
   And all was silent in that ancient hall,
Save when by fits on the low night-wind came
   The murmur of the distant waterfall.

And lo! the fairy queens who rule our birth
   Drew nigh to speak the new born baby's doom:
With noiseless step, which left no trace on earth,
   From gloom they came, and vanished into gloom.

Not deigning on the boy a glance to cast
   Swept careless by the gorgeous Queen of Gain;
More scornful still, the Queen of Fashion passed,
   With mincing gait and sneer of cold disdain.

The Queen of Power tossed high her jewelled head,
   And o'er her shoulder threw a wrathful frown:
The Queen of Pleasure on the pillow shed
   Scarce one stray rose-leaf from her fragrant crown.

Still Fay in long procession followed Fay;
   And still the little couch remained unblest:
But, when those wayward sprites had passed away,
   Came One, the last, the mightiest, and the best.

Oh glorious lady, with the eyes of light
   And laurels clustering round thy lofty brow,
Who by the cradle's side didst watch that night,
   Warbling a sweet strange music, who wast thou?

"Yes, darling; let them go;" so ran the strain:
   "Yes; let them go, gain, fashion, pleasure, power,
And all the busy elves to whose domain
   Belongs the nether sphere, the fleeting hour.

"Without one envious sigh, one anxious scheme,
   The nether sphere, the fleeting hour resign.
Mine is the world of thought, the world of dream,
   Mine all the past, and all the future mine.

"Fortune, that lays in sport the mighty low,
   Age, that to penance turns the joys of youth,
Shall leave untouched the gifts which I bestow,
   The sense of beauty and the thirst of truth.

"Of the fair brotherhood who share my grace,
   I, from thy natal day, pronounce thee free;
And, if for some I keep a nobler place,
   I keep for none a happier than for thee.

"There are who, while to vulgar eyes they seem
   Of all my bounties largely to partake,
Of me as of some rival's handmaid deem,
   And court me but for gain's, power's, fashion's sake.

"To such, though deep their lore, though wide their fame,
    Shall my great mysteries be all unknown:
But thou, through good and evil, praise and blame,
    Wilt not thou love me for myself alone?

"Yes; thou wilt love me with exceeding love;
    And I will tenfold all that love repay,
Still smiling, though the tender may reprove,
    Still faithful, though the trusted may betray.

"For aye mine emblem was, and aye shall be,
    The ever-during plant whose bough I wear,
Brightest and greenest then, when every tree
    That blossoms in the light of Time is bare.

"In the dark hour of shame, I deigned to stand
    Before the frowning peers at Bacon's side:
On a far shore I smoothed with tender hand,
    Through months of pain, the sleepless bed of Hyde:

"I brought the wise and brave of ancient days
    To cheer the cell where Raleigh pined alone:
I lighted Milton's darkness with the blaze
    Of the bright ranks that guard the eternal throne.

"And even so, my child, it is my pleasure
    That thou not then alone shouldst feel me nigh,
When, in domestic bliss and studious leisure,
    Thy weeks uncounted come, uncounted fly;

"Not then alone, when myriads, closely pressed
    Around thy car, the shout of triumph raise;
Nor when, in gilded drawing rooms, thy breast
    Swells at the sweeter sound of woman's praise.

"No: when on restless night dawns cheerless morrow,
    When weary soul and wasting body pine,
Thine am I still, in danger, sickness, sorrow,
    In conflict, obloquy, want, exile, thine;

"Thine, where on mountain waves the snowbirds scream,
　　Where more than Thule's winter barbs the breeze,
　Where scarce, through lowering clouds, one sickly gleam
　　Lights the drear May-day of Antarctic seas;

"Thine, when around thy litter's track all day
　　White sandhills shall reflect the blinding glare;
　Thine, when, through forests breathing death, thy way
　　All night shall wind by many a tiger's lair;

"Thine most, when friends turn pale, when traitors fly,
　　When, hard beset, thy spirit, justly proud,
　For truth, peace, freedom, mercy, dares defy
　　A sullen priesthood and a raving crowd.

"Amidst the din of all things fell and vile,
　　Hate's yell, and envy's hiss, and folly's bray,
　Remember me; and with an unforced smile
　　See riches, baubles, flatterers, pass away.

"Yes: they will pass away; nor deem it strange:
　　They come and go, as comes and goes the sea:
　And let them come and go: thou, through all change,
　　Fix thy firm gaze on virtue and on me."

VI. Letters

Letters

Macaulay was a marvelous letter writer—vivid, amusing, dramatic. Anyone who wants to gain real insight into his personality should familiarize himself with the letters. A definitive edition, edited by Thomas Pinney, will be published before long by the Cambridge University Press. Meanwhile, readers must be referred to G. O. Trevelyan's Life and Letters.

The series of letters published here was written by Macaulay during the struggle over the Reform Bill. It begins with a reference to the speech he made in the House of Commons on March 2, 1831 (published elsewhere in this volume) and ends with a letter reporting royal assent to the bill. The letters are addressed to the three people whom he held in the most affectionate regard: his favorite sisters, Hannah and Margaret, and his only close friend, Thomas Flower Ellis.

To Thomas Flower Ellis, 7 March 1831

London, March 7, 1831

Dear Ellis,

I have been so busy during the last few days that I have not been able to spare a moment. The House of Commons lasts from 3 in the afternoon to 2 in the morning—and the rest of my time has been spent in preparing for the press the speech which I made on Wednesday night and which has had a great success.

I will send a copy to you under franked covers when it is published.

London is thoroughly well disposed towards us; and the country will, I hope, follow the lead of London. Give me news from Lancashire. What say the manufacturers? What say the Squires? What say the lawyers? And of the lawyers what say, in especial, Milner, Holinshed,—(or how does the brute spell his name?)—Adolphus—Henderson,—and the Devil? By the bye is not Holt's nickname an excellent illustration of the title of Ben Jonson's play—The Devil is an Ass.

How things will go seems a little doubtful. But I have a good hope. Lord Duncannon, who knows the House of Commons better than any other man in it—Billy Holmes excepted who maketh a lie and loveth it—is quite confident of success. He is sure, he says, of a majority. Peel is evidently trimming. Croker would trim, if his infernal impudence and spite were not beyond even his own controul. By the bye, you never saw such a scene as Croker's oration on Friday night. He abused Lord John Russell. He abused Lord Althorpe. He abused the Lord Advocate—and we took no notice—never once groaned or cried —no! But he began to praise Lord Fitzwilliam—"a venerable nobleman,—an excellent and amiable nobleman,—" and so forth: and we all broke out together—"Question—no—no this is too bad—don't—don't—" and such other exclamations. He then called Canning his right honourable friend. "Your friend! damn your impudent face!" said the member who sate next me.

Croker is now beyond all comparison the most impudent man in the house. I always thought him so. But some of us gave the palm to O'Gorman Mahon. O'Gorman fell greatly—Cæsar in the senate did not die with more attention to the proprieties of character. He came to hear, what few people care to hear, his own sentence read at the bar by the chairman of the Committee. To make the matter better he was expelled for bribery by his agents. The fellow sate on the Treasury bench—heard the report —and never stirred. "Sir"—said the Speaker—"you must withdraw." Up he got and swaggered off as fast as he could with his acre of ruff and his three bushels of dirty hair. Sorrow such another we will be having any how plaze God—or be wishing to have; and no great blame to us for that same—the craturs.

I will not tell you the compliments that I have received on my speech, lest you should think that I am telling lies.

Ever yours truly,

T. B. Macaulay

To Thomas Flower Ellis, 30 March 1831

London, March 30, 1831

Dear Ellis,

I have little news for you, except what you will learn from the papers as well as from me. It is clear that the Reform Bill must pass, either in this or in another Parliament. The majority of one does not appear to me, as it does to you, by any means inauspicious. We should perhaps have had a better plea for a dissolution if the majority had been the other way. But surely a dissolution under such circumstances would have been a most alarming thing. If there should be a dissolution now there will not be that ferocity in the public mind which there would have been if the House of Commons had refused to entertain the Bill at all. I confess that, till we had a majority, I was half inclined to tremble at the storm which we had raised. At present I think that we are absolutely certain of victory, and of victory without commotion.

Such a scene as the division of last Tuesday I never saw, and never expect to see again. If I should live fifty years the impression of it will be as fresh and sharp in my mind as if it had just taken place. It was like seeing Cæsar stabbed in the Senate House, or seeing Oliver taking the mace from the table, a sight to be seen only once and never to be forgotten. The crowd overflowed the House in every part. When the strangers were cleared out and the doors locked we had six hundred and eight members present, more by fifty-five than ever were at a division before. The Ayes and Noes were like two vollies of cannon from opposite sides of a field of battle. When the opposition went out into the lobby—an operation by the bye which took up twenty minutes or more—we spread ourselves over the benches on both sides of

427

the House. For there were many of us who had not been able to find a seat during the evening. When the doors were shut we began to speculate on our numbers. Every body was desponding. "We have lost it. We are only two hundred and eighty at most. I do not think we are two hundred and fifty. They are three hundred. Alderman Thompson has counted them. He says they are two hundred and ninety-nine." This was the talk on our benches. I wonder that men who have been long in parliament do not acquire a better coup d'œil for numbers. The House when only the Ayes were in it looked to me a very fair house—much fuller than it generally is even on debates of considerable interest. I had no hope however of three hundred. As the tellers passed along our lowest row on the left hand side the interest was insupportable—two hundred and ninety one—two hundred and ninety two—we were all standing up and stretching forward, telling with the tellers. At three hundred there was a short cry of joy, at three hundred and two another—suppressed however in a moment. For we did not yet know what the hostile force might be. We knew however that we could not be severely beaten. The doors were thrown open and in they came. Each of them as he entered brought some different report of their numbers. It must have been impossible, as you may conceive, in the lobby, crowded as they must have been, to form any exact estimate. First we heard that they were three hundred and three —then the number rose to three hundred and ten, then went down to three hundred and seven. Alexander Baring told me that he had counted and that they were three hundred and four. We were all breathless with anxiety, when Charles Wood who stood near the door jumped on a bench and cried out—"They are only three hundred and one." We set up a shout that you might have heard to Charing Cross—waving our hats—stamping against the floor and clapping our hands. The tellers scarcely got through the crowd: for the house was thronged up to the table, and all the floor was fluctuating with heads like the pit of a theatre. But you might have heard a pin drop as Duncannon read the numbers. Then again the shouts broke out—and many of us shed tears—I could scarcely refrain. And the jaw of Peel fell; and the face of Twiss was as the face of a damned soul; and

Herries looked like Judas taking his neck-cloth off for the last operation. We shook hands and clapped each other on the back, and went out laughing, crying, and huzzaing into the lobby. And no sooner were the outer doors opened than another shout answered that within the house. All the passages and the stairs into the waiting rooms were thronged by people who had waited till four in the morning to know the issue. We passed through a narrow lane between two thick masses of them; and all the way down they were shouting and waving their hats; till we got into the open air. I called a cabriolet—and the first thing the driver asked was, "Is the Bill carried?" "Yes, by one." "Thank God for it, Sir." And away I rode to Grey's Inn—and so ended a scene which will probably never be equalled till the reformed Parliament wants reforming; and that I hope will not be till the days of our grandchildren—till that truly orthodox and apostolical person Dr. Francis Ellis is an archbishop of eighty.

What are your movements? Mine are not absolutely determined. Have you had many briefs? At any rate you have, I suppose, been employed against the coiners. However the weightier matters of the law may fare, the tithe of mint, I hope, goes on.

As for me, I am for the present a sort of lion. My speech has set me in the front rank, if I can keep there; and it has not been my luck hitherto to lose ground when I have once got it. Shiel and I are on very civil terms. He talks largely concerning Demosthenes and Burke. He made, I must say, an excellent speech—too florid and queer; but decidedly successful.

Why did not the great Samuel Grove Price speak? He often came to the front rows, and sate making notes. Every body expected him to rise, and prepared night-caps accordingly. But he always sneaked away. On my soul, I believe that he is a craven with all his bluster. Indeed, if he is afraid, it is the best thing that I ever knew of him. For a more terrible audience there is not in the world. I wish that Praed had known to whom he was speaking. But with all his talent, he has no tact, no perception of the character of his audience; and he has fared accordingly. Tierney used to say that he never rose in the House without feeling his knees tremble under him: and I am sure that no man who has not some of that feeling will ever succeed there.

Ever yours,
T. B. Macaulay

To Hannah Macaulay, 6 July 1831

London, July 6, 1831

My love,

I have been so busy during the last two or three days that I have found no time to write to you. I have now good news for you. I spoke yesterday night with a success beyond my utmost expectations. I am half ashamed to tell you the compliments which I have received. But you well know that it is not from vanity, but to give you pleasure, that I tell you what is said about me. Lord Althorpe told me twice that it was the best speech he had ever heard—Graham and Stanley and Lord John Russell spoke of it in the same way. Grahame told me that I had surpassed myself out and out. Robert Grant said that he liked this speech far better than my speech of last Parliament. O'Connell followed me out of the house to pay me the most enthusiastic compliments, and old John Smith cried as he talked to me. But what flattered me most was to come on a knot of old members whom I did not know, and who did not see me, who were disputing whether Plunket or I were the better speaker. I delivered my speech much more slowly than any that I had before made—and it is in consequence better reported than its predecessors though not well. I send you several papers. You will see some civil things in the leading articles of some of them. My greatest pleasure in the midst of all this praise is to think of the pleasure which my success will give to my father and my sisters. It is happy for me that ambition—the fiercest and most devouring of all passions—has in my mind been softened into a kind of domestic feeling, and that affection has at least as much to do as vanity with my wish to distinguish myself. This I owe to my dear mother and to the interest which she always took in my childish successes. From my earliest years the gratification of those whom I love has been associated with the gratification of

430

my own thirst of fame, until the two have become inseparably joined in my mind.

Do not,—my love,—but of course you will not—shew this letter to anybody but my father and sisters, or talk to any body else about the compliments which I repeat to you. I should appear ridiculously conceited to people who do not understand the feeling which induces me to repeat them. Kindest love to my father, Selina, and Fanny.

Ever yours my darling,
T. B. M.

To Hannah Macaulay, 8 July 1831

London, July 8, 1831

My love,

I have not been for some days so active a correspondent as usual, owing to the pressure of parliamentary business. I ought scarcely, you will say, to make this an excuse—for I am now writing at Basinghall Street, in the middle of attorneys, bankrupts, and false witnesses.

So you want to hear all the compliments that are paid to me. I shall never end, if I stuff my letters with them. For I meet nobody who does not give me joy. Baring tells me that I ought never to speak again. The newspapers are still filled with compliments. The Herald of yesterday, in particular, contained a very flattering article. Howick sent a note to me yesterday to say that his father wished very much to be introduced to me, and asked me to dine with them yesterday—as, by great good luck, there was nothing to do in the house of Commons. At seven I went to Downing Street where Earl Grey's official residence stands. It is a noble house. There are two splendid drawing-rooms which overlook St. James's Park. Into these I was shewn. The servant told me that Lord Grey was still at the House of Lords; and that her Ladyship had just gone to dress—Howick had not mentioned the hour in his note. I sate down, and turned over two large portfolios of political caricatures—Earl Grey's own face was in every print. I was very much diverted. I had seen some of them before. But many were new to me, and their merit is extraordinary. They were the caricatures of that remarkably able artist who calls himself H. B. In about half an hour Lady Georgiana Grey, the only daughter of Earl Grey who is still unmarried, and the Countess, made their appearances. We had some pleasant talk— and they made many apologies for Howick's carelessness and their absence. The Earl, they said, was unexpectedly delayed by a question which had arisen in the Lords. Lady Holland arrived soon after, and gave me a most gracious reception—shook my hand very warmly, and told me in her imperial decisive manner that she had talked with all the principal men on our side about my speech—that they all agreed that it was the best that had been made since the death of Fox, and that it was more like Fox's speaking than any body's else. Then she told me that I was too much worked—that I must go out of town, and absolutely insisted on my going to Holland House to dine and take a bed on the next day on which there is no parliamentary business. At eight we went to dinner. Lord Howick took his father's place; and we feasted very luxuriously. At nine Lord Grey came from the House with Lord Durham, Lord Holland, and the Duke of Richmond. They dined on the remains of our dinner with great expedition, as they had to go to a cabinet council at ten. Of course I had scarcely any talk with Lord Grey. He was however extremely polite to me, and so were his colleagues. I liked extremely the ways of the family. Lady Grey and her daughter seemed to be on the easiest and kindest terms with each other. Lord Howick shewed more domestic feeling than from what I knew of his habits, I had expected—and Lord Grey, whom I had rather believed to be a domestic tyrant seemed to be very comfortable and very much beloved.

I picked up some news from these Cabinet ministers. There is to be a Coronation on quite a new plan—no banquet in Westminster Hall—no feudal services—no champion—no procession from the Abbey to the Hall and back again. But there is to be a service in the Abbey. All the Peers are to come in state and in their robes, and the King is to take the oaths and be crowned and anointed in their presence. The spectacle will be finer than usual to the multitude out of doors. The few hundreds who could obtain admittance to the Hall will be the only losers.

In the evening our cabinet Ministers went, and the Duke of

Bedford and Sam Rogers dropped in—the Duke in his blue rib-band—Sam Rogers looking, as usual, like a dead man. I came away at twelve.

I have had a very kind note from Lord Lansdowne. I dined at his house on Sunday—but not with him; for he had an attack of this influenza which kept him confined to his room and, I believe, to his bed. I called on him yesterday, and found him recovering. I am to dine with him to morrow week.

I must stop. Give my thanks to my father for his kind note—and take my thanks yourself—my darling—for your letter. I only wish that I could find words to tell you how much I love you. Kindest love [and] thanks to Selina and Fanny.

Ever yours, dearest,
T. B. M.

Sarah Anne and Meg have an order for the Ventilator to night. But I do not know that they will hear much that is worth hearing.

To Hannah Macaulay, 15 July 1831

Basinghall Street, July 15, 1831

My darling,

I will not try to tell you—because I cannot tell you—how happy your letter made me, and how much I long to see you and talk with you. My father arrived yesterday night. This morning I saw him in excellent health and spirits to all appearance. *Entre nous* Buxton has spoken to Lord Brougham—and Lord Brougham has declared himself eager to serve my father to the utmost either of his own patronage or of any influence which he may have over others. But in these times of competition and of strict retrenchment Lord Brougham, even if he be sincere—which I do not dispute—may not find it easy to fulfil his promises.

The rage of faction at the present moment exceeds any thing that has been known in our time. Indeed I doubt whether, at the time of Mr. Pitt's first becoming Premier, at the time of Sir Robert Walpole's fall, or even during the desperate struggle between the Whigs and Tories at the close of Anne's reign, the rage of party was so fearfully violent. Lord Mahon said to me yesterday that friendships of long standing were every where

433

giving way—and that the schism between the reformers and anti-reformers was spreading from the House of Commons into every private circle. Lord Mahon himself is an exception. He and I are on excellent terms. But Praed and I become colder every day. His silly, conceited, factious conduct has disgraced him even more than his bad speaking.

The scene of Tuesday night beggars description. I left the House at about three, in consequence of some expressions of Lord Althorpe's which indicated that the ministry was inclined to yield. I afterwards much regretted that I had gone away; not that my presence was necessary; but because I should have liked to have sate through so tremendous a storm. Towards eight in the morning the Speaker was almost fainting. The ministerial members however were as true as steel. They furnished the ministry with the resolution which it wanted. "If the noble lord yields," said one of our men, "all is lost." Old Sir Thomas Baring sent for his razor, and Benett, the Member for Wiltshire for his night-cap, and they were both resolved to spend the whole day in the House rather than give way. If the opposition had not yielded in two hours half London would [hav]e been in Old Palace Yard.

Since Tuesday night the opposition have been rather cowed. But their demeanour, though less outrageous than at the beginning of the week, indicates what would in any other times be called extreme violence. I have not been once in bed till three in the morning since last Sunday.

To morrow we have a holiday. I dine at Lansdowne House. Next week I dine with Littleton the Member for Staffordshire and his handsome wife. He told me that I should meet two men whom I am curious to see, Lord Plunkett and the Marquess Wellesley—let alone the Chancellor who is not a novelty to me.

I am ashamed to send you so dull a letter. But if it gratifies you half as much as the sight of your handwriting about the most insignificant thing gratifies me, you will read even this trifling with pleasure. Kindest love to my Uncle, Aunt, sisters, and Cousins.

Ever yours, my own love,
T. B. M.

To Hannah Macaulay, 20 July 1831

Library of the House of Commons, July 20, 1831

My love,

Here I am sitting, waiting for the beginning of the debate on the reform bill. Did you ever see our library? If not let me describe it to you. A handsome Gothic Room, above forty-five feet by twenty-five, very neat—with a handsome carpet in the centre and thick matting all round—two immense tables with all conveniences for writing—two fire-places, which, as you may conceive, are now filled only with shavings and tattered scraps of paper,—book cases all round fitted with journals of the two Houses, Statutes at large, and various political and historical works. The window at the end—a Gothic bow-window—looks out on a small plot of grass planted with elms. Beyond lies the Thames with its boats and barges—and on the other side the Archbishop's palace at Lambeth. In sunny days the view is very pretty. This is a dull day—all but rainy—and the prospect has nothing alluring. Then for company. In the bow-window sits Sir James Grahame talking to Tom Duncombe—a very honest good-natured fellow Tom; but none of the soberest. At the other end of the room, Lieutenant Gordon preaching to Henry Maxwell—a very dishonest ill-natured fellow Gordon, though one of the most canting. See how antitheses drop from my pen in its most rapid and unstudied movements. Robinson the Member for Worcester—a bore—is writing at one table—and Mr. Macaulay Member for Calne—no bore—but a very promising young gentleman and a rising speaker—is writing at the other. The door opens while I am writing and in comes another bore—that stupid Irishman Ruthven. "Macaulay"—who calls Macaulay—? Sir James Graham. What can he have to say to me? Take it dramatically—

Sir J. G.—Macaulay.

Macaulay—What?

Sir J. G.—Whom are you writing to that you laugh so much over your letter?

Macaulay—To my constituents at Calne to be sure. They expect news of the Reform bill every day.

Sir J. G.—Well writing to constituents is less of a plague to you than to most people, to judge by your face.

Macaulay—How do you know that I am not writing a billet-doux to a lady?

Sir J. G.—You look more like it by Jove.

Cutler Fergusson, MP for Kircudbright—Let Ladies and Constituents alone, and come to the House. We are going on the case of the Borough of Great Bedwin immediately.

So away goes Sir James Graham—and away must I go too. And why do I sit writing this nonsense? And why do I not tear it up now that it is written?—Because no[thing] is worthless which affection send[s to] affection, and therefore nothing can be worthless which I send to you, my darling.

My uncle will be surprised if you tell him of our library. It has been established, I think, since his time.

We are cruelly worked. I never get to bed till three in the morning—and "Wednesday shines no Sabbath to our toils." Lady Holland has asked me out on Saturday to recruit, and I have accepted her invitation.

Kindest love to Selina, Fanny, my Uncle, aunt, and Cousins.

Ever yours, dearest,

T. B. M.

To Hannah Macaulay, 5 August 1831

London, August 5, 1831

My love,

I need not tell you that I was delighted with your letter which arrived yesterday and with the shorter note which I received to day. I am quite lonely now—except when I am in the House, where indeed I could well spare some of the company: for the crowd and heat are beyond all endurance. The compression of a slave-ship can hardly be worse. Five hundred people are often there in a space which will not conveniently accommodate more than four hundred, with a thermometer at something less than boiling heat, and this from four or five in the afternoon till midnight and long after. Yet I keep my health, and am still, I blush to say, a dumpling of a fellow, as my friend Blackwood has it.

I said a few words the night before last: they were merely in reply and quite unpremeditated. They were not ill received. I feel that much practice will be necessary to make me a good debater on points of detail. But my friends tell me that I have raised my reputation by shewing that I was quite equal to the work of extemporaneous reply. My manner, they say, is cold and wants ease. I feel this myself. Nothing but strong excitement and a great occasion overcomes a certain reserve and *mauvaise honte* which I have in public speaking—not a *mauvaise honte* which in the least confuses me or makes me hesitate for a word—but a *mauvaise honte* which keeps me from putting any fervour into my tone or my action. This is perhaps in some respects an advantage. For when I do warm, I am the most vehement speaker in the House—and nothing strikes an audience so much as the animation of an orator who is generally cold.

I ought to tell you that Peel was very civil, and cheered me loudly—and that impudent leering scoundrel Croker congratulated the House on the proofs which I had given of my readiness. He was afraid—he said—that I had been silent so long on account of the many allusions which had been made to Calne. Now that I had risen again he hoped that they should hear me often. See whether I do not dust that lying varlet's jacket for him in the next number of the Blue and Yellow. I detest him more than cold boiled veal.

After the debate I walked about the streets with Bulwer till near three o'clock. I spoke to him about his novels with perfect sincerity—praising warmly, and criticising freely. He took the praise as a greedy boy takes apple pie, and the criticism as a good dutiful boy takes senna-tea. He has one eminent merit—that of being a most enthusiastic admirer of mine—so that I may be the Hero of a novel yet, under the name of Delamere or Mortimer. Only think what an honour.

Bulwer is to be editor of the New Monthly Magazine. He begged me very earnestly to give him something for it. I would make no promises; for I am already over head and ears in literary engagements. But I may possibly now and then send him some trifle or other. At all events I shall expect him to puff me well.

I do not see why I should not have my puffers as well as my neighbours.

Write to me, my love—and make Margaret write—and tell me all about the books that you read, the company that you see, the quarrels between the Temple, the Vicarage, and the Grange —the mysteries, the secrets, and all the other delightful things which make Rothley so happy a place. I am glad that you have read Madame de Staël's Allemagne. The book is a foolish one in some respects—but it abounds with information and shews great mental power. She was certainly the first [wom]an of her age— Miss Edgeworth, I think the second, and Miss Austen the third.

But I must give over this idle rattling. Kindest love to all.

Ever yours, my love,

T. B. M.

To Hannah Macaulay, 12 August 1831

London, August 12, 1831

My love,

I am recovering, but slowly—and am still under sentence of confinement and starvation. It is three days since I have tasted any food except milk and water—except indeed that this morning I ate three mouthfuls of bread. I am on my sofa—as weak as Mary's baby and quite solitary. The treasury has found me a pair for a fortnight—to wit—my uncle's old colleague Sam Smith. I still expect to be with you next Wednesday. I fear or perhaps I should say I hope that I shall come down to you thinner than I have been for a long time.

Write to me my darling—and since I cannot have your society during this time of weakness and seclusion let me have your handwriting.

I shall not be sorry to be out of the way of the miserable proceedings in the House of Commons. One is ashamed to support such a government—and, in my situation, I cannot attack it. The weakness, dulness, cowardice, and tergiversation of the ministers —those I mean who sit in the House of Commons—have begun to disgust their most devoted friends. I will tell you instances of their fatuity and infirmity of purpose when we meet which are absolutely astounding. Do not trumpet what I say to every body. But nothing can save them from ruin if they do not speedily alter their course. The Chancellor has written to me a private letter expressing this opinion in language much stronger than what I am now using, and intreating me to put myself forward to defend them. He must feel the pressure of the danger strongly, when he treats me with so much civility. But my course is taken; indeed the cholera has settled it [wi]thout any reference to my pleasure. [And i]t is no business of mine whether [they] stand or fall. There is not one of them [in] the House of Commons except Lord Althorp who is not either useless or worse than useless— and I do not see that it would be either for my interest or my honour to thrust myself between them and the public contempt. This, I repeat, in secret. What I mean by secret I leave it to your discretion to judge.

Love to all.

Ever yours my darling
T. B. M.

To Hannah Macaulay, 29 August 1831

London, August 29, 1831

My darling,

Here I am again settled, sitting up in the House of Commons till three o'clock five days in the week, and getting an indigestion at great dinners on the remaining two. I dined on Saturday with Lord Althorp and yesterday with Sir James Graham. Both of them gave me exactly the same dinner; and, though I am not generally copious on the repasts which my hosts provide for me, I must tell you, for the honour of official hospitality, how our ministers regale their supporters. Turtle, turbot, venison, and grouse, formed the principal part of both entertainments—the effect of which is that I had the heartburn all last night, and have solemnly vowed never to eat of such a variety of good things again.

Lord Althorp was extremely pleasant at the head of his own table. We were a small party—Lord Ebrington, Hawkins, Captain Spencer, Stanley, and two or three more. We all of us congratulated Lord Althorp on his good health and spirits. He told us that he never took exercise now, that from his getting up till four o'clock he was engaged in the business of his office—that at four he dined, went down to the house at five, and never stirred till the house rose, which is always after midnight, that he then went home, took a basin of arrow-root with a glass of sherry in it; and went to bed—where he always dropped asleep in three minutes. "During the week," said he, "which followed my taking office I did not close my eyes for anxiety. Since that time I have never been awake a quarter of an hour after taking off my clothes."

Stanley laughed at Lord Althorp's arrow-root and recommended his own supper—cold meat and warm negus—a supper which I will certainly begin to take when I feel a desire to pass the night with a sensation as if I was swallowing a nutmeg-grater every third minute.

We talked about timidity in speaking. Lord Althorp said that he had only just got over his apprehensions. "I was as much afraid," he said, "last year as when first I came into parliament. But now I am forced to speak so often that I am quite hardened. Last Thursday I was up forty times." I was not much surprised at this in Lord Althorp—as he is certainly one of the most modest men in existence. But I was surprised to hear Stanley say that he never rose without great uneasiness. "My throat and lips," he said, "when I am going to speak are as dry as those of a man who is going to be hanged." Nothing can be more composed and cool than Stanley's manner. His fault is on that side. A little hesitation at the beginning of a speech is graceful; and many eminent speakers have practised it merely in order to give the appearance of unpremeditated reply to prepared speeches. Stanley speaks like a man who never knew what fear or even modesty was. Tierney, it is remarkable, who was the most ready and fluent debater almost ever known, made a confession similar to Stanley's. He never spoke, he said, without feeling his knees knock together when he rose.

Sir James Graham's official house is much finer than Lord Althorp's, and indeed than Lord Grey's. It is really a palace. The rooms in which we dined and took coffee look out on St. James's park. They are very handsome and are hung round with the paintings from which the prints in Cook's Voyages were taken—of scenes in Otaheite and New Zealand. Cook's Voyages you are aware, were undertaken under the direction of the Admiralty.

Lord Althorp was at Graham's. James, the member for Carlisle, the Attorney and Solicitor General, and the Lord Advocate were also there. There was a little more constraint than at Lord Althorp's, who is simplicity itself. I came away with Jeffrey who brought me in his carriage to the entrance of Gray's Inn.

My opinion of Lord Althorp is extremely high. In fact his character is the only stay of the ministry. I doubt whether any person has ever lived in England who, with no eloquence, no brilliant talents, no profound information—with nothing in short but plain good sense and an excellent heart, possessed so much influence both in and out of Parliament. His temper is an absolute miracle. He has been worse used than any minister ever was in debate; and he has never said one thing inconsistent, I do not say with gentlemanlike courtesy, but with real benevolence. His candour is absolutely a vice in debate. He is perpetually shewing excuses and ways of escape to his adversaries which they would never find of themselves. Lord North perhaps was his equal in suavity and good nature. But Lord North was not a man of strict principles. His administration was not only an administration hostile to liberty; but it was supported by vile and corrupt means—by direct bribery, I fear, in many cases. Lord Althorp has the temper of Lord North with the principles of Romilly. If he had the oratorical powers of either of those men, he might do any thing. But his understanding, though just, is slow; and his elocution painfully defective. It is however only justice to him to say that he has done more service to the Reform Bill even as a debater than all the other ministers together, Stanley excepted. Graham is either afraid or idle. Grant and Palmerston are idle, and, I suspect, not very hearty. Lord John Russell gives all that he has—to wit two mites which make a farthing. I must in fairness say, however, that Lord John made a better speech on Saturday than any that I have heard from him for a long time.

We are going—by *we* I mean the Members of Parliament who are for reform—as soon as the Bill is through the Commons, to give a grand dinner to Lord Althorp and Lord John Russell as a mark of our respect. Some people wished to have the other Cabinet Ministers included. But Grant and Palmerston are not in sufficiently high esteem among the Whigs to be honoured with such a compliment. Where we [are to] hold our festivities— whether at the Albion or the City of London Tavern, or whether we shall go to Greenwich to eat white-bait is undecided.

But I must stop. Kindest love to all at the Temple.

Ever yours, my love
T. B. M.

To Hannah Macaulay, 13 September 1831

London, Septr. 13, 1831

My love,

I am in high spirits at the thought of soon seeing you all in London and of being again one of a family—and of a family which I love so much. It is well that one has something to love in private life. For the aspect of public affairs is very menacing— fearful, I think, beyond what people in general imagine. Three weeks however will probably settle the whole, and bring to an issue the question, Reform or Revolution. One or the other I am certain that we must and shall have. I assure you that the violence of the people, the bigotry of the Lords, and the stupidity and weakness of the ministers, alarm me so much that even my rest is disturbed by vexation and uneasy forebodings—not for myself; for I may gain and cannot lose—but for this noble country which seems likely to be ruined without the miserable consolation of being ruined by great men. All seems fair as yet, and will seem fair for a fortnight longer. But I know the danger from informa- tion more accurate and certain than, I believe, any body not in power possesses—and I know, what our men in power do not know, how terrible the danger is.

All this is strictly confidential. I called on Lord Lansdowne on Sunday. He told me distinctly that he expected the bill to be lost in the Lords, and that if it were lost the ministers must go out. I told him with as much strength of expression as was suited to the nature [of] our connection, and to his age and rank, that if the ministers receded before the Lords, they and the Whig party were lost—that nothing remained but an insolent oligarchy on the one side and infuriated people on the other—that Lord Grey and his colleagues would become as odious and more contemptible than Peel and the Duke of Wellington. "What could be done?" "Make more peers," said I. Lord Lansdowne objected to such a course with the feeling natural to a nobleman of such ancient descent and such high rank. But why did he not think of all this earlier? Why put his hand to the plough and look back? Why begin to build without counting the cost of finishing? Why raise the public appetite, and then baulk it?

I told him that the House of Commons would address the King against a Tory ministry. I feel assured that it would do so. I feel assured that if those who are bidden will not come, the highways and hedges will be ransacked to form a reforming ministry. To one thing my mind is made up. If no body else will move an address to the Crown against a Tory ministry—I will.

This is all strictly secret. I cannot tell you how it vexes and alarms me. Kindest love to all.

Ever yours my dearest,
T. B. M.

To Hannah Macaulay, 15 September 1831

London, September 15, 1831

My love,

I have been very busy since I wrote last, moving heaven and earth to render it certain that, if our ministers are so foolish as to resign in the event of a defeat in the Lords, the Commons may be firm and united: and I think that I have arranged a plan which will secure a bold and instant declaration on our part, if necessary. Lord Ebrington is the man whom I have in my eye as our leader. I have had much conversation with him and with several of our leading county members. They are all staunch: and I will answer for this; that if the Ministers should betray us, we will be ready to defend ourselves.

We are to have a magnificent dinner in a week or ten days to commemorate the passing of the Bill through the Commons.

There will be three hundred Members or thereabouts present. It will cost us, I am sorry to say, three pounds a piece. We are to dine in Stationers' Hall, the Company having lent it to us for the occasion. The Landlord of the Albion Tavern is to furnish the dinner; and, by all that I can hear of that eminent person, we may think ourselves very lucky to get off for £3 each. Everything is to be in the first style. Sir Francis Burdett is to take the chair. The Newspapers will be full of it, no doubt, whenever it does take place. There is to be a table for the reporters.

My father has received very kind and ardent assurances from the Chancellor of attention to his interests—Lord Brougham charges himself absolutely with John's fortune. He told Buxton that, whether he went out or staid in, he would take care to provide for John before he gave up the Seals. He means also, in case a Bill for appointing Commissioners of Public Charities, now under discussion, should pass into a law, to make my father a Commissioner. This will be £800 a year. He is negociating with Lord Goderich an arrangement which will secure to Henry the place, (not in itself, I think, very desirable), of Commissioner of Prizes at Sierra Leone.

My father seems to wish that you were in town. I asked him to day when you were to come up. He said, "I wish them to come immediately but I do not like to interfere with their pleasures. I hinted what I desire. But they seem to like the country." Do not mention to him what I tell you. But make your arrangements as you think best under these circumstances.

Farewell, my dear, dear, love. How delightful it is in the middle of intrigues and tumults and ambitious competitions [to] feel that there are some whose [affec]tion is unalterable— Lord [Byron   ]¹ his sister in the midst of his tro[uble]

[["Th]ere yet are two things in my destiny
     A world to roam through—and a home with thee."
Go the world as [it] will—rise or fall who may,—a quiet home with those who are dearest to me will at last be within my reach: —and to that home I shall carry the best lesson which a man can learn in the great world—to despise it.

---

1. The paper has been torn.

Not that I have any special reason for cynicism at this moment. I receive warm assurances of the enthusiasm in my favour at Leeds. But I must stop. Kind loves to every body.

Yours ever, darling,
T. B. M.

Thank Margaret for her letter.

To Thomas Flower Ellis, 17 October 1831

London, October 17, 1831

My dear Ellis,

I should have written to you long ago—but that I mislaid your letter and forgot your direction. When shall you be in London? Of course you do not mean to sacrifice your professional business to the work of numbering the gates and telling the towers of boroughs in Wales. What you mean by saying that you are hard worked, I do not very well understand. I should have thought that your duties would be very easy.

You will come back, I suppose, with your head full of ten-pound hous[e]holders instead of ἔρωες, and of Caermarthen and Denbigh instead of Carians and Pelasgians. I expect to hear you talk of nothing but limits and population returns. Is it true, by the bye, that the Commissioners are whipped on the boundaries of the boroughs by the beadles, in order that they may not forget the precise line which they have drawn? I deny it wherever I go, and assure people that some of my friends who are in the Commission would not submit to such degradation. Indeed I believe that the story originates solely in the circumstance that Bellenden Kerr has been horsewhipped at every place to which he has yet gone.

You must have been hard-worked indeed and soundly whipped too, if you have suffered as much for the reform bill as we who debated it. I believe that there are fifty members of the House of Commons who have done irreparable injury to their health by attendance on the discussions of this Session. I have got through pretty well. But I look forward, I confess, with great dismay to the thought of recommencing; particularly as Wetherell's cursed lungs seem to be in as good condition as ever.

As to myself—I have every reason to be gratified by the manner in which my speeches have been received. To say the truth the station which I now hold in the house is such that I should not be inclined to quit it for any place which was not of considerable importance. My modesty, which, as you well know, is my great weakness, will not allow me to repeat all the compliments which I have received. You will see my two last speeches excellently reported and corrected by myself in the Mirror of Parliament.

What you saw about my having a place was a blunder of a stupid *reporther's*. Croker was taunting the government with leaving me to fight their battle and to rally their followers; and said that the honourable and learned member for Calne, though only a practising barrister in title, seemed to be in reality the most efficient member of the government. *Entre nous* they would have made a poor hand of it without me. Our meeting at Willis's rooms and Lord Ebrington's motion were wholly brought about by me. I really believe that, but for the stir which I made among our county-members, the ministers would have resigned. This is all in the strictest confidence. You shall hear particulars when we meet.

By the bye—my article on Croker has not only smashed his book, but has smashed the Westminster Review incidentally. The utilitarians took on themselves to praise the accuracy of the most inaccurate editor that ever lived—and gave as an instan[ce] of it a note in which, as I have shewn, he makes a mistake of twenty years and more. John Mill is in a foaming rage, and says that they are in a worse scrape than Croker—John Murray says that it is a damned nuisance: and Croker looks across the House of Commons at me with a leer of hatred which I repay with a gracious smile of pity. Most of the readers of the Edinburgh Review are as much pleased to see Croker trounced as the spectators on a memorable occasion at Covent Garden Theatre were to see Westmacott beaten; and are on my side without knowing why. You will see that I have stolen a hint from you to embellish my article.

I am ashamed to have said so much about myself. You will think me as great an egotist as Sir John Malcolm. But you asked for news about me. No request is so certain to be granted, or so certain to be a curse to him who makes it as that which you have made to me.

Ever yours,
T. B. Macaulay

To Hannah and Margaret Macaulay, 8 June [1832]

London, June 8

My dear Girls,

To night I set out. When I shall be able to write again I hardly know. I expect not to have a single moment to myself, except indeed while I am in the post chaise during the next week. If I can I will snatch a moment or two at Calne on Monday to let you know my movements.

The royal assent was given yesterday afternoon to the English Reform Bill. It was given by Commissioners. The King unfortunately for himself has been induced by that wretched Court faction which surrounds him to give this proof of his impotent enmity to his ministers and his people. If the matter were merely one of party, I should rejoice at the course which he has taken. It has had this effect—that Lord Grey and the Whigs have all the honor of the reform-bill and the King none of it. If we are to have a quarrel with the Court we shall be far stronger and the Court far weaker than if William the Fourth had on this occasion acted in such a way as to make himself popular throughout the country. I fear—I fear—that he has entered on the path of Charles and Louis. He makes great concessions; but he makes them reluctantly and ungraciously. The people receive them without gratitude or affection. What madness!—to give more to his subjects than any King ever gave, and yet to give in such a manner as to get no thanks!

Remember to keep to yourselves what I say about politics. In my present situation it would not do for me to promulgate opinions unfavourable to the Prince whom I serve.

I shall expect as soon as my franking privilege returns full details of your journey—how the Quaker threw Margaret's eggs out of the coach window; how he sent Hannah's novel after them; how you met Cook the murderer handcuffed half-way

447

between Liverpool and Leicester; how you admired the scenery of Matlock and the architecture of Buxton; how you thundered along the rail-road—with every etc., as Mrs. Meeke would say. Did you meet any old sinner of a Landlady? Were you shewn into any horrible taproom like that described in Conscience? Were you detained by any villainy on the part of the Coach-proprietors? I shall expect all the conversation that passed in the stage to be detailed dramatically, between inverted commas; so that I may be able to judge whether my darlings will ever produce a good novel.

But I must stop. Ever, my dear loves, your affectionate friend and brother.

TBM

Index

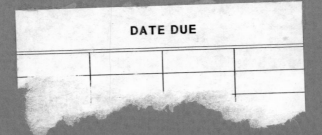

DATE DUE